More Common Ground for International Competition Law?

Edited by

Josef Drexl

Director, Max Planck Institute for Intellectual Property and Competition Law, Munich, Germany

Warren S. Grimes

Southwestern Law School, USA

Clifford A. Jones

University of Florida, USA

Rudolph J.R. Peritz

New York Law School, USA

Edward T. Swaine

George Washington University Law School, USA

ASCOLA COMPETITION LAW
The Fourth ASCOLA Workshop on Comparative Competition Law

Edward Elgar

Cheltenham, UK • Northampton, MA, USA

Published by
Edward Elgar Publishing Limited
The Lypiatts
15 Lansdown Road
Cheltenham
Glos GL50 2JA
UK

Edward Elgar Publishing, Inc.
William Pratt House
9 Dewey Court
Northampton
Massachusetts 01060
USA

A catalogue record for this book
is available from the British Library

Library of Congress Control Number: 2011925785

MIX
Paper from
responsible sources
FSC® C018575

ISBN 978 1 84980 394 6

Typeset by Servis Filmsetting Ltd, Stockport, Cheshire
Printed and bound by MPG Books Group, UK

Contents

Contributors

Steven Anderman Emeritus Professor of Law at the University of Essex; Guest Professor of Law at Stockholm University.

Neil W. Averitt JD (Harvard); MSc (London School of Economics); BA (Harvard); member of the planning staff at the US Federal Trade Commission.

Caron Beaton-Wells PhD (Melb); LLM (Melb); Associate Professor, Director of Studies, Competition Law, and Director, Competition Law and Economics Network, Melbourne Law School, University of Melbourne, Australia.

Josef Bejček Professor of Commercial Law at Masaryk University Brno; Director of the Department of Commercial Law; member of the Appellate Commission of the Czech Antitrust Authority.

Josef Drexl Dr iur (Munich); LLM (Berkeley); Director of the Max Planck Institute for Intellectual Property and Competition Law (Munich); Honorary Professor of the University of Munich.

Thomas Eilmansberger Dr phil, Dr iur, M.A.E.S. (Bruges); Professor of European Law at the University of Salzburg.

Albert A. Foer President, American Antitrust Institute.

Andreas Fuchs Professor of Law, Dr iur, LLM (University of Michigan, Ann Arbor); Director of the Institute for Commercial and Business Law, University of Osnabrück.

Michal S. Gal Professor and Co-director of the Forum for Law and Markets, University of Haifa Faculty of Law.

Gustavo Ghidini Professor of Law at the University of Milan and at the Libera Università Internazionale degli Studi Sociali (LUISS) Guido Carli in Rome.

Deborah Healey LLM (Hons) (Syd); Senior Lecturer, Director Corporate and Commercial, LLM Programme, Faculty of Law, University of New South Wales, Sydney.

Clifford A. Jones JD, MPhil, PhD (Cantab); Professor of Law, Center for Governmental Responsibility, University of Florida Levin College of Law.

Robert H. Lande Venable Professor of Law, University of Baltimore School of Law; a Director of the American Antitrust Institute.

Marina Lao Professor of Law, Seton Hall University School of Law.

Paul L. Nihoul Jean Monnet Professor of Law, University of Louvain-la-Neuve, Belgium.

Rudolph J.R. Peritz Professor of Law and Director, IProgress Project, New York Law School; Visiting Professor, Departments of Law and Economics, LUISS Guido Carli (Spring 2010); Fernand Braudel Senior Research Fellow, European University Institute (Spring 2011).

Maurice E. Stucke Associate Professor, University of Tennessee College of Law; Senior Fellow, American Antitrust Institute.

Preface

This book assembles 17 contributions based on talks given at the fourth conference of the Academic Society for Competition Law (ASCOLA) which was held at the Competition Law Center of the George Washington University Law School in Washington DC on 16–17 June 2009. All the contributions take account of the legal development until the end of 2010.

The choices of conference venue and topic were very timely. After the collapse of the financial markets in the fall of 2008, scepticism toward what economic theory can explain and predict has increased enormously, also in the field of competition law. The beginning of the financial crisis coincided with the election of a new US president and the coming into office of new decision-makers at the US antitrust agencies, which raised the question whether the new administration would turn away from its former lenient approach in the field of unilateral conduct, with regard to intellectual property in particular, and increase its enforcement activities. In this regard, the conference, above all, aimed to investigate whether those changes would increase the potential for consensus across competition jurisdictions. Of course, potential for more transatlantic convergence between the US and the EU was in the forefront of the debate. Yet, given the global outreach of ASCOLA, it was important also to take account of new interesting developments in other jurisdictions that may and will have an impact on the global landscape of competition law and enforcement.

This book is divided into four parts: the first part takes a fresh look at economics by discussing alternative approaches to the classical industrial organization theories. The second part brings together a variety of specific developments that have recently taken place in individual jurisdictions and deserve international attention for assessing global trends in competition law. Part 3 concentrates on the specific interface of intellectual property and competition law. In particular, it addresses patent ambush cases and so-called pay-for-delay settlements in the pharmaceutical industry, both of which recently attracted most attention by the agencies and courts in the US and Europe. Finally, Part 4 brings together some contributions that deal with approaches on how to promote competition policy nationally and across borders.

Part 1 starts with a contribution by *Maurice E. Stucke* where, in the light of the financial crisis, he questions the main assumptions of rational behaviour underlying industrial organization theories, especially of the Chicago School, using recent insights from behavioural economics. He strongly argues against a competition policy that is based on the assumption of self-interested behaviour of individuals and that promotes such behaviour even as a virtue in the public interest. This is followed by a contribution by *Robert H. Lande* on how competition law could be reformed by taking 'consumer choice' as a benchmark for assessing cases as an alternative to the efficiency criterion. By arguing that consumers want options rather than just lower prices, he seeks to bring a variety of factors that are important to consumers from the footnotes to the text of the case evaluation. Moreover, he argues that the consumer choice approach would not only better explain the benefits of competition law for society; it could also be used for building more consensus between different jurisdictions. *Neil W. Averitt* joins Robert H. Lande in supporting a consumer choice approach by combining competition policy and consumer protection law in an integrated legal framework. This triggers *Paul L. Nihoul* to critically consider whether competition law should be integrated as part of consumer law from the perspective of the EU, where the concept of informed choice has been developed as the core concept of consumer policy.

Part 2 starts with a transatlantic debate on how to assess resale price maintenance cases after the recent US Supreme Court decision in *Leegin*. In her contribution, *Marina Lao* does not only criticize this decision; she also most broadly reviews the pro- and anti-competitive effects of RPM, criticizes the rule-of-reason approach as applied by the US Supreme Court as a de facto legality rule and finally recommends a rebuttable presumption of illegality. Her ideas find full support from *Josef Bejček* from across the Atlantic. Just like Marina Lao, he is very sceptical about whether pro-competitive effects can actually justify RPM in individual cases and encourages enforcers to work with a presumption of illegality. This seems in line with the new European regime on vertical agreements as reformed in 2010, according to which RPM remains a blacklisted restraint, whilst the potentially pro-competitive effects are now mentioned in the Guidelines on Vertical Agreements and may therefore be considered for an exemption under Article 101(3) TFEU (Treaty on the Functioning of the European Union). Then, *Thomas Eilmansberger* discusses tying arrangements and strategies, including those relating to aftermarkets, as a most complex competition law issue from the perspective of EU law. By bringing in more differentiation between different sets of cases, he seeks to better capture the competition concerns at stake.

Deborah Healey then takes the reader to the People's Republic of China, where the recent adoption of Anti-Monopoly Law has also considerably changed the global landscape of competition law. Using a thorough historical, sociopolitical as well as comparative analysis, she reviews the application of the new law to state-owned enterprises (SOEs) and government bodies, which is, given the persisting role of large state-owned conglomerates in the Chinese market and the potentially distortive influence of local governments on the economic integration of the country, one of the big challenges in enforcing the new law. Finally, *Caron Beaton-Wells* presents a most comprehensive picture of the political debate and the most problematic issues at stake surrounding the recent introduction of criminal sanctions in the field of cartel enforcement in Australia in 2009. Her analysis should interest researchers from any other jurisdictions, including those in Europe, where nowadays criminal sanctions are discussed as a further move to make cartel enforcement more effective.

Part 3 starts with a contribution by *Andreas Fuchs* in which he reviews the application of US antitrust law and EU competition law to patent ambush cases, with a particular focus on the recent *Rambus* case. In his comparison, he highlights the weaknesses of both jurisdictions in using competition policy for guaranteeing that a standard-setting process is not distorted by the deceptive conduct of individual members of SSOs. According to him, patent ambush cases should be assessed as cases on excessive pricing, in which price control is justified in light of the entry barriers created by the network and lock-in effects in markets characterized by technological standards. *Rudolph J.R. Peritz* then draws attention to the US debate on so-called pay-for-delay settlements of patent infringement cases with reverse payments, where originator pharmaceutical companies pay off generics producers for delaying the market entry of generics. His contribution presents the topic as a story of a political battle fought by the administration and the US Federal Trade Commission in particular against the courts that still uphold a presumption of legality of such settlements in applying a rule-of-reason approach. In light of the high proportion of patent invalidations in cases where courts actually make a final decision, Rudolph Peritz argues in favour of reversing the rule of reason in the sense of presumption of illegality. In his comments, *Gustavo Ghidini* agrees with the preceding contributions and highlights that in both patent ambush and pay-for-delay cases no credit should be given to the fact that patents are involved. In the first case distortion of competition arises from deceptive conduct and in the second case from the agreement and not the patent itself. *Josef Drexl* then highlights that the assessment of both patent ambush and pay-for-delay cases should take into account the dynamic aspects of competition in particular. For patent ambush cases, he recommends applying unilateral conduct rules on excessive pricing based on an incentives balance approach. Price control is needed for decreasing the incentives of the patent holder to distort the pro-competition, innovation-enhancing standard-setting process. Pay-for-delay settlements should not solely be banned in view of promoting price competition with generics, but also with the aim of preventing originator companies from distorting dynamic competition with other originator companies based on profit from unjustified patents. Finally, *Steven Anderman* goes beyond the problems of patent ambush, by analysing the different stages of organizing a patent pool and the licensing out of patents by such pools after the stage of standard setting.

In Part 4, *Michal S. Gal* presents a five-step model of international cooperation for solving competition law problems in the context of international trade. These steps range from extraterritoriality at the lowest level over bilateral agreements, regional agreements, international enforcement and cooperation to the creation of a supranational authority. This model is then discussed and applied to the most recently witnessed 'new wave of regionalism' in view of giving policy recommendations for the modelling of regional competition agreements, which the author sees as a useful tool for more effectively addressing a number of the problems caused by the internationalization of trade. Then, *Clifford A. Jones* reviews the EU policy of exporting its competition policy approach to other countries in the framework of its so-called European Neighbourhood Policy, which includes a considerable number of countries in the Balkans, Eastern Europe, South Caucasus, North Africa and the Middle East. Finally, as president of the American Antitrust Institute and with personal experience, *Albert A. Foer* is the perfect person for explaining the role that non-governmental organizations can play in promoting competition policy both on the domestic level and internationally.

At the end of this preface, the editors would like to thank a number of people at the Max Planck Institute for Intellectual Property and Competition Law who played a very important role in the preparation of this book. Mark-Oliver Mackenrodt, Markus Raeder and Ruth Claussen were in charge of ensuring that the contributions conformed to the style of the book. Olivia Raitt reviewed a number of contributions of the non-native speakers from a linguistic point of view. Delia Zirilli was responsible for organizing the whole review process and for communication with the many people involved in the production of this book. Last but not least, the editors are very grateful to the staff of Edward Elgar surrounding Tim Williams who, this time, did not only support the project, but also showed amazing patience during a very long period of editing the manuscript.

January 2011

Josef Drexl
Warren S. Grimes
Clifford A. Jones
Rudolph J.R. Peritz
Edward T. Swaine

Abbreviations

AAI	American Antitrust Institute
ACCC	Australian Competition and Consumer Commission
Am Econ Rev	*American Economic Review*
AML	Anti-Monopoly Law (China)
Antitrust LJ	*Antitrust Law Journal*
ANZJIC	*Australian and New Zealand Journal of Criminology*
Asian-Pacific L & Pol'y J	*Asian-Pacific Law and Policy Journal*
Austr Bus L Rev	*Australian Business Law Review*
Austr Fin Rev	*Australian Financial Review*
Austr J Corp L	*Australian Journal of Corporate Law*
B2B	business to business
Berkeley Tech LJ	*Berkeley Technology Law Journal*
Cal L Rev	*California Law Review*
cert.	certiorari
cf.	compare with
CFI	Court of First Instance (now: General Court)
Ch.	Chapter
China L & Pract	*China Law and Practice*
CLR	Commonwealth Law Reports (Australia)
Col Bus L Rev	*Columbia Business Law Review*
Col J Eur L	*Columbia Journal of European Law*
COMESA	Common Market for Eastern and Southern Africa
Comp Pol'y Int'l	*Competition Policy International*
Comp & Cons LJ	*Competition and Consumer Law Journal*
Comp'y & Sec LJ	*Company and Securities Law Journal*
Cong Rec	Congressional Record (US)
Contemp Pol'y Iss	*Contemporary Policy Issues*
CUTS	Consumer Unity and Trust Society
DC Cir.	US Court of Appeals for the District of Columbia

DCFTA	Deep and Comprehensive Free Trade Agreements
DoJ	Department of Justice (US)
DPP	Commonwealth Director of Public Prosecutions (Australia)
EC	European Community; Treaty on the European Community (Amsterdam and Nice versions)
ECJ	European Court of Justice
ECLR	*European Competition Law Review*
ECR	European Court Reports
ECSC	European Coal and Steel Community
ed./eds	editor(s)
edn	edition
EEA	European Economic Area
EEC	European Economic Community
EFTA	European Free Trade Agreement
e.g.	exempli gratia (for example)
ENP	European Neighbourhood Policy
et al.	et alia (and others)
et seq.	et sequens (and the following page/ paragraph)
ETSI	European Telecommunications Standards Institute
EU	European Union
Eur Comp J	*European Competition Journal*
Eur Econ Rev	*European Economic Review*
Eur LJ	*European Law Journal*
Eur L Rev	*European Law Review*
Evol & Hum Behav	*Evolution and Human Behavior*
EWS	*Europäisches Wirtschafts- und Steuerrecht*
F.3d	Federal Reporter, 3d series
FCR	Federal Court Reports (Australia)
FDA	Food and Drug Administration
Fed L Rev	*Federal Law Review*
Fin Times	*Financial Times*
Florida J Int'l L	*Florida Journal of International Law*
Fordham Int'l LJ	*Fordham International Law Journal*
FRAND terms	fair, reasonable and non-discriminatory terms
F. Supp.	Federal Supplement
FTC	Federal Trade Commission (US)

F.T.C.	Federal Trade Commission Decisions
GRUR Int	*Gewerblicher Rechtsschutz und Urheberrecht, Internationaler Teil*
GWB	Gesetz gegen Wettbewerbsbeschränkungen (Germany)
Haifa L Rev	*Haifa Law Review*
Harv Bus Rev	*Harvard Business Review*
Harv L Rev	*Harvard Law Review*
Hastings LJ	*Hastings Law Journal*
HCA	High Court of Australia
HR	House of Representatives (US)
ICFAI J Ind Econ	*ICFAI Journal of Industrial Economics*
ICN	International Competition Network
ICPAC	International Competition Policy Advisory Committee
id.	idem (the same as mentioned previously)
IDEA	*IDEA: The Intellectual Property Law Review*
i.e.	id est (that is)
IIC	*International Review of Intellectual Property and Competition Law*
INCSOC	International Network of Civil Society Organisations on Competition
Intell Prop & Tech LJ	*Intellectual Property and Technology Law Journal*
Int'l J Ind Org	*International Journal of Industrial Organization*
Int'l L	*International Law*
Int'l Tax J	*International Tax Journal*
IP	intellectual property
IPR	intellectual property rights
J Bus	*Journal of Business*
J Comp L (ZWeR)	*Journal of Competition Law (Zeitschrift für Wettbewerbsrecht)*
J Comp L & Econ	*Journal of Competition Law and Economics*
JEDEC	Joint Electron Device Engineering Council
J Econ Behav & Org	*Journal of Economic Behavior and Organization*
J Econ Lit	*Journal of Economic Literature*
J Econ Persp	*Journal of Economic Perspectives*
J Int'l Econ L	*Journal of International Economic Law*
J L & Econ	*Journal of Law and Economics*
J Pol Econ	*Journal of Political Economy*

J Pub Econ	*Journal of Public Economics*
lit.	litera (letter, item)
Loy Cons L Rev	*Loyola Consumer Law Review*
Loy U Chi LJ	*Loyola University of Chicago Law Journal*
LSE	London School of Economics
Melb U L Rev	*Melbourne University Law Review*
Mich L Rev	*Michigan Law Review*
Minn L Rev	*Minnesota Law Review*
MOFCOM	Ministry of Commerce (China)
n.	note
NEC	*Neighbourhood Economic Community*
NGO	*non-governmental organization*
NJOZ	*Neue Juristische Online-Zeitschrift*
no.	*number*
Notre Dame L Rev	*Notre Dame Law Review*
NYU L Rev	*New York University Law Review*
NZ	New Zealand
OECD	Organisation for Economic Co-operation and Development
OJ C	Official Journal of the European Union Part C
OJ L	Official Journal of the European Union Part L
p./pp.	page(s)
para(s)	paragraph(s)
Pat Tradem & Copyr J	*Patent, Trademark and Copyright Journal*
Psych Rev	*Psychological Review*
Pub L	*Public Law*
Q J Econ	*Quarterly Journal of Economics*
Rand J Econ	*Rand Journal of Economics*
RCA	regional competition agreement
Rev Ind Org	*Review of Industrial Organization*
Rev Network Econ	*Review of Network Economics*
RPM	resale price maintenance
s(s)	section(s)
Santa Clara L Rev	*Santa Clara Law Review*
SASAC	State Assets Supervision and Administration Commission (China)
S Comm	Senate Committee
S Ct	Supreme Court Reporter
SETC	State Economic and Trade Commission (China)

SOE	state-owned enterprise
SSO	standard-setting organization
Stan L Rev	*Stanford Law Review*
Sup Ct Econ Rev	*Supreme Court Economic Review*
tbl	table
Tex L Rev	*Texas Law Review*
TFEU	Treaty on the Functioning of the European Union
TP Act	Trade Practices Act (Australia)
Trade Pract LJ	*Trade Practices Law Journal*
U Ill L Rev	*University of Illinois Law Review*
UK	United Kingdom
UMTS	Universal Mobile Telecommunications System
UNSW LJ	*University of New South Wales Law Journal*
U Penn L Rev	*University of Pennsylvania Law Review*
UNCTAD	United Nations Conference on Trade and Development
US	United States
U.S.	United States Reports
USC	United States Code
v	versus
V J Int'l L	*Virginia Journal of International Law*
V L Rev	*Virginia Law Review*
V and L Rev	*Vanderbilt Law Review*
vol.	volume
Wall St J	*Wall Street Journal*
Wash Post	*Washington Post*
Wash U J L & Pol'y	*Washington University Journal of Law and Policy*
Wis L Rev	*Wisconsin Law Review*
WL	Westlaw
World Comp	*World Competition*
WRP	*Wettbewerb in Recht und Praxis*
WTO	World Trade Organization
WuW	*Wirtschaft und Wettbewerb*
Yale J Reg	*Yale Journal on Regulation*

PART 1

Economic foundations of competition law

1. Are people self-interested? The implications of behavioral economics on competition policy

Maurice E. Stucke*

1 INTRODUCTION

For 30 years, the neoclassical economic theories associated with the University of Chicago[1] have shaped American competition policies. These

* The author wishes to thank Warren Grimes, Christopher Sagers, D Daniel Sokol, Gregory M Stein, Avishalom Tor, Spencer Weber Waller, Dick Wirtz, Michael Wise and the participants of the 4th ASCOLA conference, the Competition Law Forum on Behavioral Economics, and the Max Planck Institute for Research on Collective Goods for their helpful comments, and the University of Tennessee College of Law and the W Allen Separk Faculty Endowment for the summer research grant. This chapter is based on a longer article that was published in (2010) 50 *Santa Clara L Rev* 893.

[1] It is important to recognize that the beliefs of some Chicago School theorists evolved over time. See RA Posner, 'The Chicago School of Antitrust Analysis' (1979) 127 *U Pa L Rev* 925, at 932 (noting that some ideas first advanced by one of the School's founders Aaron Director 'have been questioned, modified, and refined, resulting in the emergence of a new animal: the "diehard Chicagoan" (such as Bork and Bowman) who has not accepted any of the suggested refinements or modifications in Director's original ideas'). At times, its theorists have clashed over competition policy or in their beliefs in market forces. Nobel laureate Ronald H Coase, who is commonly associated with the Chicago School, for example, rejected the self-interest assumption as 'consumers without humanity'. He observed that the 'rational utility maximizer of economic theory bears no resemblance to the man on the Clapham bus or, indeed, to a man (or woman) on any bus'. RH Coase, *The Firm, the Market and the Law* (1988) at 3 et seq. During the recent financial crisis, Richard A Posner, another Chicago School theorist, reconsidered some of his earlier beliefs. M Baram, 'Judge Richard Posner Questions His Free-Market Faith In "A Failure of Capitalism"' (20 April 2009) *Huffington Post* (interview with Posner) (seeing 'the importance of government regulations; the need to strengthen the regulatory structure by directly funding authorities rather than the current fee-based model; the dangers of excessive executive compensation, and even expressed support for the idea of changing bankruptcy law to make it easier for homeowners

theories assume rational individuals and firms pursue their self-interest, which for this chapter's purpose, means seeking to maximize wealth and other material goals, and generally not caring about other social goals, to the extent that they conflict.[2] In effect, greed and self-interest are repackaged as virtues.[3] Self-interested behavior drives markets toward more efficient outcomes. Until the recent financial crisis, markets were assumed to self-correct. When left mostly alone by government regulators, competition would allocate resources efficiently toward users who value them the most. The government generally need not intervene in the economy since rational market participants, in pursuing their self-interest, prevent or quickly cure most market failures.[4] These economic theories assume that the 'natural laws of the market are in essence good . . . and necessarily work for the good, whatever may be true of the morality of individuals.'[5]

This economic orthodoxy is under attack. '[T]he orthodox and unvarnished Chicago School of economic theory is on life support, if it is not dead,' said Commissioner J Thomas Rosch of the US Federal Trade Commission, 'in the real world – as opposed to the worlds of political and economic theory – markets are not perfect; . . . imperfect markets

---

who face foreclosure.'), http://www.huffingtonpost.com/2009/04/20/judge-richard-posner-disc_n_188950.html (accessed December 2010); RA Posner, *A Failure of Capitalism: The Crisis of '08 and the Descent into Depression* (2009).

[2] GJ Stigler, 'Economics or Ethics?', in S McMurrin (ed.), *Tanner Lectures on Human Values*, vol. II (1981) 176 (when 'self-interest and ethical values with wide verbal allegiance are in conflict, much of the time, most of the time in fact, self-interest theory . . . will win.'); see also RH Bork, *The Antitrust Paradox: A Policy At War With Itself* (1978) at 119 (profit-maximization assumption is 'crucial' to the Chicago School's theories); RA Posner, *Economic Analysis of Law* (3rd edn, 1986) at 3 ('The task of economics . . . is to explore the implications of assuming that man is a rational maximizer of his ends in life, his satisfactions – what we shall call his "self-interest."'); Posner, *supra* n. 1, at 931 (Chicago School's theory offered 'powerful simplifications,' such as 'rationality, profit maximization, the downward sloping demand curve'); RA Prentice, 'Chicago Man, K-T Man, and the Future of Behavioral Law and Economics' (2003) 56 *Vand L Rev* 1665 n. 4 (collecting additional sources).

[3] M Jackman, *Crown's Book of Political Quotations: Over 2500 Lively Quotes from Plato to Reagan* (1982) at 31 (quoting John Kenneth Galbraith) ('The modern conservative is engaged in one of man's oldest exercises in moral philosophy; that is, the search for a superior moral justification for selfishness.').

[4] H Hovenkamp, 'Post-Chicago Antitrust: A Review and Critique' (2001) *Colum Bus L Rev* 257, at 266 (describing Chicago School policies); Bork, *supra* n. 2, at 405 et seq.

[5] J Cardinal Ratzinger, 'Market Economy and Ethics' (1985), http://www.acton.org/publications/occasionalpapers/publicat_occasionalpapers_ratzinger.php?view=print (accessed December 2010).

do not always correct themselves; and . . . business people do not always behave rationally.'[6] Likewise in shelving the Bush administration's highly-criticized Section 2 Report,[7] the new head of the US Department of Justice Antitrust Division rejected the report's underlying assumption that monopoly markets are generally self-correcting: 'The recent developments in the marketplace should make it clear that we can no longer rely upon the marketplace alone to ensure that competition and consumers will be protected.'[8] She noted how these ideologies failed:

> Americans have seen firms given room to run with the idea that markets 'self-police,' and that enforcement authorities should wait for the markets to 'self-correct.' It is clear to anyone who picks up a newspaper or watches the evening news that the country has been waiting for this 'self-correction,' spurred innovation, and enhanced consumer welfare. But these developments have not occurred. Instead, we now see numerous markets distorted. We are also seeing some firms fail and take American consumers with them. It appears that a combination of factors, including ineffective government regulation, ill-considered deregulatory measures, and inadequate antitrust oversight contributed to the current condition.[9]

The Obama administration is re-examining such fundamental issues as the efficiency of markets and the role of legal, social, and ethical norms in a market economy. This re-evaluation raises many fundamental issues, prompting policymakers in the Obama administration to examine behavioral economics literature.[10] I discuss elsewhere how behavioral economics

---

[6] JT Rosch, Commissioner, Federal Trade Commission, 'Implications of the Financial Meltdown for the FTC', New York Bar Association Annual Dinner, New York, NY (29 January 2009), http://ftc.gov/speeches/rosch/090129financial crisisnybarspeech.pdf (accessed December 2010).

[7] US Dep't of Justice, 'Competition and Monopoly: Single-Firm Conduct Under Section 2 of the Sherman Act' (2008), http://www.usdoj.gov/atr/public/reports/236681.pdf (accessed December 2010).

[8] Press Release, US Dep't of Justice, 'Justice Department Withdraws Report on Antitrust Monopoly Law: Antitrust Division to Apply More Rigorous Standard With Focus on the Impact of Exclusionary Conduct on Consumers' (11 May 2009), http://www.usdoj.gov/atr/public/press_releases/2009/245710.htm (accessed November 2009).

[9] CA Varney, Assistant Attorney General, Antitrust Division, US Dep't of Justice, 'Vigorous Antitrust Enforcement in This Challenging Era, Remarks as prepared for the Center for American Progress' (11 May 2009), http://www.usdoj.gov/atr/public/speeches/245777.htm (accessed December 2010) 4 *et seq.*

[10] FTC Commissioner Rosch, for example, has been interested in behavioral economics' implications on competition policy. JD Rosch, 'Antitrust Law Enforcement: What To Do About The Current Economics Cacophony? Before the Bates White Antitrust Conference, Washington, DC (1 June 2009), http://

can inform merger analysis[11] and cartel[12] and monopolization cases,[13] so this chapter addresses a key assumption of the Chicago School's neoclassical economic theories – namely, that people pursue their self-interest.[14] First, do people actually behave like the Chicago School's self-interested rational agents? Second, if the answer is no, should self-interested behavior be the desired norm? Third, what are the risks if governmental policies promote self-interested behavior?

2 DO PEOPLE ACTUALLY BEHAVE LIKE SELF-INTERESTED RATIONAL AGENTS?

The Chicago School's theories are derived from the assumption of humans as rational, self-interested, and with perfect willpower.[15] Behavioral economics, in contrast, uses facts and methods from other social sciences such as psychology and sociology to understand the limits of this assumption.[16]

---

www.ftc.gov/speeches/rosch/090601bateswhite.pdf (accessed November 2009); Rosch, *supra* n. 6; A Spiegel, 'Using Psychology To Save You From Yourself' (June 8, 2009) *NPR* (June 8, 2009), http://www.npr.org/templates/story/story.php?storyId=104803094 (accessed December 2010).

[11] ME Stucke, 'Behavioral Economists at the Gate: Antitrust in the Twenty-First Century' (2007) 38 *Loy U Chi LJ* 513; ME Stucke, 'New Antitrust Realism' (January 2009) *GCP (Global Competition Policy) Mag*, http://papers.ssrn.com/sol3/papers.cfm?abstract_id=1323815 (accessed December 2010).

[12] ME Stucke, 'Am I a Price-Fixer? A Behavioral Economics Analysis of Cartels', in C Beaton-Wells and A Ezrachi (eds), *Criminalising Cartels: A Critical Interdisciplinary Study of an International Regulatory Movement* (2011); ME Stucke, 'Morality and Antitrust' (2006) *Colum Bus L Rev* 443.

[13] ME Stucke, 'Should the Government Prosecute Monopolies?' (2009) *U Ill L Rev* 497.

[14] It is beyond this chapter's scope to examine whether firms (which are a collection of individuals) pursue (or should pursue) their self-interest. Just as individual behavior may differ depending upon the norms and expectations in that social setting, so, too, firm behavior may vary. Moreover, profit-maximization, as a normative corporate theory, has many packed issues.

[15] Posner, *supra* n. 1, 928; see also RA Posner, *Antitrust Law* (2nd edn, 2001) at ix (noting how everyone involved in antitrust agrees that firms 'should be assumed to be rational profit maximizers'). But as Posner admitted, 'It is a curiosity, and a source of regret, that to this day [1979] very few of [one of the Chicago School's founders Aaron] Director's ideas have been subjected to systematic empirical examination.' Posner, *supra* n. 1, at 931 n. 13.

[16] For interesting surveys of the behavioral economics research, see GA Akerlof and RJ Shiller, *Animal Spirits* (2009); D Ariely, *Predictably Irrational: The Hidden Forces that Shape our Decisions* (2008); RH Thaler and CR Sunstein, *Nudge: Improving Decisions about Health, Wealth, and Happiness* (2008); H Gintis et al.

Pioneered by Nobel laureate Daniel Kahneman and Amos Tversky, behavioral economics is fundamentally empirical. In testing the Chicago School's assumptions in lab and field experiments, and by using data from actual market transactions,[17] the behavioral economics literature shows that many individuals do not always pursue their self-interest. Human behavior is more nuanced, diverse, and complex. People generally care about treating others, and being treated, fairly. Even when not in their financial interest, many aspire toward benevolence in accordance with religious, ethical or social norms of fairness.[18] We see this everyday. Many donate blood,[19] take time to help strangers, or tip waiters in cities they are unlikely to revisit.[20] Also contrary to the Chicago School's assumption, people in these behavioral experiments sacrifice wealth to punish unfair behavior. Neoclassical economic theory predicts that the punishment mechanism, if it imposes a cost on the punisher, should not affect the outcome.[21] But in the behavioral public goods and trust experiments,

---

(eds), *Moral Sentiments and Material Interests: The Foundations of Cooperation in Economic Life* (2005); CF Camerer et al. (eds), *Advances in Behavioral Economics* (2004); C Jolls et al., 'A Behavioral Approach to Law and Economics' (1998) 50 *Stan L Rev* 1471, at 1487. For a broader survey of literature attacking the conventional economic theories, see ED Beinhocker, *The Origin of Wealth: The Radical Remaking of Economics and What it Means for Business and Society* (2007).

17 For recent surveys of the literature, see S DellaVigna, 'Psychology and Economics: Evidence from the Field' (2009) 47 *J Econ Lit* 315; A Tor, 'The Methodology of the Behavioral Analysis of Law' (2008) 4 *Haifa L Rev* 237. For an earlier informative examination of the criticisms of behavioral economics and responses thereto, see RA Prentice, 'Chicago Man, K-T Man, and the Future of Behavioral Law and Economics' (2003) 56 *Vand L Rev* 1665.

18 See D Kahneman, JR Knetsch and RH Thaler, 'Fairness as a Constraint on Profit Seeking: Entitlements in the Market' (1986) 76 *Am Econ Rev* 728, at 729 ('A central concept in analyzing the fairness of actions in which a firm sets the terms of future exchanges is the *reference transaction*, a relevant precedent that is characterized by a reference price or wage, and by a positive reference profit to the firm.').

19 Voluntary blood donations in Britain declined sharply when a policy of paying donors was instituted alongside the voluntary sector. H Gintis et al., 'Moral Sentiments and Material Interests: Origins, Evidence, and Consequences' in H Gintis et al. (eds), *Moral Sentiments and Material Interests: The Foundations of Cooperation in Economic Life* (2005) 20.

20 In one study, the mean response by those surveyed of the tip they would leave in a restaurant they frequent regularly or in another city which they do not expect to revisit was nearly identical ($1.28 versus $1.27 for a $10 meal). Kahneman, Knetsch and Thaler, *supra* n. 18, at 737; D Kahneman et al., 'Fairness as a Constraint on Profit Seeking: Entitlements in the Market' in CF Camerer et al. (eds), *Advances in Behavioral Economics* (2004) 252, at 264.

21 Because punishment is costly for the punisher (which the punisher does not recoup through cooperation), self-interested players would not punish.

participants incur costs to punish free-riding.[22] In fact the punishment mechanism has a positive effect in deterring free-riding; in repeat games, contributions steadily increase until nearly all participants contribute 100 percent of their endowment.[23] The behavioral experiments in bargaining settings, as Samuel Bowles summarizes, systematically show 'that substantial fractions of most populations adhere to moral rules, willingly give to others, and punish those who offend standards of appropriate behavior, even at a cost to themselves and with no expectation of material reward.'[24] This 'strong reciprocity' in human behavior entails 'a predisposition to cooperate with others and to punish those who violate the norms of cooperation, at personal cost, even when it is implausible to expect that these costs will be repaid either by others or at a later date.'[25]

One common behavioral experiment is the Ultimatum Game. In this experiment, you are given money (say $100) with two conditions. First you must offer another person some portion of the $100. The second condition is that the other person can accept or reject your offer. If the other person accepts, both of you keep your portions of the $100. If the other person rejects your offered amount, neither of you keep the money. So how much should you offer?

A Chicago School theorist predicts that you would offer the nominal amount. If everyone pursues their self-interest, then you want to keep as much money as possible, and the other person recognizes that one penny/cent/yen is better than nothing. But actual experiments of this Ultimatum Game in over 20 countries show the contrary. Most people offer significantly more than the nominal amount (ordinarily 40 to 50 percent of the total amount available) and recipients typically (about half

---

Recognizing this, self-interested players will not contribute to public goods games. Thus, with or without costly punishment mechanisms, the predicted response under neoclassical economic theory is zero contributions.

[22] E Fehr and U Fischbacher, 'The Economics of Strong Reciprocity' in H Gintis et al. (eds), *Moral Sentiments and Material Interests: The Foundations of Cooperation in Economic Life* (2005) 169.

[23] Id. at 169 et seq. In the last few periods of the multi-period games, the actual rate of punishment is low. Id. at 170.

[24] S Bowles, 'Policies Designed for Self-interested Citizens May Undermine "The Moral Sentiments": Evidence from Economic Experiments' (20 June 2008) *Science*, at 1606.

[25] H Gintis et al., 'Explaining Altruistic Behavior in Humans' (2003) 24 *Evolution & Hum Behav* 153, at 154. These authors argue that 'the evolutionary success of our species and the moral sentiments that have led people to value freedom, equality, and representative government are predicated upon strong reciprocity and related motivations that go beyond inclusive fitness and reciprocal altruism.' Id.

the time) reject nominal amounts (less than 20 percent of the total amount available).[26] Consequently, most receivers in this game forgo wealth to punish unfair offers, and offerors generally offer more than the nominal amount.[27]

These results cannot be explained as maximizing one's reputation. Similar results occur in anonymous one-shot games.[28] Even when the game is repeated ten times to allow for learning, similar results follow.[29] In the Dictator Game, a variation of the Ultimatum Game where the receivers must accept any offer, people still share, although the amount shared may vary depending on certain conditions, such as social isolation and whether the recipients stand up and give a few facts about themselves or are identified as a charity.[30]

Not everyone, of course, is cooperative and charitable – some act selfishly. So the outcome in the behavioral experiments can depend on several factors, including whether the participants are primed with non-conscious reminders of the concept of money.[31] Recent behavioral experiments show that even nonconscious reminders of money can cause people to be more independent in their work, but also less likely to seek help from others, less willing to spend time helping others, and stingier when asked to donate to a worthy cause.[32] Those primed with money in get-acquainted conversations put more physical distance between themselves than in the control group.[33] Unlike the people primed with a control condition (their desk faced a poster showing a seascape or flower garden), participants reminded of money (their desk faced a poster showing various currency

---

[26] RH Thaler, *The Winner's Curse: Paradoxes And Anomalies Of Economic Life* (1992) at 21–35; C Jolls et al., 'A Behavioral Approach to Law and Economics' (1998) 50 *Stan L Rev* 1471, at 1489–93; W Guth, R Schmittberger and B Schwarze, 'An Experimental Analysis of Ultimatum Bargaining' (1982) 3 *J Econ Behav & Org* 367, at 371–4, 375 tbls 4 and 5; D Kahneman, JL Knetsch and RH Thaler, 'Fairness and the Assumptions of Economics' (1986) 59 *J Bus* S285, S291 tbl 2.

[27] ME Stucke, 'Behavioral Economists at the Gate: Antitrust in the Twenty-First Century' (2007) 38 *Loy U Chi LJ* 513, at 530.

[28] C Jolls et al., 'A Behavioral Approach to Law and Economics' (1998) 50 *Stan L Rev* 1471, at 1492.

[29] Id. at 1490.

[30] N Ashraf et al., 'Adam Smith, Behavioral Economist' (2005) 19 *J of Econ Persp* 131, at 135–6; E Hoffman et al., 'Social Distance and Other-Regarding Behavior in Dictator Games' (1996) 86 *Am Econ Rev* 653–60.

[31] KD Vohs et al., 'The Psychological Consequences of Money' (17 November 2006) *Science*, at 1154–6.

[32] Id. at 1154–6; see also B Carey, 'Just Thinking About Money Can Turn the Mind Stingy' (21 November 2006) *NY Times*, at F6.

[33] Vohs et al., *supra* n. 31, at 1156.

denominations) chose more individually-focused leisure experiences and preferred to work alone rather than with a peer on a task.[34]

3 SHOULD SELF-INTERESTED BEHAVIOR BE THE DESIRED NORM?

People do not predictably and uniformly pursue their self-interest. Because social perceptions and other factors can influence behavior, the second issue is whether humans should aspire toward self-interested behavior. Is greed good? Will it improve overall well-being? The answer is not necessarily.

Few economists defend self-interest on normative grounds.[35] Milton Friedman defended the rationality assumptions not on normative grounds, but on his theories yielding sufficiently accurate predictions.[36] Judge Posner characterized earlier economists' attempts to defend wealth

---

[34] Id. at 1156. In another experiment, the participants played the board game Monopoly. After seven minutes, the game was cleared leaving the participants with one of three different amounts of Monopoly play money: $4,000 (high-money condition); $200 (low-money condition) and no money (control condition). For the high- and low-money condition participants, their play money remained in view for the rest of the experiment. Each participant in the high-money group was asked to imagine a future with abundant finances. Those in the low-money group were asked to imagine a future with strained finances. Those in the control group (which received no money at the end) were asked about their plans for tomorrow. An accident was staged: one confederate to the experiment (who did not know the participant's priming condition) spilled 27 pencils before the participant. Participants in the high-money condition on average gathered fewer pencils than the low-money participants, which gathered fewer pencils than the control group. Id. at 1155.

[35] R Skidelsky, 'How to Rebuild a Shamed Subject' (6 August 2009) *Fin Times*, at 11 ('Ever since modern economics started in the 18th century it has presented itself as a predictive discipline, akin to a natural science.'); L von Mises, *Human Action: A Treatise on Economics* (1998) 243 ('Economics is not intent upon pronouncing value judgments.'); D Lewinsohn-Zamir, 'The Objectivity of Well-Being and the Objectives of Property Law' (2003) 78 *NYU L Rev* 1669, at 1688 (criticizing law and economics scholars as typically and conveniently assuming that although ideal preferences are superior to actual preferences as a criterion of well-being, there usually will be no significant empirical differences in applying the two measures); E Zamir, 'The Efficiency of Paternalism' (1998) 84 *Va L Rev* 229, at 251 (noting that economic analysis ordinarily assumes rationality as descriptive, rather than normative or logical).

[36] M Friedman, 'The Methodology of Positive Economics' in (1953) *Essays in Positive Economics* 15; see also Bork, *supra* n. 2, at 120 et seq.

maximization as a societal goal and to make economics a source of moral guidance as 'doomed efforts.'[37] Instead, the economist's role is prescriptive.[38]

Another branch of economic research on happiness confirms the age-old wisdom that once one's basic needs are met, money has a weak influence on happiness.[39] In the US, higher-income individuals (those in the highest decile) reported on average the highest level of happiness.[40] But the happiness economic literature does not identify a correlation between self-interest and greater happiness. After one's basic needs are met, there is no strong correlation between *increases* in wealth and subjective happiness. For example, the mean income (adjusted for inflation) of the top income decile in the US increased 33 percent between 1972 and 1996, but the mean happiness rating for the wealthiest decile remained the same.[41] Personal control – the ability to control one's life or achieve a spiritual indifference[42] – according to a British life satisfaction study, is a better predictor of happiness than income.[43] This is not especially controversial as economists generally recognize the diminishing marginal utility of money.[44] Likewise, once a country's gross domestic product per capita

---

37 RA Posner, 'The Problematics of Moral and Legal Theory' (1998) 111 *Harv L Rev* 1637, 1670.

38 Id. ('What the economist can say, which is a lot but not everything, is that if a society values prosperity (or freedom or equality), these are the various policies that will conduce to that goal, and these are the costs associated with each. The economist cannot take the final step and say that a society's ultimate goal should be growth, equality, happiness, survival, conquest, stasis, social justice, or what have you.').

39 In multivariate regressions, income as it correlates to subjective happiness evaluations has a low coefficient. BS Frey and A Stutzer, 'What Can Economists Learn from Happiness Research?' (2002) 40 *J Econ Lit* 402, 410; see also E Dunn et al., 'Spending Money on Others Promotes Happiness' (21 March 2008) *Science*, at 1687.

40 Frey and Stutzer, *supra* n. 39, at 410 (on a three-point scale ranging from not too happy (1), pretty happy (2), and very happy (3), the tenth decile between 1994 and 1996 had a mean happiness rating of 2.36, which was slightly higher than the ninth decile's mean of 2.3).

41 Id.

42 Saint Ignatius of Loyola described this spiritual indifference, 'we must above all endeavour to establish in ourselves a complete indifference towards all created things, though the use of them may not be otherwise forbidden; not giving, as far as depends on us, any preference to health over sickness, riches over poverty, honour over humiliation, a long life over a short. But we must desire and choose definitively in every thing what will lead us to the end of our creation.' Saint Ignatius of Loyola, *Manresa or the Spiritual Exercises of St. Ignatius* (1881) at 22.

43 D Nettle, *Happiness* (2005) at 73.

44 M Rabin, 'Diminishing Marginal Utility of Wealth Cannot Explain Risk Aversion', in D Kahneman and A Tversky (eds), *Choices, Values, and Frames* (2000).

exceeds a moderate level of income, societies do not get happier as they get richer.[45] For example, per capita income (adjusted for inflation) in the US more than doubled between 1945 and 1991, but Americans are not necessarily happier.[46] The percentage of 'very happy' Americans has not increased; nor has the percentage of 'not very happy' Americans substantially decreased.[47]

One interesting behavioral experiment recently reaffirmed that there is more happiness in giving than in receiving.[48] The study's authors found that personal spending was unrelated to happiness, but spending more of one's income on charities or on other people predicted greater happiness. In one before-and-after field study, employees who spent more of their profit-sharing bonus on others experienced greater happiness, and how they spent their bonus (on themselves or others) was a more important predictor of their happiness than the bonus's amount. In another experiment, after rating their happiness in the morning, the study's participants were divided into two groups: the first was told to spend by 5 pm the money in the envelope (either $5 or $20) on themselves. The second group was told to give the money to someone else or a charity. After 5 pm, the participants were asked about their happiness. Although the amount of money received ($5 or $20) did not significantly affect the participants' happiness, the prosocial spending group reported greater post-windfall happiness than did the personal spending group.

So if giving leads to greater happiness, the study's authors ask, why don't we spend a little less on ourselves and donate a little more? People predict poorly. The authors found that 63 percent of the university students predicted personal spending would make them happier than prosocial spending, and that $20 would make them happier than $5.[49]

---

[45] D Kahneman et al., 'Would You Be Happier If You Were Richer? A Focusing Illusion' (30 June 2006) *Science*, at 1909; see also Nettle, *supra* n. 43, at 72 et seq.; R Di Tella and R MacCulloch, 'Some Uses of Happiness Data in Economics' (2006) 20 *J Econ Persp* 25, at 26; D Kahneman and AB Krueger, 'Developments in the Measurement of Subjective Well-Being' (2006) 20 *J Econ Persp* 3, at 15 et seq. (despite China's real income per capita increasing by a factor of 2.5 between 1994 and 2005, no increase in reported life satisfaction, and an increase in percentage who are dissatisfied); Frey and Stutzer, *supra* n. 39, at 413 (Japan's income per capita increased six-fold between 1958 and 1991, while average life satisfaction remained unchanged).

[46] Frey and Stutzer, *supra* n. 39, at 403; R Layard, *Happiness: Lessons from a New Science* (2005) at 29 et seq.; Di Tella and MacCulloch, *supra* n. 45, at 26.

[47] Layard, *supra* n. 46, at 29 et seq.

[48] Dunn et al., *supra* n. 39.

[49] Dunn et al., *supra* n. 39, at 1688.

Behavioral economists describe this 'focusing illusion' in pursuing happiness as '[n]othing in life matters quite as much as you think it does while you are thinking about it.'[50] The happiness economic studies show how people inaccurately predict first, the impact of future life events on their happiness (such as junior professors' prediction if denied tenure),[51] second their adapting to their new condition (whether a physical disability or winning the lottery),[52] and third the strong effects of relative rather than absolute wealth on satisfaction.[53] People often predict greater happiness if they were only wealthier. But 'increases in income have mostly a transitory effect on individuals' reported life satisfaction.'[54] Winners of large amounts of money in lotteries, for example, have a temporary boost in happiness.[55] Individuals may desire more goods and services, but after obtaining them, they become preoccupied with obtaining other goods and services.[56]

Many people do not care solely about absolute levels of wealth or personal consumption, but changes in their wealth and consumption relative to others.[57] One's total income is less important than relative income, namely earning slightly more than one's peers, neighbors, friends, or as

---

[50] D Kahneman and RH Thaler, 'Anomalies: Utility Maximization & Experienced Utility' (2006) 20 *J Econ Persp* 221; DA Schkade and D Kahneman, 'Does Living in California Make People Happy?' (September 1998) *Psychological Science*, at 340 et seq.

[51] Nettle, *supra* n. 43, at 72 et seq.

[52] Di Tella and MacCulloch, *supra* n. 45, at 36 n. 7 (collecting sources).

[53] Nettle, *supra* n. 43, at 73; Layard, *supra* n. 46, at 41 et seq. Similarly, humans rarely choose things in absolute terms, but their relative advantage to other things. Ariely, *supra* n. 16, at 2. As Professor Ariely discusses, by adding a 3rd more expensive choice, for example, the marketer can steer consumers to a more expensive 2nd choice. In one behavioral economic study, 100 MIT students were offered three choices for *The Economist* magazine: (i) Internet-only subscription for $59 (16 students); (ii) print-only subscriptions for $125 (0 students); and (iii) print-and-Internet subscriptions for $125 (84 students). When the 'decoy' second choice (print-only subscriptions) was removed and only the first and third options were presented, the students did not react similarly. Instead, 68 students opted for Internet-only subscription for $59 (up from 16 students) and only 32 students chose print-and-Internet subscriptions for $125 (down from 84 students). Id. at 5–6.

[54] Kahneman et al., *supra* n. 45.

[55] Nettle, *supra* n. 43, at 75. Even people with acquired disabilities or health problems show considerable, but always not complete, adaptation to happiness. Id. at 83.

[56] Id. at 15; Kahneman et al., *supra* n. 45, at 1909–10.

[57] M Rabin, 'A Perspective on Psychology and Economics' (2002) 46 *Eur Econ Rev* 657, at 661.

HL Mencken observed, one's wife's sister's husband.[58] We compete by comparing ourselves to the wealth and consumption of our peers and the socio-economic class immediately above us. After adapting to the higher rung, we strive for more.[59]

So if self-interested behavior does not necessarily promote happiness, what according to the happiness economic literature does? Although measuring happiness can be fickle,[60] drawing from large diverse samples, the literature yields consistent conclusions. In examining happiness in 50 countries in up to four years, one study identified six factors that can explain 80 percent of the variation in happiness: divorce rate, unemployment rate, level of trust, membership in non-religious organizations, quality of government, and fraction believing in God.[61] On an individual level, the primary sources of happiness are family relationships, employment, community and friends, health, self-control or autonomy, personal ethical and moral values, and the quality of the environment.[62] Individuals who look beyond their self-interest and practice religion, belong to community organizations, do voluntary work, and have rich social connections generally are healthier and happier than those who do not.[63] Likewise, the most satisfying jobs were, as one recent survey found,

58 Kahneman et al., *supra* n. 45; see also D Neumark and A Postlewaite, 'Relative Income Concerns and the Rise in Married Women's Employment' (1998) 70 *J Pub Econ* 157 (finding that women's employment decisions are positively related to sisters' employment decision; women, whose sisters live nearby and worked the past year, are all else being equal about 10 to 15 percent more likely to work than women whose sisters did not work).

59 Ariely, *supra* n. 16, at 17 et seq.

60 Individual responses can depend on the order or wording of questions, the scales applied, a fortunate event (like the individual discovering a dime before the questioning), or the current weather. Frey and Stutzer, *supra* n. 39, at 406; Kahneman and Krueger, *supra* n. 45, at 6 et seq. One study for example examined the correlation between the responses of two questions: 'How happy are you?' and 'How many dates did you have last month?' When the happiness question was asked first, no correlation was found between the responses. But when the dating question was asked first, there was a significant correlation between the two questions' responses. Likewise, in another study, individuals were first asked to report either three positive or negative recent life events. Respondents who were first asked to recall the recent positive events reported higher current life satisfaction than those who were first asked to report three recent negative events. N Schwartz and F Strack, 'Reports of Subjective Well-Being: Judgmental Processes & Their Methodological Implications' in D Kahneman et al. (eds), *Well-Being: The Foundations of Hedonic Psychology* (1999) at 63–5.

61 Layard, *supra* n. 46, at 71.

62 Id. at 62–73; Nettle, *supra* n. 43, at 85, 87.

63 Nettle, *supra* n. 43, at 156 et seq.

'especially those involving caring for, teaching, and protecting others and creative pursuits,'[64] not those jobs with the highest salaries or that reward self-interest.[65]

4 WHAT ARE THE RISKS IF THE GOVERNMENT PROMOTES SELF-INTERESTED BEHAVIOR?

The Chicago School's assumption of self-interest does not depict how people actually act or ought to act. This leads to the third and final issue: what are the risks of a government policy that promotes such self-interested behavior?

A Chicago School theorist might agree that humans do not (nor should they) invariably pursue their self-interest. Instead, the assumption of self-interested behavior is useful in the context of commercial transactions. No one quibbles when consumers seek to save money by going to the cheaper gasoline station. Manufacturers compete by offering the optimal mix of quality, price, and choices to consumers. Within these happy confines, promoting self-interested behavior is undisputed. No one contends that consumers should opt for higher-priced, inferior-quality goods and services or that a market economy benefits from cartels.

But policymakers can become restless within these confines and press further. If society benefits whenever consumers pursue their self-interest in opting for lower-priced, better-quality goods, shouldn't society likewise benefit whenever people seek to maximize their wealth? 'Greed is the foundation of much economic activity.'[66] So if self-interest is good within the happy confines of price competition, why isn't self-interest good generally?

Even without governmental prodding, profit-maximizing firms will continue to encourage consumers to pursue their self-interest. But to what extent should the government either through soft paternalism or hard policies promote self-interest for its own sake? A helpful exercise is to consider the risks from governmental policies that promote self-interested behavior

---

64 TW Smith, 'Job Satisfaction in the United States' (17 April 2007), http://www-news.uchicago.edu/releases/07/pdf/070417.jobs.pdf (accessed December 2010).

65 Heading the list were members of the clergy (87.3% very satisfied), followed by physical therapists (with the second highest mean score and 78.1% very satisfied) and firefighters (80.1% very satisfied). Occupations with the happiest reported people were the clergy (67.2% very happy) and firefighters (57.2% very happy). Id.

66 *Kumpf v Steinhaus*, 779 F.2d 1323, 1326 (7th Cir. 1985) (Easterbrook, J).

as a norm. As I elaborate elsewhere several risks of such policies,[67] this chapter will briefly discuss one risk.

Although humans engage in commerce to promote their satisfaction and at times self-interest, this collective pursuit of self-interest will not always lead to optimal outcomes. Appealing to self-interested behavior, rather than support, at times can undermine a market economy. In examining the recent financial crisis, for example, Richard Posner described how self-interested behavior of 'law-abiding financiers and consumers can precipitate an economic disaster.'[68] Judge Posner draws a distinction of self-interest as a private virtue and public vice. Self-interest is a private virtue in that competition drives businesses to profit maximization, which drives economic progress.[69] But such self-interested behavior can be, at times, a public vice. An overleveraged financial institution may ignore the small probability that its risky conduct in conjunction with its competitors' risky conduct may bring down the entire economy. Each firm in pursuing its self-interest will incur greater leverage to maximize profits. Here, Posner argues, the government must serve as a countervailing force to such self-interested private behavior by better regulating financial institutions.[70]

But Posner's conception of self-interested behavior as a private virtue/public vice is problematic. The more government policies promote self-interested behavior as a private virtue, the more difficult it will be to characterize it over time as a public vice. For example, Posner criticizes government officials for not protecting the public against the risks of self-interested behavior: government officials 'heavily invested' in the ideology of self-correcting free markets deregulated the banking industry, which increased competition and the leverage banks undertook.[71] But these government policies in a sense reflect the will of the public (or those interest groups with the greater political clout). If market participants

---

67 See ME Stucke, 'Money, Is That What I Want? Competition Policy & the Role of Behavioral Economics' (2010) 50 *Santa Clara L Rev* 893.

68 Posner, *supra* n. 1, at 107; see also id. at 111 et seq. Fielding congressional questioning during the financial crisis, the former Fed Chairman Alan Greenspan also expressed his 'distress' in discovering a 'flaw' in his free-market beliefs: 'Those of us who have looked to the self-interest of lending institutions to protect shareholder's equity (myself especially) are in a state of shocked disbelief.' K Scannell and S Reddy, 'Greenspan Admits Errors to Hostile House Panel' (24 October 2008) *Wall St J*, http://online.wsj.com/article/SB122476545437862295.html (accessed December 2010).

69 Posner, *supra* n. 1, at 107.

70 Id. at 107.

71 Id. at 130, 134–5.

personally will profit from deregulation of their industry, they will be more sympathetic to political candidates who broadly construe their self-interested behavior as virtuous, and narrowly consider the likelihood of market failure. With each election cycle, and as the earlier financial crisis loses its salience, the market participants will promote political candidates who praise the virtues of self-interest and more narrowly consider the likelihood of market failure. With each election cycle, voters who survived the last depression will be fewer in number (as they die off), replaced by more confident voters who lived what John Mills described the 'Middle or Revival Period' and the later 'Speculative Period.'[72] As greed seemingly becomes more virtuous in correcting market failures, elected officials will find it increasingly difficult to characterize self-interested behavior as both a private virtue and a public vice.

Rather than maintain this dichotomy, government policies instead can recognize that an economy 'needs other values and commitments such as mutual trust and confidence to work efficiently.'[73] There is nothing inherently virtuous about self-interested behavior. Self-interested market participants – free of legal, social and ethical institutions – are not a prerequisite for a market economy or for promoting overall happiness. Unbridled capitalism, as Professors Akerlof and Shiller write, 'does not automatically produce what people really need; it produces what they *think* they need, and are willing to pay for.'[74] It can maximize output of snake oil or products that eventually wipe out the economy.[75]

At times appealing to self-interest is less effective than appealing to social, moral, or ethical norms. In many behavioral experiments, financial rewards or penalties when displacing social, moral, or ethical norms actually decrease motivation. Behavioral economist Dan Ariely describes several experiments where he divided the participants into three groups – all performing the same mundane task.[76] But one group (the social-norm group) was not compensated, and was asked to undertake the task as a favor. In the first experiment, the social-norm group outperformed the group members who received $5 as compensation for the task, who

---

72 J Fox, *The Myth of the Rational Market* (2009), at 309 et seq.

73 A Sen, 'Adam Smith's Market Never Stood Alone' (11 March 2009) *Fin Times*, at 9; *see also* Ashraf et al., *supra* n. 30, at 136 (collecting some of the literature on importance of trust in market economies).

74 Akerlof and Shiller, *supra* n. 16, at 26.

75 See A Faiola et al., 'What Went Wrong?' (15 October 2008) *Wash Post*, at A1 (noting several Clinton and Bush administrations officials' opposition to regulation of derivatives).

76 Ariely, *supra* n. 16, at 69 et seq.

outperformed the group members who received 50 cents. In the second experiment, the two groups did not receive cash but a gift of comparable value (a Snickers bar for the 50-cents group and a box of Godiva chocolate for the $5 group). These two groups performed as hard as the social-norm group. In the third experiment, the gifts were monetized to the two groups – a '50-cent Snickers bar' or a '$5-box of Godiva chocolates' – who again devoted less effort than the social-norm group.[77]

Another implication is that a social policy that promotes the perception that its citizens are self-interested may be self-defeating. People are not inherently selfish. But if they perceive that many others are behaving selfishly (such as cheating on their taxes), then they may be more inclined to behave selfishly as well.[78] For example, one study of more than 5,000 business (mostly MBA) and non-business graduate students at US and Canadian universities found that graduate business students cheat more than their non-business student peers. The largest influence in the business students' behavior, found the study's authors, was the students' perception that their peers were also cheating.[79]

There must be a good reason why many societies internalize in their children the norms of altruism, compassion, and empathy. Before advocating self-interest, one must inquire why societies promote these other norms. Empathy, even for adults, can debias moral judgments. People at times lack the capacity to reach moral judgments through pure reason. Thus a principal pathway to moral judgments is empathy.[80] Studies find that psychopaths understand the rules of social behavior and their action's harmful consequences, but they simply do not care.[81] By putting oneself in the other person's position, one may experience multiple competing intuitions,[82] which helps mitigate self-serving bias,[83] and has been identified as the 'single most effective skill in negotiation.'[84]

---

77 Id.

78 Fehr and Fischbacher, *supra* n. 22, at 167.

79 DL McCabe et al., 'Academic Dishonesty in Graduate Business Programs: Prevalence, Causes, and Proposed Action' (2006) 5 *Academy of Management Learning & Education* 294, http://faculty.mwsu.edu/psychology/dave.carlston/Writing%20in%20Psychology/Academic%20Dishonesty/Grop%204/business2.pdf (accessed December 2010).

80 J Haidt, 'The Emotional Dog and Its Rational Tail: A Social Intuitionist Approach to Moral Judgment' (2001) 108 *Psych Rev* 814, 819.

81 Id. at 824.

82 Id. at 819.

83 C Jolls et al., 'A Behavioral Approach to Law and Economics' (1998) 50 *Stan L Rev* 1471, 1503–4.

84 W Ury, *Getting Past No* (1993), at 19.

Ultimately our survival depends upon cooperation and our ability to look beyond our self-interest. Thus the behavioral economics experiments' larger implication is in preventing society's perception of civic duties as unraveling. Once the conditional cooperators perceive others as acting selfishly, they too will act selfishly. Any social policy should discourage, rather than encourage, the assumption that most people act selfishly, and instead emphasize that others are cooperating in their civic duties.[85]

This is especially important as the Internet and global commerce over the past 20 years have broadened social relationships and increased the interdependence of citizens throughout the world. To evolve, economies must rely on complex, large-scale cooperation. When conducting their Ultimatum Game experiment in 15 small-scale economies from 12 countries on 4 continents, the researchers found that the range of offers varied more than the range of offers by university students.[86] The differences among societies in 'market integration' and 'cooperation in production' explained a substantial portion of the behavioral variation between the different economies: 'The higher the degree of market integration and the higher the payoffs to cooperation, the greater the level of cooperation and sharing in experimental games.'[87] Moreover, 'the nature and degree of cooperation and punishment in the experiments,' they found, were 'generally consistent with economic patterns of everyday life in these societies. In a number of cases, the parallels between experimental game play and the structure of daily life were quite striking.'[88] Likewise, in reviewing traits that appear with regularity in studies of cultures of high-performing and adaptive companies, a senior advisor to McKinsey & Co. identified ten

---

85 Fehr and Fischbacher, *supra* n. 22, at 167.

86 Gintis et al., *supra* n. 25, at 154.

87 The societies were rank-ordered in five categories – 'market integration' (how often do people buy and sell, or work for a wage), 'cooperation in production' (is production collective or individual), plus 'anonymity' (how prevalent are anonymous roles and transactions), 'privacy' (how easily can people keep their activities secret), and 'complexity' (how much centralized decision-making occurs above the level of the household). Using statistical regression analysis, only the first two characteristics, market integration and cooperation in production, were significant. Id. at 158.

88 Id. BM Friedman, *The Moral Consequences of Economic Growth* (2005), at 79–102 (describing whenever America was mired in economic stagnation its democratic values stagnated as well. Hostility toward immigrants, the poor, and other competing groups, whether by nationality, religion, race, or gender, increased as these groups were seemingly threatened by others stealing their fixed, or dwindling, share of the pie. In contrast, during periods of economic growth, our society slowly progressed from this zero-sum mentality toward openness, mobility, and democracy).

illustrative performing, cooperating, and innovating norms.[89] These coincide with religious and ethical norms involving respect and reciprocity (for example, do unto others as you would have them do unto you), honesty, and trust.

The recent financial crisis has provided the needed impetus for government policymakers to re-examine many assumptions underlying our current economic policies. A competition policy that assumes self-interested behavior may be misguided. It ignores how ethical, moral, and social norms may hinder undesirable conduct and promote desirable behavior more effectively than financial incentives and penalties. In understanding the drivers of behavior (beyond the assumption of wealth-maximization), competition policy can better understand how such informal norms can promote the desired objectives. Money may be an inefficient mechanism to motivate, noted behavioral economist Dan Ariely. 'Social norms are not only cheaper, but often more effective as well.'[90]

Competition policy's greatest failing, over the past 30 years, has been empirical. Policymakers do not have an effective feedback mechanism to quickly learn of and correct their mistakes when predicting a merger's or restraint's likely competitive effects. Thus they incompletely comprehend how competition works in particular markets, in particular communities, at particular time periods, and the interplay among private institutions, government institutions, and informal social, ethical, and moral norms. Rather than rely on financial incentives and disincentives, policymakers can use the behavioral economics literature to consider how ethical, moral, and social norms can assist in attaining the desired outcome. By undertaking more empirical research, competition authorities will better understand the dynamics of human motivation under different settings and how legal, social, and ethical norms interact to influence individual behavior and competition generally.

The lessons do not end there. The financial crisis has fueled outrage against greedy Wall Street bankers. But did one really expect these bankers to exercise restraint and forgo bonuses? Instead, the financial crisis's larger implication is how many of us were taken in with the notion that self-interest was somehow virtuous. Although greed may now appear repulsive, did we not ourselves once revel in it?

---

[89] ED Beinhocker, *The Origin of Wealth: The Radical Remaking of Economics and What it Means for Business and Society* (2007), at 370–71.

[90] Ariely, *supra* n. 16, at 86.

2. Consumer choice as the best way to recenter the mission of competition law

Robert H. Lande*

1 INTRODUCTION

The mission of competition law needs to be clarified, and this article shows that the best way to do this is to interpret and enforce these laws in terms of consumer choice. This reformulation is necessary due to uncertainty and instability that exist in the field. For example, even though the United States' competition laws, which it calls antitrust laws, are more than a century old, it can't decide upon these laws' overall purpose. The 'main point of antitrust' in the United States from 1890 to the 1970s was a variety of social/political/economic objectives, including the belief that big businesses were suspect and small businesses were good.[1] Then the efficiency-only paradigm emerged during the Reagan and Bush administrations.[2] More recently, the Clinton Administration seemed to care about enhancing economic efficiency and also about protecting consumers from

* This chapter is in large part a condensation and update of NW Averitt and RH Lande, 'Using the "Consumer Choice" Approach to Antitrust Law' (2007) 74 *Antitrust LJ* 175. I am grateful to Christine Carey, James Denvil and Gary Stapleton for excellent research assistance.

1 RH Lande, 'Wealth Transfers as the Original and Primary Concern of Antitrust: The Efficiency Interpretation Challenged' (1982) 34 Hastings LJ 64, at 101–105, available at http://papers.ssrn.com/so13/papers.cfm?abstract_id=1121459. See also JB Kirkwood and RH Lande, 'The Fundamental Goal of Antitrust: Protecting Consumers, Not Increasing Efficiency' (2008) 84 *Notre Dame L Rev* 191, available at http://papers.ssrn.com/so13/papers.cfm?abstract_id=1113927.

2 See Kirkwood and Lande, *supra* n. 1, at 191–6. The efficiency approach originated in the 1960s, with Robert Bork, and was spread by Judge Posner and others. This approach did not merely assert that efficiency is important, but rather asserted that efficiency is the only acceptable goal of antitrust. With Reagan's 1980 election, federal enforcement officials who adhered to the efficiency approach were appointed, and it came to dominate antitrust. Today many

paying more as a result of illegally acquired market power: the 'wealth transfer' or 'protecting consumers' property from theft by market power' reason for competition law.[3]

What does the Obama administration believe? It is too early to tell, but it is possible that its overriding concern will be different from prior administrations. Of course it will care about efficiency and about consumers paying higher prices, but it might well use as its loadstar an approach focusing on consumer choice. The consumer choice approach began being utilized during the Clinton and Bush administrations, and it often has been used by the European Union.[4] But it might well be used even more during the Obama administration.

This article will define the consumer choice approach to competition law or antitrust law and show how it differs from other approaches (at 2, below); it will discuss the types of situations where a consumer choice focus is likely to make a difference in enforcement outcomes, producing better results than the other paradigms (at 3, below); it will show that another important advantage of using the consumer choice approach would be to nudge decisions in the right direction (at 4, below); and, finally, it will offer a brief overview of implementation issues (at 5, below).

---

scholars still exclusively believe in the efficiency goal. This is especially true of economists.

[3] The Clinton administration did not adhere to any one specific approach and, during its eight years, did not speak with one voice on the subject. Efficiency was a large part of its concern, and there was no inclination to return in any way to a 'big is bad/small is good' philosophy. But it was also concerned with prices to consumers, or 'wealth transfers' from consumers to firms with market power. (When cartels raise prices they cause not only allocative inefficiency, but also a transfer of wealth from consumers to firms with market power. See Lande, *supra* n. 1, at 101–5.) This is the theft explanation for antitrust or competition law, and it asserts that these laws are at their core about corporations stealing consumers' property – consumers' surplus. Cartels are undesirable because they unfairly raise prices to consumers above the competitive level and thereby represent a taking of consumers' property by the cartel. Id. at 96.

Perhaps surprisingly, this same theft or wealth transfer approach has also been adopted by the US Supreme Court. See Kirkwood and Lande, *supra* n. 1, at 192 and 216–9. Because its last 15 antitrust cases were all decided in favor of the defendants, one might think that the US Supreme Court had endorsed the efficiency paradigm. But these cases may be explained better by a concern with protecting consumers from paying supra-competitive prices than they are with efficiency. Efficiency is important to the Court, but the transfer seems to be even more important. Id.

[4] See infra n. 38 et seq.

2 WHAT IS THE 'CONSUMER CHOICE' APPROACH TO COMPETITION LAW?

If you examine every type of competition law or antitrust law violation, from price fixing to predation, and ask what they have in common, the answer is that they all significantly restrict consumer choice. Every violation significantly and artificially distorts or diminishes the choices that otherwise would be offered by the free market.[5] This does not mean everything that significantly reduces consumer choice is, or should be, a violation of competition laws. But if you examine what these violations have in common, it is that they significantly reduce consumer choice.

How does a consumer choice approach differ from either a price approach or an efficiency approach? It is broader than both, and it includes both. First, it includes price considerations because consumers should be able to choose from among the price options a free market would provide. Additionally, it encompasses the wealth transferred from consumers to firms acquiring market power (the belief that when cartels raise prices above the competitive level this constitutes the theft of consumers' property). The consumer choice approach also includes efficiency considerations, especially the innovation concern, because optimal innovation gives rise to optimal consumer choice. Because cost savings efficiencies can affect price, these considerations are included as well. But most important, the consumer choice approach also gives a high priority to other consumer concerns such as competition in terms of quality, variety, service, and privacy.[6]

Some other crucial elements of a choice paradigm include the following idea: (1) Not every decrease in consumer choice counts as an injury to competition; only significant decreases, but not, for example, a reduction

---

[5] For example, collusion, including price fixing, and the division of markets and customers diminish the choices – usually the price choices – available to consumers, and replace price choices determined by competition with price choices determined by collusion. By contrast, procompetitive joint ventures leading to new or less expensive products do not restrict consumer choice. A second example is anticompetitive mergers, which can produce too few firms in the marketplace and thus lead to fewer choices than the free market would offer. Monopolization through predation also artificially reduces the choices available to consumers. For an analysis of every antitrust violation in choice terms see RH Lande, 'Consumer Choice as the Ultimate Goal of Antitrust' (2001) 62 *U Pittsburgh L Rev.* 503, at 506–8, available at http://papers.ssrn.com/sol3/papers.cfm?abstract_id=1478680.

[6] See NW Averitt and RH Lande, 'Using the "Consumer Choice" Approach to Antitrust Law' (2007) 74 *Antitrust LJ*, 175, at 183, available at http://papers.ssrn.com/sol3/papers.cfm?abstract_id=1121459.

in choice from ten down to nine options; (2) More choice is not necessarily good. The goal of competition policy should not be to maximize choice, but rather to eliminate practices that artificially restrict the choices the free market otherwise would have provided; (3) Although every competition law violation reduces consumer choice, not every reduction in consumer choice violates competition law. Some reductions in consumer choice – such as when a monopolist reduces its variety of offerings – do not violate any law; (4) Reductions in consumers' ability to choose from among the offerings the market provides are consumer protection violations;[7] (5) Competition law under a consumer choice perspective would continue to have efficiency defenses since efficiencies can positively affect consumer choice.

The overall approach can be illustrated by the most highly publicized US antitrust litigation of our generation – the *Microsoft* case.[8] This case illustrates the importance of choice, and illustrates how we have been moving towards a choice paradigm, because it was litigated primarily in 'choice' terms. The products in question were PC operating systems and web browsers. The pertinent briefs and court decisions reveal that both the litigants and the court focused primarily on innovation, new products, and short-term and long-term consumer choice.[9] Naturally, both sides strongly disagreed about how to maximize consumer choice, but the important point is that price and cost savings were less important concerns. In *Microsoft*, little attention was paid to the price of the operating system – over which Microsoft had a legal monopoly – or the price of the web browser, which was given away free. Nor were cost savings efficiencies the primary concern. Rather, diminished short-term consumer choices, innovation, and the resulting long-term choices innovation would have brought were the key issues.[10]

Even though this article urges that competition law should shift to employing an explicit focus upon consumer choice, *Microsoft* illustrates that the United States is engaged in a lengthy process of shifting from an efficiency or price approach towards a choice approach, even if choice terminology is not always explicitly used. This case also illustrates how a price or efficiency model is often inadequate to address our concerns in the competition or antitrust area.

---

7 Id. at 181 et seq.
8 Lande, *supra* n. 5, at 511–4.
9 Id. at 511 et seq.
10 Id. at 511.

3 WHEN WOULD THE CONSUMER CHOICE FORMULATION MAKE A DIFFERENCE?

At this point one might think: 'Of course competition law should be concerned about more than just price and cost savings. Of course quality, service, etc. should impact the analysis. However, if a market is competitive in terms of pricing issues, won't it also be competitive in terms of non-price issues? If a market has three firms, or five firms, or whatever number of firms one believes is enough to ensure price competition in a particular market, won't this same number of firms also ensure non-price competition? If so, what is the harm in using just a price standard? Won't ensuring price competition automatically give us the non-price options we want as well?'

Normally this is indeed true. Normally there is no difference between a choice approach and a price approach, and therefore little benefit to using a choice standard. For example, suppose there are four firms making cookies, that three firms are enough to have price competition, and that three firms could make them at the same cost as four. If consumers want 20 different types of cookie, or 200, three firms should be able to supply them just as well as four. If two of the four firms wanted to merge, there would be no advantage to using a choice standard over a price standard or an efficiency standard to assess this merger.

But sometimes it would make a difference. There are three broad categories of cases where a choice analysis could lead to a different (and in each case superior) result: cases in markets with little or no price competition; cases involving conduct that increase consumers' search costs or otherwise impairs their decision-making ability; and cases in markets in which firms compete primarily through independent product development and creativity, rather than through price.

3.1 Markets Lacking Serious Price Competition

The first group of cases involves conduct in markets with little or no price competition as a result of regulation, industry-wide joint ventures, or third party payers. In these situations there is no way properly to assess consumer welfare without focusing explicitly on non-price issues.

First, consider markets where prices are regulated. For example, airlines in the United States, before they were deregulated, competed in terms of quality and service, as demonstrated by their intense competition over the quality of the meals they served.[11] A price analysis of this market would

[11] Averitt and Lande, *supra* n. 6, at 196–7, n. 67–9.

have been seriously incomplete. One even could ask why the United States did not permit every airline to merge during the period when their rates were regulated. After all, they could not have raised prices. The answer is that we wanted non-price competition.

Now consider a market where all the significant firms were allowed to merge. Montgomery County, Maryland, allowed its two major taxicab companies to merge, on the theory that prices were regulated so there could be no harm from this merger.[12] Unfortunately, as a result of the merger, service and quality went down significantly.[13] This example illustrates that, even if prices are regulated, competition often leads to better service, and the potential harm to consumers in these markets from a lack of competition are often extremely difficult to quantify in price terms.

Second, consider situations involving industry-wide joint ventures.[14] There have been many United States cases, including *Aspen*[15] and *Broadcast Music Incorporated*,[16] involving all or most all of a relevant market. These joint ventures severely restricted price competition as a necessary part of their operations, and also involved activity that limited consumer choice. In these cases it would have been meaningless to decide whether the joint venture was procompetitive or anticompetitive by focusing only on price terms because there was only limited price competition in the relevant markets. In each case there was, however, significant non-price competition between the firms that entered into the joint venture. Consumers could pick from among the firms in the market on the basis of service, quality, or another dimension of competition. Alternatively, one could ask why all the firms in these joint venture cases were not allowed to merge since they were setting joint prices already? The answer is that we wanted to preserve choice competition.

Third, consider cases involving third party payers.[17] Whenever their bills are paid by someone else, consumers are likely to care more about quality, service, and variety than price. If a person knows their medical or car repair bills will be paid by their insurance company, for example, a price model would be woefully inadequate at explaining their behavior.

---

12 Id. at 233–5.

13 Id. at 234.

14 Id. at 197 et seq.

15 Id. at 197 (citing *Aspen Skiing Co. v Aspen Highlands Skiing Corp.*, 472 US 585 (1985)).

16 Id. at 198 (citing *Broadcast Music, Inc. v CBS*, 441 US 1 (1979)).

17 Id. at 198 et seq.

3.2 Conduct that Increases Consumers' Search Costs or Otherwise Impairs Their Decision-making Ability

A second broad category of cases when a consumer choice approach will work better involves conduct that increase consumers' search costs or otherwise impairs their decision-making ability. This conduct tends to cause consumers to obtain products or services less suited to their needs, at a cost higher in terms of the value of consumers' time, in addition to adversely impacting price.

In the United States there have been a large number of these cases, including the advertising restriction cases: *Bates v State Bar of Arizona*,[18] *Mass Board of Optometry*,[19] and similar cases that involve collusion to raise consumer search costs, including *National Society of Professional Engineers*,[20] and *Detroit Auto Dealers*.[21] Prices of the products and services in question – legal services, optician services, cars, etc. – probably increased as this was the restraints' purpose.[22] The restrictions against advertising also made it harder for consumers to choose the service or product that best suited their needs.[23] Moreover, consumers' selection of a less optimal engineer, lawyer, optician, automobile, etc. harmed their welfare.

In each instance, efficiencies were claimed for the practices. Depending upon the case, the efficiencies were more, or less, believable.[24]

If practices such as these were evaluated under the rule of reason, the negative effects of the practices – both the higher prices and the deleterious effects of consumers obtaining an engineer, lawyer, optician, or automobile that was suboptimal for their purposes – should be balanced against the practices' efficiencies. If only the negative price effects were included in this trade-off, the balance easily could come out in favor of the restraint. However, a trade-off that included the negative effects on consumer

---

[18] Id. at 200 (citing *Bates v State Bar of Arizona*, 433 US 350, 384 (1977) (rule forbidding most attorney advertising overturned on First Amendment grounds)).

[19] Id. (citing *Massachusetts Bd. of Registration in Optometry*, 110 F.T.C. 549 (1988) (board regulations impeding advertising by corporate providers, and prohibiting advertising of discounts, were unauthorized by statute, and condemned as antitrust violations)).

[20] Id. (citing *National Society of Professional Engineers*, 435 US 679, 681 (1978)).

[21] Id. at 200 et seq. (citing *National Society of Professional Engineers*, *Detroit Auto Dealers Ass'n*, 111 F.T.C. 417, 681 (1989)).

[22] Id.

[23] Id. at 200.

[24] Id.

choice, as well as the negative price effects, would more accurately measure the effects of the restrictions on overall consumer welfare.

3.3 Markets in which Firms Compete Primarily through Independent Product Development and Creativity, Rather Than through Price

Finally, there are some markets in which firms compete primarily through independent product development and creativity, rather than through price. These markets may involve high-tech innovation or editorial independence in the news media. Effective competition in these industries may sometimes require more independent centers of decision-making than are required to ensure price competition, so market concentration principles taken from a price context may not ensure robust competition in the respects that are actually most relevant to consumers. In these cases, competition law decision-makers should focus upon artificially diminished consumer choice even if prices are competitive. For this reason, in these markets a price standard is inadequate.

For example, the media is an area where society cares a great deal about independent judgment, decision-making and creativity. Suppose there were only four remaining media firms of a particular type (such as book publishers, TV, radio or magazine owners) and that two of them wanted to merge. Suppose they could guarantee that the prices of the remaining three firms would remain competitive following the merger. Should society approve this merger? Or would society fear the artificially diminished choice that can result from fewer independent sources of opinion and information? If so, some large media mergers might well be evaluated differently under a choice standard than under a price standard.

It might be instructive to contrast a media merger with the earlier example of a conventional merger of cookie-making firms. Recall the example where there were only four firms that made cookies, and three would be enough to yield effective price competition. Whether consumers want 20 or 200 different types of cookie the remaining three firms should supply them. For a hypothetical four to three cookie merger there would be no advantage to using a choice standard over a price standard or an efficiency standard. The key difference is that the owners of the cookie companies don't care which cookies their customers eat, so they will produce whatever kinds of cookie consumers want.

In contrast, owners of the media might have distinct preferences concerning the editorial content of the news. Within limits, they may be able to add their own slant to coverage. Moreover, the media owners might have unconscious biases and presuppositions, so even if they have the best intention they might not be able to supply the full range of views. While companies can easily make many different types of cookie, it is much more difficult to hold all sorts of different worldviews.

To emphasize the point: the United States has six major TV networks.[25] Should all six be allowed to merge the entirety of their news operations into one? Media pooling is currently permitted, and dozens of newspapers were permitted to form the Associated Press.[26] Why not allow all six of the major TV networks to merge all of their news operations? This merger would produce very significant cost saving efficiencies. But it is extremely uncertain that it would produce any anticompetitive effects on prices. Because TV news programs compete for advertising dollars and personnel with many other types of televised broadcasts and also to some extent with other forms of media, an anticompetitive price effect would be extremely difficult to demonstrate. The real harm from this news gathering merger, however, could easily be expressed in terms of choice – in terms of perspectives, quality, and varieties of approaches to news coverage. A choice model would account for this harm much better than a price or efficiency model.[27]

---

25 Id. at 235.

26 Id. at n. 226.

27 The Voter News Service (VNS) is also illustrative. See Lande, *supra* n. 5, at 519–22. At 8:00 pm on 7 November 2000, Election Day in the United States, all the major TV networks declared that Presidential candidate Al Gore won the state of Florida, and therefore the election. Later, at 10:00 pm, all the networks simultaneously declared Florida too close to call. Next, the networks called it for Presidential candidate George W Bush. Then once again, the networks later declared Florida was too close to call.

Each network called the state of Florida wrong twice – once for each candidate. Why the uniformity of incorrect results? Previously six election prediction organizations existed independently, but they gradually combined the entirety of their election polling and prediction operations to form the VNS. This produced significant cost saving efficiencies. Did it also have negative effects on prices? It is extremely difficult to find any significant price effects. Whether VNS charged the six news organizations a monopoly price is irrelevant since the six news organizations owned it.

Unfortunately, due to their combination there was no effective competition in terms of choice of information, quality, perspective, or variety of approaches to election prediction. If the VNS were analysed under the rule of reason, and all that was balanced was its considerable cost savings against its non-existent or highly uncertain price effects, VNS probably would survive an antitrust challenge. But if the balance weighed these cost savings against both the dubious price effects and also the far more certain decrease in quality, fewer independent approaches to election prediction, and less viewer choice, then the case might well come out differently. If there had been competition among six (or even between two) election polling or prediction organizations, the predictions might have been more accurate, and viewer choice would have been greater. Id.

Alternatively, consider high technology markets where innovation is crucial. It is virtually meaningless to apply a price standard to evaluate the effects of a merger or joint venture on future technology since that technology does not yet exist. For mergers in the defense, pharmaceutical, computer, or other high-tech sectors, to ensure the optimal level of future consumer choice we want divergent sources of attempts to innovate. Consumers quite often prefer innovation over low prices on existing products.[28]

These situations should be evaluated explicitly and directly as to whether research that might lead to new and better products will be enhanced or eliminated. Price effects should also be evaluated, but a consumer choice approach would, quite properly, intensify the focus on products that might never be invented but for the merger or joint venture. The practices at issue mostly affect non-price competition, so competition law should focus on these issues explicitly. Doing so might sometimes result in the recognition that more firms are needed for innovation or perspective competition than for price competition.

4 IMPLEMENTATION ISSUES

Competition law cannot seriously consider adopting an overall approach unless it can be implemented in a relatively objective, predictable manner. How does the choice focus compare to the other approaches in terms of predictability? What are the guiding principles for determining how much weight to give to significant decreases in consumer choice? How can we conduct the analysis relatively objectively?

Mergers seem to be the easiest place to discuss implementation issues. The United States Merger Guidelines express concern with the price effects of mergers 12 times, and in a footnote, acknowledge that mergers also can reduce quality, variety, and innovation.[29] Even the Efficiency section of the Guidelines largely focuses on cost savings rather than innovation.[30] But, suppose the Guidelines made innovation and the resulting consumer choices a higher priority. As a practical matter, how could it do this optimally?

The best solution might be for the Merger Guidelines explicitly to say there were certain types of market (including technology, media, fashion,

---

28 Id. at 193–5.

29 Id. at 188, n. 41.

30 Id. at 187 et seq.

entertainment, etc.) where the need for innovation or perspective competition means that a larger number of firms may be required to have effective choice competition. Mergers in these markets might be evaluated in terms of different concentration levels or different changes in concentration levels. Alternatively, if the enforcers were reluctant to say explicitly that different structural standards should apply to certain markets, as a practical matter consumer choice concerns could be accommodated into merger analysis in these markets in three different ways.

First, choice considerations could simply be used as a tie-breaker or plus factor. If a decision-maker were deciding the legality of a media merger, for example, and if they were on the margin as to whether to challenge a transaction if they only considered price effects, choice considerations could cause them to make a different decision.

Second, and very similarly, choice considerations could be used as an implicit factor that would operate within the current structure of the Merger Guidelines. Suppose that for industries where price competition was most important, the enforcers would challenge 20 percent of above-Guideline mergers. But perhaps for those industries where consumer choice issues were especially crucial – for mergers involving sectors such as high-tech industries, media, entertainment, or fashion – the enforcers would block 40 percent of above-Guideline mergers. To implement choice concerns this way, as an informal part of the enforcers' discretion, the concentration levels and changes in the Guidelines would not be changed. But the Guidelines would be enforced more vigorously whenever choice competition was especially important.

Third, the Merger Guidelines could make choice analysis a separate explicit factor in the merger review process. Under this approach, a merger should be challenged either if it were likely to lead to higher prices, or if it were likely to lead to significantly less consumer choice because the merger was likely to hinder innovation (the most important factor that determines consumer choice in the long run).

As a practical matter, this would mean that the merger investigation and decision would make a separate, high priority inquiry into both the price and the innovation effects of the merger. This is similar to the way that innovation is already a separate factor in the Federal Collaboration Among Competitors Guidelines.[31] This inquiry sometimes could lead to a different result from the current price-oriented inquiry, especially because not every company within an industry competes substantially through innovation. Some firms instead largely compete by making existing

31 Id. at 242, n. 250.

products less expensively, by superior marketing, by superior service, etc. This method of inquiry would be different from attempting to predict whether a particular merger would be likely to lead to more, or to less, innovation (another possible inquiry for the enforcers). Rather, it would mean attempting to ascertain whether particular firms historically had been centers of independent innovation.

Here is how this inquiry could work. Suppose an industry consisted of five firms: A, B, C, D, and E. Suppose the enforcers believe that three firms are enough to have effective price competition in this market, and also that three firms are enough for effective innovation competition. But suppose that only firms A, B and C compete significantly by innovating, that only these three have large research and development budgets, that only these three have a history of making significant innovations. Suppose that firms D and E compete in other ways – perhaps they are imitators that make existing products less expensively. Suppose that firms A and B (two of the firms that compete by innovating) want to merge. Under price analysis we should permit this merger because after the merger there would still be four firms left, and it is stipulated that three firms is enough for effective price competition.

But under choice analysis we should block the merger because it is likely to lead to less innovation, the long-term source of optimal consumer choice. Regardless which number of firms we believe is necessary for effective competition, choice analysis could lead to tougher merger enforcement.[32]

5 CONCLUSIONS

Nudge, a book by Cass Sunstein and Richard Thaler, stresses the importance of starting points, presumptions and the questions that are first asked.[33] This book persuasively demonstrates how actions that non-coercively tend to point decision-makers in particular directions often affect the outcome of a wide variety of situations. This principle also illustrates the importance of the choice focus: if used as a starting point, it

[32] This is analogous to a unilateral effects analysis, which proposes that we should be especially tough on mergers between two firms producing goods within the same niche of a relevant market, and more lenient on mergers between firms producing dissimilar goods. Choice analysis arguably could also be said to create a 'submarket' consisting of innovators, or an 'innovation market', within a broader market. Id. at 215 et seq.

[33] C Sunstein and R Thaler, *Nudge* (2008).

will often nudge antitrust law or competition law towards incorporating choice considerations more fully and carefully.

This would be desirable, because consumers don't just want low prices. They want options. This is an important reason why consumer choice is an emerging way to explain and analyse potential competition law violations. Consumer choice analysis in most cases would produce the same result as price or efficiency analysis. But factors like innovation, perspectives, quality, service, privacy, and safety now all too often remain in the footnotes of the analysis, where they are all too often forgotten. The consumer choice approach would, in effect, move them into the text, where they would play a more prominent role in the evaluation. As noted throughout this chapter, the consumer choice mission could lead to better case analysis in several important and general types of situation.[34]

The consumer choice approach also has the advantage of explaining accurately and simply, in a way that everyone can understand, why competition is good for consumer welfare. It is the best, the most intuitive way, to explain the advantages of free competition to a diverse array of audiences, including judges, legislators, the media, and the public.

As a final example, to show how much clearer and easier to understand the choice formulation is, and how awkward and non-intuitive the other approaches to competition policy can be, consider an old case brought by the US Federal Trade Commission (FTC) against firms' jointly set advertising restrictions concerning the safety of bulletproof vests.[35] A trade association of manufacturers of bulletproof vests adopted a rule that it was unethical for members to advertise safety or to claim their products were safer. The FTC's concern was that without safety advertising consumers might purchase bulletproof vests that were less safe than they would prefer.[36]

Would anyone be satisfied if their bulletproof vest performed poorly so long as it was sold at a competitive price? In theory, we could translate safety harms caused by advertising restrictions into price harms or efficiency harms using complex Procrustean intellectual gymnastics.

---

[34] In addition, the 'choice' approach will not lead to a worse analysis than a price or efficiency approach. See, generally, Averitt and Lande, *supra* n. 6. Moreover, the choice approach is as easy to implement, and as predictable, as a price or efficiency approach. Id. at pt V.

[35] See discussion at NW Averitt and RH Lande, 'Consumer Sovereignty: A Unified Theory of Antitrust and Consumer Protection Law' (1997) 65 *Antitrust LJ* 713, at 750, available at http://papers.ssrn.com/so13/papers.cfm?abstract_id=1134798.

[36] Id.

But, wouldn't it be better for the enforcers straightforwardly to say that consumers care about safety, so the enforcers are going to focus on that form of competition explicitly?

The Bush administration was dominated by the belief that competition laws should be analysed only in terms of economic efficiency. For this reason, during the last eight years there has been very little chance of arriving at an international consensus as to the main goal of competition policy. By contrast, the European Union seems to have given choice issues a higher priority, as demonstrated by its recent Article 82 policy statement[37] and the relevant case law.[38]

---

[37] The European Commission's Directorate General for Competition's recent so-called Guidance Paper on Article 82 EC of 3 December 2008 states: '[i]n applying Article 82 to exclusionary conduct by dominant undertakings, the Commission will focus on those types of conduct that are most harmful to consumers. Consumers benefit from competition through lower prices, better quality and a wider choice of new or improved goods and services.' Communication from the Commission – Guidance on the Commission's enforcement priorities in applying Article 82 of the EC Treaty to abusive exclusionary conduct by dominant undertakings [2009] OJ C 45/7, para 5. The document recognizes that 'competitors who deliver less to consumers in terms of price, choice, quality and innovation will leave the market.' Id. at para 6. 'In this document, the expression "increase prices" includes the power to maintain prices above the competitive level and is used as shorthand for the various ways in which the parameters of competition – such as prices, output innovation, the variety or quality of goods or services – can be influenced for the profit of the dominant undertaking and to the detriment of consumers.' Id. at para 11. Additionally, the paper clarifies that '[t]he aim of the Commission's enforcement activity in relation to exclusionary conduct is to ensure that dominant undertakings do not impair effective competition by foreclosing their rivals in an anticompetitive way and thus having an adverse impact on consumer welfare, whether in the form of higher price levels than would have otherwise prevailed or in some other form such as limiting quality or reducing consumer choice.' Id. at para 19.

[38] See Case T-464/04 *Independent Music Publishers & Labels Association (Impala) v Commission* [2006] ECR II-2289, para 107 ('The Commission also failed to consider whether the concentration might result in an ability to reduce supply, in terms of numbers of new titles or in terms of originality of new releases, or whether it would impoverish creativity, quality and diversity in musical choice . . . or would have an impact on consumer choice, . . . as it had done in the statement of objections in the EMI/Time Warner case (see point 55, which deals with marginalization of the independents and its impact on the choice and diversity of music being offered to the public). Last, the analysis took no account of Article 151(4) EC or of cultural diversity.'); Case T-65/98 *Van den Bergh Foods Ltd v Commission* [2003] ECR II-4653, para 152 ('The exclusivity clause constitutes a barrier to market entry and to the expansion of the relevant market . . . . Retailers are prevented from exercising their freedom of choice with regard to the products that they wish to stock and to the optimization of space at the sales

Today there is optimism that United States antitrust enforcers might well vigorously adopt the consumer choice formulation and mission. If they do, there might be a chance that the international community could at least think about working together towards a common understanding about the primary goal of competition policy.

outlets. Moreover, consumer choice is reduced.'); T-25/99 *Roberts and Roberts v Commission* [2001], ECR II-1881, para 40 ('In this respect, the Commission rightly observes in its pleadings that the consumer's choice between those establishments is influenced primarily by their environment and atmosphere, even within the sub-category of pubs distinguished by the applicants.').

3. Protecting consumer choice: Competition and consumer protection law together

Neil W. Averitt*

1 INTRODUCTION

Another chapter in this volume has discussed the role of choice in antitrust, and has suggested that competition law should begin to more explicitly protect the non-price qualities of variety, choice, and innovation, as well as protecting competitive prices per se.[1] This chapter concurs in that assessment, and will propose a larger context into which that suggestion will fit. It proposes that the concept of choice actually underlies both antitrust and consumer protection law. Viewing both of these bodies of law together in the larger, more inclusive perspective of 'choice' will lead to a number of enforcement advantages as well as to benefits for consumers. It will integrate the two bodies of law; confirm the validity of the choice perspective of antitrust; and from the new context it will suggest some particular legal principles of competition law and possible new areas of enforcement interest.[2]

The discussion that follows is divided into five principal sections: What

* The author is a member of the planning staff at the US Federal Trade Commission. The views expressed here are the author's own, and are not necessarily the views of the FTC or of any individual Commissioner.

[1] See RH Lande, 'Consumer Choice as the Best Way to Recenter the Mission of Competition Law', Ch. 2, above. For a more elaborate treatment see NW Averitt and RH Lande, 'Using the "Consumer Choice" Approach to Antitrust Law' (2007) 74 *Antitrust LJ* 175, http://papers.ssrn.com/so13/papers.cfm?abstract_id=1121459.

[2] For a fuller discussion of this thesis, with particular reference to the situation under United States law, see NW Averitt and RH Lande, 'Consumer Sovereignty: A Unified Theory of Antitrust and Consumer Protection Law' (1997) 65 *Antitrust LJ* 713, http://papers.ssrn.com/so13/papers.cfm?abstract_id=1134798 (accessed November 2009).

is consumer protection law (at 2, below)? How does it relate to competition law (at 3, below)? Does this permit a single unified theory of choice (at 3, below)? How could such a choice model help create more relevant theories of liability for both antitrust and consumer protection law (at 4, below)? How could choice concepts lead to better remedies (at 5, below)? What other practical benefits might it bring to European enforcement agencies (at 6, below)?

2 WHAT IS CONSUMER PROTECTION LAW?

The discussion of a unified theory must begin with an introduction to consumer protection law.

The 'choice' construction of antitrust law called our attention to the importance of non-price as well as price competition. This was an important step toward making antitrust policy better attuned to the subject of consumer preferences. It made antitrust policy increasingly aware of the complexities of consumer demands – to the fact, for example, that consumers do not generally pursue a single goal of minimum prices, but rather a more complex hierarchy of goals that includes variety, individualism, and innovation. In doing so, however, this insight also sensitized enforcement agencies to the possible relevance of complex consumer behavior in other fields as well. The most closely related such field is consumer protection law.[3]

While antitrust enforcement involves government agencies in safeguarding competition on a market-wide basis, consumer protection law helps empower consumers to protect themselves purchase-by-purchase. It does this by protecting consumers in the exercise of their decisions in the marketplace. It is through these decisions that consumers express the complex trade-offs among price, convenience, and various intangible attributes that give value to a product, and also through these choices that they avoid undesirable products.[4] Consumer protection enforcement aims to prevent business conduct that might otherwise distort this process of free selection.

---

[3] In the United States the law on consumer protection is also enforced by the Federal Trade Commission, making the connection between the two particularly close.

[4] Thus, for example, an enforcement agency may require firms to disclose enough information about their policies on privacy and data security 'to provide consumers with meaningful choice' as to whether to give personal information to them. See US Federal Trade Commission, 'Protecting Consumer Privacy in an Era of Rapid Change', Preliminary Staff Report (December 2010) at 53.

The greatest threat to consumer decision-making is deception. If consumers are given false information their decisions will inevitably suffer. Actionable deception can take a number of different forms. It may involve explicit falsehoods ('Our medicine will grow hair'). Or it may involve a false implication ('Do you hate growing bald? Buy our medicine'). Or it may involve an implication by silence (Saying nothing in response to a question, 'I assume that your product is scientifically proven?').

Consumer decision-making can also be harmed in other, less common ways. Sometimes a seller can withhold the material information that is needed for an informed choice. For example, a seller of home insulation may fail to provide the quantitative measures of insulating power that are needed for an objective comparison of different brands.[5] Or sometimes a seller may engage in actual coercion of a consumer's decision. This is extreme conduct, but it can happen. One manufacturer of furnaces, for example, sent salesmen to perform free home inspections, and the salesmen disassembled furnaces for examination, professed to have found a problem, announced that they could not ethically reassemble a potentially dangerous product, left the consumer without a heat source for the home, and then announced that they could provide suitable new parts or services.[6]

Consumer protection violations are reached under different parts of the Federal Trade Commission Act, depending on the exact nature of the conduct. The FTC Act prohibits 'unfair or deceptive acts or practices.'[7] Deception is thus specifically covered by the Act. It has been defined by the agency as 'a representation, omission, or practice that is likely to mislead the consumer.'[8] The other forms of consumer protection violation are reached under the prohibition against 'unfair practices.' That has been described in more general terms as 'seller behavior that unreasonably creates or takes advantage of an obstacle to the free exercise of consumer decisionmaking.'[9]

In short, consumer protection law is directed against any form of seller

---

[5] See Labeling and Advertising of Home Insulation, 16 Code of Federal Regulations s 460 (1981); cf. Automotive Fuel Ratings, Certification and Posting (the 'Octane Rating Rule'), 16 Code of Federal Regulations s 306 (1981).

[6] See *Holland Furnace Co. v FTC*, 55 FTC 55 (1958), *aff'd*, 295 F.2d 302 (7th Cir. 1961). See also *Arthur Murray Studio v FTC*, 458 F.2d 622 (5th Cir. 1972) (high-pressure sales pitches to elderly consumers).

[7] 15 United States Code s 45(a)(1).

[8] FTC Policy Statement on Deception (1983), http://www.ftc.gov/bcp/policystmt/ad-decept.htm (accessed December 2010).

[9] FTC Policy Statement on Unfairness (1980), http://www.ftc.gov/bcp/policystmt/ad-unfair.htm (accessed December 2010).

conduct that is likely to materially distort the exercise of consumer choice in the market.

3 HOW DOES CONSUMER PROTECTION RELATE TO COMPETITION LAW?

It is obvious that competition and consumer protection law are both in some way addressed to the exercise of 'choice'. The question is whether there is a sufficiently close relationship between the two concepts to permit a single theory that encompasses both.

The answer is that there is. Antitrust and consumer protection law are both part of a single effort to support a market economy. They are therefore closely related to each other in both functional and economic terms.

On a functional level, they can be understood as working together to provide the conditions that a market economy requires. A market economy requires two basic things – an array of options in the marketplace, and an ability on the part of consumers to select freely and effectively from among those options. Antitrust and consumer protection law can be functionally understood as addressed to those two needs. Antitrust protects the array of options in the marketplace, keeping the options undiminished by artificial conduct such as price-fixing or anticompetitive mergers. Consumer protection then protects purchasers' ability to select from among those options, ensuring that the selection process is not distorted by conduct such as deception or coercion.

Alternatively, antitrust and consumer protection can be understood in economic terms, as protecting against the two types of market failure that pose the greatest threats to a market economy. One type of market failure occurs in the external environment that surrounds the consumer. These failures include departures from competitive conditions caused by business actions, such as price-fixing and mergers. No individual consumer, no matter how shrewd or well-informed, can protect himself against these failures, and they are therefore the stuff of public competition enforcement. A second market failure occurs 'inside the head' – in the consumer's inability to process information correctly. These failures can be caused or aggravated by conduct such as deception or coercion. In theory a sufficiently shrewd consumer could compensate for such conduct through more careful pre-purchase research, but that can be difficult and it does not always happen. For this reason, public consumer protection enforcement also addresses these kinds of market failures.

Whether viewed from the standpoint of function or of market failures, therefore, there is a close relationship between competition and consumer protection law. Each is responsible for one half of a larger venture of protecting a market economy based on consumer choice.[10]

4 A UNIFIED THEORY OF CHOICE WILL HELP TO BRING BETTER CASES

The unified theory of choice is not just a pleasing theoretical construct, although it is certainly that. If adopted and consistently applied by the enforcement agencies it would also help them at the practical tasks of identifying better cases, and of more effectively pleading the cases that they bring. It would do this by ensuring that agency cases are framed in terms of the most relevant and helpful body of law, and that the essential elements of proof can be clearly known and satisfied.

Choice theory draws a clear line between competition and consumer protection law, and clearly distinguishes their fields of application. This allows investigations to be assigned to the appropriate legal theory. It will help to avoid the imprecise dual pleading of the sort prevalent a few years ago, when matters were routinely alleged to be both 'unfair methods of competition and unfair or deceptive acts or practices'.[11] Keeping the routine cases instead focused on the one most relevant theory will contribute to a clear perspective and make it easier to keep the essential elements of proof in mind.

Establishing clear definitions for antitrust and consumer protection is also useful in a second way. In situations where both theories might legitimately be applicable, agencies will, for institutional reasons, often focus primarily on only one. Choice theory, however, calls attention to both bodies of law simultaneously, as the two parts of a single venture. It will therefore make it easier for agencies to consider the full range of their options, and to be alert to the possibility of reframing a case in different, more effective terms.

This would have been particularly useful in the FTC's cases involving the deception of standard-setting organizations. In systems where the products of different manufacturers need to work together – such as audio equipment or computers – industry-wide standards are commonly developed by a trade association. Usually the association demands that a

---

[10] Companion Statement on the Commission's Consumer Unfairness Jurisdiction (1980) 4 *Trade Regulation Reporter (CCH)* Para 13203 at p. 20,909-03 (the agency's elaboration of certain issues raised in the Policy Statement on Unfairness).

[11] See, e.g., *Amway Corp.*, 93 FTC 618, 629 (1979).

standard either not use any patented technology, or else that the patent holder promise to charge only reasonable and non-discriminatory royalties. Sometimes, however, a patent holder will sit silent, fail to disclose its patents, wait until the industry is locked into its technology, and then demand large royalties.

The FTC's most recent case on this theory was *Rambus*.[12] Because the case involved business-to-business conduct, and was brought by the agency's Bureau of Competition, it not surprisingly was grounded on an antitrust theory. The agency alleged that Rambus had engaged in monopolization by means of deception. The appeals court rejected that argument, however, because it had trouble seeing how conduct could be characterized as 'monopolization' if it did not necessarily lead to a change in market structure. The case could have been easy, however, if it had been framed as a simple deception matter.[13] Rambus deceived the standard-setting organization, in a way that affected the organization's decision on which technology to acquire, and that is a completed offense at that point without any need to show market power. Thus the choice approach could have pointed the Commission toward a more promising legal theory.

A key step in this approach is recognizing that a business corporation can be a 'consumer'. This is something of a conceptual leap, since consumer protection law has traditionally focused on protecting individual natural persons. In principle, however, the agencies should care about protecting market processes, rather than favoring one or another type of participant in those processes. Prosecutorial discretion may often counsel in favor of letting corporations handle their own legal disputes, but if public action seems warranted on the merits it should not be ruled out by the mere identity of the parties involved.[14]

Once agencies become comfortable with this approach, then they will find a number of useful opportunities to rethink and recategorize cases. Another traditional business matter that might be usefully approached

---

[12] *Rambus v FTC*, 522 F.3d 456 (DC Cir. 2008).

[13] There could still be complexities in establishing the relevant facts, but the legal theory would be simple.

[14] The FTC's Bureau of Consumer Protection is already moving in this direction. It has been willing to treat at least small businesses as consumers. See, e.g., *FTC v National Supply & Distribution Center* (press release 5 February 2001) (consent order) (misrepresentation of the existence of prior business relationship when selling photocopier toner to small businesses). See also *McGregor v Chierico*, 206 F.3d 1378, 1380–81, 1388 n. 11 (11th Cir. 2000) (deceptive acts by telemarketers to induce businesses to pay for unordered toner).

in consumer protection terms is the coerced purchase of a license. If such a purchase is coerced by the threat of bad-faith litigation, then the wrongful effect is felt 'inside the head' of the purchaser and constrains his or her decision-making ability, rather than necessarily being based on market power. Such a matter is more akin to the consumer protection violation involving furnace sales than to a traditional antitrust theory.

Sometimes a case might be reframed in the other direction, and conduct that has traditionally been treated as a consumer protection violation could be approached in competition terms instead. Some years ago, for example, the Commission sought to challenge the restrictions on the commercial practice of optometry that were imposed by state statutes and administrative regulations. These were restrictions on things like practice under a trade name or in a retail setting. The Commission took the view that state regulators who imposed these restrictions were guilty of an unfair consumer practice, and that the Commission's rule to this effect could be cited to forestall any state disciplinary proceeding.[15] The appellate court reversed, finding that the Commission's rule-making authority in consumer protection matters did not authorize it to override the policy of a state in this way.[16] A better outcome might have been reached on a competition theory, however. For one thing, the theory of the case would have been more persuasively framed, since restrictions on commercial practise affect the variety of retail optometry formats that are available in the marketplace, the core concern of antitrust. And once the matter is presented in competition terms, then the path toward a possible rebuttal of the state action defense becomes more visible. Competition cases over the years have worked out a number of limitations on the state action doctrine. For example, state administrative actions are only exempt from the antitrust laws if they are supported by a clearly articulated legislative policy, and if the members of a state regulatory board are themselves members of the industry they may also have to be actively supervised by a higher level of state government.[17] These considerations would have made an antitrust theory a more promising one to litigate.

---

15 Ophthalmic Practice Rules (13 March 1989) 54 *Federal Register* 10 285.

16 *California Board of Optometry v FTC*, 910 F.2d 976 (DC Cir. 1990).

17 See *California Retail Liquor Dealers Ass'n v Midcal Aluminum*, 445 US 97 (1980) (clear articulation); *Town of Hallie v City of Eau Claire,* 471 US 34 (1985) (considering when governmental bodies must be supervised).

5 A UNIFIED THEORY OF CHOICE WILL HELP TO DESIGN BETTER REMEDIES

The choice model will also help enforcement agencies design better remedies – once again by means of reminding agencies of the full range of the available legal theories.

Remedies have traditionally been framed in the same terms as the violation they are designed to correct. Thus an antitrust violation, which restricts the range of options, is usually corrected by an order increasing that range. A familiar example would be an order requiring the divestiture and re-creation of an improperly acquired asset. Similarly, consumer protection violations are usually corrected by orders that support the decision-making process in some way, such as by orders banning the use of an ad that was found deceptive.

Sometimes, however, the most effective remedy will be one involving the other side of an agency's jurisdiction. Thus, for example, antitrust remedies might sometimes be framed in terms that will also enhance consumers' ability to make choices. This path has already been followed in a number of individual cases. The antitrust agencies have challenged horizontal trade-association agreements that made comparison shopping more difficult.[18] The resulting orders, removing these restrictive terms, clearly served to enhance consumer decision-making as well as to end the illegal agreement itself. But such an approach might be kept in mind more systematically for the future, and then it may suggest some novel approaches to antitrust litigation. For example, one harmful effect that may flow from resale price maintenance is that it provides sales personnel with an incentive to mislead consumers into buying the most profitable, price-maintained product.[19] If such facts are proven in a particular case, then the appropriate remedy might be framed and justified, not solely by reference to the traditional antitrust element of price agreement, but also by a showing that it will remove the contract terms that encouraged and led to consumer deception.

Similar innovations may be possible in the area of consumer protection remedies. There the agencies can become alert to the possibility that the most effective remedy will be aimed at increasing the number of options in

---

[18] See, e.g., *National Society of Professional Engineers v United States*, 435 US 679 (1978) (agreement against competitive bidding); *Detroit Auto Dealers' Ass'n v FTC*, 955 F.2d 457 (6th Cir. 1992) (agreement to restrict operating hours available for comparative shopping).

[19] See WS Grimes, 'Spiff, Polish and Consumer Demand Quality: Vertical Price Restraints Revisited' (1992) 80 *Cal L Rev* 815.

the marketplace – a traditional antitrust goal. This approach has already been followed in a few matters. For example, the Commission's R-Value Rule was not only intended to produce better information about insulating values and to facilitate comparison shopping. The Commission also intended that this process would eventually lead to better products in the marketplace – to better options.[20] Similarly, the Commission's Franchise Rule was intended not only to give better information about business opportunities, but also, by means of this competition, to encourage the development of better opportunities in the future.

The choice model will help to keep all these kinds of cross-theory effects more fully in view, and will make it easier for the agencies to consider them as soon as they begin to think about remedies.

6 OTHER ADMINISTRATIVE BENEFITS OF THE CHOICE MODEL

The choice model can provide a number of other practical administrative benefits as well. Two of these may be particularly relevant for enforcement agencies outside the United States.

First of all, the choice model suggests that the agencies that enforce antitrust and consumer protection law should become more closely linked in national systems that have not yet taken this step. The linkage could be made by statute or, in countries where separate agencies are already well established, it could be accomplished by a memorandum of understanding between them. The closer coordination would have a number of benefits. These include not only the prospect of more effective law enforcement, as discussed above, but also the important advantage of framing an institutional mission that is clear and intuitive, and that can be readily explained to the legislature and the general public. Everyone understands the value of free choice, and that can translate into more widespread public support for the mission of trade regulation.

Second, the choice model may provide a logical midpoint on which the American and European approaches to trade regulation can converge. European law has traditionally focused on abuse of dominance. American law has emphasized economic efficiency, or, more recently, efficiency as

---

[20] This goal was explicitly stated. Information failures 'diminish comparison shopping, and create unwarranted competitive parity or advantage for inferior products. Thus, a market that functions in this way not only harms consumers but also lessens fair and open competition.' Statement of Basis and Purpose, Labeling and Advertising of Home Insulation, (1979) 44 *Federal Register* 50218, at 50223.

tempered by choice.[21] A full use of the choice model is likely to be broadly acceptable to both groups – being neither exclusively focused on efficiency to the exclusion of other social values, nor cut off from all economic moorings.[22]

7 CONCLUSION

Large-scale, integrating legal concepts have always exercised an appeal to academics. The choice model has merit in these terms, because it helps to unify antitrust and consumer protection at a basic conceptual level. The model also has a number of intensely practical benefits, however, pointing the way toward better selection and more effective articulation of legal theories. For this reason it is worth examining as a possible point of convergence for jurisdictions throughout the world.

---

[21] See TJ Muris, 'The Federal Trade Commission and the Future Development of US Consumer Protection Policy', Remarks of the FTC Chairman to the Aspen Summit on Cyberspace and the American Dream (19 August 2003), http://www.ftc.gov/speeches/muris/030819aspen.shtm (accessed December 2010).

[22] In the past year, new policy statements on both sides of the Atlantic have made use of 'consumer choice' concepts. See US Dep't of Justice and Federal Trade Commission, Horizontal Merger Guidelines section 6.4 (August 2010) (considering merger's likely effects on 'innovation and product variety'); European Commission, Guidelines of 14 December 2010 on the applicability of Article 101 of the TFEU to horizontal co-operation agreements, C(2010) 9274/2, para 119 ('The effects on competition in innovation are important . . . [but may] not be sufficiently assessed by analysing actual or potential competition in existing product/technology markets').

4. Is competition law part of consumer law?

Paul L. Nihoul

1 INTRODUCTION

I would like to thank the authors of the preceding chapters for their important contributions to the role of consumer choice in competition law. In their contributions, they have sketched a proposal to establish a rational link between the market process – the process of economic competition – and a category of people: the consumers.

The proposals appear to me to be a logical step, me being a European academic spending my professional life studying the decisions adopted by the European Commission and the judgments issued by the European courts in the field of competition. Both types of instances indeed emphasize in the documents they produce that competition should aim at producing opportunities for consumers.[1]

The proposals made also strike a sympathetic cord within me, since my main academic interests are precisely competition law and consumer protection. The authors could not find a more sympathetic commentator to their proposals eager to work in the same direction. In this context, I will ask *three questions* relating to *three important concepts* that might have to be worked upon if we want to further the work on the said proposals, which have been submitted in the preceding chapters.

2 THE CONCEPT OF COMPETITION

I would certainly agree that competition is necessary to provide consumers with choice. To me, it appears that *real* choice for consumers is equivalent

---

[1] See, e.g. Commission Decision (EC) 2007/53, Case COMP/C-3/37.792 – *Microsoft* [2004] OJ L 32, p. 3, para 706; Case T-201/104 *Microsoft v Commission* [2007] ECR II-3601, para 652.

to *effective competition* on markets. Where consumers have a choice, they can play the suppliers off against one another. They do not even have to claim more favourable business terms vis-à-vis their current supplier. Their mere capability of shifting to competitors implies that the supplier will feel the pressure and will consequently devote important resources to the satisfaction of their customers.

It appears from that brief description that consumer choice lies at the heart of the competitive process. Competition entails rivalry among firms – and that rivalry aims at winning the confidence of consumers.[2]

Here is my first question. I would like to ask whether this process is limited to consumers or whether it extends to yet other market players. If the competitive process is aimed at providing consumers specifically, with particularly interesting conditions, then we can rightly assert that competition is directed towards them. This statement, however, becomes less convincing if consumers are not the only ones to benefit from competition. If the latter statement is correct, the most we can say is probably that competition is beneficial to various actors – whether consumers are among those beneficiaries and to what extent – remains to be determined.

2.1 The Economic Chain

In this regard, it must be emphasized that competition is by no means limited to the final level of the economic chain where businesses deal with end consumers. It opposes firms, in principle, at *all* levels of the economic chain – thus providing advantages to other economic actors at the various levels of the economic chain. Think of distributors playing producers off against one another in the hope of getting a better bargain. Such distributors also have a choice between various suppliers. As we have already stated, this choice provides the distributors with bargaining power vis-à-vis their suppliers and, accordingly, the competition process entails in most situations an improvement of the market conditions available to them.

Concededly, the excellent conditions that distributors may obtain as a result of their choice in the competitive process between potential suppliers should also benefit consumers, at least if effective competition exists on the distribution market. On such a market, and because consumers have a choice between distributors, the latter will normally strive to provide the

---

2 On this topic, see P Nihoul, *La concurrence et le droit – La position occupée par les entreprises, les consommateurs et les autorités* (2001).

goods and services at the lowest possible price. Lower prices obtained by the distributors from their suppliers will thus translate, in a second step, into lower consumer prices as well.

In such a scenario, consumers benefit from competition – as do other actors too. Consumers, thus, are not the only ones taking advantage of the competitive process. Based on this illustration, we would probably go *too* far if we said that an exclusive link exists between competition and consumers.

2.2 Both Ways – Upward and Downward Competition

In the scenario we have just examined, competition plays 'upwards'. Actors located at a lower level of the economic chain play actors off against other actors located at a superior level of the chain. For example, distributors bargain with producers in order to obtain better supply conditions to the same extent that consumers play distributors off against one another in order to obtain a better bargain.

This scenario of upward competition is classical in its traditional presentations of the virtues associated with competition. These presentations suggest that consumers are, in effect, the main beneficiaries of the competitive process – either directly, as a result of the existence of a choice between distributors, or indirectly, because they are located at the final stage where they benefit from the excellent conditions resulting from the presence of competition at higher levels.

However, the question is whether competition only plays upwards? Does competition also play 'downwards'? Do producers sometimes play distributors off against one another in order to increase their profit margin? Similarly, do distributors sometimes play consumers off against one another to obtain higher profits?

The answer is yes. On some markets, scarcity is used as a marketing argument to obtain higher prices from customers. In such a scenario, competition involves rivalry among customers or final consumers which strive to obtain a product or service that would otherwise escape them. Think of the queues in the US when the first I-phones were commercialised, that is, in limited numbers. Think of fashion companies that limit their product line to a given number of pieces and make that limitation an essential marketing argument. Think of the fashion shop called the 'Billionaire' in California – a name that subconsciously suggests 'do *not* enter here if you are *not* a billionaire', 'do not enter here if, whatever your *real* resources, you are not able nor ready to spend money', as if, being a billionaire, you had unlimited financial resources; and even 'by spending much give yourself the feeling and give others the impression that you are a member of the financial elite, even though you are not'.

The more I think about competition, the more I have the impression that consumer competition is the *rule* rather than the *exception* – and the more I have the impression that competition may not at all be favourable to the persons located at the final level of the economic chain. As consumers, we do not define our needs independently but in connection with, and, in fact, in comparison with what our peers have. This is precisely what firms play upon in their commercial strategy when they attempt to induce consumers to purchase products and services from them, rather than from an alternative supplier. The strategies consist of putting consumers under pressure to purchase the same as, and possibly even more than the persons with whom they want to be associated.

At the end of the day, we can probably state that the level of competition existing between firms in a given country depends on, or at least provides a good indication of the level of competition existing between consumers in that country, and the extent to which people combat with one another to ensure that they, in fact, have the most numerous and beautiful possessions. Consumers compete harshly in their professional activities, and thus accelerate competition among firms in order to collect the financial resources needed to make these purchases.

2.3 Competition as a Process

In answering the first question, I would submit that competition is neither specifically nor exclusively related to consumers. It is rather a process whereby:

- natural and legal persons in demand of given resources – goods or services – present their demand to potential suppliers possessing these resources,
- and thereby place these suppliers in a position of arbitrators
- where several demands are formulated concurrently.

In this process, the concept of 'choice' is essential – but consumers are not the only ones to benefit from it. Any person or firm possessing resources is placed in the position as an arbitrator between conflicting demands where the market is organised along competitive lines. Competition is just *one* illustration of a much larger process where people negotiate, some in a better position than others, and can use their position to obtain a more attractive bargain.

3 THE CONCEPT OF CONSUMER

The authors propose consumer choice as the cornerstone of a comprehensive theory including both competition law and consumer law. These two areas of law would be united through a common denominator. Competition would become a part of consumer law. Since consumer law aims at protecting consumers, and competition creates choice for consumers, competition would then have to be considered as part of consumer law. According to this proposal, competition law would protect consumers from external defects owing either to an imperfect functioning of markets or to the absence of sufficient choice. Consumer law would react to internal defects where, for example, consumers do not have all the necessary data in order to make enlightened choices owing to insufficient information or deceptive business practices.

For reasons I have expressed at the outset of these comments, I can hardly resist the temptation to applaud the idea of making competition law part of consumer law.

However, I must also draw the attention to the fact that, currently, the consumers referred to here may not be the same in the two fields of law. To put it in the form of a question: are the consumers aimed at in *competition law* the same as those that are protected by *consumer law*?

3.1 Consumer Law

In consumer law, the term 'consumer' receives a meaning close to that referred to in the ordinary language. In most instruments of EU law, consumers are defined as being natural persons active on the market in a private capacity. This definition excludes the application of consumer protection to legal entities such as firms and to those natural persons acting in the professional sphere.[3]

The general idea behind this is that the law should provide protection to consumers defined as such, because they are not in the same position as the undertakings. Firstly, the latter have access to information that is not always available to the former, which gives rise to an asymmetry of information. For instance, a business selling a technical device is better placed to know whether that product is solid or not. Unless provided by the seller or the manufacturer, this information is not available to the consumer

[3] See, for instance, European Parliament and Council Directive (EC) 1999/44 of the European Parliament and the Council on certain aspects of the sale of consumer goods and associated guarantees [1999] OJ L 171, p. 12, Article 1(2)(a).

who, therefore, may be deceived. Secondly, businesses often have legal resources that are not available to consumers, giving rise to an asymmetry in the availability of legal means. Often, the cost of legal action is an obstacle for consumers trying to enforce their rights.

However, these considerations also raise concerns. An information asymmetry exists vis-à-vis all 'customers' whether they are business entities or final consumers. Why should protection be excluded for customers who are not final consumers? Similarly, many businesses face an asymmetry regarding their capacity to legally pursue their rights. For instance, case law shows that dominant firms sometimes initiate judicial proceedings with the sole purpose of pushing competitors out of business because the latter cannot devote the same amplitude of resources in such proceedings.

Hence, it appears that the reasons why protection *should* be granted are also present in situations where the customers are not individual persons acting in a private capacity. Yet, the law limits protection to such customers defined as consumers. This can probably be explained by the political decision to address only market interactions that involve final consumers. In other situations, a similar protection is not granted because that same political will does not exist, even though rational arguments could be articulated in support of extending protection to all customers.[4]

3.2 Competition Law

We now have to examine whether the concept of 'consumer' is the same when used in the context of competition law. Looking at the website of the European Commission, or at political documents coming from the Directorate General for Competition, one may have the impression that, indeed, the concept is the same in both environments. For instance, the site contains a declaration emphasizing that:

> Competition Policy is basically applying rules to make sure that companies compete with each other and, in order to sell their products, innovate and offer good prices to consumers. The risk if there's no competition policy is that companies will do deals with each other to split up the market between them, or will act in a way which doesn't allow competitors on to the market; and in either

[4] On the notion of consumer see I Ramsay, *Consumer Law and Policy: Text and Materials on Regulating Consumer Markets* (2nd edn, 2007) 53; S Weatherill, *EU Consumer Law and Policy* (2005); G Howells and S Weatherill, *Consumer Protection Law* (2005) 1.

> case the result can be that consumers are denied access to innovative products and pay higher prices.[5]

In this statement, an opposition is made between, on the one hand, 'companies', which do not always comply with the rules of competition and, on the other hand, 'consumers', who may suffer from such infringements. The conclusion is inevitably that the consumers for whom *competition law* cares about are those whom *consumer law* seeks to protect – the 'people in the street' – natural persons acting in a private capacity.

This position, however, needs to be revised taking into account other, more technical, Commission statements. One such statement can be found in the guidelines issued by the European Commission regarding the application of Article 81(3) EC (now Article 101(3) TFEU). As appears in these guidelines, consumers are defined as 'users', that is, legal or natural persons acting in a private or professional capacity:

> . . . The concept of 'consumers' encompasses all direct or indirect users of the products covered by the agreement, including producers that use the products as an input, wholesalers, retailers and final consumers, i.e. natural persons who are acting for purposes which can be regarded as outside their trade or profession. In other words, consumers within the meaning of Article 81(3) are the customers of the parties to the agreement and subsequent purchasers. These customers can be undertakings as in the case of buyers of industrial machinery or an input for further processing or final consumers for buyers of ice-cream or bicycles . . .[6]

As it appears from this statement, the concept of 'consumer' does not contain, in the sense of EU competition law provisions, any reference whatsoever to a person acting for any particular purpose. Consumers are defined as those located 'downwards' in the economic chain who purchase or obtain a good or service from another actor located 'upwards'. In this context, consumer choice may be interpreted as meaning that 'an economic actor purchasing on the demand curve' should have a choice between goods or services provided by 'another economic actor offering, this time, on the supply curve'. Thus, the concept of consumer does *not* refer, in this context, to any specific category of people. It rather relates to a function, that is, the function of demand.

---

5 http://ec.europa.eu/competition/consumers/index_en.html (accessed November 2009).

6 EC, Guidelines on the application of Article 81(3) of the Treaty [2004] OJ C 101, p. 97, para 84.

3.3 Political Stake

Is this all politically neutral? Not by any means! The variation in vocabulary[7] has political implications. The ambiguity described above – since the word has two different meanings – has consequences. When people interested in consumer protection hear that competition enhances the welfare of consumers, they believe that the welfare in question is one of the *consumer* as defined in *consumer law*. Owing to the high technicality of competition law, they are usually not able to ascertain the necessary semantic distinction. Yet, using the concept of 'consumer' in the context of competition law makes competition more acceptable and even more attractive in the circles of people interested in consumer protection.

At this stage, it is important to draw the attention to the existence of two conflicting political currents regarding competition in the EU.

One current welcomes competition as the ideal cornerstone for the organisation of the economy. This corresponds, in general, without nuance, to 'rightwing' political circles. In these circles, economic freedom is seen as an essential value. Firms should in principle be free to develop their economic projects without having to face intervention. Interventions by authorities should be limited.

The other current considers competition as evil. Competition is only associated with rivalry that leads to the disintegration of society. The perception is that competition pushes both people and firms to fight against one another instead of uniting their fate against common challenges that undertakings and consumers have to face. Hence, competition is perceived as disrupting various forms of solidarity that may exist within society and may justify the intervention of authorities in the economy. Accordingly, public monopolies have been used by governments as a means to implement particular policies in many sectors on the European continent such as telecommunications, energy, transportation, water distribution, social insurances, etc. In contrast, competition is seen to imply that regulatory barriers to entry should be abolished.

It will come as no surprise that those seeing competition with reluctance generally support the adoption of rules protecting consumers. With regard to both fields of law, the idea is that free markets should not generally be presumed to reach satisfactory social results by themselves. Instead, political representatives are called to define such social objectives and the legal instruments for their realisation.

---

[7] Or better said, in the meanings given to different words depending on the context.

In this context, referring to consumers within the ambit of competition law inevitably creates confusion. The supporters of the second current have the impression that competition and, hence, free markets aim at protecting consumers just as the legal rules do in that second current.

Going one step further, one may wonder whether reference to consumers in the field of competition is not a political strategy used in an attempt to convince one part of the population, which would otherwise reject competition, of its value as a cornerstone for the organisation of the economy and society in general. It is difficult to interpret differently constant reference by Commission officials to the benefits accruing from competition to consumers' daily life. The intention is probably to convey political legitimacy to competition policy . The Commission seems to tell European citizens: 'You may feel that we are not acting in the interest of the people when we enact and implement rules of competition. Yet, these rules have a positive effect on your situation as consumers. You should therefore support us in our work!'

4 THE CONCEPT OF CHOICE

The third concept I would like to address is that of choice. There is a trend to consider that, in substance, consumer issues can be regarded as information-related issues.[8] Since suppliers know that consumers make informed choices, they are, thereby, induced into behaving better. It is argued that the rules adopted in the field of consumer protection should thus be limited to the introduction of information-related obligations. Suppliers should be obliged to inform consumers correctly and/or possibly organise the provision of third party independent information. Consumers will then make informed choices.

Certainly, we should not reject the idea that granting a choice to consumers is positive and that consumers should be provided with information so that they make correct choices. To recall, the existence of a choice makes it possible for consumers to shift to other suppliers when they are not satisfied with their current one. We have all experienced the satisfaction that one can feel in finding a supplier who offers a better deal.

However, the ability to switch to another supplier does not, in itself, solve the problems of the past. Suppose you are not satisfied with your supplier of Internet services. Switching to another provider will not

---

[8] On that topic see M Radeideh, *Fair Trading in EC Law: Information and Consumer Choice in the Internal Market* (2005).

necessarily guarantee that the problems you had with the previous supplier will automatically disappear. Imagine that the previous supplier had overcharged you. Competition is not going to help you solve that specific difficulty. If you want your money back, you will have to sue that firm – or use another mechanism provided by non-information-related rules imposed under consumer law. Such mechanisms do not depend on information, nor do they mainly ensure the provision of necessary information. Information does not help us deal with suppliers we leave behind.

Furthermore, we can never be sure to encounter any problem with the *new* supplier. In coming back to our example, let us assume that we have now chosen another Internet provider. The shift to this new provider does not imply, in itself, that we will never face any difficulty with this new supplier. Indeed, we may even discover that we have ended up with an even worse provider?

Information cannot solve all difficulties for the very good reason that such information is not available. A major contribution of linguistics has been to show that language does not exist as a source of objective representation. Languages are composed of statements, all of which originate from speakers with specific intentions. Commercials often say more about the willingness of the seller to sell than they inform on the product or service they are supposed to promote.

Finally, emphasizing the role of information may also create a danger. In the trend described above, consumer law should mainly consist of obligations of suppliers to inform appropriately and correctly. With this information, the argument goes, consumers will make correct choices and, therefore, quite rightly also have to bear the consequences of their choices. It appears from this analysis that an information-based approach to consumer law paves the way for a transfer of risk from the suppliers to the consumers.

Take, for example, product liability. If consumer law consists of information-related obligations, consumer law would predominantly oblige manufacturers to warn consumers about the existence of possible risks. Based on these warnings, consumers would then make their choices – and then have to live with the damages possibly resulting from the realisation of these risks.

Would this constitute a good basis for a sound consumer policy?

PART 2

Individual jurisdictions and international perspectives

5. Resale price maintenance: A reassessment of its competitive harms and benefits

Marina Lao*

1 INTRODUCTION

In a sharply divided five to four decision in *Leegin Creative Products, Inc. v PSKS, Inc.*,[1] the US Supreme Court in 2007 overruled the nearly century-old precedent of *Dr. Miles*[2] to end per se condemnation of resale price maintenance (RPM)[3] in favor of a rule of reason analysis. But the case has hardly settled the debate on the economics of, or the appropriate legal treatment for, RPM. While some commentators view RPM as often procompetitive and *Leegin* as long overdue,[4] others disagree with the majority's decision.[5] Indeed, bills were introduced in Congress to

* I would like to thank Josef Drexl, Warren Grimes, Rudolph Peritz, Robert Steiner, Charles Sullivan and participants in the 2009 ASCOLA conference for helpful comments. Thanks are also due to Eric Wolf and especially Nicholas Dimakos (Seton Hall, Class of 2011) for excellent research assistance.

1 551 US 877, 127 S Ct 2705 (2007).

2 *Dr. Miles Med. Co. v John D. Park & Sons Co.*, 220 US 373 (1911).

3 For convenience, unless otherwise specified, I use the term RPM without the qualifier 'minimum' to refer *only* to minimum resale price maintenance (not maximum RPM), since minimum RPM is the focus of this chapter.

4 See, e.g., B Klein, 'Competitive Resale Price Maintenance in the Absence of Free-Riding' (2009) 76 *Antitrust LJ* 431; JD Wright, 'Overshot the Mark? A Simple Explanation of the Chicago School's Influence on Antitrust' (2009) 5 *Comp Pol'y Int'l* at 14–23, also available at http://ssrn.com/abstract id=1370641 (accessed December 2010); RA Winter, 'Resale Price Maintenance with and without Free-riding' http://www.ftc.gov/opp/workshops/rpm/docs/rwinter0217.pdf (accessed December 2010).

5 See, e.g., 'The Discount Pricing Consumer Protection Act: Do We Need to Restore the Ban on Vertical Price Fixing?', Hearing on s 148 before the Subcommittee on Antitrust, Competition Policy and Consumer Rights of the S. Comm. on the Judiciary, 111th Cong. (2009) (statement of P Harbour, Comm'r, Federal Trade Commission); 'The Leegin Decision: The End of the

reverse *Leegin*.[6] However, though they were approved by the Judiciary Committees of both congressional bodies, the full House and Senate never voted on them,[7] probably owing to the press of other more urgent matters facing them.

At the state level, most states favor the per se illegality rule against RPM – a vast majority had joined in the filing of an *amicus* brief in *Leegin* opposing the overruling of *Dr. Miles*,[8] and later urged passage of the Congressional bills.[9] The state of Maryland has already passed a 'Leegin repealer' that effectively reaffirms the per se illegality rule against RPM under state antitrust law notwithstanding *Leegin*.[10] Moreover, some states such as New York, California and New Jersey already have state antitrust

---

Consumer Discounts or Good Antitrust Policy?' Hearing on s 2261 before the Subcommittee on Antitrust, Competition Policy and Consumer Rights of the S. Comm. on the Judiciary, 110th Cong. (2007) (statement of Robert Pitofsky); RM Brunell, 'Overruling Dr. Miles: The Supreme Trade Commission in Action' (2007) 52 *Antitrust Bull* 475; WS Grimes, 'The Path Forward After Leegin: Seeking Consensus Reform of the Antitrust Law of Vertical Restraints' (2008) 75 *Antitrust LJ* 467; M Lao, 'Free Riding: An Overstated, and Unconvincing, Explanation for Resale Price Maintenance' in Pitofsky (ed.), *How the Chicago School Overshot the Mark* (2008) 196; ED Cavanaugh, 'Vertical Price Restraints After Leegin' (2008) 21 *Loy Cons L Rev* 1.

6 Discount Pricing Consumer Protection Act, s 148, 111th Cong. (2009); Discount Pricing Consumer Protection Act of 2009, HR 3190, 111th Cong. (2009). A similar bill was introduced in the Senate in 2007 but was not acted upon. See Discount Pricing Consumer Protection Act, s 2261, 110th Cong. (2007). *See infra* notes 52–6 and accompanying text.

7 The House Bill was approved by the House Judiciary Committee on 13 January 2010, see www.govtrack.us/congress/bill.exd?bill=h111-3190, while the Senate Bill was approved by the Senate Judiciary Committee on 18 March 2010, see www,govtrack.us/congress/bill.xpd?bill=s111-148 (accessed December 2010).

8 Thirty-seven states joined in an *amicus* brief in *Leegin* in support of retaining the per se rule against RPM. See Brief for the State of New York et al. as *Amici Curiae* Supporting Respondent, *Leegin Creative Leather Prods., Inc. v PSKS Inc.*, 551 US 877, 127 S Ct 2705 (2007), 2007 WL 621851.

9 The State Attorneys General of 38 states submitted to Congress joint letters, dated 27 October 2009, strongly supporting the passage of s 148 and HR 3190, the Discount Pricing Consumer Protection Act that would repeal *Leegin*. See Letter from Thirty-Eight State Attorneys General to Sen. Herb Kohl and Sen. Orrin G Hatch (27 October 2009), http://naag.org/assets/files/pdf/signons/20091027.S_148.pdf (accessed December 2010); Letter from Thirty-Eight Attorneys General to Rep. John Conyers and Rep. Lamar Smith (27 October 2009), http://naag.org/assets/files/pdf/signons/20091027.HR_3190.pdf (accessed December 2010).

10 Maryland Code Annotated Commercial Law § 11–204 (LexisNexis 2009).

laws that specifically ban RPM agreements.[11] And, at least California has already shown that it has no intention to defer to federal law on the issue.[12] Thus, the battle in the United States over RPM is far from over.

Leegin also places the United States at odds with the European Union and most advanced industrialized countries,[13] furthering the absence of consensus. For example, under EU law, RPM is considered a 'hard-core' restraint, which is presumed unlawful unless the RPM proponent shows the restriction is indispensable to promoting technical or economic progress or improving the production or distribution of goods, and that consumers receive a fair share of the resulting benefits.'[14]

In this chapter, after providing a short history of RPM and a synopsis of *Leegin* and post-*Leegin* developments, I will explore theories relating to RPM's competitive harms and benefits. In addition to briefly commenting on the more widely acknowledged anticompetitive theories, I will develop arguments on two less recognized effects: to explain why evidence of higher prices under RPM should not be viewed as neutral or irrelevant, but should be read to presume anticompetitive effect; and to focus attention on RPM's often overlooked adverse effect on the retail sector. With respect to the procompetitive theories, I argue that the free-rider explanation for RPM, though theoretically elegant, has limited application. As for the more recently advanced non free-rider procompetitive theories, I identify and analyse a few common problems: their failure to show that the theories are socially efficient and not merely privately efficient for the manufacturer, and the lack of consideration of less restrictive alternatives. Furthermore, their explanation as to why RPM is necessary in a competitive retail market absent free-riding is unpersuasive since it seems contrary to common experience. Given the dearth of empirical evidence behind the theories,[15] it may be wiser to place the onus on those seeking to impose RPM – which is essentially a limitation on price competition – to demonstrate that it is procompetitive in a given case.

---

[11] California Business and Professional Code § 16720(d)–(e) (Deering 2009); New York General Business Law § 369 a (Consol. 2009); New Jersey Statutes Annotated § 56:4-1.1 (West 2009).

[12] On 14 January 2011, the California Attorney General's Office announced that it had stopped a cosmetics manufacturer's RPM practice of prohibiting retailers from selling its cosmetics online at a discount. See http://ag.ca.gov/newsalerts/print_release.php?id=2028 (accessed January 2011).

[13] See OEDC, 'Policy Roundtables – Resale Price Maintenance' (2008) at para 2, http://www.oecd.org/dataoecd/39/63/43835526.pdf (accessed December 2010).

[14] Article 101(3) TFEU.

[15] See *infra* Part 3.3.

2 BACKGROUND

2.1 History of RPM Leading to Leegin

The per se rule against RPM traces its origins in the United States to *Dr. Miles*, a 1911 Supreme Court case that condemned an agreement between a manufacturer and its distributors setting the product's resale prices.[16] Though the Court tempered the harshness of *Dr. Miles* shortly thereafter by holding, in *Colgate*, that a manufacturer can legally pre-announce its suggested retail prices and then unilaterally cut off distributors who refuse to adhere to them,[17] it interpreted Colgate very narrowly until the mid-1980s.[18] Meanwhile, during the depths of the Great Depression, the US Congress decided to allow states to experiment with RPM by enacting the Miller-Tydings Act of 1937 (and later the McGuire Act of 1952) – legislation that permitted states to legalize RPM agreements within their states.[19] However, it later determined the states' foray into RPM to be anti-consumer,[20] and repealed both Acts by passing the Consumer Goods Pricing Act of 1975.[21]

Interestingly, shortly after *Dr. Miles* was reinstated nationwide, the Court swung swiftly toward tolerance of vertical restraints largely owing to the influence of the Chicago School. In 1977 it adopted the rule of reason for vertical non-price restraints in *Sylvania*.[22] In the 1980s, it aggressively limited the application of the per se rule against RPM by elevating the standard of proof of 'agreement' in *Monsanto*[23] and by construing the term 'price' agreement narrowly in *Business Electronics*.[24] And in 1997, it overturned the per se rule in favor of the rule of reason approach for *maximum* vertical price fixing in *Khan*.[25]

---

16 *Dr. Miles Med. Co. v John D. Park & Sons Co.*, 220 US 373, 409 (1911).

17 *United States v Colgate & Co.*, 250 US 300 (1919).

18 See, e.g., *United States v Parke, Davis & Co.*, 362 US 29 (1960); *Simpson v Union Oil Co.*, 377 US 13 (1964).

19 Miller-Tydings Fair Trade Act, Pub. L. No. 314, Ch. 690, Title VIII, 50 Stat. 690 (1937); McGuire Act, Pub. L. No. 542, 66 Stat. 631 (1952). The McGuire Act was passed to close a perceived loophole in Miller-Tydings. Both Acts were repealed in the Consumer Goods Pricing Act of 1975, Pub. L. No. 94–145, 89 Stat. 801.

20 See 121 Cong. Rec. at 23, 662 (1975) (Statement of Rep. Seiberling) ('[T]he fair trade laws have clearly become anti-consumer. In an economic system built on the principle of competition, they are an anachronistic anomaly whose repeal is long overdue.').

21 Pub. L. No. 94–145, 89 Stat. 801 (1975).

22 *Cont'l T.V., Inc. v GTE Sylvania Inc.*, 433 US 36 (1977).

23 *Monsanto Co. v Spray-Rite Serv. Corp.*, 465 US 752 (1984).

24 *Bus. Elecs. Corp. v Sharp Elecs. Corp.*, 485 US 717 (1988).

25 *State Oil Co. v Khan*, 552 US 3 (1997).

Through it all, however, perhaps in deference to Congress, which made clear after repealing Miller-Tydings its opposition to overturning the per se rule against RPM,[26] the Court remained respectful of the core of *Dr. Miles* until *Leegin* – that is, RPM, *if* it could be proven, remained per se illegal. In terms of public enforcement, after a long hiatus during the Reagan administration, the FTC and the Department of Justice resumed investigation of RPM cases. Between 1990 and 2000 (the latter part of the first Bush's second term and the Clinton years), they brought and settled approximately 15 RPM cases.[27] The states, too, have successfully brought many RPM cases relying on *Dr. Miles*.[28]

2.2 Synopsis of Leegin

The material facts in *Leegin* were largely undisputed. Leegin, a manufacturer of women's leather accessories, had RPM agreements with its retailers and later terminated one retailer, Kay's Kloset, when it sold below the required minimum prices.[29] By all accounts, Kay's Kloset was a successful Leegin retailer against which there were no credible claims of inadequate service. Kay's Kloset sued Leegin for RPM on a theory of per se liability

26 After the Department of Justice, under the Reagan administration, filed an *amicus* brief on behalf of the petitioner/defendant in *Monsanto* seeking to overturn the per se rule against RPM, Congress passed appropriation measures in four years specifically prohibiting the Department from using its appropriations for this purpose. See Judiciary Appropriation Act, Pub. L. No. 98–166, § 510, 97 Stat. 1071, 1102 (1983); Judiciary Appropriation Act, Pub. L. No. 99–180, § 605, 99 Stat. 1136, 1169 (1985); Act of 18 October 1986, Pub. L. No. 99–500, § 605, 100 Stat. 1783, 1783; Act of 22 December 1987, Pub. L. No. 100–202, § 605, 101 Stat. 1329, 1329–38.

27 *Nintendo of America Inc.*, 114 F.T.C. 702 (1991); *Kreepy Krauly USA, Inc.*, 114 F.T.C. 777 (1991); *The Keds Corp.* 117 F.T.C. 389 (1994); *Reebok Int'l, Ltd.*, 120 F.T.C. 20 (1995); *FTC v Onkyo U.S.A. Corp.*, 1995-2 Trade Cas. (CCH) 71, 111 (D.D.C. 1995); *New Balance Athletic Shoe, Inc.*, 122 F.T.C. 137 (1996); *American Cyanamid Co.*, 123 F.T.C. 1257 (1997); *Nine West Group, Inc.*, No. C-3937, 2000 WL 250227 (F.T.C.); and *Sony Music Entm't, Inc.*, No. C-3971, 2000 WL 1257799 (F.T.C.) (minimum advertised price agreement). DOJ cases include: *United States v Canstar Sports USA, Inc.*, 1993-2 Trade Cas. (CCH) 70, 372 (D. Vt. 1993); *United States v Cal. SunCare, Inc.*, 1994-2 Trade Cas. (CCH) 70, 843 (C.D. Cal. 1994); *United States v Playmobil USA, Inc.*, 1995-1 Trade Cas. (CCH) 71,000 (D.D.C. 1995); *United States v Anchorshade, Inc.*, 1996-2 Trade Cas. (CCH) 71, 640 (S.D. Fla. 1996); and *United States v Brush Fibers, Inc.*, 1997-2 Trade Cas. (CCH) 71, 915 (E.D. Pa. 1996).

28 See Brief for the States, *supra* n. 8, at 1 (listing some of the cases).

29 *Leegin Creative Leather Prods., Inc. v PSKS Inc.*, 551 US 877, 127 S Ct 2705, 2710-2712 (2007).

and prevailed in the lower courts. Reversing and remanding in a five to four decision, the Supreme Court overruled *Dr. Miles* and held that the rule of reason standard was applicable.

Justice Kennedy, writing for the majority, took the position that the per se rule should be limited to restraints 'that would always or almost always tend to restrict competition and decrease output.'[30] He then noted that the 'economics literature is replete with procompetitive justifications' for RPM[31] – ameliorating free-rider effects and facilitating new entry being two principal ones.[32] Consequently, while he acknowledged that RPM may have anticompetitive effects and that 'the empirical evidence on the topic is limited,'[33] Kennedy concluded that the rule of reason was appropriate and that *stare decisis* did not compel affirming *Dr. Miles*.[34]

In his dissent, joined by Justices Souter, Ginsburg, and Stevens, Justice Breyer focused on the anticompetitive uses of RPM. Though agreeing that RPM can sometimes be beneficial,[35] he rejected the conclusion that courts should consequently adopt a rule of reason when there was no economic consensus or empirical evidence showing how often the harms or benefits occur and how easy or difficult it is to 'separate the beneficial sheep from the antitrust goats.'[36] Clearly skeptical of the free-rider theory,[37] a main justification asserted for RPM, Breyer emphasized the lack of empirical data showing that free-riding is a common occurrence or has serious competitive effects, and noted disagreement among economists on this issue.[38] He also dismissed claims that, even absent free-riding, RPM may be the most efficient way to increase market share by inducing dealer services, saying that he found the arguments incomprehensible.[39] Finally, placing greater weight on *stare decisis*, Breyer found 'no change in circumstances' that would support changing the long-established per se rule against RPM by overturning *Dr. Miles*.[40]

---

[30] Id. at 2713 (citing *Bus. Electr. Corp. v Sharp Electr. Corp.*, 485 US 717, 723 (1988)).

[31] Id. at 2714.

[32] Id. at 2715–16.

[33] Id. at 2717.

[34] Id. at 2721.

[35] Id. at 2729 (Breyer, J, dissenting).

[36] Id.

[37] Id. at 2730 ('We do, after all, live in an economy where firms, despite *Dr. Miles'* per se rule, still sell complex technical equipment (as well as expensive perfume and alligator billfolds) to consumers.').

[38] Id. at 2729.

[39] Id. at 2733.

[40] Id. at 2731.

2.3 Post-Leegin Developments

In the only two RPM cases that have reached the federal appellate courts post-*Leegin*, the Fifth and the Eleventh Circuits have both upheld the dismissal of plaintiffs' complaints for failure to sufficiently allege a plausible relevant product market (and, thus, defendants' market power).[41] This is not entirely surprising when *Leegin* is read together with the strict pleading standards articulated by the Supreme Court in *Twombly*[42] in 2007. But it suggests that the rule of reason may devolve into a *de facto legality* rule for RPM, just as it has for vertical non-price restraints after *Sylvania*, despite the fact that the Court had admonished lower courts 'to be diligent in eliminating [RPM's] anticompetitive uses.'[43]

Some manufacturers have lost little time in embracing *Leegin*. Nine West, in reliance on *Leegin*, quickly and successfully petitioned the FTC to be released from a consent order entered in 2000 that had prohibited it from entering into RPM agreements with its retailers.[44] There is also anecdotal evidence that many suppliers have already acted on *Leegin* to require retailers to enter into minimum-pricing pacts and have cut them off when they price below the set minimums.[45] A provider of price comparisons for consumers, ConsumerWorld.org, said that the impact of the new ruling on consumer pricing is already evident, particularly in baby goods, consumer electronics, home furnishings, and pet food.[46] In a series of recent articles, the *Wall Street Journal* provided further details on the post-*Leegin* resurgence of RPM and minimum advertised price (MAP) policies, and their effect on discounters and consumers alike.[47] Manufacturers, ranging from

---

41 *PSKS, Inc. v Leegin Creative Leather Prods., Inc.*, 615 F.3d 412, 417 (5th Cir. 2010); *Jacobs v Tempur-Pedic Int'l.*, F.3d (11th Cir. 2010), 2010 WL 4880864 at 4-6. See also *Spahr v Leegin Creative Leather Prods., Inc.*, 2008 WL3914461 (E.D. Tenn. 2008). But see *BabyAge.com v Toys 'R' Us, Inc.*, 558 F Supp 2d 575 (E.D. Pa. 2008).

42 *Bell Atlantic Corp. v Twombly*, 550 US 544 (2007). See also *Ashcroft v Iqbal*, 129 S Ct 1937 (2009).

43 *Leegin*, 127 S Ct at 2719–2720. The majority offered three relevant factors to be considered in a rule of reason analysis – the number of producers within the market engaged in RPM, the source of the restraint, and market power – and further suggested that lower courts 'devise rules over time for offering proof, or even presumptions when justified,' to ensure that the rule of reason is effectively implemented. Id.

44 *Nine West Group, Inc.*, No. C-3937, 2008 WL 2061410 (F.T.C.).

45 See J Pereira, 'Price Fixing Makes Comeback After Supreme Court Ruling' (18 August 2008) *Wall St J* at A1.

46 Id.

47 See, e.g., id.; J Pereira, 'State Law Targets "Minimum Pricing"' (28 April 2009) *Wall St J* at D1; J Pereira, 'Why Some Toys Don't Get Discounted

Sony to the lesser-known, are reported to be aggressively policing and enforcing RPM and MAP agreements covering a wide variety of products, usually with help from outside firms that specialize in scouring the Internet for non-conforming prices.[48] Even the US discount giant, Wal-Mart, has apparently accepted RPM goods.[49]

The debate over whether the per se approach or the rule of reason is more appropriate for RPM clearly has not abated. And the state of California has signaled its intention to continue to enforce its own state antitrust law which treats RPM as a per se violation by filing suit, and obtaining a settlement, against a manufacturer that had implemented RPM post-Leegin.[50] Given that the law and policy relating to RPM are in flux, a reassessment of its competitive harms and benefits is warranted.

3 A COMPETITIVE ASSESSMENT

Whether they approve or disapprove of RPM, virtually all economists, legal commentators, and the established bar seem to agree that the practice may have anticompetitive harms as well as procompetitive justifications.[51] The two sides disagree primarily on the issue of how often those benefits or harms occur and how significant their impact; and there is, unfortunately, very little empirical evidence that can shed light on this issue.[52] This

– Manufacturers Set Minimums that Retailers Must Follow or Risk Getting Cut Off' (24 December, 2008) *Wall St J* at D1; J Pereira and JR Wilke, 'Instruments, Audio Gear Scrutinized in Price Probe' (23 October 2008) *Wall St J* at B1; J Pereira, 'Discounters, Monitors Face Battle on Minimum Pricing' (4 December 2008) *Wall St J* at A1.

48 See Pereira, 'Discounters, Monitors Face Battle', *supra* n. 47. See also G Tarr, 'Sony Adds New Premium-Goods Sales Policy' (5 May 2008) *TWICE: This Week in Consumer Electronics*, http://www.twice.com/article/244551-Sony_Adds_New_Premium_Goods_Sales_Policy.php?rssid=20328&q=%27Sony+Adds+New+Premium-Goods+Sales+Policy%E2%80%99 (accessed December 2010).

49 See Pereira, 'State Law Targets 'Minimum Pricing', *supra* n. 47.

50 See http://ag.ca.gov/newsalerts/print_release.php?id=2028 (accessed January 2011).

51 See *Leegin Creative Leather Prods., Inc. v PSKS Inc.*, 551 US 877, 127 S Ct 2705, 2716 (2007); id. at 2729 (Breyer, J, dissenting).

52 Even the *Leegin* majority conceded that 'the empirical evidence on the topic is limited,' though it concluded that 'it does not suggest efficient uses of the agreements are infrequent or hypothetical.' Id. at 2717. See also *infra* Part 3.3 (discussing the weakness of the few empirical studies and surveys of empirical studies that are available).

section will briefly critique the more widely recognized economic theories underlying RPM, and discuss a few that are often overlooked.

3.1 Anticompetitive Theories and Effects

RPM has a few competitive harms that are seldom recognized, namely higher consumer prices even when there is no evidence of an upstream or downstream cartel, and adverse impact on the retail sector. Additionally, even those sympathetic to RPM generally concede that RPM can be used to facilitate a cartel or otherwise stabilize prices at either the manufacturer or dealer level.[53] Moreover, the *Leegin* Court acknowledged that, even absent concerted action, RPM can be anticompetitive if it is imposed by a dominant manufacturer or is adopted owing to pressure from one or more powerful dealers acting alone.

3.1.1 Price effects

A troubling fact about RPM is that virtually all studies show it leads to higher consumer prices.[54] For almost 40 years under Miller-Tydings, some states experimented with RPM while others did not,[55] and subsequent

---

[53] See *Leegin*, 127 S Ct at 2716–2717; see also R Posner, *Antitrust Law* (2nd edn 2001) 172; TR Overstreet, Jr., *Resale Price Maintenance: Economic Theories and Empirical Evidence* (1983) at 12–23; HP Marvel and S McCafferty, 'The Welfare Effects of Resale Price Maintenance', (1985) 28 *J L & Econ* 363, at 373 (providing a historical example of resale price maintenance being used to facilitate a horizontal cartel of retail drug stores).

[54] For studies, analyses, and literature indicating that resale price maintenance almost always raises prices, see, e.g., Overstreet, *supra* n. 53, at 160; P Areeda and H Hovenkamp, *Antitrust Law* (2nd edn 2004) 1604b, at 40 ('The evidence is persuasive on this point.'); 'Brief for WS Comanor and FM Scherer as *Amici Curiae* Supporting Neither Party' at 4, *Leegin Creative Leather Prods., Inc. v PSKS, Inc.*, 127 S Ct 2705 (2007), 2007 WL 173679; Hearing on HR 2384 before the Subcomm. on Monopolies and Commercial Law of the H. Comm. on the Judiciary, 94th Cong. 122 (1975) (statement of KI Clearwaters, Deputy Assistant Att'y Gen., Antitrust Division, DOJ); Hearing on s 408 before the Subcomm. on Antitrust and Monopoly of the S. Comm. on the Judiciary, 94th Cong. 174 (1975); RL Steiner, 'Sylvania Economics – A Critique' (1991) 60 *Antitrust LJ* 41, 56; WF Mueller, 'The Sealy Restraints: Restrictions on Free Riding or Output?' (1989) *Wis L Rev* 1255, at 1293–1296. Even commentators who view vertical restraints as generally procompetitive implicitly concede that RPM tends to raise consumer prices. See, e.g., FH Easterbrook, 'Vertical Arrangements and the Rule of Reason' (1984) 53 *Antitrust LJ* 135, at 156 ('[T]he manufacturer can't get the dealer to do more without increasing the dealer's margin.'). But see H P Marvel and S McCafferty, 'The Political Economy of Resale Price Maintenance' (1986) 94 *J Pol Econ* 1074, at 1075.

[55] See Hearings on s 408 before the Subcomm. on Antitrust and Monopoly of

empirical studies showed consumer prices to be 19 to 27 percent higher in states where RPM was legalized.[56] These price effects are bound to become more significant when RPM is adopted today given the growing importance of Internet retailers, who typically start out at lower price points.[57]

Proponents and opponents of RPM have substantially different reactions to the unambiguous evidence of higher prices under RPM. The *Leegin* majority and other RPM supporters attach no significance to it, arguing that it can support either procompetitive or anticompetitive theories.[58] For example, higher prices would not be anticompetitive if they reflect enhanced value for the product, or if the wider retail margin induced more dealer services that increased demand for the good. Underlying this reasoning is their assumption that the manufacturer's interests are aligned with the consumers' and, hence, there is probably a procompetitive explanation for any observed price increase that is not the result of a cartel.[59]

While it is true that even strong empirical evidence of higher prices under RPM cannot actually *prove* anticompetitive effect, since the data does not demonstrate whether consumers received net enhanced value in return for paying more, it seems reasonable to presume anticompetitive effect when a practice consistently results in substantially higher prices on a wide range of products. It strains the imagination to wonder what sort of enhanced value consumers could possibly have received in return for high-priced music CDs, light bulbs, men's underwear, pet food, or shampoo, to name some of the many items for which higher prices were observed under RPM.

From a theoretical perspective, there are various possible anticompetitive explanations for higher retail prices under RPM, even absent evidence of a manufacturer's or dealer's cartel. First, a manufacturer may 'impose' RPM to placate a powerful retailer if the manufacturer needs the retailer's distribution network.[60] Even if the powerful retailer is less efficient than a more innovative newcomer, the manufacturer may have to accommodate

---

the S. Comm. on the Judiciary, 94th Cong. 173 (1975) (statement of TE Kauper, Assistant Att'y Gen., Antitrust Division).

[56] See *Leegin*, 127 S Ct at 2727–2728 (Breyer, J, dissenting); Hearings on HR 2384, Statement of KI Clearwaters, *supra* n. 54; FM Scherer, 'Comment on Cooper et al's "Vertical Restrictions and Antitrust Policy"' (2005) 1 *Comp Pol'y Int'l*, 65, at 72–4 (citing studies showing substantial price decreases after termination of RPM in light bulbs, over-the-counter drugs, jeans, and other items).

[57] See M Lao, 'Resale Price Maintenance: The Internet Phenomenon and Free Rider Issues' (2010) 55 *Antitrust Bull* 473.

[58] See *Leegin*, 127 S Ct at 2718.

[59] See id. at 2718 et seq.

[60] See id. at 2717.

the powerful dealers who typically have larger operations and account for more sales.[61] Moreover, a multibrand retailer's ability to substitute one brand with another gives the retailer substantial leverage over a manufacturer,[62] even if it may not have sufficient market share to be considered a retailer with market power in the traditional antitrust sense.

Second, a manufacturer may set RPM prices to protect against downward pressure on its own wholesale prices. Economist Robert Steiner, who has written extensively on the anticompetitive effects of restricting intrabrand competition, observes that intense intrabrand competition on a brand minimizes retail markup of that brand.[63] It is logical to expect these retailers to then turn to the manufacturer and press for wholesale price cuts.[64] A manufacturer's self-interest in preventing discounting in order to relieve this pressure is incongruent with consumers' interest and cannot be considered welfare-enhancing. Furthermore, when RPM agreements are adopted for this reason, they often lead to a related, more serious, likely anticompetitive effect – higher prices across the board for *all* brands even without any upstream or downstream conspiracy. That is because retail price competition on a brand, particularly a popular brand, is likely to also reduce retail prices for competing brands sold by the multibrand retailers, as those brands attempt to compete. It follows that preventing price competition on a popular brand would have the opposite result – higher prices on competing brands as well, including those that have not adopted RPM.

Third, in a market with substantial brand differentiation, higher prices under RPM may reflect the joint maximization of a manufacturer and its retailers' profits (to be shared among them), which is not beneficial for consumers. Strong brand name acceptance insulates a brand from interbrand competition to a certain extent, giving the manufacturer some power to raise prices even in a relatively competitive market. In this situation, the economic presumption that restrictions on intrabrand competition are benign because of the existence of interbrand competition is questionable.

---

61 See *Toys "R" Us, Inc. v FTC*, 221 F.3d 928 (7th Cir. 2000).

62 See, e.g., Areeda and Hovenkamp, *supra* n. 58, 1604d3, at 48 et seq.

63 See, e.g., RL Steiner, 'How Manufacturers Deal with the Price-Cutting Retailer: When Are Vertical Restraints Efficient?' (1997) 65 *Antitrust LJ* 407, at 441 (citing case studies involving Levi's jeans); RL Steiner, 'Jeans: Vertical Restraints and Efficiency' in L Duetsch (ed.), *Industry Studies* (1993) 182.

64 See S Robson Walton, 'Antitrust, RPM, and the Big Brands: Discounting in Small-Town America (II)' (1983) 15(2) *Antitrust L & Econ Rev* at 11, 16 (speaking of Wal-Mart's experience when it was a new discounter: 'I don't have any question but that competitive pricing at the retail level creates more pressure on manufacturers' factory prices than is present when they're able to set retail prices as well. . . .').

Justice Douglas said many years ago that price is the 'central nervous system of the economy.'[65] A basic antitrust assumption is also that consumers should have a choice in price/quality tradeoffs. Given these fundamental principles and the existence of various non-consumer friendly reasons for higher retail prices, it is best not to assume that higher prices must have a procompetitive explanation unless the plaintiff proves otherwise under the rule of reason.

3.1.2 Effects on retail sector

Competitive assessments of RPM tend to focus almost exclusively on the manufacturer's perspective, with little or no attention paid to the retail sector.[66] Intuitively, that makes little sense because the United States has a vibrant retail sector that has greatly benefited the nation's economy. Over the years, we have seen a succession of innovative retailers emerging with new sales formats that consumers have embraced. These retail innovations include department stores (for example, Macys), chain stores (for example, Walgreen), self-service supermarkets (for example, Safeway), catalog stores (for example, Sears);[67] and, more recently, mass-merchandize discounters such as Wal-Mart, specialty stores such as Home Depot, warehouse or 'big box' stores such as Best Buy and Costco, and now online stores such as Amazon.com.

Retailers are neither fungible nor equally efficient. In the absence of RPM, they have incentives to improve or develop innovative sales systems that cut costs, reduce prices, and increase sales. Permitting price discounting, particularly of popular brands, encourages new or existing multi-brand retailers to develop novel and cost-effective ways of performing normal retailing functions. In so doing, they may offer consumers different services. The phenomenal success of each new type of store, as it was introduced, demonstrates that it met with many consumers' desires and that its cost-reducing package of different services was considered attractive and not inferior.

In banning discounting, RPM prevents efficient retailers from achieving a higher volume of sales by passing along their cost savings to consumers, and thereby minimizes the incentive for retail innovation. In the United States, stores such as Amazon.com, Costco, and Wal-Mart owe their success largely to their innovative retail concepts, and their ability

[65] *United States v Socony-Vacuum Oil Co.*, 310 US 150, 224 n. 59 (1940).

[66] One notable exception is economist Robert Steiner. See Steiner, *supra* n. 63.

[67] See id. at 419–23 (discussing the introduction of department stores, chain stores, mail order houses, and supermarkets as new forms of distribution).

to offer sought-after products at discount prices. It is worth noting that major discounters, including Costco and eBay, were among those urging passage of the 2009 Congressional Bill to statutorily override *Leegin*.[68] If stores such as Costco initially had no hope of increasing sales of popular brands by sharply reducing retail margins, they would have had less reason to conceive of the warehouse-club format – relying on high volume sales at narrow margins in large, no-frills settings – that has proven to be immensely successful. While the already established discount giants probably have sufficient power to resist RPM (if they so choose) and continue to prosper, *Leegin* may have an untold effect on the next generation of discount retail innovators – the future Costcos, Wal-Marts, and Amazons. Indeed, if *Leegin* stands, it is conceivable that the current innovative retailers may, in the future, use their buying leverage to pressure manufacturers to adopt RPM in order to prevent the *next* retail innovation from emerging and supplanting their dominance.

3.1.3 Facilitating dealer or manufacturer cartel; Dealer or manufacturer market power

Since much has already been written about the cartel theories of RPM, I will only summarize them here. Ward Bowman, a distinguished economist, first introduced the theory that RPM can be used to facilitate a dealer cartel, noting that dealer groups can pressure a manufacturer to help enforce their horizontal price-fixing agreements under the guise of resale price maintenance.[69] Though some skeptics have questioned why a manufacturer would acquiesce,[70] historical examples show clearly that dealer-initiated RPM is not merely a theoretical concern but a real one.[71] In fact, some commentators view *Dr. Miles* as a case involving an RPM 'imposed'

---

[68] Pereira, 'Discounters, Monitors Face Battle', *supra* n. 47.

[69] W Bowman, 'The Prerequisites and Effects of Resale Price Maintenance' (1955) 22 *U Chi L Rev* 825.

[70] See, e.g., Easterbrook, *supra* n. 54, at 142; WF Baxter, 'Vertical Practices – Half Slave, Half Free' (1983) 52 *Antitrust LJ* 743, at 751 et seq; H Hovenkamp, 'Vertical Restrictions and Monopoly Power' (1984) 64 *Boston U L Rev* 521, at 544 n. 110 (arguing that the facilitation of dealer cartel theory is impossible when the manufacturer is not a monopolist and unlikely when it is).

[71] See *Leegin Creative Leather Prods., Inc. v PSKS Inc.*, 551 US 877, 127 S Ct 2705, 2717 (2007). Even strong supporters of vertical restraints concede that. See Marvel and McCafferty, *supra* n. 53, at 373. See also I Paldor, 'Rethinking RPM: Did the Courts Have it Right All Along?' (2007) 61–89 (unpublished S.J.D. thesis, University of Toronto), http://papers.ssrn.com/sol3/papers.cfm?abstract_id=994750 (accessed December 2010) (recounting the historical impetus for RPM and instances of RPM that came from organized dealers).

by the manufacturer at the behest of retailers seeking to implement their horizontal price-fixing agreement.[72]

From a theoretical perspective, a manufacturer's acquiescence can perhaps be explained by its expectation of higher wholesale prices in return for cooperation, that is, the colluding dealers would share their excess profits with the manufacturer by paying higher wholesale prices. Another possible explanation could be the manufacturer's concern, in a competitive upstream market, that multibrand dealers would otherwise drop its products in favor of its rivals.[73] Even in the case of a dominant manufacturer, dealers acting in concert can have collective monopsony power which gives them bargaining leverage.[74]

The theory of RPM as a device to facilitate a manufacturer's cartel posits that RPM removes the cartel participants' incentive to 'cheat' on their explicit or implicit price-fixing agreement, thereby stabilizing the cartel or oligopoly pricing behavior. In a normal market, each manufacturer in a cartel would be tempted to grant secret price concessions to retailers who would then likely reduce the products' retail prices, leading to higher sales. But if RPM makes retail discounting impossible or very difficult, the temptation to cheat would be removed because the manufacturer knows that any wholesale price reduction granted to a retailer would not lead to additional sales. Because retail prices are transparent, a manufacturer's attempt to couple a clandestine wholesale price cut with reduced RPM would not work as it would be detected. Knowing that, a manufacturer is unlikely to destabilize a manufacturer cartel or oligopoly pricing system by cheating.[75] Despite the coherence of this theory, there are admittedly few RPM cases clearly attributable to it.[76]

Even without concerted action, as the *Leegin* Court recognized, RPM can still be anticompetitive if it results from the flexing of either a manufacturer's or a dealer's market power. A powerful manufacturer's adoption

---

[72] See, e.g., H Hovenkamp, *The Antitrust Enterprise: Principle and Execution* (2005) at 186. Professor Rudolph JR Peritz, however, has provided a compelling counter-narrative of *Dr. Miles*, showing that the case in fact involved a manufacturer who sought to control prices and differentiate its brand through standard form contracts. RJR Peritz 'The Life and Times of Dr. Miles Medical Company' in EM Fox and D Crane (eds), *Antitrust Stories* (2007) at 61–90.

[73] See Areeda and Hovenkamp, *supra* n. 58, 1604d3, at 48 et seq.

[74] See Paldor, *supra* n. 71, at 96 et seq.

[75] See R Pitofsky, 'In Defense of Discounters: The No-Frills Case for a Per Se Rule Against Vertical Price Fixing' (1983) 71 *Geo LJ* 1487, at 1490 et seq.

[76] There are only a handful of such cases, involving General Electric. *See United States v General Elec. Co.*, 82 F. Supp. 753, 765–6, 771–5 (1949); *United States v General Elec. Co.*, 358 F. Supp. 731 (1973).

of RPM agreements on its own initiative is anticompetitive if it induces retailers not to carry the products of the manufacturer's smaller, but innovative, up-and-coming rivals.[77] RPM agreements that result from pressure from one or more dominant dealers acting alone are also anticompetitive since they tend to forestall innovation or competition from more nimble or innovative retailers.[78]

3.2 Procompetitive Theories

As earlier mentioned, the *Leegin* majority and those who approve of RPM generally concede that the practice has anticompetitive risks, but they assert that those risks are outweighed by its procompetitive effects. The primary efficiency claim is that RPM enhances welfare by eliminating free-riding. More recently, a few non free-rider procompetitive claims have also been advanced.

3.2.1 The free rider explanation

3.2.1.1 The classic theory Eliminating free-rider effects is the principal economic explanation most often offered for RPM.[79] In a nutshell, the classic free-rider theory posits that effective marketing for some products requires special point-of-sale dealer services that cannot be separately sold, such as in-store demonstrations.[80] However, if consumers can use the services provided by one retailer but buy at a discount from another retailer offering no such services, there would be an underprovision of the desired services because few retailers would be willing to provide them. RPM remedies this problem by prohibiting price competition, thereby inducing retailers to provide the needed services.

While this hypothesis is theoretically valid, the claim that it explains most RPM agreements is overstated and unconvincing. In his *Leegin* dissent, Breyer noted that free riding is ubiquitous in our economy and questioned 'how often the "free riding" problem is serious enough to significantly deter dealer investment.'[81] Many other commentators are

---

77 *Leegin Creative Leather Prods., Inc. v PSKS Inc.*, 551 US 877, 127 S Ct 2705, 2717 (2007).

78 See id.

79 See id. at 2716. For a critique of the free rider theory, see Lao, *supra* n. 5.

80 See LG Telser, 'Why Should Manufacturers Want Fair-Trade?' (1960) 3 *J L & Econ* 86; Bowman, *supra* n. 69; BS Yamey, *The Economics of Resale Price Maintenance* (1954) at 3–27.

81 *Leegin*, 127 S Ct at 2729–2730 (Breyer, J, dissenting).

similarly skeptical of the free-rider explanation, observing that few products require demonstrations and other special dealer services and few dealers actually provide them.[82] Yet, RPM has been used in the sale of a wide range of products, including boxed candy, pet foods, jeans, vitamins, hair shampoo, knit shirts, men's underwear,[83] music CDs, and women's fashion accessories (*Leegin*). Moreover, even where free-riding is a legitimate concern, RPM cannot truly provide an effective solution. Retailers inclined to shirk can still free-ride off of services provided by others and use their RPM margin to attract customers from the service-providing retailers through gifts or discounts on other products.[84]

3.2.1.2 'Quality-certification' free-riding 'Quality certification' free-riding, a variant of the classic free-rider theory, posits that a reputable retailer's carrying of an item certifies its quality or stylishness, and that free-riding occurs when discounters who did not invest to develop this reputation sell to customers who want the product because it has the reputable retailer's stamp of approval. And, this free-riding is said to deter retailers from investing in quality certification.[85]

One weakness of this theory is that most RPM cases seem to involve well-established brands, which do not particularly need a prestige retailer's certification.[86] A Sony product, for example, does not need Macy's quality certification. Nor does a Vera Wang dress require Neiman's style endorsement. Even for lesser-known brands, it is questionable how important certification is today. In this Internet age, other sources of independent information about quality are readily available. There are numerous

---

[82] See, e.g., Brief of Amici Comanor and Scherer, *supra* n. 54, at 6; Areeda and Hovenkamp, *supra* n. 58, 1601e, at 13; R Pitofsky, 'Why Dr. Miles Was Right' (1984) 8 *Regulation* 27, at 29; S Orstein, 'Resale Price Maintenance and Cartels' (1985) 30 *Antitrust Bull* 401, at 428; K Arquit, 'Resale Price Maintenance: Consumers' Friend or Foe?' (1991) 60 *Antitrust LJ* 447, at 452; Lao, *supra* n. 5, at 201 et seq. Even some supporters of RPM agree with this critique. *See* B Klein, 'Distribution Restraints Operate by Creating Dealer Profits: Explaining the Use of Maximum Resale Price Maintenance in State Oil v. Khan' (1999) 7 *Sup Ct Econ Rev* 1, at 7 et seq.

[83] See Pitofsky, *supra* n. 82, at 29 et seq; E Corey, 'Fair Trade Pricing: A Reappraisal' (1952) 30(5) *Harv Bus Rev*, 47.

[84] See B Klein and KM Murphy, 'Vertical Restraints as Contract Enforcement Mechanisms' (1988) 31 *J L & Econ* 265, at 266.

[85] HP Marvel and S McCafferty, 'Resale Price Maintenance and Quality Certification' (1984) 15 *Rand J Eco*. 346.

[86] Even the theory's proponents acknowledge there is less need for reliance on retailers for certification 'as the manufacturer's brand becomes better known.' Id. at 349.

product review websites covering an extensive variety of products and services upon which consumers can now rely.[87] Whether quality certification free-riding poses a serious problem in deterring investment is probably not a question that can be answered empirically, but there is at least no evidence of an underprovision of luxury or quality goods or of upscale stores in our economy. Nor is there indication of a trend, among such stores, toward failure or compelled conversion to no-frills formats.

More importantly, even assuming that quality certification free-riding is a credible and serious problem, RPM cannot effectively solve it. Under the theory, unlike the prestige retailers who have a certification role, non-prestige retailers have *no* service obligations at all. RPM would only give them an even greater cost advantage over the quality certification retailer. It would allow them to continue to free-ride on the prestige retailer's quality certification and use their windfall to attract more customers from the prestige retailer through non-price inducements such as coupons, giveaways or discounts on other items and so forth.

A related procompetitive theory sometimes also asserted for RPM is that it enables a manufacturer to promote and protect a prestigious image for its product.[88] While it is most likely true that RPM can enhance the elite status of a product, I disagree that this is a clear consumer benefit that warrants condoning private restrictions on price competition. My argument is not that antitrust law should affirmatively *regulate* high-image marketing strategies – I agree it should not. Rather, it is simply that antitrust law should not treat the promotion of status marketing as a procompetitive justification for restricting price competition through RPM. Professor Warren Grimes goes further in his criticism and argues that RPM in this context encourages deception of consumers and is anticompetitive.[89]

3.2.1.3 New market entry Another procompetitive justification identified by the *Leegin* Court is facilitation of new entry,[90] which can be

---

[87] Some of the well-known websites that provide product reviews include Amazon.com, ConsumerReports.org, consumersearch.com, and epinions.com among others.

[88] See, e.g., BR Henry and EF Zelek, Jr., 'Establishing and Maintaining an Effective Minimum Resale Price Policy: A *Colgate* How-To' (Summer 2003) *Antitrust* 8.

[89] See WS Grimes, 'Spiff, Polish, and Consumer Demand Quality, Vertical Price Restraints Revisited' (1992) 80 *Cal L Rev* 815, at 834–6. Grimes argues that the excess retail margin provided by RPM encourages retailers to mislead customers and steer them to the RPM product, even when another brand may be better for the customer. Id.

[90] *Leegin*, 127 S Ct at 2716.

considered a variation of the free-rider theory. This argument explains that new entrants (or existing firms seeking to introduce a new brand or expand into a new region) generally need the assistance of competent dealers in launching a product. But attracting such dealers may be difficult if dealers fear that their market development investments would be unprofitable. Without RPM, later-appointed dealers, who have incurred no market development costs, would be able to undercut the pioneer dealers' prices making it difficult for the pioneer dealers to reap the benefits of their efforts.[91] To the extent that RPM may help manufacturers recruit competent dealers for new products, the practice could be efficient.

Some skeptics have contended that this theory makes sense only for vertical non-price restraints, such as exclusive territories, but not for RPM.[92] With exclusive territories, new dealers cannot enter a pioneering dealer's territory and take away sales generated by the pioneering dealer's efforts.[93] In contrast, RPM gives new dealers an unearned windfall that they can then use to subsidize non-price competition against the pioneering dealer who actually earned the RPM margin through its market development. In any event, to the extent this justification does have merit, any reformulation of the legal rule for RPM should take it into account.[94]

3.2.2 Non free-rider explanations

Perhaps recognizing that few instances of RPM can be justified under the free-rider theory, economists have more recently developed a few non free-rider justifications for the practice. The three best-known are: (1) RPM as a private self-enforcement mechanism to induce dealer performance of their express or implied service obligations;[95] (2) RPM as a means to induce dealers to carry more inventory when demand is uncertain;[96] and (3) RPM as a correction for dealers' bias toward price competition that is said to result from consumer heterogeneity.[97]

---

[91] See Areeda and Hovenkamp, *supra* n. 58, 1617a, 1631b, at 193–6, 308.

[92] See Steiner, 'How Manufacturers Deal with the Price-Cutting Retailer', *supra* n. 63, at 430; Areeda and Hovenkamp, *supra* n. 58, 1617a3, at 195–6.

[93] See Steiner, 'How Manufacturers Deal with the Price-Cutting Retailer', *supra* n. 63, at 430.

[94] See Pitofsky, 'In Defense of Discounters', *supra* n. 75, at 1495.

[95] Klein and Murphy, *supra* n. 84.

[96] R Deneckere, HP Marvel and J Peck, 'Demand Uncertainty and Price Maintenance: Markdowns as Destructive Competition' (1997) 87 *Am Econ Rev* 619.

[97] RA Winter, 'Vertical Control and Price Versus Nonprice Competition' (1993) 108 *Q J Econ* 61.

3.2.2.1 Summaries of the three major non-free-rider theories RPM as contract enforcement mechanism. Offered by Klein and Murphy, this hypothesis asserts that it is difficult for manufacturers to make and enforce contracts with retailers specifying the required services. RPM is therefore adopted to provide monopoly rents to retailers to induce their performance of their explicit or implicit service obligations.[98] The theory is that the threat of losing these future excess profits for non-performance incentivizes retailers to provide the expected services.[99] Implicit in this theory is the notion that the threat of termination may not be a sufficient motivator if retailers are making only normal profits.[100] Klein and Murphy further suggest that the theory is particularly applicable in situations where consumers cannot ascertain quality until after purchase and cannot correctly assign blame after detecting poor quality.[101]

RPM as incentive to increase inventory when demand is uncertain. This Deneckere, Marvel and Peck theory posits that RPM is welfare enhancing because it provides an incentive to retailers to stock more inventory when consumer demand is uncertain.[102] RPM assures retailers that, if demand turns out to be at the low end of the expected range, they will not be forced to sell their excess inventory, assumed to have little or no scrap value, at fire-sale prices. This induces retailers to stock sufficient inventory to cover demand at the high end of the range.

RPM for correcting retailer bias toward price competition. This theory, developed by Ralph Winter,[103] says that consumer heterogeneity leads to retailer bias toward price competition that is corrected by RPM. According to Winter, retailers focus on the 'inter-retailer margin' – attracting buyers of a product from other retailers. These consumers, price-sensitive and time-insensitive,[104] are more easily won over by low price than by service. Manufacturers, however, benefit from attracting buyers *into* the market (those on the 'product margin') and are indifferent as to which retailer makes the sale.[105] Winter asserts that achieving this objective requires more time-reducing services from retailers. Thus, there is a mismatch in manufacturer-retailer incentives in the provision of dealer

---

98 Klein and Murphy, *supra* n. 84.
99 Id. at 267–9.
100 Id. at 268–9.
101 Id. at 281.
102 Deneckere et al., *supra* n. 96.
103 Winter, *supra* n. 97.
104 Id. ('Consumers with low opportunity costs of time are *overrepresented* on interretailer margins.').
105 Id. at 63.

services. RPM would correct the problem and maximize the joint profits of the manufacturer and retailers.[106]

3.2.2.2 Critique of these non-free-rider theories I see a few common problems with these theories. First, while the theories may all demonstrate *private* efficiency, they do not necessarily demonstrate *social* efficiency: that is, they explain why RPM would benefit manufacturers and some retailers, but do not adequately explain why and how it would necessarily enhance consumer welfare. Second, they do not persuasively explain why RPM is necessary in a competitive retail market absent free-riding. Third, they include almost no consideration of less restrictive alternatives.

Private efficiency versus social efficiency. The central focus of antitrust law is, or should be, on *consumer* welfare. In the RPM context, it means asking whether the practice, under a particular theory, usually results in net consumer benefit. However, economic theories of competitive benefits seem to all focus on *total* welfare – a theory is considered procompetitive as long as the manufacturer's gains exceed consumers' losses, even if those gains come principally from consumer surplus. There is no concern with distribution issues. Thus, while the non-free-rider theories of benefits may show that RPM is privately efficient for the manufacturer, they do not satisfactorily show that it is socially efficient.

This is most evident in Deneckere et al.'s inducement of increased inventory theory. It is safe to assume that, under this theory, RPM is indeed optimal for the manufacturer. In fact, RPM (unless it is dealer-driven) is probably always privately efficient for the manufacturer or it would not have been adopted. But the manufacturer's benefits under this theory often come at the expense of consumers – from consumer surplus.[107] If demand turns out to be high, consumers pay the high RPM price. If demand turns out to be low, they still pay the high RPM price instead of having the benefit of lower prices that should otherwise prevail in a competitive retail market with low demand. Thus, while RPM benefits manufacturers and some retailers under this theory, it is often not welfare enhancing for consumers.

Winter's theory of RPM as correction for retailer bias toward price competition, likewise, is not necessarily beneficial for consumers. It is true that buyers on the inter-retailer margin are probably time-insensitive and

---

[106] Id. at 61.

[107] See Deneckere, *supra* n. 96, at 887 (acknowledging that the manufacturer's gains under their inventory theory 'can often come principally from consumer surplus').

price-sensitive, or they would not be spending time searching for the store with the best bargain. However, there is no basis to assume that all or even most buyers on the verge of buying a product (on the 'product margin') necessarily prefer services to low prices, which is a premise of the model. Naturally, if a manufacturer adopts RPM on its own initiative, we can assume that it is optimal for the manufacturer. But it does not follow that *consumer* welfare is also enhanced – unless one accepts the assumption made by most economists that manufacturers' and consumers' interests are aligned. The reasoning behind the assumption is that manufacturers should want retailers to sell at the lowest possible retail price in order to increase sales. Therefore, if the manufacturer establishes higher retail prices through RPM, there must be a procompetitive reason – perhaps RPM will encourage dealer services leading to higher demand for the product.

Economist William Comanor, however, has compellingly challenged the basis of that assumption.[108] He explains that, in deciding on the level of services to offer consumers for a higher price, manufacturers respond only to the preferences of marginal consumers.[109] However, if the average or infra-marginal consumer does not desire the extra services but is nonetheless willing to pay the higher RPM price because she is relatively price-insensitive, and if relatively few marginal consumers benefited from the additional services, RPM would result in net consumer harm. Regardless of whether *total* welfare is adversely affected, antitrust law should be concerned with the transfer of consumer surplus to manufacturers and retailers even if economists consider this issue irrelevant from the standpoint of pure economics.

Why wouldn't retailer competition provide appropriate price/service mix? In his *Leegin* dissent, Breyer rejected claims that RPM was needed to induce dealer services even absent free-riding, saying that he failed to understand why retailer competition would not incentivize dealers to provide services valued by consumers so long as free-riding were not an issue.[110]

According to economists Benjamin Klein and Ralph Winter, normal retail competition does not generate optimal services, even in the absence of free-riding, because of a mismatch in manufacturer-dealer incentives.[111]

---

108 WS Comanor, 'Vertical Price-Fixing – Vertical Market Restrictions, and the New Antitrust Policy' (1985) 98 *Harv L Rev* 983 (demonstrating conflicts between the interests of consumers and manufacturers).

109 Id. at 990–2.

110 *Leegin Creative Leather Prods., Inc. v PSKS Inc.*, 551 US 877, 127 S Ct 2705, 2733 (2007) (Breyer, J, dissenting).

111 Klein, 'Competitive RPM' *supra* n. 4; Winter, *supra* n. 97.

Klein argues that a manufacturer's incremental profit margin from retailer services is often significantly larger than the retailer's.[112] Therefore, in a competitive retail market, a retailer's incentive to provide services will be lower than the manufacturer's and will not lead to the correct price/service mix.[113] RPM corrects for this incompatibility and leads to an optimal level of dealer services, at least from the manufacturer's perspective.

Winter offers a roughly similar explanation in his procompetitive theory of RPM as a means to correct for retailer bias toward price competition instead of sales efforts.[114] He argues that retailers focus on attracting consumers from other retailers (consumers on the 'inter-retailer margin') and that these consumers are price-sensitive and time-insensitive.[115] Manufacturers, however, benefit from attracting buyers into the market (those on the 'product margin'), and he asserts that this is best achieved if time-reducing services are provided by retailers.[116] Thus, there is a mismatch in manufacturer-retailer incentives in a competitive retail market.

The mismatch-in-incentives argument seems to assume that retailers are generic when common knowledge tells us that that is untrue. Winter's theory also implicitly assumes that, even absent free-riding, *all* retailers of a product would compete for buyers who value low prices over time-saving or other sales efforts. This assumption does not appear to be supported by any empirical data and is contrary to common experience. In reality, we have a rich retail market offering a wide spectrum of price/service mix. There are low-service stores catering to customers who are tolerant of minimal sales efforts and are willing to expend time and effort in search of the lowest price. There are also high-service stores designed to attract buyers who value sales efforts and are time-sensitive. And, consumers generally choose the type of store they patronize based on the level and the kind of service they prefer.

The full mix of retailers existing in our marketplace today is the culmination of customers' and manufacturers' desires at a time when RPM was *not* permitted. It has functioned well in a non-RPM regime that has existed since *Dr. Miles*. Unless there is supporting empirical evidence, and there is none, I am skeptical of the premise that, absent RPM, retailers would all gravitate toward competition for the price-sensitive buyers and ignore customers who prefer service, so long as the services are not free-rideable.

---

112 Klein, 'Competitive RPM' *supra* n. 4, at 5 et seq.
113 Id. at 11 et seq.
114 Winter, *supra* n. 97.
115 Id. at 62 et seq.
116 Id.

Where the manufacturer chooses a good mix of retailers for the distribution of its products, it is difficult to see why RPM is beneficial in the absence of free-riding. It would only prevent some retailers from offering price-sensitive consumers the option of lower price and minimal service, without particularly benefitting those who value services since there is no evidence of shortage of high-service stores even in the absence of RPM.

Less restrictive alternatives. Another common problem with the proffered non-free-rider procompetitive theories is that they fail to consider less restrictive alternatives. For example, with respect to the inducement to increase inventory theory, if the objective is truly to encourage retailers to carry more inventory to meet the possibility of high demand, there is at least one obvious less restrictive alternative: a reasonable return policy for unsold inventory. Proponents of the inventory theory have argued that return policies are too costly to administer,[117] but that argument, unsupported by data, is unpersuasive.[118] Shipping costs should not be costly since the theory assumes zero value for unsold inventory and, therefore, there is no reason for their physical return. The manufacturer only has to verify the number of unsold units, perhaps by asking for the return of the items' barcodes. This task seems quite manageable, especially as compared to the manufacturer's need to enforce RPM if demand turns out to be low. If demand falls in the low range, retailers would have huge incentives to sell excess inventory by directly 'cheating' on the RPM agreement, or by engaging widely in various forms of non-price competition such as offering giveaways on related products and services. For the manufacturers' inventory objective to be achieved in this environment, they would have to closely monitor and enforce RPM agreements, which would likely be as costly as administering a return/refund policy.

With respect to the contract enforcement theory, even accepting Klein and Murphy's assumption that increasing the rents earned by retailers is beneficial, there are other less restrictive alternatives that can be used, such as direct and periodic lump sum payments.[119] Direct payments would provide an incentive to retailers to provide needed services – the claimed benefit – but would not stifle innovative retailing or bar efficient retailers from passing along their cost savings to consumers.

A manufacturer's choice of RPM over an alternative strategy does not necessarily mean that the former is better for consumers. A strategy

[117] Deneckere et al., *supra* n. 96, at 890 n. 9.

[118] For a comprehensive critique of the argument that return policies are too costly to administer, see Paldor, *supra* n. 71, at 218–20.

[119] See Paldor, *supra* n. 71, at 204–8.

that is privately efficient for the manufacturer may not be socially efficient because the manufacturer's interests may not coincide with the consumers'. The consideration of less restrictive alternatives is particularly important given the lack of solid empirical evidence supporting the procompetitive theories underpinning RPM and the almost certainty of higher consumer prices that RPM brings.

3.3 Lack of Strong Empirical Evidence

Aside from data (mostly from the Miller-Tydings era) showing higher prices under RPM and some historical cases of RPM being used to facilitate dealer cartels, there is little reliable empirical evidence supporting any of the various economic theories either approving or disapproving of RPM. Even the *Leegin* Court conceded as much, though it cited two studies to say that the limited empirical evidence at least 'does not suggest efficient uses of the agreements are infrequent or hypothetical.'[120]

In one of the studies, Pauline Ippolito analysed a sample of all litigated RPM cases from 1976 to 1982[121] and concluded that they were generally inconsistent with dealer or manufacturer cartel theories.[122] But, as Justice Breyer and other critics have noted, the study 'equates the failure of plaintiffs to *allege* collusion with the *absence* of collusion – an equation that overlooks the superfluous nature of allegations of horizontal collusion in a resale price maintenance case and the tacit form that such collusion might take.'[123] There were also other methodological problems with the sample, which Ippolito herself apparently acknowledges.[124]

In the other study, Thomas Overstreet reviewed 68 RPM cases brought and resolved by the FTC between 1965 and 1982,[125] and noted that the use of RPM in the majority of cases 'was not likely motivated by collusive

120 *Leegin Creative Leather Prods., Inc. v PSKS Inc.*, 551 US 877, 127 S Ct 2705, 2717 (2007).

121 PM Ippolito, 'Resale Price Maintenance: Empirical Evidence from Litigation' (1991) 34 *J L & Econ* 263. Ippolito's sample consisted of 130 private and 73 government (federal or state) cases, 30% of which involved maximum RPM. See id. at 268 et seq.

122 Id. at 281 (noting that only 13% of the cases in the sample included allegations of horizontal price fixing).

123 *Leegin*, 127 S Ct at 2732 (Breyer, J, dissenting) (citing H Hovenkamp, *Federal Antitrust Policy: The Law of Competition and its Practice* (3rd edn 2005) § 11.3c, at 464 & n 19).

124 See Ippolito, *supra* n. 121, at 280 et seq.

125 Overstreet, *supra* n. 53.

dealers who had successfully coerced their suppliers.'[126] But Overstreet acknowledged elsewhere in the study that the data he relied on was generally 'inadequate to determine rigorously whether the associated economic conditions correspond best with procompetitive or anticompetitive hypotheses about the use of RPM.'[127] He also observed in a later study that 'the historical experience, or practice of RPM [is] largely a sorry record of abuses'.[128]

The weakness of these two empirical studies is evident from the fact that, while the *Leegin* majority cited them, it also specifically acknowledged that historical examples suggest that the use of RPM to implement and enforce dealer cartels is a legitimate concern.[129] In short, Ippolito's conclusion seems to be inconsistent with history, and Overstreet's conclusion is substantially qualified by his other contrary observations.

In addition to these empirical studies cited by the *Leegin* Court, there are two other more recent surveys of empirical studies on RPM: one by four members of the FTC staff (Cooper et al.),[130] and the other by Francine Lafontaine and Margaret Slade.[131] The Cooper et al. paper, published in 2005, concluded from an analysis of 22 studies that vertical restraints are likely to be benign or welfare enhancing. Criticism of the Cooper et al. survey, however, has been scathing. Economist Frederic M Scherer described it as 'severely biased, ignoring important cases in which vertical restraints had significant anti-consumer consequences.'[132] After summarizing cases and detailing other data that were completely left out of the *Cooper* et al. paper, Scherer concluded that the authors' survey method 'systematically overlooked or excluded the cases [. . .] and other examples at odds with their conclusion.'[133] Calling their sample 'severely biased,'

---

126 Id. at 80.

127 Id. at 66.

128 TR Overstreet, Jr. and AA Fisher, 'Resale Price Maintenance and Distribution Efficiency: Some Lessons from the Past' (1985) 3 *Contemp Pol'y Iss* 43, at 45.

129 *See Leegin Creative Leather Prods., Inc. v PSKS Inc.*, 551 US 877, 127 S Ct 2705, 2717 (2007). Even strong supporters of vertical restraints concede that. *See* Marvel and McCafferty, 'Welfare Effects of RPM' *supra* n. 53, at 373.

130 J Cooper, L Froeb, D O'Brien and M Vita, 'Vertical Antitrust Policy as a Problem of Inference' (2005) 23 *Int'l J Ind Org* 639; J Cooper, L Froeb, D O'Brien and M Vita, 'Vertical Restrictions and Antitrust Policy: What About the Evidence' (2005) 1 *Comp Pol'y Int'l* 45.

131 F Lafontaine and M Slade, 'Exclusive Contracts and Vertical Restraints: Empirical Evidence and Public Policy' in *Handbook of Antitrust Economics* (2008) 391.

132 Scherer, *supra* n. 56, at 66.

133 Id. at 74.

Scherer remarked that '[n]o amount of decision theory and weighting of prior beliefs will yield good decisions if the evidence that goes into formulating the prior beliefs is biased.'[134] Another review of the survey, by the American Antitrust Institute, is similarly critical.[135]

In the second survey, Lafontaine and Slade reviewed 23 empirical papers on vertical restraints and concluded that manufacturer and consumer interests tend to be congruent.[136] However, unlike Cooper et al., Lafontaine and Slade acknowledged clear problems with the set of available studies they surveyed, including its small number, the techniques used, and industry coverage. Indeed, Slade later observed that 'the most important lesson that can be learned from an examination of the empirical evidence on vertical restraints is how *scant* that evidence is.'[137] And she noted that only when more evidence is gathered – from use of restraints in different industries, use of different empirical techniques, and replication of results in different settings – will it be possible to draw strong conclusions.[138]

4 A PROPOSAL AND CONCLUSION

Were it not for the inconvenient realities of antitrust litigation in the United States, the application of a rule-of-reason standard for RPM might seem relatively sensible. After all, if there is consensus in the economic literature that RPM may have procompetitive uses, it might not be unreasonable to ask the plaintiff to prove that, on balance, a specific RPM arrangement is anticompetitive. The problem is that, in real-world antitrust litigation, a full-blown rule of reason analysis often operates as a de facto legality rule, which even the *Leegin* Court did not favor.

A complete reinstatement of the per se ban against RPM, however, may not be ideal, because economists seem to agree that RPM agreements may *sometimes* be economically justified. Instead, it may be preferable to

---

134 Id.

135 See WS Comanor, FM Scherer and RL Steiner, 'Vertical Antitrust Policy as a Problem of Inference: The Response of the American Antitrust Institute' AAI (18 April 2005), http://papers.ssrn.com/sol3/papers.cfm?abstract_id=1103589 (accessed December 2010). But see Wright, *supra* n. 4, at 21 et seq. (summarizing Cooper et al.'s conclusions without criticism).

136 Lafontaine and Slade, *supra* n. 131.

137 See ME Slade, 'The Effects of Vertical Restraints: An Evidence Based Approach' in Konkurrensverket (Swedish Competition Authority) (ed.), *The Pros and Cons of Vertical Restraints* (2008) 12, at 28 (emphasis added).

138 Id.

apply a presumption of illegality to RPM agreements, which a defendant can rebut by showing that the restraint is reasonably necessary to achieve a legitimate business purpose that benefits consumers, and that no less restrictive alternative would achieve that purpose. This would resemble the EU approach.[139]

It is appropriate to place the burden on the RPM proponent to demonstrate factually that the arrangement is reasonably necessary to achieve demonstrable consumer benefits in a given case for a few reasons. If there is one thing that both RPM supporters and opponents usually agree on, it is that RPM raises consumer prices. Moreover, market competition is the norm in the economies of most advanced industrialized countries, and price is an important dimension of competition. Since resale price maintenance is essentially a restraint on price competition, albeit intrabrand price competition, presuming illegality to the practice and placing the onus of rebuttal on the RPM proponent would strike a proper balance. This is particularly true given the absence of reliable empirical evidence on the prevalence and significance of RPM's procompetitive effects.

---

139 See, in particular, the most recently revised European Commission's 'Guidelines on vertical restraints' of 19 May 2010 [2010] OJ C 130/1, paras 223–9.

6. The *Leegin* case: A US antitrust chief event versus a storm in a European teacup?

Josef Bejček

1 GENERAL REMARKS

I am afraid that all arguments have been made already. Now, it is merely about balancing them, accepting some of them and denying others. It is, to a great extent, a question of beliefs, trust and value-based prejudices.

The *Leegin* case has reopened the old and, many times and in different variations, repeated question whether some judicial activism working against the legislative intent has occurred or whether a final sound step in removing a rigid per se obstacle to potentially procompetitive vertical restraints has been made.

The key headline of this case might be: another lap in the balancing of legal certainty, justice and the suitability of antitrust law.

The overruling of *Dr. Miles*[1] is less dramatic than it might appear. *Leegin* represents only a slight erosion of the Sherman Act's historical prohibition of RPM.[2] *Leegin* did not hold that RPM is per se legal – at least not formally; however, the real social, psychological and factual impact may yet be another story.

The undertakings may well believe that practicing RPM is not connected with a real risk of sanction so that therefore it will always pay off. It is interesting to note that according to some lawyers there has also been a decrease of interest on behalf of companies in both the creation and introduction of compliance programs in recent times.[3] Therefore, there is

---

[1] *Dr. Miles Medical Co. v John D. Parke & Sons Co.*, 220 US 373 (1911).

[2] See J Mitnick, J Lavelle, W Reiss and O Smith, 'On Life Support from Leeginaire's Disease: Can the States Resuscitate *Dr. Miles*?' (2008) 22(3) *Antitrust* 63.

[3] The Czech Antitrust Authority learned about a decrease in the interest of companies in the creation and introduction of compliance programmes in recent

enough reason to worry about a gradual alteration and even weakening of RPM policies of companies.

The US Supreme Court rejected per se illegality of RPM, but did not introduce per se lawfulness of RPM – at least not formally. The question remains whether the Supreme Court intended to make RPM per se legal without actually saying so? The Court failed to provide any practical guidance on this matter.[4]

The Court's guidance for applying the rule of reason is as follows:[5] (i) RPM, when adopted by only a few manufacturers lacking market power, is not likely to be anticompetitive; (ii) if the impetus for a vertical price restraint originates from the retailers, there is a greater likelihood of anti-competitivness of RPM;[6] and (iii) market power of both the manufacturer and the distributors is certainly a reason for concern and more careful scrutiny.

2 THE HYPOCRISY OF THE COLGATE POLICY AS A HIDDEN RPM?

Even before the *Leegin* case, there was a kind of de facto RPM hidden behind the so-called *Colgate* policy. On the one hand, according to Dr. Miles, RPM was banned, yet on the other, according to *Colgate*, it was allowed. It was a two-faced dance between words: if the dealers were only requested to assure and promise adherence to a given price, it is argued that the dealers had not agreed to maintain the retail price and therefore remained free to sell the product at any price. [7]

Indeed, *Colgate*[8] differed from *Dr. Miles* to the extent that the latter

times. Cf. 'Roundtable on resale price maintenance', Note by the Czech Republic, OECD, DAF/COMP/WD(2008)9.

4 R Blair, 'The demise of Dr. Miles: Some troubling consequences' (2008) 53 *Antitrust Bull* 133, at 151.

5 See MA Denger and J Lipton, 'The rule of reason and "*Leegin* Policies": The Supreme Court's Guidance' (2007) 22(1) *Antitrust* 45, at 46.

6 However, in my opinion, it is not very difficult to arrange things in such a way that it looks like an initiative of the manufacturer. In addition, one should not induce the anticompetitive character of the conduct from the facts that provoked that conduct. Rather, the case should only be assessed in the light of the effects of the conduct on the market.

7 LA Graglia, 'Leegin Creative Leather Products, Inc. v PSKS, Inc.: *The Strange Career of the Law of Resale Price Maintenance*' (2008) 53 *Antitrust Bull* 803, at 817.

8 *United States v Colgate & Co.*, 250 US 300 (1919).

involved written contracts, while *Colgate* involved only a unilateral request by the manufacturer. According to the *Colgate* policy, the reseller is free to sell at whatever price, but the manufacturer can lawfully refuse to resupply if the reseller sells below the MSRP (manufacturer's suggested resale price). The game is a sham, as Warren Grimes explains: 'The conduct in issue cannot be genuinely unilateral – some interaction between dealer and supplier is required. Liability should turn on whether the conduct is anticompetitive, not on whether the conduct can be repackaged to appear more unilateral in nature.'[9]

Warren Grimes's correct recommendation[10] is that idiosyncratic results of a unilateral conduct defence should no longer be tolerated. A defence of unilateral conduct cannot be justified by economic analysis; the *Colgate* unilateral conduct is anticompetitive regardless of the subterfuge of 'no agreement'.

Forty years later, the US Supreme Court recognized that *Colgate* permits a manufacturer to achieve 'the same economic effect as is accomplished by a prohibited combination to suppress price competition'.[11] Thereby, 'Colgate rights' turn out to be illusory.

A European 'Colgate policy' would hardly be possible.[12]

3 PER SE ILLEGALITY V HARDCORE BAN

Per se illegality in the US is not tantamount to a hardcore ban in the EU. The Court of First Instance (CFI) and the European Commission state that

---

9 WS Grimes, 'The Path Forward after *Leegin*: Seeking Consensus Reform of the Antitrust Law of Vertical Restraints' (2008) 75 *Antitrust LJ* 467, at 491.

10 Id.

11 *United States v Parke, Davis & Co.*, 362 US 229 (1960).

12 See Guidelines on vertical restraints [2010] OJ C 130/1, para 48:

> . . . RPM can also be achieved through indirect means. Examples of the latter are an agreement fixing the distribution margin, fixing the maximum level of discount the distributor can grant from a prescribed price level, making the grant of rebates or reimbursement of promotional costs by the supplier subject to the observance of a given price level, linking the prescribed resale price to the resale prices of competitors, threats, intimidation, warnings, penalties, delay or suspension of deliveries or contract terminations in relation to observance of a given price level. Direct or indirect means of achieving price fixing can be made more effective when combined with measures to identify price-cutting distributors, such as the implementation of a price monitoring system, or the obligation on retailers to report other members of the distribution network that deviate from the standard price level . . .

there are no anticompetitive agreements that could *ever* meet the requirements of Article 101(3) TFEU (ex-Article 81(3) EC).[13] Nevertheless, RPM was only sporadically exempted from the ban.[14]

Unlike Article 101(3) TFEU, in its application under Regulation 1/2003, there is no *ex lege* excemption in the US. In the EU, under Article 2 of the Implementation Regulation 1/2003, the burden of proof is shifted to the alleged infringer who, accordingly, has to produce convincing evidence for the fulfilment of the legal requirements for an exemption under Article 101(3) TFEU.[15]

In my opinion, the *Leegin* decision enables US courts to follow the same policy as in the EU. It does not assert that minimum RPM is generally an efficient instrument to achieve efficiences in distribution agreements, nor does it assert the opposite. There is no pre-judicial 'black and white' or 'either/or' dichotomy; instead, individual cases should be assessed according to a differently structured rule of reason.

4 MINIMUM AND MAXIMUM (RECOMMENDED) RPM

Regarding RPM, it is necessary to discern between minimum RPM on the one hand, and maximum RPM or mere price recommendations on the other.

Maximum RPM may be procompetitive as it removes the problem of double marginalization where each commercial level adds its own margin.

Recommendations, which may, in principle, be exempted,[16] may produce the same effect as actual price fixing when the supplier somehow motivates the distributor not to sell below the 'recommended' level.[17]

---

13 Case T-17/93 *Matra Hachette v Commission* [1994] ECR II-595, para 85; Commission Decision of 15 September 1999, Case No. IV/36.748 – *REIMS II* [1999] OJ L 275/17, paras 63–5; Commission Decision of 24 July 2002, Case No. COMP/29.373 – *Visa International – Multilateral Interchange Fee* [2002] OJ L 318/17, para 79.

14 Case 243/83 *Binon v AMP* [1985] ECR 2015, para 46: The ECJ suggested that RPM for newspapers and periodicals may be exempted under Article 101(3) TFEU since it constitutes 'the sole means of supporting the financial burden resulting from the taking back of unsold copies and . . . the sole method by which a wide selection of newspapers and periodicals can be made available to readers'.

15 See also L Peeperkorn, 'Resale Price Maintenance and its Alleged Efficiences' (2008) 4 *Eur Comp J* 201, at 204.

16 Cf. Guidelines on vertical restraints, *supra* n. 12, paras 48 and 226–9.

17 See Case T-208/01 *Volkswagen v Commission* [2001] ECR II-5141, where a printed warning to distributors not to depart from 'recommended' retail prices were assessed as vertical price fixing.

Recommending a resale price to an important supplier or requiring the reseller to respect a maximum resale price is covered by the Vertical Agreements Block Exemption Regulation provided that the market share neither of the supplier nor the purchaser does exceed the 30 percent threshold. For cases above this market share threshold, the possible risks of competition between maximum and recommended prices – such as creating a focal price point for the resellers or the facilitating of collusion between suppliers or purchasers – should be taken into account.

A most important factor in assessing possible anticompetitive effects of maximum or recommended prices is the market position of the supplier. The stronger the market position of the supplier, the higher the risk that a maximum resale price or a recommended resale price leads to a more or less uniform application of that same price level by the resellers because they may use it as a focal point.

Another important factor in assessing possible anticompetitive effects of maximum or recommended prices is the market position of the competitors. In a narrow oligopoly, competitors are more likely to exchange information on the preferred price level that may lead to a possible infringement of Article 101(1) TFEU.

5 COMMENTS ON SOME PROCOMPETITIVE ARGUMENTS IN FAVOUR OF MINIMUM RPM

Solving the *free-rider problem* through RPM is not always fair: minimum RPM does not create an incentive to spend the extra profit on promotion, as it is still possible to make use of the promotional investments made by other distributors and to pocket the higher margin. Nor does minimum RPM, unlike maximum RPM, remove the 'double marginalization' problem, it merely shifts the higher end price onto the final consumer.

Keeping more stocks may indeed be facilitated by RPM, but at the expense of the consumer. By shifting the commercial risk and operating costs on to the consumer, the higher price of the goods stored could lower demand and, hence, slow down turnover, which should not be financed by consumers. It is possible that the consumers will just pay for the more risky behaviour of the distributors who are allowed, thanks to the higher prices resulting from RPM, to cover losses from unsold higher stocks.

Facilitating entry into new markets: a price floor would allow for maintaining the same price level even after the later entry of new distributors, and, in this way, the costs of first distributors may be recovered. A lump sum payment supporting entry would be the better option. Similarly, some kind of territorial protection may have the same effect so that RPM is not the only means for enhancing market entry.

Higher efficiency in the distribution of products as a result of RPM is not provable and, moreover, even if it *were* true, there is neither evidence of the positive impact on consumer welfare nor on the level of competitiveness.

Higher quality of presale services for products sold under RPM might be achievable; yet there is a kind of 'tying' of product and services. Therefore, many consumers are prevented from choosing the product at a lower price without this addition service. Consumer choice is reduced in this way.

The assertion that RPM, in addition to removing the free-rider problem, brings about *advantages for manufacturers* as a result of enhanced demand for their products caused by the stronger competitive efforts in non-price areas, such as regarding the extent and quality of pre-sale services, may be true, but only for the group of inframarginal customers. However, marginal customers, who are sensitive to price changes, would be forced to buy what they do not need at a higher price. The welfare of these consumers will not be enhanced if they are forced into buying more expensive products that would be cheaper *without* the additional unsought services. The exclusion of price competition is undoubtedly detrimental to competition. Shifting competition to other parameters is not guaranteed, and the impact of competition with regard to other parameters may not be the same as in price competition. Minimum prices, implemented through RPM policies, work as a benchmark or a price standard that increases the general price level within whole industries and facilitate cartelization.

Another common assertion is that higher margins, enabled by RPM, may *keep more distributors in the marketplace* or enable less effective distributors to enter the market. My heretical question would be: does it make sense for the consumer to have a higher number of distributors who deprive the same consumers of their money owing to higher supra-competitive margins? Is it useful for competition, which seems to be more intensive because of the higher number of competiting distributors, if the most important parameter of competition, namely price, is excluded from competition?[18]

---

[18] The introduction of RPM for books in the Netherlands (see M Kneepkens, 'Resale Price Maintenance: Economics Call for a More Balanced Approach' (2007) 28 *ECLR* 656, at 660) was justified by the need to enhance the number of bookstores. However, there was no convincing economic argument; the introduction of RPM was very much part of a cultural policy. It is at least disputable whether consumers are better off if they buy a more expensive book sold in a larger number of bookstores, if the same book would be cheaper in a more limited number of bookstores or on the Internet. In this case, consumer welfare is defined by the

6 COMMENTS ON SOME ANTICOMPETITIVE ARGUMENTS AGAINST MINIMUM RPM

It is worth mentioning that the *Leegin* decision also recognized the general anticompetitive potential of vertical restraints, and that of vertical price restraints more specifically.

The problem is how to exclude the common interest of manufacturers and distributors to exploit the consumers.

RPM policies promote a high quality image through uniform retail prices, although there is no direct causal link between price and quality. Consumers simply pay more for high-image brands, without any justification arising from procompetitive distribution benefits.[19] The issue here is how to assess consumer welfare in the sense of Article 101(3) TFEU: according to RPM proponents, pre-sale services and advertising appear as a kind of consumer 'welfare' enforced by higher prices. But does RPM really lead consumers to their 'happiness' even against their own will?

How should competition law enforcers assess a situation, where enhanced (pre)sale services coupled with higher prices set by RPM *decrease demand* and, thereby, hamper access of consumers to the respective products? Should enforcers aim to lower prices or to enhance better services in the framework of the goal of consumer welfare? How about a situation where the decrease of demand owing to higher prices outweighs higher demand caused by better services?

The problem of *higher prices* as a result of RPM is substantial. There was a period of time in the US when RPM was allowed on a state level. There were states with and without a ban on RPM. Those states, where RPM was made legal, observed a substantial price increase compared with those states where RPM was considered illegal.[20] This is, in my opinion, a very rare example of a legal and social experiment. Identical products were investigated. Owing to varying economic conditions in the different

---

possibility to buy the book at a higher price because of the declared necessity to offer the same book in a larger number of bookstores – even for those consumers who will *never* buy the book. In form of a 'cultural engineering', the state prefers the physical availability of the book to making books available at lower prices.

[19] Peepercorn, *supra* n. 15, stating that the price of many products is to a large extent (up to 50 percent) made up by the margin and costs of distribution.

[20] R Brunell and A Foer, 'Brief of the American Antitrust Institute as Amicus Curiae in Support of Respondent, Supreme Court of the United States, *Leegin Creative Leather Products, Inc.* (*Petitioner, v PSK, Inc.*, (Respondent)' (February 26, 2007) at p. 14, http://www.antitrustinstitute.org/files/AAI-percent20Leeginpercent20vpercent20percent20PSKS,percent20amicuspercent20briefpercent20FILEDpercent202-26-07_022620071820.pdf (accessed December 2010).

states, such as buying power, buying customs and traditions as well as consumer preferences, it may be debated whether the conditions of *ceteris paribus* (other things being equal) were preserved. Nevertheless, comparably lower consumer prices in all US states that practiced a ban on RPM was detected, which makes it very probable that different RPM policies were the only (or at least the main) reason for the variations. Similarly, immediately after the abolition of the system of unified (bound) prices for books in Switzerland on 30 April 2007, the prices of books substantially fell by 10 to 40 percent while prices of other goods generally increased. Recommended prices (*Richtpreise*) must not be presented any longer in Switzerland.[21]

Snobbish, prestigious consumption by certain types of inframarginal consumers might be better served by a system of exclusive distribution or by sufficiently high wholesale prices charged by the manufacturers to the distributors forcing, in turn, the distributors to sell the goods at accordingly high wholesale prices to the retailers and consequently forcing the retailers to sell the goods at accordingly high retail prices. Individual demand for high-image consumption goods decreases with the rising number of consumers. Lowering the price of the 'prestigious' goods leads enhances demand by marginal customers while it decreases demand by inframarginal consumers. The total impact on both the manufacturer and distributor alike depends on the proportion between these two groups of customers. It is generally not acceptable to assert that the interest of a 'snobbish' group of consumers to pay high prices takes priority over the interest of a broader group of consumers to pay low prices for an equally first-rate quality product.

Intra-brand (price) competition is reputedly excluded without guaranteeing the transfer of economic benefits by means of pre-sale services and promotion. I suppose that, in contrast, disincentives for manufacturers to lower their costs, to innovate and to enhance efficiency may occur because they have a sure 'margin cushion'. RPM may be seemingly innocent in the beginning when manufacturers start to bring a new product to the market. Later, however, the market conditions may change, in particular when a hardly assessable cumulative effect of parallel RPM restraints in the sense of Article 8 of the Commission's *de minimis* notice arises in the relevant market.[22]

---

21 See 'Und plötzlich diese Freiheit?' (2007) *WuW* 1007.

22 Commission Notice on agreements of minor importance that do not appreciably restrict competition under Article 81(1) of the Treaty establishing the European Community (de minimis) [2001] OJ C 368/13.

Apart from price competition between its distributors, a supplier with a very small market share cannot harm competition by implementing RPM without adequate services for customers. But does it contribute to more inter-brand competition by enabling consumers to distinguish between branded goods based on prices?

If a large part of the competing producers implement RPM practices, *ceteris paribus* (other conditions being equal), the requirements of Article 101(3) TFEU will probably not be met since those very agreements will eliminate competition in respect of a substantial part of the products in question.

7 CONCLUSION

- RPM practises are more likely to distort competition and decrease consumer welfare than to increase efficiency. RPM has a virtually negative impact on competition in an overwhelming majority of cases, while the procompetitive impacts are rather theoretical or even hypothetical.
- Therefore, a principal ban of RPM – with the possibility of exemptions – is more appropriate because the number of cases where RPM will *really* be procompetitive and indispensible for enhancing consumer welfare will be lower than the number of detrimental cases of RPM.
- Illegality of RPM supports manufacturers against strong distributors and enables price reductions for consumers, which, in turn, contributes to greater consumer welfare.
- The question is not whether to prefer fixed to flexible rules, but to what extent these rules are economically sound.
- Even a *general* ban should not exclude an exemption for RPM in substantiated circumstances. In the EU, the classification as a hardcore restraint just means a rebuttable presumption of illegality but not an absolute ban. The rebuttable presumption of illegality is an expression of the proportionality principle that allows an appropriate weighing of the anticompetitive and procompetitive cases that corresponds to the potential effects of RPM in the real world.
- The application of the rule of reason does not necessarily mean arbitrariness. There is the possibility of a structured rule of reason, including safe harbours based on market shares like in the framework of the European Vertical Agreements BER, which enable an economic assessment of each individual case.

- The radical proposal[23] to assess both price and non-price vertical restrictions as legal, unless the contrary is proven, is not sufficiently reasoned and does not take into account the actual risks of anticompetitive effects of many vertical restraints.
- Undertakings with a negligible market share may not fall under the prohibition of Article 101(1) TFEU because the restriction is not appreciable for realistically endangering competition.[24]
- Granting exemptions according to Article 101(3) TFEU is hypothetically possible[25] even if block exemptions categorize vertical price restraints as hardcore restraints.[26] However, the application of Article 101(3) TFEU may come very close to a complete ban of such practices.[27] Article 101(3) TFEU still allows for a *de iure* application of the rule of reason, whereby the particular anticompetitive potential of hardcore restraints need to be taken into account in applying the requirements for an exemption.[28]
- Hence, an exemption of RPM as a blacklisted category of vertical price agreements in block exemption regulations can never been excluded.[29]
- On the other hand, all conditions of Article 101(3) TFEU have to be met, including the indispensability of RPM in order to achieve the efficiency enhancing objectives of the agreement regardless of whether the other measures are more or less costly or effective.
- Under certain conditions, it would be possible to adopt a block exemption for RPM in the future. Under the condition of low market share thresholds and low market coverage of the RPM

---

23 F Alese, 'Unmasking the Masquerade of Vertical Price Fixing' (2007) 28 *ECLR* 514, at 525.

24 See Case 5/69 *Völk v Vervaeke* [1969] ECR 295. In this case, the manufacturer's market share of 0.2 percent and 0.5 percent in Germany was held to be insufficient for applying Article 101(1) TFEU (ex-Article 85(1) EEC Treaty).

25 Different opinion by referring to the Guidelines on the application of Article 81(3) of the Treaty [2004] OJ C 101/97, para 46, P Gey and H-G Kamann, 'The assessment of minimum resale price maintenance in Europe in the aftermath of Leegin' (2008) *J Comp L* (*ZWeR*) 208, at 218. Even these Guidelines do not ban black-listed restrictions, they only declare them to be unlikely to fulfil the conditions of Article 101(3) TFEU (ex-Article 81(3) EC).

26 E.g., Vertical Agreements Block Exemption Regulation No. 230/2010, Article 4a).

27 Gey and Kamann, *supra* n. 25.

28 On RPM, see in particular the new Guidelines on vertical restraints of 2010, *supra* n. 12, paras 223–9.

29 Gey and Kamann, *supra* n. 25, at 224.

for the respective product[30] the parties to the agreement should be granted the possibility to prove that the efficiency-enhancing justification outweighs the anticompetitive effects. In fact, no reliable safe harbour should be adopted as the parties may fail to bear the onus of proof.

- I fully share the opinion of Professor Eleanor Fox: 'Don´t shy from use of presumptions when it makes economic or administrative sense and the party with knowledge of all the facts gets a full and fair chance to rebut.'[31] Such a policy could be implemented through a structured rule of reason whereby a firm may show how using RPM is procompetitive.
- My suggested approach is to maintain the contemporary legal regime for RPM agreements as a hardcore provision with an irrebuttable presumption of the anticompetitive impact of RPM and with a rebuttable presumption of non-fulfilment of the conditions required for the exemption.
- The parties to the agreement should bear the burden to prove the positive effects and their passing-on to the consumers, as well as the absence of less restrictive possibilities of solving the same problem.
- In a situation of uncertainty of the need for changing the rules, a conservative approach is preferable. Do not change settled rules unless it is *obvious* that the change will be for the better. The need for change in the approach towards RPM agreements is far from being *obvious*.

---

30 Gey and Kamann, *supra* n. 25, at 225.

31 E Fox, 'Perspectives on the Future Direction of Antitrust' (2008) 22(3) *Antitrust* 23.

7. Competition law issues concerning related markets and their treatment under EU competition law

Thomas Eilmansberger

1 INTRODUCTION

Most products are useless on a stand-alone basis and depend on other products (or services) to fulfil their function. The mere fact, however, that a good can be used only together or in connection with another good does not as such impact on consumer choice and competition in the markets concerned. The situation may be different if such necessarily combined use makes significant demands on the design or functionality of one or both products in question. Such compatibility requirements frequently arise with regard to products ('secondary products') that are complementary in the sense that their purpose is to make another product or service ('primary product') function in a better way or at all.[1] There appear to be basically two types of secondary product that have to meet such compatibility demands (typically created by certain technical properties of the primary product), namely (i) products that are destined to eventually either become an integral part of or be attached to another product,[2] and (ii) products enabling another product to do its job and fulfil its basic function.[3]

It is obvious that such compatibility requirements, or more precisely, the resulting interfaces, have the potential to restrict access to the product markets concerned. That applies, in particular, if the interface can somehow be controlled by the maker of the primary product. It is thus not surprising that antitrust enforcement in the EU has often had to deal with practices,

[1] For an antitrust analysis from a US perspective see, e.g. J Bauer, 'Antitrust implications of aftermarkets' (2007) 52 *Antitrust Bull* 31, at 45 et seq.

[2] E.g. aftermarket products such as consumables, spare parts, repair services, accessories and add-ons, and product components.

[3] E.g. consumables, CD- or DVD-players, mobile phones or coffee machines.

where such interface control has been exercised to exclude rivals from the secondary market in question. Such practices, which in this chapter shall be referred to as 'practices establishing a technical tie', include refusals to license IP rights concerning the interface or to disclose relevant primary product information,[4] refusals to supply goods required to produce the secondary product or perform services with regard to the primary product,[5] as well as random changes of primary product specifications that render secondary products of competitors useless or give the producer of the primary product a significant head start on the secondary product market.[6]

Compatibility requirements, however, do not always yield an interface that can be used, or, as the case may be, abused to control access to the secondary product market. This may be owing to the existence of standards regarding either the primary or secondary product[7] or because the interface in question is just not sufficiently sophisticated to be protectable by IP.[8] In such cases, where technical ties are not possible and supply-side restrictions, consequently, do not work,[9] strategies to capture a related secondary market have to rely on more indirect, but at the same time, also, somewhat less subtle methods. That is, less subtle in the sense that they involve some sort of customer coercion. The bond between the primary and secondary product of a given brand must then be created either by a contractual tie, forcing the buyer to purchase the additional product or service,[10] or by offering the two products exclusively as a bundle. Even less surprisingly, EU antitrust enforcement has also had to deal with such indirectly foreclosing practices in a number of cases.[11]

---

4 Case 238/87 *Volvo v Veng* [1988] ECR 6211, para 9; Case 53/87 *Maxicar v Renault* [1988] ECR 6039, para 16; Case T-201/04 *Microsoft v Commission* [2007] ECR II-3601, paras 312–36; XIV. Report on Competition Policy 1984 (1985), *IBM*, paras 94 et seq.

5 Case T-30/89 *Hilti v Commission* [1991] ECR II-1439, paras 4 and 67; Case 22/78, *Hugin v Commission* [1979] ECR 1869, paras 7 et seq.

6 Commission decision 89/113/EEC, Case IV/31394 – *Decca Navigator System* [1989] OJ L 43/27, para 108.

7 E.g. CD and CD-player.

8 E.g. measurements for bed sheets.

9 I.e. where rivals on the secondary market cannot be directly excluded.

10 This is how a contractual tie is understood and defined in this chapter: the sale of a tying product under the condition that a tied product is purchased as well, either at the moment of purchasing the tying product or subsequently.

11 See, e.g. *Volvo*, *supra* n. 4, para 9; *Maxicar*, *supra* n. 4, para 16; *IBM*, *supra* n. 4, paras 94, 95; *Hugin*, *supra* n. 5, paras 7–8; *Decca Navigator System*, *supra* n. 6, para 108; Commission decision 88/138/EEC, Cases IV/30.787 and 31.488 – *Eurofix-Bauco v Hilti* [1988] OJ L 65/19, para 75; *Hilti*, *supra* n. 5, para 16; Commission decision 92/163/EEC, Case IV/30.043 – *Tetra Pak II* [1992] OJ L

This chapter focuses on the analysis and critique of this case law and the decisional practice in the EU and also attempts to systematically describe how these various tying practices were, or should have been, treated under EU competition law. This seems a particularly suitable topic because it is illustrative of the somewhat different approaches to abuse of dominance issues in the EU and the US.[12] While, in the US, welfare effects and efficiencies still seem to be central in defining the basic content of the antitrust prohibitions, the EU institutions under Article 102 TFEU (as well as Article 101 TFEU), despite a significantly stronger reliance on economic analysis in recent years, still tend to protect competition for its own sake, that is, irrespective of the immediate negative economic or welfare effects of the practice at issue.[13] In the field of abuse control, that means that the EU courts adopt a more 'abstract', one could also say 'structural' approach. 'Structural', not in the sense of a protection of specific competitors, however, but merely of their opportunities to succeed 'on the merits' on the market.[14] As will be seen, this emphasis also has important implications for the treatment of tying practices.

2 BASIC LEGAL FRAMEWORK

In the EU, the basic legal framework for tying practices consists of the following rules and principles: (i) Article 102(2) lit d) TFEU, which

---

72/1, para 184; Case T-83/91 *Tetra Pak v Commission* ('Tetra Pak *II*') [1994] ECR II-755, para 242; Case C-333/94 P *Tetra Park v Commission* ('*Tetra Pak II*') [1996] ECR I-5951, paras 34–7; *Microsoft*, *supra* n. 4, paras 312 et seq.

[12] See, e.g. E Fox, 'We Protect Competition, You Protect Competitors' (2003) 26 *World Comp* 149, at 157 et seq.

[13] Cf. R Whish, *Competition Law* (6th edn, 2009) at 188 et seq.

[14] See most recently Case C-202/07 P *France Télécom v Commission* [2009] ECR I-2369, paras 104 et seq.:

> In that context, in prohibiting the abuse of a dominant market position in so far as trade between Member States is capable of being affected, Article 82 EC [now Article 102 TFEU] refers to conduct which is such as to influence the structure of a market where the degree of competition is already weakened and which, through recourse to methods different from those governing normal competition in products or services on the basis of the transactions of commercial operators, has the effect of hindering the maintenance of the degree of competition still existing in the market or the growth of that competition . . . Article 82 EC refers not only to practices which may cause damage to consumers directly, but also to those which are detrimental to them through their impact on an effective competition structure. . . .

specifically mentions tying as abusive conduct caught by this prohibition; (ii) the essential facilities doctrine (EFD) developed under Article 102(1) TFEU and applied to aftermarket situations;[15] (iii) the prohibition of indirect foreclosure practices such as single-branding arrangements contained in Article 101 and 102 TFEU; and (iv) the prohibition of direct foreclosure practices such as predatory pricing under Article 102 TFEU.

3 THE TYING PROHIBITION IN ARTICLE 102(2) LIT D) TFEU

3.1 General Remarks

According to Article 102(2) lit d) TFEU, an abuse of a dominant position may, in particular, consist of 'making the conclusion of contracts subject to acceptance by the other parties of supplementary obligations which, by their nature or according to commercial usage, have no connection with the subject of such contracts'.

Thus, there is an express, and also a per se prohibition of the classic and maybe purest form of tying, and arguably of market power leveraging in general, namely contractual tying. It should be noted that this form of tying is prohibited not only because of its presumed (distortive) effects on performance-based competition on the secondary product market, but also because of its exploitative effect.[16] This is consistent with Article 102 TFEU, which prohibits other types of exploitative conduct such as excessive prices and unfair sales conditions as well, and it is also significant because it is for this reason alone that the Chicago 'single economic rent' doctrine could not gain any support in the EU.

The per se prohibition of this market power leveraging practice, or to be precise, the prohibition regardless of immediate welfare effects or consumer welfare implications, apparently so central to the tying analysis under the Sherman Act (and the doctrinal discussion in the US[17]), but even regardless of its significant foreclosure effects,[18] however, also makes

---

[15] See, e.g. A Capobianco, 'The essential facility doctrine: similarities and differences between the American and the European approach' (2001) 26 *Eur L Rev* 548.

[16] Cf. L Ritter and D Braun, *European Competition Law: A Practitioner's Guide* (3rd edn, 2005) at 420.

[17] See, e.g. C Shapiro and DJ Teece, 'Systems competition and aftermarkets: an economic analysis of *Kodak*' (1994) 39 *Antitrust Bull* 135.

[18] Although those may be relevant for the Commission to give the case an enforcement priority; see Commission, Guidance on the Commission's

perfect sense under the merits-based competition logic briefly described above. Using market power, and the corresponding customer dependence, instead of superior performance, to succeed on and capture a related but separate market evidently constitutes such a business method 'different from those governing normal competition'[19] or 'other than those falling within competition based on merits'[20] to which Article 102 TFEU applies. Given this emphasis on the protection of performance-based competition on the tied product's market and the argument brought forward in the US that 'tying' is unproblematic because producers will compete away aftermarket profits in the primary good market so that consumers will normally pay competitive prices for the package,[21] would not, even if factually correct[22] and furthermore applicable in the case of a dominant firm, be relevant in the EU context.

This 'per se prohibition' does not, however, mean that Article 102(2) lit d) TFEU (or the general clause in Article 102(1) TFEU) can be applied without an economic analysis of the pertinent facts. Apparently not dissimilar to US practice, which I understand to provide for a per se illegality of tying practices under certain conditions only,[23] the prohibition in Article 102(2) lit d TFEU only applies if certain factual requirements are met, an assessment that necessitates an often fairly thorough economic analysis. More specifically, in order for this prohibition to apply, the following test must be met: (i) the tied product must be a separate product and the tied product must belong to a separate product market; (ii) there must be an element of coercion; and (iii) connected to the latter requirement, there must be a dominant position on the market for the tying product (the establishment or strengthening of a dominant position on the market for the tied market would not even be caught by Article 102(2) lit d) TFEU if the latter formed a separate relevant market). I shall

enforcement priorities in applying Article 82 of the EC Treaty to abusive exclusionary conduct by dominant undertakings [2009] OJ C 45/7, para 50.

19 Case T-203/01 *Michelin v Commission* ('*Michelin II*') [2003] ECR II-4071, para 54; Case 85/76 *Hoffmann-La Roche v Commission* [1979] ECR 461, para 91; *France Télécom*, *supra* n. 14, para 104.

20 Case T-228/97 *Irish Sugar v Commission* [1999] ECR II-2969, para 111; Case T-111/96 *ITT Promedia v Commission* [1998] ECR II-2937, para 138; Case T-65/89 *BPB Industries v Commission* [1993] ECR II-389, para 94; similarly Case C-62/86 *AKZO v Commission* [1991] ECR I-3359, paras 69 et seq.

21 See, e.g. Shapiro and Teece, *supra* n. 17, at 143, B Klein, 'Market Power in Aftermarkets' (1996) 17 *Managerial and Decision Economics* 143.

22 For doubts in this respect see L Coppi, 'Aftermarket monopolization: the emerging consensus in economics' (2007) 52 *Antitrust Bull* 53, at 59 et seq.

23 *Jefferson Parish Hospital Dist. No. 2 v Hyde*, 466 US 2 (1984).

now discuss the first two requirements (which are the only tying-specific requirements) in more detail.

3.2 Separate Product Requirement

In my view, this test should comprise two related but ultimately distinct elements. The first element or condition to be met is that the tied product constitutes a product separate[24] from the tying product, and not an integral part thereof; the second condition is that it also belongs to a separate relevant, and thus separately exploitable, market, which would not be the case if the interconnection and interdependence between the two products were such that they naturally form or are viewed as a system.

3.2.1 Is the tied product a separate product or a constitutive component of the tying (primary) product?

The tying prohibition in Article 102(2) lid d) TFEU applies only to products or services that have 'no connection with the subject of such contracts'. In other words, the tied product must be a separate product. According to established case-law and practice, the central criterion in this respect is consumer perception:[25] does the consumer perceive the secondary product as a component of the tying product so that he or she would consider the product to be incomplete without the tied or bundled component,[26] or would the consumer, given the choice, rather purchase the two products or services separately?[27]

---

[24] See, e.g. M Dolmans and T Graf, 'Analysis of Tying Under Article 82 EC: The European Commission`s Microsoft Decision in Perspective' (2004) 27 *World Comp* 225, at 227.

[25] See *Hilti*, *supra* n. 5, paras 64 et seq.; *Tetra Pak II*, *supra* n. 11, paras 82–5; *Microsoft*, *supra* n. 4, para 918; Guidance paper, *supra* n. 18, para 51, Commission, Guidelines on the application of Article 81 of the EC Treaty to technology transfer agreements [2004] OJ C 101/2, para 191.

[26] Such as in the proverbial example of the shoe and the shoelace or countless other products that are composed of different components.

[27] Guidelines on Vertical Restraints [2010] OJ C 130/1, para 215:

> Whether products will be considered as distinct depends on customer demand. Two products are distinct where, in the absence of the tying, a substantial number of customers would purchase or would have purchased the tying product without also buying the tied product from the same supplier, thereby allowing stand-alone production for both the tying and the tied product. Evidence that two products are distinct could include direct evidence that, when given a choice, customers purchase the tying and the tied products separately from different sources of supply, or indirect evidence, such as the presence on the

Obviously, the separate product test is, or should be, a very dynamic concept that already can and should accommodate certain efficiency claims, especially as regards bundles and package tie-ins. The finding that the secondary or aftermarket product constitutes a separate product depends on a number of aspects, such as the money and time to be saved by the own purchase and assembly of the tied or bundled product (which is why the equipment of electronic devices such as remote controls with batteries is generally unproblematic), or the difficulty posed by the assembly of the two products at issue (which may be low in case of a car radio but considerably higher in the case of an air-conditioning system), the relevance of which has not only to be assessed for each primary and secondary product concerned individually, but may also change over a period of time.[28]

The existence of independent producers of the tied product is an indicator of a product being separate but it does certainly not exclude a finding to the contrary: there may be a separate demand for the product as consumable (for example, battery) or wear part (for example, shoelace) only.[29] The fact that consumers may find it convenient to purchase two separately offered products as a package instead of assembling the finished product themselves, or to purchase the primary product with a certain amount of consumables but are reluctant to also commit to an obligation to purchase these secondary products (as aftermarket products) from the supplier of the primary product in the future, already suggests that the legality of a tie under of Article 102(2) lit d) TFEU depends on whether the tie is accomplished by a bundled sale or by a contractual or requirement tie.[30] Another constellation where the existence of independent producers does not imply

market of undertakings specialised in the manufacture or sale of the tied product without the tying product, or evidence indicating that undertakings with little market power, particularly on competitive markets, tend not to tie or not to bundle such products. For instance, since customers want to buy shoes with laces and it is not practicable for distributors to lace new shoes with the laces of their choice, it has become commercial usage for shoe manufacturers to supply shoes with laces. Therefore, the sale of shoes with laces is not a tying practice.

[28] See, for example, P Rey, P Seabright and J Tirole, 'The Activities of a Monopoly firm in Adjacent Competitive Markets: Economic Consequences and Implications for Competition Policy' (2001), http://idei.fr/doc/wp/2001/activities2.pdf (accessed 4 July 2011); concerning plugs see Dolmans and Graf, *supra* n. 24, at 228.

[29] Cf. DS Evans and AJ Padilla, 'Tying Under Article 82 EC and the Microsoft Decision: A Comment on Dolmans and Graf' (2004) 27 *World Comp* 503, at 511.

[30] I.e. with regard to the same combination of products, it may be legal to bundle but not to impose a contractual or requirement tie.

the existence of a separate product is when a product, which is evidently composed of a set of different (and separately offered) products, actually defines itself by combining these different functionalities (for example, a smart phone with a camera, or a cutlery set). A much more reliable indicator of relevant consumer preferences than the existence of independent producers is, therefore, the fact that firms lacking market power do not tend to offer the primary product as a package with another product.[31]

Finally, as has been already alluded to above, the type of tie may be indicative of whether the separate product test is met. It is probably fair to presume that this condition is, as a rule, met in the case of contractual ties. This type of tie presupposes a separately traded secondary product. It would not be necessary to force a second purchasing obligation on the customer if the secondary product in question were considered to be an integral part of the tying product to begin with. However, as will also be discussed in more detail below, there is no such presumption in the case of bundling.[32]

3.2.2 Do the two products belong to two different relevant markets?

A further requirement is that the tied or bundled secondary product, in addition to being separate, belongs to a separate, and thus separately exploitable, product market.[33] Thus, if the secondary product forms part of the market for the primary product, tying should not be considered abusive under Article 102 TFEU.[34] As far as can be seen, this condition has not yet been applied or confirmed in the cases decided by the Commission or the European Courts.[35] Its relevance, however, in my view necessarily follows from the very concept of market power leveraging underlying the prohibition in Article 102(2) lit d) TFEU. As the abuse charge here consists of the non-merit-based transfer of market power, that is, of the use of market power to achieve the 'capture of second empire' in the words of the Supreme Court in *Kodak*,[36] this 'second empire' must be a market that

---

31 Guidance paper, *supra* n. 18, para 51.

32 See 3.3.2, below.

33 Cf. J Goyder and A Albors-Llorens, *Goyder's EC Competition Law* (5th edn, 2009), at 365; see also *Microsoft*, *supra* n. 4, para 927.

34 See *Microsoft*, *supra* n. 4, para 918: 'The Commission was also correct to state, at the same recital, that in the absence of independent demand for the allegedly tied product, there can be no question of separate products and no abusive tying.'

35 See Commission decision *Eurofix-Bauco/Hilti*, *supra* n. 11; CFI judgment in *Tetra Pak II*, *supra* n. 11; ECJ judgment in *Tetra Park II*, *supra* n. 11; CFI judgment in *Hilti*, *supra* n. 5; *Microsoft*, *supra* n. 4.

36 To use the famous language of the US Supreme Court in *Eastman Kodak Company v Image Technical Services, Inc. et al.*, 504 US 451 (1992).

is *distinct* from the market for the primary product market dominated by the firm imposing the tie. If that were not to be the case, that is, if the two markets were interconnected to a degree that excludes the possibility of consumer exploitation with regard to the secondary market – both before and after the purchase – regulatory intervention to stimulate competition on the secondary product market would neither be necessary nor justified.

This 'system-defence', as I would like to call it here,[37] is a significant limitation of the scope of the tying prohibition. It applies if the tying and the tied product, even if constituting separate products, are viewed by the consumer to form two constitutive and formative elements of a system in the sense that the consumer can be assumed to take the total system cost, that is, the cost of both the primary and the secondary product into account when making the purchasing decision.[38] This will typically be the case if and when it is not even possible to clearly identify the primary product in a given combination.[39] Even in this case, however, the secondary product may be so expensive or determinative of the quality of the performance of the primary product[40] that consumers immediately perceive the two products as forming a whole system.[41] In such cases, it is submitted that firms should also be allowed to compete on the market for the whole system; therefore, it should not be considered abusive if the firm were to 'close' the system by tying its constitutive elements or excluding rivals from the secondary product market.

Although, as discussed above, there do not appear to be any cases in which a dominant firm had to rely on this theory to defend itself against a tying charge; there are some cases in which the central aspect of this defence, namely the issue of whether the tied product forms or belongs to a separate relevant market, has been discussed in more detail and useful criteria to assess this question have been developed.[42] The question arose in

---

37 Being aware, of course, that the term 'system' usually has a wider meaning referring to every combination of products working together (see, e.g. GT Gundlach, 'Aftermarkets, systems, and antitrust: a primer' (2007) 52 *Antitrust Bull* 17, at 18 et seq.).

38 I.e. when deciding whether to buy at all or when choosing between competing systems.

39 E.g. in a smartphone package and/or a mobile phone subscription.

40 Cf. also Guidelines for technology transfer, *supra* n. 25, para 191.

41 E.g. Polaroid camera and film.

42 *Info-Lab/Ricoh* (1999), Competition Policy Newsletter No. 1, p. 35; *Pelikan/Kyocera* (1995), *Competition Policy Newsletter* No. 6, p. 13; *Digital Equipment*, para 69, XXVII. Report on Competition Policy 1997 (1998) (see analysis of P Chevalier, 'Dominance sur un marché de produits secondaires' (1998) *Competition Policy Newsletter* No. 1, p. 26); and most recently Case T-427/08 *Confédération*

these cases because the firms at issue lacked market power on the market for the primary product so that the applicability of Article 102 TFEU turned on whether there was at least a dominant position on the market for the secondary product market which, in turn, presupposed that this market constituted a separate relevant market.

In *Info-Lab/Ricoh* and *Pelikan/Kyocera*,[43] the Commission (echoing the approach of the Supreme Court in Kodak) basically inquired whether the markets at issue are interrelated in such a way that competition on the primary market exercises effective discipline in the secondary market. It considered the following criteria to be relevant or at least strongly indicative in this respect:[44] (i) can the consumer make an informed choice with regard to lifecycle pricing, (ii) is the consumer also likely to make such an informed choice, that is, does he or she sufficiently care[45] (this will often crucially depend on the price difference between the two products); (iii) would a relevant number of customers adapt their purchasing behaviour at the level of the primary market in case of an apparent policy of exploitation being pursued in one specific aftermarket; (iv) within a reasonable period of time?[46]

Also with regard to the separate market condition, there is a (rebuttable) presumption that the requirement is met where there is contractual tying (for example, a requirement-tie), especially if there is no minimum purchasing requirement or an otherwise fixed ratio between the primary and the secondary products (for example, servicing in fixed intervals). With regard to bundling, however, again, no such presumption can be made and a considerably more complex analysis is required. The transparency concerning the total system cost brought about by this tying technique may even support the contrary conclusion (that is, the existence of an integral market), but does not of course exclude a finding of a separate market for the secondary product, for example, if the consumer, even if aware of the price increase of the primary product caused by the forced purchase of the secondary product, does not really care, because of the relatively low cost of the latter.[47]

---

européenne des Associations d'Horlogers-Réparateurs (CEAHR) v Commission [2010] ECR II-0000 (not yet officially reported).

43 Commission Decision *Info-Lab/Ricoh*, *supra* n. 42; *Pelikan/Kyocera*, *supra* n. 42; see also *Digital Equipment*, *supra* n. 42.

44 *Info-Lab/Ricoh*, *supra* n. 42.

45 See also M Hartmann-Rüppel and PP Engelhoven, 'Kartellrecht und Eigentum – Die Soda-Club-II-Entscheidung des BGH' (2008) *J Comp L* (*ZWeR*) 290, at 298.

46 Similar analysis in *Confédération européenne des Associations d'Horlogers-Réparateurs (CEAHR)*, *supra* n. 42, paras 65 et seq.

47 As would probably be the case in the above example of the car radio.

An important implication of this system defence is that the tying element of loss-involving strategies, that is, low-price, or even below-cost sales of devices necessary to consume or utilise the supplier's other product, will,[48] as a rule, not qualify as an abuse even if there is a dominant position with regard to either product. The low-price strategy with regard to the tying product suggests that it is the tied product or service where the firm intends to earn its profits, and the consumer will typically be aware that prices for this product will be a relevant, if not the crucial, cost factor when using the tying product. While in the absence of a separate relevant (and exploitable) market, the imposition of the tie, that is, the locking of the two products and the offering of the whole system on the market only, would not be abusive as such, but the way in which the firm competes on the systems market could be. This will be discussed in more detail in section 5, below.

3.3 Coercion

For tying or bundling to be abusive, there must be a coercive element.[49] The tie must somehow be imposed on the customer who, were it not for the tie, could be expected to purchase the primary or tying product only. Coercion clearly is the conceptually crucial element of the tying abuse under Article 102(2) lit d) TFEU, as it is the customer's compulsion that brings about the relevant distortion of competition. For the prohibition to apply, a foreclosure effect, while typically achieved by successful tying practices, is not required; the coercion itself justifies a finding of abuse.

Also with respect to this tying element, the analysis differs for the various tying techniques, that is, whether the practice at issue is a contractual tie, a bundle, or a technical tie. It has been pointed out that both the separate product and the separate market requirement are considerably easier to establish in the case of contractual ties. The same applies to the coercive element. It is only possible to operate with a more or less robust presumption with regard to this condition in the case of a contractual tie. The analysis of bundles and technical ties is, for different reasons, considerably more complex.

3.3.1 Contractual tying

In the case of a contractual tie, the coercion requirement is quite easily established. This tying variant defines itself by the fact that the sale of

---

48 E.g. coffee machine and capsules; gaming hardware such as the play-station, or the content for mp3-players.

49 See also Dolmans and Graf, *supra* n. 24, at 228 et seq.

the (dominant) primary product or service is conditioned upon the purchase of the secondary product. Coercion is, therefore, almost an inherent element and it is this type of tie to which Article 102(2) lit d) TFEU squarely applies. Since the other conditions (separate product and separate market) are, as a rule, also met in such cases, it is not surprising that the analysis in the decisional practice of contractual ties imposed by firms dominating the primary market has been fairly straightforward so far.[50]

3.3.2 Bundling

The coercion analysis in bundling cases is considerably more complex.[51] Though it is obviously possible, it cannot be simply presumed that the purpose and effect of offering two separate products as a bundle is to force an additional purchase upon the customer. After all, bundling is an ubiquitous business practice that evidently does not require market power with regard to the primary (and supposedly tying) product, and for that reason alone should not be assumed to aim at and achieve the leveraging of market power (that is, to force a second product or service on the customer with a view to capturing a secondary market). It must be borne in mind that the addition of the secondary product, for example, of an accessory product, could also serve a perfectly legitimate end, namely to make the primary product more competitive on its market. Therefore, even if there is a dominant position on the primary product market, it is necessary to show that the bundling of these two separate products was, in fact, designed to and is capable of accomplishing the leveraging of market power.

It is submitted that the only way to establish leveraging through customer coercion in the case of bundling would be to show that the addition of the secondary product was accompanied by a corresponding increase in the price of the primary product.[52] In such a scenario, bundling should be considered a form of economic tying where, just as in the case of contractual tying, customer dependence is abused in order to capture and exploit

---

[50] See, e.g. Commission decision in *Tetra Pak II*, *supra* n. 11, paras 117 et seq; CFI judgment in *Tetra Pak II*, *supra* n. 11, para 137.

[51] Cf. Bauer, *supra* n. 1, at 47; Whish, *supra* n. 13, at 728; B Nalebuff, 'Bundling, Tying and Portfolio Effects' (2003) *DTI Economics Paper No. 1*, http://www.berr.gov.uk/publications/economicsstatistics/economics-directorate/page14636.html (accessed 4 July 2011).

[52] See Dolmans and Graf, *supra* n. 24, at 231 according to whom the choice to buy products separately is, for example, denied if the stand-alone tying product is sold at the same price as the bundled version. But that is only persuasive if this price is really a bundled price, i.e. includes both price components; see also Evans and Padilla, *supra* n. 29, at 508.

an additional market.[53] It should be noted, however, that it is not necessarily through customer coercion that bundling will achieve the leveraging of market power. Customer compulsion *indirectly* forecloses the market for the secondary product. Bundling can also be used, however, to directly foreclose rivals on that market as well as on the primary product market. This effect can be accomplished if the bundled product is offered essentially for free, that is, added to the primary product without a corresponding price increase. The monopolisation of the secondary product market is likely to harm consumers in the following three scenarios: (i) if competitors in the market for the secondary product depend on the profits from that market to be able to compete on the market for the primary product;[54] (ii) if the competing secondary product itself might pose a competitive threat to the dominant primary product;[55] or (iii) if the exclusion of rivals from the secondary product market threatens to distort competition on present or emerging adjacent markets.[56]

3.3.3 Technical tying

Technical tying is not covered by Article 102(2) lit d) TFEU. That applies to both relevant variants, namely arbitrary changes in the specifications of the primary product designed to cause compatibility problems for rivals on the secondary product markets on the one hand, and refusals to share information, supply products (for example, spare parts) or grant licences necessary to offer compatible secondary products on the other. While there may be a coercive element in these practices, it is typically somewhat indirect, resulting from the exclusion of rivals and the ensuing narrowing of consumer choice. More importantly, in these cases there is no leveraging effect in the ordinary sense because the ability to restrain competition on the secondary product market is not based on the dominant position on the primary product but comes with the control of the

---

[53] Whish, *supra* n. 13, at 727 (arguing that it may be possible to achieve the same effect as a tie-in agreement through pricing practices).

[54] For the application of this theory in a different context see Commission decision 87/500/EEC, Case IV/32.279 – *BBI/Boosey & Hawkes* [1987] OJ L 286/36, para 19.

[55] An example would be the US Microsoft/Explorer case where the strategy to eliminate Netscape appears to have been motivated by Netscape's threat to become an alternative platform and diminish the application barrier to entry that governs operating systems markets; see Dolmans and Graf, *supra* n. 24, at 233.

[56] As was the Commission's charge with respect to the bundling of the MediaPlayer with Microsoft's Windows Operating System (see Commission decision 2007/53/EC, Case COMP/C-3/37.792 – *Microsoft* [2007] OJ L 32/23, paras 835–954); see also Evans and Padilla, *supra* n. 29, at 504.

technical interface between primary and secondary product that naturally follows from the production or design of the primary product. Thus, the power of Microsoft to control a software market attached to its dominant operating system is not owing to its dominance in that market but to the superior knowledge and IP protection of its interface with software applications.

Technical ties relying on a control of the interface are also analytically too complex to be dealt with under the simple tying prohibition in Article 102(2) lit d) TFEU.[57] To the extent, an exercise of such control involves or results in the exclusion of (potential) competitors from information, technology or other input necessary for competing on the secondary product market, the practice should rather be analysed under the essential facility doctrine that permits a much more nuanced balancing of the various interests involved.[58] However, as will be seen, while a more differentiated analysis of that type of technical tie may restrict the application of the prohibition in Art. 102 TFEU with regard to firms dominating the primary market, it does at the same time permit the finding of an abuse in the absence of such a dominant position on the primary product market and thus very significantly increases the scope of abuse control in this area.

3.4 Defences

Article 102(2) lit d) TFEU does not, properly speaking, provide for a defence. The prohibition contained therein applies per se if the conditions are met. Because some of these are negative conditions that must not be present for the prohibition to apply, they, de facto, constitute a form of defence. Particularly relevant is the requirement that the two products or services concerned have no connection 'by their nature or according to commercial usage'. The first of these two negative conditions contained therein (no connection by their nature) is, of course, the analytical basis for the separate product requirement discussed at length above.[59] The second negative condition (no connection according to commercial usage), on the other hand, has almost no practical relevance. Not only is the Commission reluctant to accept that there is an according commercial usage (not established by the firm itself), but it has also made clear, and

---

[57] See also F Etro, 'Market Leaders. Antitrust Policy and the Software Market' (2008) V(1) *ICFAI J Ind Econ* 1, at 22.

[58] See also Whish, *supra* n. 13, at 699; Rey, Seabright, and Tirole, *supra* n. 28, at 39.

[59] See 3.2, above.

was backed in this regard by the CFI, that it would in such a case simply apply Article 102(1) TFEU instead of Article 102(2) lit d) TFEU.[60]

In the context of these two requirements, security and quality requirements can also be, and have already been argued. Furthermore, with regard to these arguments, the decisional practice has been rather restrictive. While they were, in principle, recognised as possible justifications both in Commission practice and secondary legislation[61] they were usually rejected with reference to the facts at hand.[62] Both the Commission[63] and the ECJ[64] now recognise an efficiency justification under the condition that these efficiencies are somehow passed on to and benefit the consumer. It is too early to assess the potential relevance of this defence but it seems to me that it will have only a limited impact. Efficiency claims would appear to be mostly relevant with regard to bundling practices but will be, in that context, often obsolete because such efficiency considerations will regularly also lead to the conclusion that either the separate product or the separate product market requirements are not met. It will, however, be interesting to see whether this development will encourage parties to invoke price discrimination more frequently[65] (or other allegedly output-increasing practices) as a defence.

3.5 First Conclusion

The tying variant, which is most likely to be caught by Article 102(2) lit d) TFEU, is the contractual tie. In connection with this type of tie, the basic elements of this prohibition, and in particular the separate product and the separate product market requirement, as well as the element of coercion,

---

[60] Commission decision in *Tetra Pak II*, *supra* n. 11, paras 117 et seq; backed in this regard by the CFI in *Tetra Pak II*, *supra* n. 11, para 137 and the ECJ in *Tetra Pak II*, *supra* n. 11, para 37.

[61] Guidelines on vertical restraints, *supra* n. 27, para 222 (only if positive effects cannot be realised equally efficiently by imposition of quality standards); see also Guidelines on technology transfer, *supra* n. 25, para 191.

[62] Commission decision in *Eurofix-Bauco v Hilti*, *supra* n. 11, para 88; backed in this regard by CFI in *Hilti*, *supra* n. 5, paras 115–19 and the ECJ in Case C-53/92 P *Hilti v Commission* [1994] ECR I-667; Commission decision in *Tetra Pak II*, *supra* n. 11, para, 119; backed, in this regard, by the CFI in *Tetra Pak II*, *supra* n. 11, paras 131, 139 and 141 and the ECJ in *Tetra Pak II*, *supra* n. 11.

[63] Guidance paper, *supra* n. 18, para 30.

[64] Case C-95/04 P *British Airways v Commission* [2007] ECR I-2331, paras 84 et seq.

[65] Which, so far, has not been accepted; see, e.g. Guidelines on vertical restraints, *supra* n. 27, para 216.

will typically be present. The tying in the form of bundling, however, calls for a considerably more sophisticated and differentiated analysis under Article 102(2) lit d) TFEU (as well as under the general clause in Article 102(1) TFEU). In addition, technical ties require a more comprehensive analysis that will often have to include a separate assessment of exclusionary practices aimed at controlling the interface between the primary and secondary product.

3.6 Contractual and Other Forms of Ties Imposed by Firms Not Dominating the Tying Product's Market

3.6.1 Applicability of Article 102 TFEU

Article 102(2) lit d) TFEU requires both a dominant position and coercion based on that dominance.[66] The prohibition does not apply to ties by which firms merely exercise their market power below the dominance threshold, that is, their ability to charge somewhat supra-competitive prices. In this context, in my view, a variation of the 'single monopoly profit' doctrine applies: it should not make a difference whether such firms make use of their limited pricing discretion by charging supra-competitive prices for the primary product or by forcing the customer to purchase a somewhat overpriced add-on.

That means that Article 102 TFEU can be applied only to ties imposed by firms not dominant on the tying product's market if a dominant position can at least be established for the market for the tied product. This will often be possible if, according to the criteria discussed above,[67] the secondary product market constitutes or forms part of a separate relevant product market. It is, however, unclear whether tying practices would constitute an abuse of that dominant position.

As far as can be seen, no cases have yet been brought in which this approach was tested in practice. There are only some policy statements touching upon this question. The guidelines on vertical agreements are somewhat ambiguous in this respect. While they do not differentiate between the primary and the secondary market and argue that the benefit of the block exemption provided for by Regulation 330/2010 is lost if the market share threshold of 30 per cent is exceeded in either market,[68] they assume that anti-competitive effects only arise if there is a strong position

---

66 Goyder and Albors-Llorens, *supra* n. 33, at 364; Dolmans and Graf, *supra* n. 24, at 266 et seq.

67 See 3.2.2, above.

68 Guidelines on vertical restraints, *supra* n. 27, para 218.

on the tying product market.[69] In its Guidance Paper, the Commission takes a clearer position. It expresses its intention only to take action against tying practices if there is a dominant position with regard to the tying product,[70] but softens this condition for tying in aftermarkets stating that in this special case the condition is that the firm is dominant in the tying market and/or the tied aftermarket.[71]

At first sight, the Commission's intention to challenge tying practices even if dominance exists only on the secondary product market has a sound analytical basis. While Article 102 TFEU does not, in principle, ban practices creating a dominant position (presupposing the existence of dominance at the moment the relevant acts were performed) there can be little doubt that the strengthening of an already existing dominant position could be found abusive under Article 102 TFEU. Consequently, tying practices used to strengthen that dominance would, in principle, be caught by the Article 102 TFEU prohibition. Upon closer analysis, however, doubts arise. It is unclear whether, in such situations, the abuse element is really present given the absence of any customer coercion. The supplier of the primary product will only be able to impose the tie (creating or defending his dominance with regard to the proprietary secondary product) if the firm, while not being dominant, at least enjoys some market power enabling it to extract the extra profit gained by the forced sale of the secondary product. As was argued above, however, an exploitation of market power below the dominance level cannot be considered abusive under Article 102 TFEU.

3.6.2 Applicability of Article 101 TFEU

Article 101(1) lit e) TFEU prohibits agreements which 'make the conclusion of contracts subject to acceptance by the other parties of supplementary

---

69 Guidelines on vertical restraints, *supra* n. 27, para 219: 'The market position of the supplier on the market of the tying product is obviously of main importance to assess possible anti-competitive effects. In general, this type of agreement is imposed by the supplier. The importance of the supplier on the market of the tying product is the main reason why a buyer may find it difficult to refuse a tying obligation.' Para 220: 'The market position of the supplier's competitors on the market of the tying product is important in assessing the supplier's market power. As long as its competitors are sufficiently numerous and strong, no anti-competitive effects can be expected, as buyers have sufficient alternatives to purchase the tying product without the tied product, unless other suppliers are applying similar tying. In addition, entry barriers on the market of the tying product are relevant to establish the market position of the supplier. When tying is combined with a non-compete obligation in respect of the tying product, this considerably strengthens the position of the supplier.'

70 Guidance paper, *supra* n. 18, para 50.

71 Guidance paper, *supra* n. 18, para 34.

obligations which, by their nature or according to commercial usage, have no connection with the subject of such contracts'. Although the question has not yet been resolved by the Courts,[72] there is a strong consensus in the literature that this rule does not apply to individual (vertical) ties but only to (horizontal) agreements to tie.[73]

Individual (vertical) ties with a bilateral element, that is, contractual ties,[74] may, however, constitute a vertical restraint and fall under the general prohibition in Article 101(1) TFEU. Since vertical ties certainly do not constitute a hardcore offence (which is presumed to have an anti-competitive object), anti-competitive effects, more precisely a relevant foreclosure effect, must be proven.[75] It may be recalled that in its earlier decisional practice, the Commission had adopted a more form-based approach. Article 101 TFEU was considered to be applicable if the agreement restrained the economic freedom of one of the parties and a requirement tie, of course, did just that. In a few older cases, the Commission did, indeed, consider such ties imposed by non-dominant firms to be restrictive of competition,[76] and the earlier generation of block exemption regulations treated requirement ties as restrictive agreements for which an exemption under Article 101(3) TFEU was granted under certain conditions only.[77] However, under the new economic approach, as well as under the new generation of block exemption regulations, there is a much stronger reliance on foreclose effects and, consequently, on market shares. The vertical guidelines emphasise that tying may constitute a vertical restraint falling under Article 101 TFEU only where it results in a single branding type of

72 A Jones and B Sufrin, *EU Competition Law* (4th edn, 2011) at 678; Whish, *supra* n. 13, at 681.

73 See Whish, *supra* n. 13, at 681.

74 Which is not present in the case of bundling so that bundling by non-dominant firms cannot be challenged under Article 101 TFEU either, bundling is thus not challengeable at all in cases of non-dominance.

75 Guidelines on vertical restraints, *supra* n. 27, para 214.

76 Commission decision 79/86/EEC, Case IV/C-29.290 – *Vaessen/Moris* [1979] OJ L 19/32, para 15; Commission decision 85/410/EEC, Case IV/4.204 – *Velcro/Aplix* [1985] OJ L 233/22; Case 193/83 *Windsurfing v Commission* [1986] ECR 611, para 57.

77 Commission Regulation 1984/83 on the application of Article 85(3) of the Treaty to categories of exclusive purchasing agreements [1983] OJ L 173/5, Article 3 c); Commission Regulation 2349/84 on the application of Article 85(3) of the Treaty to certain categories of patent licensing agreements, [1984] L 219, p. 15, Article 2(1)(1), only if necessary for proper technical exploitation, and express blacklisted certain forms of bundling; Commission Regulation (EC) No. 240/96 of 31 January 1996 on the application of Article 85(3) of the Treaty to certain categories of technology transfer agreements [1996] OJ L 31/2, Article 2(5).

obligation for the tied product, and they suggest that the methodology used to assess foreclosure effects of distribution agreements be applied.[78] Another expression of this approach is that now requirement ties generally fall within the block exemptions under Regulations 330/2010 and 772/2004 if the market share of the firm imposing the tie is below 30 per cent.[79]

4 AFTERMARKETS AND THE ESSENTIAL FACILITY DOCTRINE (EFD)

4.1 General Remarks

It is well established under EU competition law that there is, under certain conditions, a duty to grant access to a product or service that is indispensable for the offering of a product or service on a downstream or otherwise related market.[80] In case of IP-protected information or know-how, the refusal to license must prevent the emergence of a new product for which there is consumer demand.[81] This essential facility doctrine (although it has never been referred to under this name by the courts) has already been applied to all different sorts of facilities such as harbour and airport infrastructures,[82] network infrastructures,[83] spare parts,[84] raw materials,[85]

[78] Guidelines on vertical restraints, *supra* n. 27, para 214.

[79] Commission Regulation 330/2010 on the application of Article 101(3) of the Treaty on the Functioning of the European Union to categories of vertical agreements and concerted practices [2010] OJ L 102/1, Article 3; Commission Regulation 772/2004 on the application of Article 81(3) of the Treaty to categories of technology transfer agreements [2004] OJ L 123/11, Article 3(2).

[80] Leading case: Case C-7/97 *Bronner v Mediaprint* [1998] ECR I-7791, para 41, according to which access must be granted if the refusal is incapable of being objectively justified and the service in itself is indispensable to carrying on that person's business, inasmuch as there is no actual or potential substitute in existence.

[81] Case C-418/01 *IMS Health* [2004] ECR I-5039, para 38.

[82] Commission decision 94/19/EC, Case IV/34.689 – *Sea Containers v Stena Sealink* [1994] OJ L 15/8, para 66; Commission decision 94/119/EC *concerning a refusal to grant access to the facilities of the port of Rødby (Denmark)* [1994] OJ L 55/52, para 12; Commission decision 98/190/EC, Case IV/34.801 – *Flughafen Frankfurt/M AG* [1998] OJ L 72/30, paras 73 et seq.

[83] XXII. Report on Competition Policy 1997 (1998), *S.W.I.F.T.*, at 161; Commission Decision 2004/33/EC, Case COMP/37.685 – *GVG/FS* [2004] OJ L 11/17.

[84] Commission decision 78/68/EEC, Case IV/29.131 – *Hugin/Liptons* [1978] OJ L 22/23, at 32; ECJ judgment in *Hugin*, *supra* n. 5.

[85] Joined Cases 6 and 7/73 R *Istituto Chemioterapico Italiano and Commercial Solvents v Commission* [1974] ECR 223, para 25.

information,[86] as well as IP-protected technologies,[87] and more importantly, in the context of this chapter, it has already been applied numerous times to interfaces controlling access to aftermarkets.[88]

It is easy to see why the essential facilities doctrine is relevant for the topic at hand, that is, competition on related markets. Access to aftermarkets is frequently restricted either by IP-protected (or secret) technologies or simply information necessary to achieve interoperability between the primary and secondary product,[89] or by products required to perform certain services,[90] both of which are controlled by the producer of the primary good. It should, therefore, not be surprising that, in recent years, aftermarket interfaces appear to have been the main field of application of the essential facilities doctrine in the EU.[91] After all, besides natural monopolies such as network infrastructure, access to which is now subject to a special regulatory regime established by secondary legislation, it is really only IP-protected interfaces for secondary products that easily meet the strict non-duplicability condition contained in the indispensability test set out in *Bronner*.[92]

4.2 Assessment under Article 102 TFEU

As was already mentioned above, the refusal to grant access to interface information is not a classic market power leveraging abuse in that it is not the dominant position on the primary product market that gives the firm the power to restrict access to the aftermarket. Rather, it is the production and more familiar knowledge of the primary product that typically yields the IP protection (or other form of exclusive power) regarding the interface. Consequently, the relevant abuse element, that is, the distortion of performance-based competition in these cases is not,

---

[86] Commission Decision 89/205/EEC, Case IV/31.851 – *Magill TV Guide/ITP, BBC und RTE* [1989] OJ L 78/43; backed by CFI in Case T-69/89 *RTE v Commission* [1991] ECR II-485 and the ECJ in Joined Cases C-241/91 P and C-242/91 P, *RTE and ITP v Commission* [1995] ECR I-743.

[87] *IMS Health*, *supra* n. 81, para 82.

[88] *Hilti*, *supra* n. 5, para 77; *Volvo*, *supra* n. 4, para 9; see most recently Commission decision in *Microsoft*, *supra* n. 56, paras 568–72; and the CFI judgment in *Microsoft*, *supra* n. 4, paras 331 et seq.

[89] E.g. interface information for software applications or the design of replacement parts.

[90] E.g. spare parts for repair services or cartridges necessary to sell toner.

[91] See, e.g. Commission decision in *Microsoft*, *supra* n. 56 and CFI judgment in *Microsoft*, *supra* n. 4.

[92] *Bronner*, *supra* n. 80, para 41.

or at least is not primarily, the transfer or extension of dominance on the primary market. Rather, it is the exploitation of the advantage that comes from controlling a gatekeeper input for the aftermarket product. Again, this is an input that is typically not the fruit of superior business acumen or, indeed, any business effort at all, but is simply the by-product of the development and manufacture of the primary product.[93] A further important implication of this idea is that the finding of an abuse does not presuppose the existence of a dominant position on the primary product market. It suffices that the secondary product constitutes a separate market comprising only the aftermarket for the particular brand under the criteria discussed above.[94] If this condition is met, the interface information or product, being a necessary input for the secondary product, constitutes or belongs to a separate relevant market as well, and it is on *this* market that the dominant position necessary to apply Article 102 TFEU can be found.

This is no mere theory. In the decisional practice of the Commission as well as in the case-law of the Community Courts, this type of abuse has already been condemned in a number of cases, and it has been clarified that the finding of such an abuse does not require dominance on the primary market.[95] While the latter aspect does significantly increase the scope of the essential facilities doctrine with regard to aftermarkets, a consistent application of this doctrine and its various requirements should prevent an overly liberal application to aftermarket situations. These requirements are as follows.

Firstly, the aftermarket product must, as was just pointed out, constitute or belong to a separate relevant market. If that is not the case, the input for this product can not be considered to constitute or belong to a separate relevant product market either and it will not be possible to establish a dominant position necessary to apply Article 102 TFEU.[96]

---

[93] It should be noted that the fact that the 'facility' (here the interface information or product) is a component of the primary product and destined for use by its owner only, does not, as such, hinder the application of the essential facility doctrine in the EU. This doctrine has been applied many times to such inputs for which there was, strictly speaking, no market because their owner never intended to market them independently; see in particular *IMS Health*, *supra* n. 81, paras 43 et seq.

[94] See 3.2.2, above.

[95] Notably *Hugin*, *supra* n. 5, paras 3 et seq; *Volvo*, *supra* n. 4, para 9.

[96] See, e.g. *Info-Lab/Ricoh*, *supra* n. 42, in which the Commission rejected a complaint by Info-Lab contending that Ricoh abused its dominant position by refusing to sell empty toner cartridges which would permit it to compete on the filled-cartridges consumable market inter alia with the argument that those

More importantly, however, in the absence of a separate market to capture and subsequently to exploit, there would be no abusive distortion or competition either.

Secondly, the interface must be a bottleneck for the particular aftermarket. Access to the IP-protected information, form, or to the product in question, must be indispensable for being able to enter the aftermarket.

Thirdly, the two markets concerned, namely the input constituting the interface and the final aftermarket product, must be sufficiently distinct. If the bottleneck defines the product and its essential qualities, and if, therefore, the imposition of a duty to share would not open the way to quality-based competition (but only to competition on price), a refusal to share this input with potential competitors cannot be viewed as an improper and abusive extension of the dominant position on the input market to a downstream market. It is, however, not necessary that access to the input would enable rivals to offer an entirely new product. Furthermore, in the aftermarkets context, the new product criterion formulated by the ECJ with respect to IP-protected inputs[97] should be understood merely to confirm the requirement that the two markets involved are not *too* close in the sense described above.[98] This is also how the CFI appears to have interpreted this criterion in the *Microsoft* case when it was satisfied that the Commission demonstrated that access to the interface information at issue would permit some quality competition and not a mere cloning of Microsoft's own software application.[99]

5 ABUSIVE 'SYSTEM COMPETITION'

As discussed in more detail above, the exclusion or hindering of rivals on secondary markets through tying, bundling, or refusals to deal, should not be considered abusive if the secondary product concerned would either not constitute a separate product but rather an integral part of the primary

consumables did not constitute a separate relevant market. Also in *Pelikan/Kyocera*, *supra* n. 42, the Commission rejected a similar complaint by pointing out that Kyocera was subject to intense competition on the primary market which restrained its behaviour on the secondary market.

97 *IMS Health*, *supra* n. 81, para 48.

98 See also J Vickers, 'A Tale of Two EC Cases: *IBM* and *Microsoft*' (2008) 4 (1) *Comp Pol'y Int* 1, at 19; *IMS Health*, *supra* n. 81, paras 44 et seq.

99 *Microsoft*, *supra* n. 4, paras 655 et seq.

product,[100] or does not form or belong to a separate (and separately exploitable) product market.[101] It is submitted that, in these two constellations, even firms dominating the primary product market may, without running afoul of Article 102 TFEU, compete with the whole bundle composed of the primary and the secondary product.

The focus of abuse control, however, would then shift to the marketing of this system. Thus, while it would be legal under Article 102 TFEU to only offer the primary and secondary product as a bundle, the addition of the secondary product without according price increase could render the price for the whole package abusively low. The test for establishing whether this price is predatory is a straightforward one. The question would be whether, after the addition of the secondary product, the price for the main product (that is, the whole package) is still cost-covering under the criteria developed in the case-law.[102]

Another issue concerns below cost sales of one system component[103] aiming at creating or increasing demand for the other system component.[104] If the two components really do form a system within the meaning of this paper, and do not belong to two separate relevant markets, the predatory pricing test must again be applied to the whole system. Given that it is the whole system that competes on the market, looking at the cost/price relation of the loss-producing component in isolation would be inappropriate, and a prohibition of that practice would also not be necessary to protect efficient competitors on the system market. That means that a certain cross-subsidisation of system components, and a certain price discrimination of heavy users, is, in principle, acceptable under Article 102 TFEU. It is, however, also clear that a predatory pricing charge focusing on the whole system cost will be very difficult to prove. The criteria developed in the case-law do not really fit a constellation where the total price of using the system varies according to the intensity of use and where a certain degree of cross-subsidisation is therefore an inherent element. The most convincing approach is probably to look at the prices paid by average-intensity

---

[100] See 3.2.1, above.

[101] See 3.2.2, above.

[102] *AKZO v Commission*, *supra* n. 20, para 72; CFI judgment in *Tetra Pak II*, *supra* n. 11, paras 148–9; backed by the ECJ in *Tetra Pak II*, *supra* n. 11, para 41; *France Télécom*, *supra* n. 14, para 130; backed by the ECJ in *France Télécom*, *supra* n. 14.

[103] E.g. of gaming hardware or cellphones.

[104] E.g. the software products or telecommunication services requiring such hardware to function.

users and determine whether they cover the combined average total cost of both system components.

If the loss-producing conduct in the above sense is not predatory, could it be viewed as a practice that distorts competition by indirectly foreclosing the market? In principle, the manipulation of future purchasing patterns through exclusive purchasing agreements and fidelity rebate schemes can be abusive.[105] Incentivising the consumption of own products or services by below-cost sales of required hardware does, however, differ from those practices. Contrary to the mentioned exclusivity and loyalty enhancing arrangements, using loss-producing hardware does not inherently hinder or exclude competitors, at least as long as the taking advantage of that benefit is not contingent on the customer not using another system. The assessment of the practice may be different, however, if there are significant switching costs between the systems, or if, despite being supplied below cost, the incurred loss still represents a significant sunk cost.

6 MAIN CONCLUSIONS

Article 102(2) lit d) TFEU will almost always apply to contractual tying in case of dominance in the primary product because in that case the separate product and separate product market test will typically be met. Bundling is an entirely different story, and it is mainly *this* tying practice that calls for a more complex analysis and a rejection of per se treatment under Article 102(2) lit d) TFEU. Technical ties in the form of refusals to grant access to relevant interface information or to supply products necessary to perform aftermarket services must be analysed under the essential facility doctrine. Such a refusal can be abusive even if the firm controlling the interface is not dominant on the primary product market. If the primary and secondary products do not constitute separate products from the point of view of consumers, or if consumers view them as a system, taking the cost of either both products or services into account when making their purchasing decision, practices aiming at excluding

[105] *Hoffmann La-Roche*, *supra* n. 19, para 90; Case T-65/98 R *Van den Bergh Foods v Commission* [2003] ECR II-4653, para 160; *BPB Industries and British Gypsum*, *supra* n. 20, para 68; Case 322/81 *Michelin v Commission* ('*Michelin I*') [1983] ECR 3461, paras 83 et seq; *Michelin II*, *supra* n. 19, para 111; Case C-163/99 *Portugal v Commission* [2001] ECR I-2613, para 53; Case T-219/99 *British Airways v Commission* [2001] ECR II-6917, para 272; backed by the ECJ in *British Airways v Commission supra* n. 64, para 74.

rivals from offering one system component, that is, practices closing the system, are legitimate under Article 102 TFEU. Abuse investigations under that provision would in such cases have to focus on the marketing of the system as a whole.

8. A comparative look at the competition law control of state-owned enterprises and government in China

Deborah Healey

1 INTRODUCTION

The enactment of a competition law in China in 2007 was a notable achievement in a number of respects. The process of lawmaking was lengthy: consultations were numerous and the approach changed many times. The Anti Monopoly Law (AML), operative 1 August 2008, prohibits monopoly conduct,[1] which it defines as abuse of dominance,[2] monopoly agreements[3] and certain mergers and acquisitions,[4] and shows the influences of both European and US competition laws. The fourth category of prohibition in the AML is, however, more unusual – the law prohibits the exploitation of administrative power, known in China as 'administrative monopoly'.[5]

This chapter examines the application of the AML to government bodies and operations: state-owned enterprises (SOEs) and administrative monopoly. It outlines factors that are likely to influence the way the AML will be interpreted, particularly in relation to SOEs. It considers whether the picture is any clearer after more than a year of operation.

1 See Article 3.
2 Chapter III.
3 Chapter II.
4 Chapter IV.
5 Chapter V.

2 THE STATE AND BUSINESS IN CHINA

2.1 System Reform

A very brief snapshot of the historical, economic, commercial and legal factors that form the background to the AML and are likely to influence its interpretation and application generally and in particular to government follows.

2.2 Economic Reform

Until 1978 the economy in China was dominated by the State. Factories and other SOEs were units of state production, and the State set prices for key goods, and a floating price within a range in response to supply and demand for most other goods.[6] In 1978 a decision was made to open up the economy. Special Economic Zones were set up where socialist economics were not practised and customs duties, taxes and employment regulations did not apply.[7] In 1992, China accelerated the reform process by adopting a market system.[8]

A Company Law was enacted in 1994, and SOEs and town and village enterprises (TVEs) were reorganised as corporations, with shares that could be sold to non-government entities.

Some SOEs were shut down and others privatised. The central government kept control of the larger and more profitable SOEs in sectors characterised as important, such as telecommunications, banking, energy, transportation, natural resources, military industry, energy and utilities. Non-controlling interests were often sold to the private sector.

A significant new government restructuring programme commenced in 1998, reducing the number of central government ministries, downsizing party organisations and restructuring some industrial ministries into trade associations. By that stage most prices were set by the market, administrative and business functions of SOEs were separated

---

[6] Its Constitution was amended in 1993 when the concept of 'socialist market economy' was introduced. J Yang, 'Market Power in China: Manifestations, Effects and Legislation' (2002) 21 *Rev Ind Org* 167.

[7] See M Williams, *Competition Policy and Law in China, Hong Kong and Taiwan* (2005) at 111.

[8] See PRC Constitution, Article 15. Other references to 'socialist market economy' were subsequently added. See DL Yang, *Remaking the Chinese Leviathan: Market Transition and the Politics of Governance in China* (2004), at 7 ff.

and government generally no longer directly administered enterprises.[9] The more important SOEs were under the direct control of the State Assets Supervision and Administration Commission under State Council (SASAC), with the control of smaller enterprises left to local government (with SASAC in a supervisory role). In some cases, entities were privatised.[10] Importantly, insolvent SOEs do not go out of business – state banks are generally required to continue to support local politically sponsored producers.[11]

In 2006, the State Council released a list of strategic industries in which the State would retain control: military related manufacturing, power production and grids, petroleum, gas and petrochemicals, telecom manufacturing, coal, civil aviation and shipping.[12] These industries are known as 'lifeline industries', characterised as key to the country's national security and economic development.[13]

In 2009 SASAC announced that the adjustment and reorganisation of central state-owned enterprises will continue.[14] The number of directly SASAC-controlled SOEs has reduced from 196 in 2003 to 138 in 2009.[15] Seventy per cent of these bodies have been 'reconstructed', a large number are listed on domestic and overseas stock markets, and many are 'fully competitive market entities'.[16] Corporate management structures have been improved with a 'standard board of directors' implemented in 24 enterprises. Many have set up overseas branches, are exploring international markets and carrying out strategic mergers and acquisitions.[17] The business imperatives of SOEs are, however, still not solely focussed on profitability.[18]

---

9 See Yang, id. at 41.

10 F Deng and GK Leonard, 'Incentives and China's New Antimonopoly Law' (2008) 22(2) *Antitrust* 73, at 75. Examples given are Lenovo, China Mobile and Sinopec.

11 See Williams, *supra* n. 7, at 215.

12 (31 August 2008) *China Daily*. See SASAC, 'Guiding Opinions for Promoting the Adjustment of State Assets and Restructuring of State-Owned Enterprises' (5 December 2006), http://finance.sha.com.cn/g/20061218/11133173443.shtml (accessed 15 March 2008).

13 Id.

14 Statement of SASAC (31 August 2009). Available with author.

15 Id. The SASAC website still lists 150 'Central SOEs': http://www.sasac.gov.cn/n2963340/n2971121/n4956567/4956583.html (accessed December 2010).

16 Id.

17 Id.

18 S Li and J Xia, 'The Roles and Performance of State Firms and Non-State Firms in China's Transition' (2008) 36 *World Development* 39, at 42.

2.3 Administrative Monopoly

Administrative monopoly is a major challenge to competition and has been a significant factor in China. It goes beyond the mere use of market power by SOEs. China devolved power and financial control and responsibility to its provinces in the transition to the market economy. In response the provinces erected protective barriers to keep out the goods of other provinces and to avoid sharing tax revenue. The provincial barriers erected in a myriad ways are a major impediment to the creation of a single market and a level playing field for market participants in China. Many beneficiaries of local protectionism are SOEs. Rectification of administrative monopoly requires action under a broader range of competition policies.

2.4 Systemic Legal Problems

The explosion of new laws and regulations that has come with the opening up of the country, with inconsistent and often unsatisfactory enforcement, impacts on the move to a market economy and potentially the effective operation of the AML.[19] More than one agency often has authority to enforce laws, which results in a fragmented and inconsistent approach to decision making.[20] Judicial review is generally limited, with narrow scope, convoluted procedures and bias in favour of government agencies.[21] The vague language of Chinese legislation and use of broad administrative discretion in interpreting the law does not assist certainty. Policy laws consisting of administrative regulations, meetings, instructions and speeches that become legally binding simply because they emanate from authoritative government or party bodies add to the regulatory confusion.[22]

---

[19] See R Peerenboom, *China's Long March toward Rule of Law* (2002) at 239, noting that by 2002 more than 350 laws and 6,000 lower level regulations had been passed.

[20] See B Owen, S Sun and W Zheng, 'China's Competition Policy Reforms: The Anti-Monopoly Law and Beyond' (2008) 75 *Antitrust LJ* 5.

[21] Id. at 13, citing CX Liu, 'A Quiet Revolution: An Overview of China's Judicial Reform' (June 2003) 4 *Asian-Pacific L & Pol'y J* 9.

[22] H Blanchard, 'Seeking Truth from Facts: Constitutional Revisionism in the PRC' (2005) 17 *Florida J Int'l L* 365, at 373. On China's legal environment generally, see Peerenboom, *supra* n. 19, particularly at Ch. 6.

2.5 Importance of Personal Relationships

Informal *guanxi* interpersonal networks and relationships are an important part of the legal system and operate alongside law and legal institutions. They provide a complementary mechanism for dealing with formal institutions. The move to the market economy and the growth of client relationships reinforce this position.[23] This will be very relevant to the stance in competition law on the issue of collaboration.

2.6 Competition – An Unknown Concept

Importantly for current purposes, the concept of 'competition' was not part of the political vocabulary in China until after 1979, and the language of international competition law is even less familiar to Chinese.[24]

2.7 'Excessive' Competition

A separate issue aligned to the lack of familiarity with competition as a concept is the problem of so-called excessive competition, which is a subject of much concern in China. The ability of SOEs to absorb unlimited losses because of government support fuels many well-documented examples of excessive competition. Purely commercial entities would not be able or willing to absorb all losses arising from robust competition and in another environment would be forced to compete less aggressively or leave the market. Reported examples of excessive competition have included shipping between China and Japan, dairy products (resulting in product safety issues), household appliances, the travel industry and airlines.[25] Measures taken by the government to deal with excessive competition include 'industrial self-discipline', mentioned within the AML.[26] Industrial self-discipline is undertaken with direct government supervision, and allows major companies in an industry to reach a floor price

---

[23] PS Potter, *The Chinese Legal System: Globalization and Local Legal Culture* (2001) at 12 et seq.

[24] DJ Gerber, 'Economics, Law and Institutions: The Shaping of Chinese Competition Law' (2008) 26 *Wash U J L & Pol'y* 290.

[25] See Owen, *supra* n. 20, at 12 et seq. As to airlines see Yang, *supra* n. 6, at 167.

[26] See State Economic and Trade Commission (SETC), 'Opinions on Self Disciplinary Prices Adopted by Some Industries' (17 August 1998), http://www.law99.net/law/doc/c001/1998/08/17/00107286html, referred to in Owen, *supra* n. 20, at 21.

agreement or limit production. Trade associations play an important part in imposing industrial self-discipline.

It has been suggested by Chinese commentators that excessive competition means that there is no need for a competition law. Closer analysis of the issue reveals that there are other issues involved, such as lack of innovation, domestic consumption, lack of enforcement of rules and other market imperfections.[27]

It is against this political, legal and commercial background that the AML was enacted in 2007.

3 OBJECTS OF THE AML

This consideration of the AML proceeds on the basis that a competition law should generally be a law of universal application, applying to both private and state-owned enterprises, and that any exemptions should be thoroughly justified in economic and public benefit terms, be minimal in scope and be as least restrictive of competition as possible.[28]

Analysis of the objects of the AML reinforces the view that the Chinese view of competition is different from that of other countries and that competition alone is unlikely to be the paramount consideration in its interpretation. The express objects of the AML include the usual prevention of anticompetitive conduct, promotion of market competition and economic efficiency, and protecting the rights of the consumer.[29] The AML also has the more unusual purposes of 'protecting the public interest' (whatever that is) and 'promoting the healthy development of the socialist market economy'. These diverging objectives indicate the priority in enforcing and applying the AML are not solely the competitive process. Other provisions reinforce this view. Article 4, for example, states: 'The State shall make and implement competition rules appropriate for the socialist market economy and strengthen and improve macroeconomic measures for a united, open, competitive and well-ordered market system.'

---

[27] See Owen, *supra* n. 20, at 23 et seq.

[28] See, for example, United Nations Committee for Trade and Development (UNCTAD) 'Application of Competition Law: Exemptions and Exceptions' (2002), UNCTAD/DITC/CLP/Misc.25, at 36, http://www.unctad.org/en/docs/ditcclpmisc25_en.pdf (accessed December 2010); OECD 'Competition Assessment Toolkit' (2007), at 13.

[29] See AML Article 1. The objects of the Australian Act (s 2) are to enhance the welfare of Australians through the promotion of competition and fair trading and provisions for consumer protection.

This provision gives rule makers significant discretion as to the types of rule that may be made, focussed against the background of the socialist market economy. The words 'well-ordered market system' introduce an element that shows a completely different focus on market. Market competition should be the regulator – competition laws are designed to foster vigorous competition. Whether the market is well-ordered is not relevant, and a well-ordered market may be a comfortably inefficient market, or a coordinated or cartel market. The Chinese views on 'excessive competition', coupled with traditional practices such as price regulation and industrial self-discipline, have the capacity to impact significantly the interpretation of the law and the workings of the market.

The idea of orderly markets is also recognised in relation to industry associations (Article 11). Industry associations are a traditional risk area for competition contraventions because of the seemingly legitimate close proximity of competitors, and the ability for coordinated conduct to occur, particularly in relation to pricing. On the one hand Article 11 exhorts industry associations to encourage their members to compete, but on the other encourages them to do so 'protecting the order of market competition'.

Orderly marketing is clearly an element of the socialist market economy, and will have an impact on the application of the AML. The parameters of the distinction between a socialist market economy and a free market provide the major distinction between the competition law in China and other competition laws. This distinction presents the major challenge to the adoption and implementation of a competition law in China: how does competition work in a socialist market economy? It was inevitable that China would enact a competition law reflecting its national philosophy on market rather than merely adopting the law of other jurisdictions. It plainly makes it more difficult to predict legal outcomes in an area that is always one of divergent views and decision making, particularly in the initial stages of the new law.

4 APPLICATION OF THE AML

The application of the AML to SOEs is unclear. Arguably, if they are engaged in business and competing in the marketplace, SOEs should be subject to the AML. To exempt them from the application of the law would distort the processes of competition that the AML is designed to foster. It would entrench bodies with significant market power in markets to the detriment of consumers and possible new entry. It would also create situations where other entities in competition with SOEs would be required to comply with a different set of rules.

Prohibitions in the AML on monopolistic conduct[30] apply to 'undertakings',[31] which are defined as natural persons, legal persons or other organisations that engage in manufacturing or supplying commodities or services.[32] SOEs are 'undertakings' on a strict construction of the provisions of the AML. SOEs are described as undertakings, for example, in Article 7, although ironically that provision may remove a good number of them from the reach of the AML.[33] The specific prohibitions on administrative monopoly are limited to the administrative functions of SOEs and do not include their business functions.[34]

There appears to be no reason why the general prohibitions aimed at undertakings do not apply to most SOEs to the extent that they are engaged in production or business and abuse their commercial monopoly power, as opposed to using their administrative power. This distinction between use of business power and administrative power will often be difficult to discern in particular situations, however, given the mixed functions of SOEs.[35] Many SOEs are both business operators and industry administrators, making it difficult to determine the real issue of power in competition law terms:[36] the government is 'not only the maker of the rules but also the sportsman competing in the game and the referee of the game at the same time'.[37]

---

30 Monopoly agreements, abuse of a dominant position and concentration (acquisitions and related conduct) (Article 4).

31 This is the same terminology as under EU law.

32 Article 12. The EU provisions apply to entities engaged in commercial activity, including SOEs. See P Craig and G de Burca, *EU Law: Text, Cases and Materials* (2003) at 939.

33 Chinese legal interpretation is not generally so focussed on strict construction as common law countries. See also Z Wu, 'Perspectives on the Chinese Anti-Monopoly Law', (2008) 75 *Antitrust LJ* 94, at 98, which assumes that they are undertakings.

34 Article 32.

35 A new Law of State-Owned Assets of Enterprises was passed in November 2008, operative 1 May 2009.

36 See W Wen, 'Market Dominance by China's Public Utility Enterprises' (2008) 75 *Antitrust LJ* 151, at 152.

37 Y Guo and A Hu, 'The Administrative Monopoly in China's Economic Transition' (2004) 37 *Communist and Post-Communist Studies* 265, at 272.

5 LIFELINE AND OTHER REGULATED INDUSTRIES CARVE-OUT

There is a carve-out of significance from application of the AML to certain SOEs, although the size of the excluded group is undetermined at this stage. Article 7 was added in June 2007 just before the AML was passed. The scope of the carve-out has been the subject of much discussion and debate, and the wording of the provision is ambiguous at best but set out here in full for consideration:

> Industries controlled by the State-owned economy and relied upon by the national economy and national security or industries implementing exclusive operation and sales in accordance with the law shall be protected by the State to conduct lawful operation by the undertaking. The State shall supervise and control the price of commodities and services provided by these undertakings and the operation of these undertakings so as to protect the interests of the consumer and facilitate technical progress.

Thus, where State-controlled and owned industries are important to the national economy or to national security, or where other industries operate 'exclusively in accordance with law' (presumably given monopoly rights by the government) they will fall within Art. 7 and will be allowed to continue under the supervision and protection of the State, rather than under the focus of the AML. In these situations, the State may fix prices for commodities and services and regulate their operations to protect consumer interests and facilitate progress.

A second part of Article 7 contains the following rejoinder:

> Undertakings of industries under the previous paragraph shall conduct their business in accordance with law in an honest and trustworthy manner, impose strict self-discipline, and accept supervision from the public. These undertakings shall not harm the interests of consumers by making use of their position of control or their position of exclusive and monopolistic sales.

This provision requires these bodies to operate within the law and not exploit their positions. It is difficult to understand how they will 'accept supervision from the public', although this is likely to mean accepting State supervision. The last words indicate that the State will not allow these bodies to take advantage of their favoured market position, but there is no designation about which body will ensure this. Note that the second part of this Article applies to the actual undertakings and not to the industries.[38]

---

[38] This provision has some similarities with Art. 106(2) TFEU (Treaty on the Functioning of the European Union).

In this provision legislators have recognised that in some industries state ownership and control may be 'vital to national security and the economy', particularly while reform of SOEs is ongoing and will take some time to complete. It reflects a policy decision that it is not desirable to have multiple operators in selected industries at this stage, and allows the government to implement industry policy.[39]

This provision encompasses three groups:

- industries vital to the national economy;
- industries vital to national security; and
- industries subject to exclusive operations and sales under the law.

The wording focusses at the outset on national issues, which suggests that SOEs operating at a provincial or local level would not be protected. If a number of local SOEs constitute an important national industry, the answer may be different. It seems that this provision is aimed at 'life-line industries'. Other competition laws grant particular industry groups special treatment, although it is generally accepted that industry-based exemptions, as opposed to exemptions for specific types of conduct, 'should almost always be treated with suspicion'.[40] In the context of China, however, this provision will have particular impact owing to the size of the state-owned economy and the nature of the bodies potentially exempted here.

The critical issue is whether the first group involves all SOEs directly supervised by SASAC. A review of the 2009 Law on State Owned Assets (Assets Law)[41] provides further clues but does not completely resolve the issue. The Assets Law deals with a number of important basic issues about SOEs such as the responsible person for decision making and board appointments, account keeping, restructuring and reorganisation. The Assets Law basically recognises two categories of SOEs. The first is the local SOE, with the contribution or shareholder function performed by the State Council and the local government concerned. The second category refers to 'larger sized state-invested enterprises that have bearing on the national economic lifeline and state security determined by State Council' where the contributor or shareholder function is performed by the State Council.[42] This suggests that all 138 SOEs supervised by

---

[39] Wu, *supra* n. 33, at 98.

[40] UNCTAD, *supra* n. 28, at 32.

[41] Law of the People's Republic of China on the State-Owned Assets of Enterprises, operative 1 May 2009.

[42] Article 4.

SASAC fall inside the lifeline category and potentially within Article 7 of the AML. However, by way of contrast, Article 30 of the Assets Law says that state invested enterprises must comply with laws and regulations on major matters listed, and that these specifically include 'mergers' and 'restructuring'.

This carve-out has significant implications even if it is restricted to the recognised lifeline industries. The first and second categories of Article 7 will be determined on the width of the definitions given to 'importance to the national economy' and to 'national security'. Whether it is appropriate to exempt all these SASAC or lifeline industries from application of the AML is open to question. The list is quite extensive and not all of these industries are considered to be of national importance requiring special rules in other countries. In the US, for example, most of these industries are not owned or operated by government. Some are subject to sector-specific regulation in other countries, although this would not of itself qualify them for a competition law exemption. Whether Article 7 catches all the SASAC SOEs as 'lifeline industries', or only part of that group, and whether they are the only 'lifeline industries' or whether that group could potentially include some of the provincial level SOEs, is still unclear.

The third category catches companies in those state-controlled industries where the state has granted monopolies. Presumably this group involves SOEs and also private companies. In these industries the State will continue to control price and the operation of the monopoly undertakings[43] – presumably this means those state-regulated monopolies such as petroleum and tobacco and other monopoly industries subject to specific regulation. The companies in these industries are not necessarily state-owned but the industries are state-regulated. The idea of 'lawful operation' indicates that the State, not the AML and its regulators, will ensure the lawful operations of these entities.

Two examples of conduct in lifeline industries illustrate the issues involving market power that can arise and may need rectification. The power of vertically integrated SOEs is well illustrated by the rise of the China National Petroleum Corp (CNPC) subsidiary Kunlin, in China's urban energy sector. Kunlin has reportedly 'managed to force out several small and medium-sized gas distributors' in a number of provinces in China. CNPC does not compete in downstream gas services, but recent reports allege that Kunlin leverages its parent CNPC's market position and access

---

43 There are provisions in the EU law dealing with exclusive rights but these also incorporate a competition analysis, discussed below.

to natural gas to advance its commercial position in the growing commercial and domestic markets. The urban gas market was deregulated and opened to outside investment in 2004, and local state-owned gas companies, private and joint-venture companies and large-scale enterprises now compete for customers. Whether the conduct of Kunlin would constitute an abuse of a dominant position clearly depends upon the true market definition and Kunlun's degree of market power in that market. However absent the application of the AML to SOEs of this kind, there is not a level playing field for competition with private providers.[44]

In another example, it has been suggested that the government has authorised only two firms, which are both SOEs, to sell gasoline, and that this is a potential violation of the prohibition on requiring purchases from designated firms that could be protected by Article 7.[45] It has also been suggested that this 'oil monopoly' could be attacked under the AML.[46] Clearly the extent of application of the AML will be extremely relevant to the latter issue.

Another important outstanding issue is whether SOEs falling within the categories listed in Article 7, whatever its full extent, have to comply with the provisions of the AML requiring notification of mergers or acquisitions. The actual wording of Article 7 focusses more on their other market behaviour than on issues of restructure or merger. This question is particularly relevant when one considers the ongoing work of SASAC in reducing the number of SOEs it controls. It is an interesting issue on a number of levels. Firstly, these bodies are owned and controlled by the State.[47] If they were related corporate bodies, under most competition laws they could engage in anticompetitive conduct without risk. There also may be very good reasons, having regard to efficiency, why these restructurings are taking place, so in any event many of them would likely pass the test under

[44] See Y Yue, 'Showdown for China's Urban Gas Sector' (4 May 2009), http://english.caijing.com.cn/2009-05-04/110159485.html (December 2010).

[45] Deng and Leonard, *supra* n. 10, at 73. See also Z Hao, 'The Claim of Abuse of Dominance and its Interpretation' (November 2008) *China L & Pract*, http://www.chinalawandpractice.com/Article/2043176/Channel/16143/The-Claim-of-the-Abuse-of-Dominance-and-its-Interpretation.html (accessed December 2010), where it is stated that 'a regulation was issued in 1999 by government departments stating that the wholesale of oil products is monopolised by CNPC and Sinopec, which related to concerns surrounding national economic security'.

[46] T Lei, 'Non-State enterprises may sue oil giants' (13 October 2008) *China Daily*, http://www.chinadaily.com.cn/bizchina/2008-10/13/content_7100917.htm (accessed December 2010).

[47] The reorganisation of all SOEs or companies must be approved at the relevant level of government. See Assets Law, Art 34.

the monopoly law, that is, they may not have the effect of eliminating or restricting competition.

The issue is, however, whether they are caught by the AML and hence subject to the filing requirements based on turnover that apply to undertakings.[48]

A number of relevant mergers have taken place since the AML became operative. Notable examples include:

- the merger between China Eastern Airlines and Shanghai Airlines in July 2009, the latter becoming a wholly owned subsidiary of China Eastern in a move described by MOFCOM as involving a 'consolidation of regional airlines;[49]
- the merger of telecommunications companies China Unicom and China Netcom in May 2009 and the sale of the CDMA business to China Telecom;[50] and
- the approval granted by 'China' to three units of Hebei Steel for a merger to form the country's No. 2 listed steel-maker in September 2009.[51]

It appears that of the 58 mergers formally considered by MOFCOM to date, none have involved SOEs. On the one hand, these facts suggest that there is no intention for SOEs to notify mergers and reconstructions under the AML. Concerns about transparency, however, suggest that it would be better for notification to be made, or alternatively some information released about mergers and reconstructions and their likely effect in the marketplace, having regard to the prominent position that many of the subjects will occupy in the marketplace.

On the other hand there may be a different intention. A different indicator of the approach that might be taken in relation to sector-specific laws and to the whole question of application of the AML to state-owned enterprises is presented by the MOFCOM view on the merger in the telecommunications industry between Unicom and Netcom. Prior to the merger in 2009, Unicom was one of China's leading mobile carriers and

---

[48] See Regulation on Notification Threshold of Concentration between Undertakings, adopted 3 August 2008.

[49] See MOFCOM Statement (13 July 2009).

[50] See (26 May 2009) *Economic Observer*, www.eeo.cn (copy with author). This article noted that the merger came within the AML notification thresholds.

[51] See MOFCOM, 'Units of Hebei Steel win approval for merger', press release, Forbes.com (23 September 2009) (copy with author).

Netcom a leader in the fixed-line and broadband market.[52] Following this merger, MOFCOM indicated that, where one SOE takes over another SOE, the usual notification process under the AML should be observed and should have been observed in that case. This suggests that SOEs are not exempted from the AML provisions under a blanket rule, and that the sector specific regulation may not in all cases override the AML, but that the relevant AML provisions will rather be selectively employed to advance the Constitutional agenda.[53] This approach would be consistent with the changing nature of the economy in China.

Many other countries restructure their own undertakings at will without recourse to their competition laws, and some do so under other industry laws that take them outside the scope of competition laws. The focus is on China in this regard more because of the concerted nature of their restructurings. Clearly many restructurings would pass a test based on weighing up any anticompetitive impact with their public benefit. The apparent removal of SOE mergers from the scope of the AML is a significant shortcoming in its operation. Transparent information on this issue would assist in understanding the approach to Article 7, and implementing a comprehensive approach to competition issues.

6 OTHER RELEVANT PROVISIONS

There are other exclusions from the AML that are not exclusive to government but that could apply.

Article 51 of the AML provides that anticompetitive conduct specifically mandated by other laws overrides the AML and this is also cause for concern. It allows for additional parallel regulations that complicate the legal landscape. This provision clearly has the flexibility to operate more broadly than Article 7 because it is not constrained by the categories of national security, national importance or legislative monopoly – it can

---

[52] See 'China Unicom unveils details of merger with China Netcom' (2 June 2008) *China Daily*, http://www2.chinadaily.com.cn/photo/2008-06/02/content_6739610.htm (accessed December 2010). The deal was completed on 16 October 2008.

[53] A report of the Economic Observer outlined in Hogan & Hartson LLP, 'China Antitrust Update' (11 May 2009), states that a written indication to the newspaper by MOFCOM confirmed that the parties should have notified MOFCOM of the merger. http://www.hhlw.com.files/Publication/d614a44e-5001-4785-8576-e5309e868043/Presentation/PublicationAttachment/83263da6-9b5f-4042-8f6c-555f54594bdd/ChinaAntitrust_May1109.pdf (accessed 14 November 2009). See also www.eeo.com.cn (1 May 2009).

apply to any conduct specifically mandated by law. It potentially applies to any SOE set up under a specific law.

There are also some specific provisions in the AML aimed at 'industry associations'. During the process of restructuring the economy from one where all industries were directly owned or controlled by government to a market economy, the government retreated from non-essential industries such as textiles, electronics, machinery and chemicals that were not natural monopolies. Government ministries that had previously overseen these industries were replaced with trade associations and chambers of commerce representing and coordinating various interests in the industries.[54] These bodies are able to engage in 'industrial self-discipline'.

A number of provisions within the AML allow laws to be made and the State Council to override the prohibitions of the AML. These include:

- Article 15(7), which provides that monopoly agreements falling within Articles 14 or 15 shall be exempt in 'other circumstances as stipulated by law and the State Council'.
- Acquisitions of domestic enterprises by foreign investors that concern national security are given a national security review in addition to consideration under the AML (Article 31).

7 ABUSE OF ADMINISTRATIVE POWERS: 'ADMINISTRATIVE MONOPOLY'

Administrative monopoly encompasses a number of behaviours by government bodies that inhibit the distribution of goods or services and create duplication at national, provincial and local level, such as:

- monopolies intended to restrict competition in an industry or measures that compel anticompetitive conduct;
- measures that mandate the use of particular products or services; and
- governmental actions that restrict market entry.[55]

Besides the State Council, China has some 660 local governments, including those for municipalities directly below State Council, provincial capital cities, cities, counties and towns. Local governments are important – they

---

[54] Owen, Sun and Zheng, *supra* n. 20, at 11 and 14.

[55] See, for example, Owen, Sun and Zheng, *supra* n. 20, at 17; see also Yang, *supra* n. 6, at 171; Williams, *supra* n. 7, at 139.

are responsible for economic regulation in their area.[56] The diversity of administrative monopoly is described by the following examples:

> differential taxation applied to goods from outside the 'home' territory, outright boycotts of 'foreign' goods, physical blockades at provincial or municipal boundaries, the use of administrative permits in a discriminatory fashion, orders to all state businesses answerable to the local government only to purchase supplies from local manufacturers. Forced tie-in sales of unrelated goods to benefit favoured producers and discriminatory administrative directions to local state banks to support local state enterprises with credits are also common . . . [A]buses include the creation of profits seeking enterprises within the local government structure which also act as the local administrative organs responsible for regulating a particular trade.[57]

It has been suggested that the most serious restrictions on competition in China arise from administrative monopoly.[58] Significant reforms have taken place but the problem is still huge.[59]

A recent report gives an example that highlights the pervasive nature of the problem. The county of Gongan in Hubei Province issued a circular stipulating:

> what brand and how many cigarettes local departments should consume every year, and what punishments would be meted out for unfulfilled targets. The decree would require nearly 4 million yuan worth of cigarettes to be consumed for meeting the target . . . Patently against the anti-monopoly law, the order is the result of local protectionism.[60]

As noted previously, various State Council departments in 1999 issued a regulation prohibiting any company except SinoChem and PetroChina from selling wholesale petrol products, and again in 2001 prohibited any other company from selling at retail level.[61]

Article 8 of the AML expressly prohibits administrative monopoly. The

---

56 Q Wu, 'The Making of a Market Economy in China: Transformation of Government Regulation of Market Development' (2007) 13 *Eur LJ* 750.

57 Williams, *supra* n. 7, at 139.

58 See, for example, X Wang, 'Challenges in Enforcing Chinese Antimonopoly Law – the Conflicting Goals of the Law' presented at 3rd Asian Competition Law Forum, Hong Kong (2 December 2007), on file with the author.

59 See, for example, Yang, *supra* n. 8, at 186 et seq. where a number of significant reforms in a range of areas are outlined in detail.

60 'Strange decree on cigarettes' (6 May 2009) China Daily, http://www.chinadaily.com.cn/cndy/2009-05/06/content_7746766.htm (accessed December 2010).

61 See X Zhang and VY Zhang, 'The Antimonopoly Law in China: Where do we stand?' (2007) 3 *Comp Pol'y Int'l* 185, at 199.

AML nominates a comprehensive variety of conduct by government and administrative bodies which would, by implication, lessen competition or affect the market. Without traversing Articles 32–37 (which are lengthy, detailed and quite specific in their designation of the prohibited practices) in full detail, the prohibitions in the AML outline a number of specific abuses related to designated dealings, creating regional barriers to entry by discriminatory rules and regulations, including both physical barriers and barriers by creation of standards, entry requirements and monopoly activities. Each of the provisions also requires proof that the conduct involves an abuse of power.

While the provisions on administrative monopoly are comprehensive, enforcement, discussed more fully in the next section, is likely to prove very difficult given the strength of local governments and lack of a mandate in the general regulator to enforce these provisions at all. The critical issue in relation to administrative monopoly will be whether those enforcing the provisions have sufficient independence and authority to do so.

Of significant concern in this context is also the second part of Article 51, previously mentioned, which provides that where other laws or regulations specifically make provision for the regulation of conduct that would otherwise be anticompetitive, they will prevail over the AML. This creates further capacity for duplication, fragmentation and confusion in relation to policing administrative monopoly conduct, and subjugates the AML to other laws that may have been implemented without any consideration of the implications of particular conduct on competition, or are in fact designed to circumvent it.

8 ENFORCEMENT

Issues with the legal system generally raised earlier impact significantly on the ability of the authorities to enforce the AML. There are, however, additional and significant issues in relation to the AML. The Anti Monopoly Enforcement Authority (AMEA) is the body responsible for enforcing the AML, imposing fines and performing a number of other specific functions.[62] Article 10 allows the AMEA to delegate its powers to enforce to government authorities, autonomous regions and municipalities. This of itself means that the power to enforce is fragmented, being shared between those three bodies. However, to exacerbate the problem, while the designation of the AMEA in the AML suggests that a single agency is responsible

[62] See Article 10.

for the enforcement and performance of its functions, in practice the existing agencies NDRC, SAIC and MOFCOM enforce the AML. MOFCOM is responsible for mergers and acquisitions, NDRC for pricing issues and SAIC for monopoly agreements, abuse of dominance and administrative monopoly (excluding price-related issues). The potential for overlap and inconsistency in these circumstances is profound.

In carrying out its duties the AMEA is given broad powers to investigate suspected conduct. Parties are required to cooperate[63] and have a right of reply.[64] The AMEA must make its determination in accordance with the law and publicise the determination.[65] There is power for a decreased penalty where parties make admissions.[66] There is, however, no tradition of negotiated legal outcomes in China, which will make AML enforcement quite different from that which occurs in other jurisdictions.[67]

There is a right to appeal by applying for administrative reconsideration or filing an administrative suit, unless the determination relates to a concentration issue, in which case the process is slightly different.[68]

It is clear that it would be more effective for there to be one agency, and for the AMEA to have power to enforce against administrative monopoly as well as other areas.[69]

Administrative monopoly is a more serious problem. Provisions relating to administrative monopoly are not enforced by the AMEA. Article 51 provides that, in cases involving administrative monopoly, the superior agency of the offender must order it to correct its behaviour. There is no fine or other sanction for an organisation, despite the serious effect on competition of many of these behaviours. Individuals may, however, face personal disciplinary sanctions. The AMEA investigates and may propose options or outcomes to the superior agency, but it is not given responsibility for any other enforcement of these provisions.[70] Procedural rules issued in June 2009 by SAIC outline a detailed hierarchy of procedures and the

---

63 Article 41.

64 Article 42.

65 Article 43.

66 Article 43.

67 RH Pate, 'What I Heard in the Great Hall of the People – Realistic Expectations of Chinese Antitrust' (2008) 75 *Antitrust LJ* 195.

68 Article 52.

69 Experts at the International Symposium on Anti Monopoly Enforcement in Beijing in December 2007 advocated a unified and independent enforcement agency: see J Wu, 'Calls for single anti-monopoly agency' (14 December 2007) *China Daily*, http:// www.china.org.cn.english/GS-e/235609.htm (accessed December 2010).

70 Article 51.

correct entity to be proposing remedial action for administrative monopoly, depending upon the nature of the relevant body that has offended the provisions.[71]

Given the multitude of provincial and municipal levels of the SAIC it is likely that the bulk of investigations will be taken at lower levels. An obvious result of this delegation is the prospect of local decision-making and resultant issues of lack of uniformity, localism and response at that level to the power of other local officials which might prevail. Given the administrative hierarchies that exist at local level, local enforcement bodies may find it extremely hard to make themselves heard against a powerful administrative department in their region.

9 SANCTIONS

The AMEA imposes sanctions under the AML for provisions other than those relating to administrative monopoly. As well as the power to issue cease and desist orders and order confiscation of illegal gains, the AMEA may impose substantial fines.

In determining the amount of fines the AMEA must consider the nature, extent and duration of the illegal conduct.[72] Penalties may be reduced or parties exempted from punishment if undertakings report their conduct and give evidence.[73] There is civil liability for damages caused by contravention.[74] Owing to difficulties previously noted with enforcement, whether these penalties will ever be recovered remains to be seen.

10 OTHER JURISDICTIONS

10.1 Brief Consideration

While a comprehensive overview of other jurisdictions is beyond the scope of this chapter, some brief points in relation to the EU, the United States, Australia, Hong Kong and Singapore are noted for the purposes of comparison.

---

71 Rules on Procedures for Administrations of Industry and Commerce on Prohibiting Abuses of Administrative Powers to Eliminate or Restrict Competition.

72 Article 49.

73 Article 45.

74 Article 49. Previous drafts of the AML nominated liability as criminal.

10.2 European Union

EU law covers 'undertakings', and this applies to public authorities, municipalities and other entities entrusted with regulatory or administrative functions when they are engaged in 'economic activity', although this does not necessarily involve a profit motive or economic purpose.[75] Non-commercial activities or exercising powers of a public authority are not caught, and an entity may be an 'undertaking' for part of its functions and not for others.[76]

There are additional specific exclusions for public activities that are classified as being 'non-economic'. Entities engaged in activities involving so-called 'solidarity' in the form of social security, pensions or health care not in a market context are not undertakings. Where these activities are provided in a market context they are provided by undertakings and will not be exempt.[77] Procurement that is ancillary to non-economic activities is also excluded.

In the EU, a mix of provisions deals with coverage of the Treaty on the Functioning of the EU (TFEU), the ability of Member States to regulate out of the Treaty and other issues relating to exemptions. The Treaty itself institutes a system 'ensuring that competition in the internal market is not distorted',[78] and Member States are obliged to conduct their economic policy in accordance with the principles of an 'open market economy with free competition'.[79] Member States must take all appropriate measures to fulfil the Treaty obligations[80] and abstain from all measures that would jeopardise the Treaty obligations.[81] The position of Member States and their obligations under the Treaty in respect of some activities of

---

[75] Associations of football clubs may be undertakings despite the fact that some of the member clubs are in fact amateur. See R Whish, *Competition Law* (6th edn, 2009), at 85 (referring to Case T-193/02 *Piau v Commission* [2005] ECR II-209).

[76] So, for example, a public authority may have power to adopt by-laws on parking and also to run a commercial car park. Only the latter would be caught. See id. at 83.

[77] Cases have differentiated, for example, between pension funds paid to all, regardless of contributions made, and funds with benefits dependent on contributions and in competition with life insurance companies. Id. at 87 (citing Cases C-159/91 *Poucet v Assurances Generales de France* [1993] ECR I-63. Cf. also Case C-244/94 *Fédération Française des Sociétés d'Assurance* [1995] ECR I-4013.

[78] Former Art. 3(1)(g) EC; now 'Protocol on the internal market and competition' (Protocol to the Lisbon Treaty).

[79] Art. 119(1) TFEU.

[80] Art. 4(3)(2) TEU.

[81] Art. 4(3)(3) TEU.

undertakings is not totally clear. The extent to which Member States themselves may be liable under Articles 101 and 102 TFEU for granting special and exclusive rights to undertakings is still inconclusive. The right of Member States to grant special or exclusive rights is constrained by various Treaty provisions, including those mentioned above. There are some exemptions from the general application of Treaty provisions where the services concerned are of general economic interest or where revenue-producing monopolies are involved and the application of competition rules would obstruct the performance of particular assigned tasks. A competition test, however, still applies.[82] The Commission also has power to take action against a Member State that is involved in granting state aids that could distort competition.[83] There are exemptions for aids having a social character or provided, for example, in times of national disaster, or where economic development is abnormally low or unemployment high.[84]

10.3 United States

Historically there is far less involvement by government in commercial activities in the United States. State-owned enterprises do not form a significant part of the US economy.

There are statutory immunities or exemptions from some or all of the antitrust laws that are implemented or implied under laws and by courts, limitations on the full application of antitrust law as a consequence of the continued industry regulation, and a state action doctrine based in part on the workings of its federal system, which permits some anticompetitive conduct authorised or supervised by the state. Most of these exemptions have existed for a long time.

These exemptions were reviewed as part of work undertaken by the Antitrust Modernization Commission in 2007,[85] and the findings and recommendations of the Commission are largely consistent with the views expressed in other jurisdictions about appropriate coverage of competition laws.

---

[82] Art. 106(2) TFEU. See Case C-320/91 *Corbeau* [1993] ECR I-2533.

[83] Art. 107(1) TFEU.

[84] Art. 107(2) TFEU. The procedural powers of the Commission in this respect are contained in Council Regulation (EC) No. 659/1999 of 22 March 1999 laying down detailed rules for the application of Article 93 of the EC Treaty [now Article 108 TFEU] [1999] OJ L 83/1.

[85] See Antitrust Modernization Commission, 'Report and Recommendations' (2007), http://govinfo.library.unt.edu/amc/report_recommendation/amc_final_report.pdf (accessed December 2010).

The Commission concluded that statutory exemptions should be granted rarely, and only for so long as a clear case had been made that the conduct in question resulted in a public benefit.[86] Statutory exemptions should use the least anticompetitive method of achieving the regulatory objective. The Commission recommended that Congress review the exemptions with these objectives in mind.

In relation to regulated industries, the Commission concluded that antitrust law should continue to apply to the industry to the maximum extent possible.[87]

The state action doctrine was the subject of a recommendation by the Commission to the courts: that they should apply the doctrine more precisely and with greater attention to both Supreme Court precedents and potential consumer law harm from immunised conduct.[88]

10.4 Australia

Thorough consideration was given to the application of competition law to SOEs and government in Australia 16 years ago as part of a general review of competition policy. At that time, major government services such as electricity and port services were sheltered from international competition but provided key inputs to businesses competing both nationally and internationally. State government activities and a range of other persons and businesses were exempt mainly for constitutional reasons. Following the review, a National Competition Policy (NCP) was adopted. The Trade Practices Act (TPA) now applies to government bodies at all levels to the extent that they carry on business, and mirror state legislation provides back-up for those areas that cannot be constitutionally covered.[89]

NCP was clear on the application of the TPA: it should apply to all as a matter of policy and any exemptions should be granted only on demonstrated public interest grounds and following a transparent process of review and justification. [90]

---

[86] Id. recommendation 57. A full list of exemptions is appended to the Report at Annexure A to Ch IV. At this stage the recommendations have not been implemented.

[87] Id. recommendation 63.

[88] *Antitrust Modernization Commission*, id., recommendation 75.

[89] See, for example, *NT Power Generation Pty Ltd v Power and Water Authority & Anor.* [2004] HCA 48 (6 October 2004). Whether bodies are carrying on business will depend upon the nature of their activities, and they may be carrying on business in respect of some activities and not others.

[90] See 'National Competition Policy', Report of an independent inquire into the Trade Practices Act (so-called Hilmer Report) (1993), http://ncp.ncc.

Issues akin to administrative monopoly are dealt with in several ways. Two key principles of NCP adopted at that time were:

- competitive markets will generally serve the interests of consumers and the wider community by providing strong incentives for efficiency; and
- arrangements detracting from competition should be retained only if they can be shown to be in the public interest.

In summary, NCP provided for:

> the extension of the . . . TPA to previously excluded businesses to make them more commercially focussed and expose them to competitive pressure; regulatory arrangements to secure third-party access to 'essential' infrastructure services and, more generally, to guard against overcharging by monopoly service providers, especially in the infrastructure area; and a process for reviewing, and where appropriate amending or rescinding, a wide range of legislation which restricted competition.[91]

NCP was implemented through legislation, intergovernmental agreements and a package of financial incentives paid by the Australian government to the States and Territories.

By agreement, all existing laws were reviewed to see whether their anticompetitive aspects could be removed or were justified in the public interest. All new laws are reviewed prior to enactment to ensure that unnecessarily anticompetitive laws are not enacted. Specific exemptions are subject to a transparent process and must have a two-year sunset clause.

10.5 Singapore and Hong Kong

By way of contrast to other jurisdictions, the Competition Act of Singapore expressly does not apply to the Government, statutory bodies or anyone acting on their behalf. The Hong Kong Competition Law proposals for a competition law take a very broad approach to exempting government.

Neither of these countries has a comprehensive approach to dealing with areas of administrative monopoly.

---

gov.au/docs/Hilmer-001.pdf (accessed December 2010). See also Productivity Commission, 'Review of National Competition Policy Reforms', Productivity Commission Inquiry Report No. 33 (28 February 2005), http://www.pc.gov.au/__data/assets/pdf_file/0016/46033/ncp.pdf (accessed December 2010).

91 See Productivity Commission, id. at xi.

11 CASES UNDER THE AML INVOLVING SOEs AND GOVERNMENT

The first action under the AML was made in the area of administrative monopoly. The claim was against the General Administration of Quality Supervision, Inspection and Quarantine for the PRC (AQSIQ), a government body. The claim alleged that AQSIQ required companies to pay annual fees to register for an online quality monitoring network administered by a commercial company in which it had a 30 per cent stake breached the AML.[92] In other words, AQSIQ required the use of a technology in which it had a financial interest, to the detriment of other technologies, including the technology of the person making the complaint (the plaintiff). Beijing No. 1 People's Court ruled that the limitation period for the complaint under the Administrative Litigation Law had expired.[93] While there was some talk of an appeal, it was reported that the rule in question was ultimately withdrawn

A second case in Yuyao (Zhejiang Province) involved an accounting firm that alleged it was discriminated against when setting up a service centre for a new business. Its competitor, Yangming, was allowed to set up in an advantageous position despite a notice by the State Administration of Taxation to the effect that tax offices and tax agents were not allowed to share the same space. Yuyao complained, citing Article 8 and Chapter V of the AML. The matter was settled out of court with the municipal government promising equal space for Yuyao.[94]

A third case involved a complaint about a unilateral rate increase against the government-operated digital broadcaster in Hangzhou City.[95]

Another reported case involved action against China Mobile by Mr Zhou Ze alleging abuse of dominance. He had been paying 50 yuan per month as a rental fee under the 'GoTone' phone plan to lease a phone, but owned his own mobile. He argued that the lack of flexibility in the plan

---

92 O'Melveny & Myers LLP, 'The Antimonopoly Law Takes Effect', http://www.omm.com/the-anti-monopoly-law-takes-effect-08-07-2008/ (accessed 1 November 2008).

93 See 'Court turns down first Anti-Monopoly case' (5 September 2008) *China View*, http://news.xinhuanet.com/english/2008-09/05/content_9802041.htm (accessed December 2010).

94 P Jones, 'Initial Cases Under China's AML' (2008) *International Committee, ABA Section of Antitrust Law*, vol. 4, at 21.

95 No reports of its progress or resolution could be found.

was an indicator of abuse of China Mobile's dominant position.[96] The lawsuit conducted before the Beijing Dongcheng District People's Court in March 2009 demanded reimbursement of 1,200 yuan paid over the past two years and an order to cease charging users the monthly fees. The matter was reportedly settled in October 2009, with the claim withdrawn and a 1,000 yuan payment to Mr Zhou, characterised as a '. . . token of the company's gratitude for his suggestions'.[97]

The handling of these claims has provided no useful clues about the utility of the AML and the approach that will be taken to its enforcement in this area. Favourable outcomes appear to have been reached in the first two examples, however, outside the courtroom, apparently initiated by the impact of the complaints.

It does not appear at this stage that there has been a case successfully argued under the AML, and not against an SOE or in relation to administrative monopoly.

12 CONCLUSION

It has been suggested on more than one occasion that the approach of the Chinese to competition law is somewhat ambivalent. As one author puts it, while the statute that has been adopted looks 'Western', at a basic level the incentives to apply and enforce it are less compelling in China, and: 'This dichotomy between form and actual operation may also be attractive to Chinese officials because it provides a way of reducing conflicts and aligning interests among various elements of the bureaucracy.'[98]

Arguably the place of the AML against the background of the socialist market economy is the real point of distinction. The provisions of the AML as enacted are broad enough to encompass the activities of SOEs and government, but the AML contains a carve-out of indeterminate size

---

96 (6 April 2009) *Wall St J*, Technology News and Insights, http://www.wsj.com/digits/2009/04/06/anti-monopoly-law-inspires-consumer-suit-against-china-mobile (last visited September 2009).

97 B Perez and Reuters 'China Mobile settles monopoly case' (28 October 2009) *South China Morning Post* at B1.

98 See DJ Gerber, *supra* n. 24, at 298. See also Williams, *supra* n. 7, at 146, suggesting that the motivation could be 'reassertion of control by the bureaucracy over the wayward private sector'; cf. comments of W Blumenthal, General Counsel, Federal Trade Commission, 'Looking Towards Implementation of China's Anti-Monopoly Law: Remarks before the ABA Section of International Law', 2008 Spring Meeting, New York (4 April 2008), http://www.ftc.gov/speeches/blumenthal/20080404ABAIntlSecNYreChinaAML.pdf (accessed December 2010).

for the most important SOEs and also provides for the co-existence of regulated industries. What little indication there is in the AML suggests that other laws will have precedence over it in a number of situations. There are as yet no transparent principles indicating how these issues of precedence will be determined. These factors indicate that the Government still expects to play a significant role in market competition.

The provisions dealing with enforcement in relation to the general prohibitions and particularly to action in relation to administrative monopoly are cumbersome and fragmented. Despite the detailed provisions in relation to administrative monopoly, there are no real sanctions provided for it.

The traditional role of government in the economy, the significance of SOEs and the endemic nature of administrative monopoly make the application of the AML to government critical to the success of the AML as a robust and effective competition law. This chapter concludes that the true intentions of the legislators and the enforcement authorities are still unclear. Whether the supporting structures for the AML are suitable to the particular economic, legal and political environment, whether there is real ongoing commitment to the development of competitive markets in China, and whether these can truly develop against the background of its socialist market economy, are issues that are yet to be determined.

It is likely that it will be some time before the role and effectiveness of the AML in relation to government and its business activities can be comprehensively assessed.

9. Australia's criminalization of cartels: Will it be contagious?

Caron Beaton-Wells*

1 INTRODUCTION

The international movement in favour of criminal sanctions for 'serious' cartel conduct over the last decade has been well-documented.[1] In 2009, Australia became the latest convert in the campaign led by the United States to have this type of anti-competitive activity seen and dealt with as a crime. Australia's conversion may be taken as further evidence of 'common ground' if not convergence in both substantive antitrust law and enforcement strategy with respect to cartel conduct. However, it should be seen as commonality or convergence at the highest level of generality or abstraction only.[2] The Australian experience supports equally the view that the approach taken by a particular country in deciding whether to criminalize and, if so, how to define and enforce a cartel offence is likely to be distinctive in various respects. There will be multiple complex forces at work in such matters, requiring insight from at least the disciplines of political science, sociology, regulation, organizational behaviour, psychology and history, in addition to orthodox legal and economic analysis.[3]

---

* The author is grateful to Brent Fisse for comments on an earlier draft and to Christopher Tran for editorial and research assistance. Errors or omissions are the sole responsibility of the author.

[1] C Harding, 'Business Collusion as a Criminological Phenomenon: Exploring the Global Criminalisation of Cartels' (2006) 14 *Critical Criminology* 181.

[2] Perhaps as general as the principle that competition law should be effectively enforced: one of the 11 'emerging principles of international competition law' identified in C Noonan, *Emerging Principles of International Competition Law* (2008) 566.

[3] As attested to by the range of contributions in C Beaton-Wells and A Ezrachi (eds), *Criminalising Cartels: Critical Studies of an International Regulatory Movement* (2011).

This paper does not attempt to map exhaustively the Australian criminalization project to date.[4] Instead it focuses on three particular aspects or issues that have marked the process over a period of eight years:

- political prevarication and compromise (*infra* 3);
- legislative overreach and undue complexity (*infra* 4); and
- enforcement bifurcation and excessive discretion (*infra* 5).

These factors are not unique to the Australian experience. But an understanding of each and their interplay are central to understanding both the Australian decision to criminalize and also the ultimate statutory scheme and enforcement policy that have been established in Australia. Going forward, these factors will continue to be influential in the implementation of the new cartel regime and the determination of whether it delivers on the promise of greater deterrence of serious cartel conduct in the Australian economy.

It is concluded that Australia's decision to criminalize serious cartel conduct may prove infectious, at least to some countries that are geographically, economically, socially and legally proximate to Australia.[5] But those countries may be well advised to approach criminalization in a manner that vaccinates them from the pathology infecting Australia's new criminal cartel regime.[6] A degree of immunity may be secured by ensuring that definitional and enforcement issues are examined in detail early on, preferably at the same time that the general question of whether to criminalize is considered.

It may be useful first to outline the key tenets of Australia's new cartel regime.[7]

---

[4] Cf. the research project described at http://www.cartel.law.unimelb.edu.au (accessed December 2010).

[5] In 2010 it became apparent, for example, that New Zealand would follow Australia's suit in criminalizing cartel conduct: see Ministry of Economic Development (NZ), 'Cartel Criminalisation, Discussion Document' (January 2010).

[6] See C Beaton-Wells and B Fisse, 'The Cartel Offences: An Elemental Pathology', http://denning.law.ox.ac.uk/lawvle/users/ezrachia/CCLP%20L%2022%20Beaton-Wells%20%20Fisse.pdf (accessed December 2010).

[7] For a detailed critique of the regime, see C Beaton-Wells and B Fisse, *Australian Cartel Regulation: Law, Policy and Practice in an International Context* (2011).

2 THE NEW CARTEL REGIME

Australia's long-standing civil prohibitions on cartel conduct are in s 45 of the Trade Practices Act 1974 (TP Act). Section 45 covers not only 'contracts' but also 'arrangements' and 'understandings', to which at least two of the parties must be competitors. The terms 'contract', 'arrangement' and 'understanding' have been interpreted as representative of a spectrum of consensual dealings,[8] ranging from the most formal and explicit at the 'contract' end to the most informal and implicit at the 'understanding' end. No significant distinction has been drawn between an 'arrangement' and an 'understanding' and, importantly, both require an undertaking of some form of commitment or obligation by one or more of the parties.[9] In 2007, in an attempt to widen the scope of the prohibition to address tacit collusion, the regulator, the Australian Competition and Consumer Commission (ACCC), proposed amendments to remove commitment as a condition of establishing an 'understanding'.[10] That proposal was criticized heavily by commentators[11] and was overtaken in 2010 by a proposal by the Australian Government to introduce new prohibitions on information disclosures and signalling by competitors.[12]

The focus of Australia's cartel prohibitions is on a provision contained in the contract, arrangement or understanding. Per se liability under s 45 attached to a price fixing provision[13] or an exclusionary provision.[14] Otherwise the provision must be shown to have the purpose, effect or likely effect of substantially lessening competition in a market within Australia.[15] It is a contravention either to make a contract, arrangement

---

8 *ACCC v Leahy Petroleum Pty Ltd* (2007) FCR 321, 331 para 24.

9 *Apco Service Stations Pty Ltd v ACCC* (2005) 159 FCR 452, 464 para 47.

10 ACCC, 'Report: Petrol Prices and Australian Consumers: Report of the ACCC into the price of unleaded petrol' (December 2007) at 228–89, http://www.accc.gov.au/content/item.phtml?itemId=806216&nodeId=d5fc6a56fb589b453abc58f22e0b78bd&fn=Petrol%20prices%20and%20Australian%20consumers%20all%20chapters.pdf (accessed December 2010).

11 See Australian Government – The Treasury, 'Discussion paper – Meaning of "understanding" in the Trade Practices Act 1974' (2009), and submissions to this Discussion paper, available at: http://www.treasury.gov.au/contentitem.asp?NavId=037&ContentID=1459 (accessed December 2010).

12 See C Beaton-Wells and B Fisse, 'The Competition and Consumer Amendment Bill (No. 1) (Exposure Draft): A Problematic Attempt to Prohibit Information Disclosure' (2011) 39(1) *Austr Bus L Rev* 28.

13 As defined in TP Act, s 45A.

14 As defined in TP Act, s 4D.

15 TP Act, ss 45(2)(a)(ii), 45(2)(b)(ii).

or understanding containing such a provision or to give effect to such a provision contained in a contract, arrangement or understanding.

The amendments brought about by the Trade Practices Amendment (Cartel Conduct and Other Measures) Act 2008 (CC & OM Act) introduce cartel offences and a new set of parallel civil per se prohibitions. The general provisions of s 45 remain, although the per se prohibition on price fixing has been removed as this is the subject of one of the new per se prohibitions.

The new offences and civil per se prohibitions reflect the 1998 OECD *Recommendation of the Council concerning Effective Action against Hard-Core Cartels* in that they are addressed to four types of provisions, broadly categorized as involving price fixing, output restriction, market allocation and bid rigging.[16] These types of provisions are classified as 'cartel provisions'.[17] It is now an offence – subject to proof of the mental (fault) elements referred to below – or a civil per se violation to make a contract, arrangement or understanding that contains a cartel provision or to give effect to a cartel provision contained in a contract, arrangement or understanding.[18] The only difference in the elements of the offences and the civil prohibitions is that the former require the proof of certain mental elements generally associated with criminal provisions, namely the intention to make a contract or arrangement or arrive at an understanding, or to give effect to a cartel provision with the knowledge or belief that the cartel provision is contained in a contract, arrangement or understanding.

There is a range of exceptions and defences that will apply to conduct that otherwise would be subject to the new statutory prohibitions, criminal and civil.[19] Exemption or immunity may be obtained for provisions in contracts, arrangements or understandings on a case-by-case basis through the long-standing authorization or notification processes in Pt VII of the TP Act.[20] Notification in this context is available only for collective bargaining and then only for contracts where the total value of the transactions under the contract over a 12-month period will not exceed

---

16 C(98)35/FINAL (14 May 1998) 3, http://www.oecd.org/dataoecd/39/4/2350130.pdf (accessed December 2010).

17 As defined in TP Act, s 44ZZRD.

18 Despite the fact that the amendments will not be retrospective, there is no temporal limitation on the idea of giving effect in this context. Conceivably, therefore, it could catch conduct that gives effect to an agreement reached in the distant past.

19 See TP Act, Pt IV Div 1 sub-Div D.

20 See the exceptions for conduct notified and cartel provisions subject to a grant of authorization in TP Act, ss 44ZZRL-44ZZRM.

AU$3 million.[21] In addition, pre-existing exemptions from the per se prohibition on price fixing continue for provisions in relation to the price of goods or services to be collectively acquired or for the joint advertising of the price for the re-supply of goods or services collectively acquired.[22]

Exemptions also aim to prevent overlap between the various prohibitions under the TP Act. For example, exemptions remove an agreement that involves a vertical exclusive dealing or resale price maintenance provision from the per se compass of the cartel prohibitions and allow it to be dealt with under the prohibitions specific to such restraints.[23] The main exception to the cartel offences and new civil prohibitions is for joint venture activity. This exception is confined to contracts that relate to the joint production and supply of goods or services.[24]

A dual criminal/civil regime with wide-ranging offences and prohibitions and substantial overlap between them means that policy and enforcement outcomes depend on the exercise of prosecutorial discretion by enforcement agencies. Those agencies are the body responsible for the enforcement of the TP Act, the ACCC and the general centralized prosecutions agency responsible for prosecutions of all indictable federal offences in Australia, the Commonwealth Director of Public Prosecutions (DPP).[25]

The roles of and relationship between these agencies in the context of the new cartel regime are outlined in a Memorandum of Understanding (ACCC/DPP MOU).[26] Under the ACCC/DPP MOU, in broad terms, the ACCC is responsible for investigation and the DPP for prosecution.[27]

The ACCC retains its coercive information-gathering powers for the purposes of criminal investigations.[28] It may also draw on its entry, search

---

21 TP Act, ss 93AB-93A.

22 TP Act, s 44ZZRV.

23 TP Act, ss 44ZZRR-44ZZRS.

24 TP Act, ss 44ZZRO-44ZZRP. A person will not be entitled to rely on the defence in relation to the cartel offences unless they have given the prosecutor certain information within 28 days after the day of committal for trial (s 44ZZRO(2)).

25 http://www.cdpp.gov.au (accessed December 2010).

26 'Memorandum of Understanding between the Commonwealth Director of Public Prosecutions and the Australian Competition and Consumer Commission regarding Serious Cartel Conduct' (2009), http://www.accc.gov.au/content/item.phtml?itemId=882220&nodeId=ef73337d44a8c8ee9ffd593f93cb0699&fn=Memorandum%20of%20understanding%20%20between%20CDPP%20and%20ACCC.pdf (accessed December 2010).

27 Id. at paras 2.2–2.3.

28 TP Act, s 155.

and seizure powers that have been broadened by the CC & OM Act.[29] In addition, for criminal investigations, the ACCC has new surveillance and telecommunications interception powers that it will use in joint operations with the Australian Federal Police.[30]

Both corporations and individuals may be liable for cartel offences under the TP Act. Individuals may be liable either as primary offenders or as accessories to an offence committed by a corporation. For corporations, upon conviction, the maximum fine is the greatest of AU$10 million; three times the total value of benefits reasonably attributable to the offence; or if unascertainable, 10 per cent of the corporation's annual turnover over a 12-month period.[31] For individuals, conviction for a cartel offence exposes them to a maximum fine of AU$220,000 and/or a maximum term of ten years' imprisonment.[32] Disqualification orders are also available.[33]

Provision has been made for bars on proceedings and use of evidence to minimize double jeopardy concerns under a dual civil/criminal regime for substantially the same conduct.[34] While the Federal Court of Australia has primary jurisdiction to determine cases brought under the TP Act,[35] for constitutional reasons relating to Australia's federal system, State and Territory courts traditionally have dealt with all criminal offences, including offences under Commonwealth legislation. In a further significant development associated with Australia's criminalization of serious cartel conduct, jurisdiction to deal with indictable criminal offences is to be conferred upon the Federal Court for the first time to enable it to hear cartel trials.[36] As indictable offences, the constitutionally guaranteed right to a jury trial will apply,[37] and unanimous verdicts based on proof beyond a reasonable doubt will be necessary for conviction.

---

29 TP Act, Pt XID.

30 See ACCC, 'ACCC Approach to Cartel Investigations' (July 2009) at para 28, http://www.accc.gov.au/content/item.phtml?itemId=882220&nodeId=cd1644c035c1d07db8c9ce05b09e21fd&fn=Guideline%20-%20ACCC%20approach%20to%20cartel%20investigations.pdf (accessed December 2010).

31 TP Act, ss 44ZZRF(3), 44ZZRG(3).

32 TP Act, s 79.

33 TP Act, ss 86E, 44ZZRI.

34 TP Act, s 76B.

35 TP Act, s 86(1).

36 Federal Court of Australia Amendment (Criminal Jurisdiction) Bill 2008 (Cth). For the submissions to and report by the Senate Standing Committee on Legal and Constitutional Affairs on the Bill: see http://www.aph.gov.au/senate/committee/legcon_ctte/criminal_jurisdiction/index.htm (accessed 29 May 2009).

37 See Commonwealth Constitution, s 80.

3 POLITICAL PREVARICATION AND COMPROMISE

Since at least the mid-1990s, competition policy in broad terms has enjoyed bipartisan support in Australia, as well as support at both the Commonwealth (federal) and State and Territory levels of government. Historically, however, Conservative governments in Australia have resisted tough penalties for anti-competitive conduct, particularly criminal penalties.[38] Perhaps unsurprisingly, therefore, the criminalizing legislation has been passed in 2009 on the watch of a Labour government.

While the idea was born in the term of a Conservative government, it was both hatched and championed, not by the government, but by the ACCC.[39] That the then conservative government fell into line, albeit reluctantly, was in large part owing to the high profile and strong public support for the fiercely independent regulator under its then leader, the charismatic Professor Allan Fels.[40] The ACCC called for criminalization in a submission to a government-instigated review of Australia's competition legislation by an independent committee (Dawson Committee) in 2002.[41] In 2003 the then Treasurer accepted 'in principle' the recommendation of the Dawson Committee,[42] albeit emphasizing the need for any new criminal penalty regime not to impose 'significant additional uncertainty and complexity for business' and to 'work well in the context of the Australian legal system'.[43] The process adopted subsequently to develop the legislative proposals was marked by secrecy, obfuscation and delay.[44]

A working party was appointed and reported to the government in

---

[38] See C Beaton-Wells, 'The Politics of Cartel Criminalisation: A Pessimistic View from Australia' (2008) 29 *ECLR* 185, at 187 et seq.

[39] See C Beaton-Wells, 'Criminalising Cartels: Australia's Slow Conversion' (2008) 31 *World Comp* 205.

[40] See generally F Brenchley, *Allan Fels: A Portrait of Power* (2003).

[41] Australian Competition and Consumer Commission, 'Submission to the Trade Practices Act Review Committee' (June 2002) 51–2, http://tpareview.treasury.gov.au/submissions.asp (accessed December 2010).

[42] See Trade Practices Review Committee, 'Review of the Competition Provisions of the Trade Practices Act' (2003) at 161 et seq. http://tpareview.treasury.gov.au/content/report/downloads/PDF/Chpt10.pdf (accessed December 2010).

[43] Treasurer, 'Commonwealth Government Response to the Review of the Competition Provisions of the Trade Practices Act 1974' (2003), http://www.treasurer.gov.au/Ministers/phc/Content/publications/pub_downloads/TPAResponse.pdf (accessed December 2010).

[44] Cf. the process in Britain in relation to the creation of a cartel offence under the Enterprise Act 2002, s 188, as summarized in Beaton-Wells, *supra* n. 38, at 191.

2004.[45] It did not call for submissions publicly and the extent of its consultation beyond the bodies represented upon it (those being the ACCC, DPP and the responsible government department, the Treasury) is not clear. It did not release its report or its recommendations for public consideration and a subsequent request for access to its report under freedom of information legislation was refused.[46] No public discussion paper was issued,[47] nor a reference made to the highly respected Australian Law Reform Commission (ALRC).[48]

The Treasurer outlined the legislative proposals in a sketchy 13-page press release in 2005.[49] Significantly, it was proposed that the new cartel offence include an element of dishonesty (akin to the offence in the Enterprise Act 2002). This particular aspect of the proposal signalled ambivalence on the part of the government as to the moral basis for criminalization and a concern about the challenges of communicating the criminality of cartel conduct to others.[50] Further indicia of political wavering were found in the proposed penalties for individual offenders and the questions as to whether the ACCC would have the necessary powers and resources to enforce the new criminal provisions.[51] An exposure draft of the Bill was not released for comment and the Bill was not introduced to Parliament before a federal election intervened and the Bill lapsed.

Significantly, in the course of the election campaign, the ACCC scored a major victory with record-breaking penalties against a cartel in the

---

[45] Treasurer, 'Working Party to Examine Criminal Sanctions for Cartel Behaviour', Press Release (3 October 2003), http://www.treasurer.gov.au/tsr/content/pressreleases/2003/086.asp (accessed 29 May 2009).

[46] See *Fisse v Secretary, Department of the Treasury* (2008) 172 FCR 513. The report was released in December 2010 in response to a second request, and is available at http://www.brentfisse.com/publications.html (accessed January 2011).

[47] Cf. the policy on best practice processes in regulation issued by the Australian Government's Office of Best Practice Regulation, http://www.obpr.gov.au/consultation.html (accessed December 2010).

[48] See recently Australian Law Reform Commission, 'Principled Regulation: Federal Civil and Administrative Penalties in Australia', Report No. 95 (2002); Australian Law Reform Commission, 'Same Crime, Same Time: Sentencing of Federal Offenders', Report No. 103 (2006).

[49] Treasurer, 'Criminal Penalties for Serious Cartel Behaviour', Press Release (2 February 2005), www.treasurer.gov.au/tsr/content/pressreleases/2005/004.asp (accessed December 2010).

[50] See the discussion of dishonesty as an indicium of moral wrongfulness in C Beaton-Wells, 'Capturing the Criminality of Hard-Core Cartels: The Australian Proposal' (2007) 31 *Melb U L Rev* 675, at 694–701.

[51] See the discussion in Beaton-Wells, *supra* n. 38, at 193 et seq.

cardboard packaging industry.[52] It took down Visy Ltd, one of Australia's largest manufacturing companies, and, with it, Australia's fourth richest man, renowned philanthropist, political donor and Visy Chairman, Richard Pratt. In the media frenzy that accompanied the announcement of the settlement and Pratt's public apology, the then Prime Minister John Howard praised the Visy Chairman for his contributions to Australian business and society and not coincidentally, it may seem, at the same time declined to re-commit the government to criminalization.[53]

The then Labour opposition capitalized on the political opportunity to voice its public support for criminalization, promising if elected to introduce criminal penalties in its first year in office.[54] Upon election, consistent with a general commitment to renewing competition policy in Australia, the Labour Government appointed the country's first Minister for Competition Policy and Consumer Affairs – Christopher Bowen. With the change from a Conservative to a Labour government came a change in the approach taken to the development of the criminalizing legislation. While remaining inherently political and hence imperfect from the standpoint of principle, there was a clear shift from an approach marked by ambivalence and prevarication to one of consultation and compromise.

In keeping with his party's election promise, Bowen released an Exposure Draft Bill of the criminalizing legislation, together with a discussion paper and a draft of the ACCC/DPP MOU, in January 2008.[55] In particular, he sought submissions on the questions as to whether dishonesty should be an element of the new offence and whether the ACCC should have telecommunications interception powers.[56] The submissions on both questions were divided,[57] but also raised a host of other complex legal and practical issues relevant to the proposed legislation.[58] So began a

---

[52] See *ACCC v Visy Industries Holdings Pty Ltd [No. 3]* (2007) 244 ALR 673.

[53] See 'PM back-pedals on cartel penalties' (10 October 2007) *Austr Fin Rev* 1.

[54] C Bowen, 'Howard and Costello take conflicting positions on criminal penalties for cartel behaviour' (Press Release, 9 October 2007), http://www.alp.org.au/media/1007/msat090.php (accessed 29 May 2009).

[55] See Treasury, 'Criminal penalties for serious cartel conduct: Draft Legislation' (11 January 2008), http://www.treasury.gov.au/contentitem.asp?NavId=037&ContentID=1330 (accessed December 2010).

[56] See Treasury, 'Criminal penalties for serious cartel conduct: Discussion Paper' (11 January 2008), http://www.treasury.gov.au/documents/1330/PDF/Cartels_Bill_Discussion_paper.pdf (accessed December 2010).

[57] The submissions are available at http://www.treasury.gov.au/contentitem.asp?ContentID=1350&NavID=037 (accessed December 2010).

[58] For a detailed critique of the issues, see C Beaton-Wells and B Fisse,

protracted and, at times, heated process of consultation and revision, the results of which were finalized only 18 months later.

In October 2008 Bowen released a second Exposure Draft Bill.[59] Dishonesty had been removed, it having been conceded that such an element would be problematic from an enforcement perspective.[60] The ACCC would have telecommunications interception powers, and in a further sign that the Labour Government was seeking to remove any doubt about its criminalization credentials, the proposed maximum jail term had been lifted from five to ten years. Australia was thus to stand shoulder-to-shoulder in this regard with the world's leading criminal cartel-buster, the United States.[61]

However, despite the consultative stance, Bowen found himself fending off criticisms on account of failure to address many of the issues highlighted in the first round of consultations. In particular, the much-criticized breadth of the proposed cartel offences and their mirror civil prohibitions was not off-set by important exceptions and defences.[62] Moreover, concerns remained as to how the involvement of the DPP would affect the operation of the ACCC Immunity Policy, another issue highlighted early in the year but on which there had been no further announcement.[63]

'Criminalising Serious Cartel Conduct: Issues of Law and Policy' (2008) 36 Austr Bus L Rev 166.

59 See Treasury, 'Trade Practices Amendment (Cartel Conduct and Other Measures) Bill 2008' (27 October 2008), http://www.treasury.gov.au/contentitem.asp?ContentID=1426&NavID=037 (accessed December 2010)

60 See P Pyburne, 'Trade Practices Amendment (Cartel Conduct and Other Measures) Bill 2008' (Bills Digest No. 90, 2008–09, 4 February 2009) at 6 et seq. http://www.aph.gov.au/library/pubs/bd/2008-09/09bd090.pdf (accessed December 2010). For a more thorough critique see B Fisse, 'The Cartel Offence: Dishonesty?' (2007) 35 *Austr Bus L Rev* 235.

61 See Commonwealth, 'Parliamentary Debates', House of Representatives (3 December 2008) 12310 (C Bowen, Minister for Competition Policy and Consumer Affairs), http://parlinfo.aph.gov.au/parlInfo/search/display/display.w3p;adv=;db=;group=;holdingType=;id=;orderBy=;page=1;query=Title%3Acartel%20Database%3Achamber%20Title%3A%22second%20reading%22%3F%20%20Context_Phrase%3Abill%3F%20Speaker%3A%3F;querytype=;rec=12;resCount=Default (accessed December 2010).

62 See, for example, the comments of N Berkovic, 'Practices bank on anti-cartel law bonanza' (31 October 2008) *The Australian* 31.

63 This was an issue highlighted in several of the submissions in response to the first Exposure Draft of the Bill released in January, available at: http://www.treasury.gov.au/contentitem.asp?ContentID=1350&NavID=037 (accessed December 2010). See further C Beaton-Wells, 'Forks in the Road: Challenges Facing the ACCC's Immunity Policy for Cartel Conduct: Part 1' (2008) 16 *Comp & Cons LJ* 71, at 75–91.

Yet more consultations were embarked upon. Then, on 3 December 2008 – still within its first year of office – the Government fulfilled its promise, introducing the CC & OM Bill into Parliament.[64] The Bill reinstated the so-called anti-overlap exemption for vertical conduct that had been missing from the Exposure Drafts. At the same time, a revised MOU between the ACCC and DPP was released and adjustments made to both the ACCC's Immunity Policy and the DPP's Prosecution Policy to address the immunity issue.[65] Even so, the critics would not be silenced.

The Bill was referred to a Senate Economics Committee that received submissions and held a public hearing. In this process two issues dominated. The first was whether the proposed scheme differentiated adequately between conduct warranting criminal treatment and conduct to be treated as a civil contravention. The second was whether the proposed joint venture exception was too narrowly drawn. The Committee was not persuaded that either of these issues necessitated amendments to the Bill and recommended that it be passed unamended.[66] However, it did recommend that the ACCC prepare guidelines to ameliorate uncertainty about the approach that will be taken to enforcement of the dual criminal/civil regime.[67]

The CC & OM Bill was passed on 16 June 2009 and took effect on 28 July 2009. Its enactment marks one of the most dramatic and potentially far-reaching reforms of Australian competition law. Yet, despite extensive consultation, compromise and consequential amendment, the Government remains subject to scathing criticism by commentators in relation to the reform. Much of the criticism is directed at the so-called issue of overreach of the statutory scheme and the perceived failure of the policy-makers and the legislative drafters to define sufficiently narrowly and clearly the conduct to be criminalized. Dishearteningly no doubt for

64 Parliamentary Debates, *supra* n. 61, at 12309.

65 See ACCC/DPP MOU, *supra* n. 557; ACCC, 'Immunity Policy for Cartel Conduct' (2009), http://www.accc.gov.au/content/index.phtml/itemId/879795 (accessed December 2010); DPP, 'Prosecution Policy of the Commonwealth' (1992) at paras 2.7–2.10, http://www.cdpp.gov.au/Publications/ProsecutionPolicy/ProsecutionPolicy.pdf (accessed December 2010).

66 The Committee's report is vulnerable to criticism for its superficial treatment of the issues and weak conclusions: see J Clarke, 'Review misses bill's key point' (21 April 2009) *Austr Fin Rev* 26.

67 Senate Standing Committee on Economics, 'Report on the Trade Practices Amendment (Cartel Conduct and Other Measures) Bill 2008' (2009), at para 4.11 Recommendation 1, at http://www.aph.gov.au/senate/Committee/economics_ctte/tpa_cartels_09/report/report.pdf (accessed December 2010).

the Government, this failing prompted calls to 'return to the drawing board' and to delay the process further in the interests of 'getting it right'.[68]

4 LEGISLATIVE OVERREACH AND UNDUE COMPLEXITY

Complaints about the overly inclusive and complex nature of the new cartel regime are not novel in the context of Australian competition law, even if they are heightened in the context of the introduction of a criminal regime. In fact, they are symptoms of entrenched and distinctive features of the approach taken to competition legislation generally in this country, relating both to the substance of the law as well as to the style of its drafting.

4.1 Legislative Substance

There is a history of formulating prohibitions for the TP Act that are overreaching in their terms and/or attach per se liability in circumstances in which it is arguably not warranted. In the cartel context, this is no more true than of the long-standing per se prohibition on exclusionary provisions.[69] Paraphrasing, an exclusionary provision is defined as a provision that has the purpose of preventing or limiting dealings with third parties.[70] The essential flaw in this formulation is that it imposes a per se ban on conduct that is not necessarily anti-competitive or without any redeeming economic or social virtue in the sense generally assumed to attract strict liability in antitrust law.[71] Not surprisingly, the application of the prohibition has generated some strange results, most notably in the context of assessing whether it should prohibit sporting authorities from deciding which players and how many teams to have in their competitions.[72]

---

[68] See, for example, 'Legal experts urge delay on ACCC cartel power boost' (17 February 2009) *Business Spectator*; 'Council attacks cartel proposal' (15 May 2009) *The Australian* 29; R Miller, 'Cartel bill risks tying up the courts' (8 May 2009) *The Australian* 28.

[69] Another example is the per se prohibition on third line forcing in TP Act, s 47.

[70] See the full definition in TP Act, s 4D.

[71] The classic statement on the rationale for per se illegality is found in *Northern Pacific Railway v US* 356 US 1, 5 (1958). See also F Easterbrook, 'The Limits of Antitrust' (1984) 63 *Tex L Rev* 1; J Baker, 'Per se rules in the antitrust analysis of horizontal restraints' (1991) 36 *Antitrust Bull* 641.

[72] See generally I Wylie, 'What is an Exclusionary Provision? Newspapers, Rugby League, Liquor and Beyond' (2007) 35 *Austr Bus L Rev* 33.

The scope of the prohibition has been criticized.[73] Recommendations that it be narrowed have been ignored.[74] The problem has been aggravated by the absence of sufficient exceptions or defences to the prohibition to recognize and balance competing policy interests. The anti-overlap exemptions referred to above have their limitations (for example, they do not save supply agreements between competitors from the per se reach of s 45),[75] and a joint venture exception involving a competition test was introduced only in 2007.[76] Moreover, a broader doctrine or defence of ancillary restraints, excluding from per se liability anti-competitive conduct that is ancillary to cooperative efficiency-enhancing activity, is foreign to Australian competition law.[77]

The reason for this in large part is because competition and economic efficiency are treated as two separate concepts under the TP Act. Competition assessments are the province of the statutory prohibitions enforced by the courts, whereas more general efficiency assessments are the domain of the administrative agencies empowered to exempt conduct from the prohibitions under a procedure of authorization.[78] Moreover, the availability of authorization has not been seen as a satisfactory response to the overreach of the per se prohibition on exclusionary provisions. As a matter of principle, it has been argued, legitimate business conduct should not be subject to a procedure that requires parties to demonstrate public benefits when the conduct may not be even anti-competitive and that imposes conditions and time limitations on the protection that is granted. Authorization is also impractical, imposing costs, delays, public-

---

[73] See, for example, C Oddie and L McKeown, 'Joint Ventures and exclusionary provisions: Anticompetitive purpose or unintended effects?' (2002) 10 *Comp & Cons LJ* 192; W Pengilley, *Price Fixing and Exclusionary Provisions* (2001) at pt 10.

[74] See the recommendations in Trade Practices Review Committee, *supra* n. 42, at 127 et seq. Recommendations 8.1–8.2.

[75] See B Fisse, 'Unjustified Per Se Criminal and Civil Liability under the Trade Practices Act 1974 (Cth) for Supply Agreements between Competitors' (2009) 15 *UNSW LJ* 17.

[76] TP Act, s 76C.

[77] See generally PE Areeda and H Hovenkamp, *Antitrust Law: An Analysis of Antitrust Principles and Their Application* (2nd edn, 2005) Vol XI, 19B, at 61 et seq. 1904 et seq.; J Faull and A Nikpay, *The EC Law of Competition* (2007) at paras 3.181–3.214.

[78] While some commentators have argued against retention of this separation and for explicit incorporation of efficiencies into judicial analysis (see, for example, P Williams and G Woodbridge, 'The Relation of Efficiencies to the Substantial Lessening of Competition Test for Mergers: Substitutes or Complements?' (2002) 30 *Austr Bus L Rev* 435), the argument appears to have little traction in wider circles.

ity and uncertainty in circumstances in which such imposts are evidently unwarranted.[79]

The approach that has been taken in formulating the new cartel offences and civil per se prohibitions not only perpetuates the problems with the per se prohibition on exclusionary provisions but aggravates it given the imposition of criminal liability. The difficulties are compounded by the new overlapping civil per se prohibitions and those relating to output restriction and market allocation in particular.[80] Illustrations of conduct inappropriately caught by these overreaching prohibitions proliferate.[81] The overreach is not cured by the anti-overlap exemptions or the authorization procedure, for the reasons cited above. This is even more so in the context of the cartel offences given the importance of confining indictable offences to unambiguously serious conduct.[82] Further, there is no apparent prospect of the prohibitions being judicially 'read down'. In Australia, where the same statutory language is used for both criminal and civil prohibitions, the same interpretation must be adopted in both contexts.[83]

The disquiet caused by the scope of the prohibitions has been heightened by the approach taken to formulation of the joint venture exception. The exception does not involve a competition test.[84] While this may be explicable in relation to the cartel offences, it does not explain why the test has been removed in relation to the new civil per se prohibitions (while it remains in relation to the joint venture exception for exclusionary provisions).[85] The exception is also confined to joint ventures formalized in contracts, or arrangements or understandings intended to have

---

[79] See the criticisms in W Pengilley, 'Collective boycotts under the Australian Trade Practices Act: What our policy-makers have failed to understand and what the Dawson Committee should do about it' (2002) 10 *Comp & Cons LJ* 144, at 184.

[80] Apparently s 4D is being retained 'as a backstop for the new cartel provisions' given that it is wider in scope. See M Bezzi, 'The conduct of cartel litigation: The ACCC enforcement perspective on serious cartels – some key issues and practical considerations', Paper presented at the Competition Law Conference, Sydney (23 May 2009) at 4.

[81] See Law Council of Australia, 'Submission to Senate Standing Committee on Economics on the Trade Practices Amendment (Cartel Conduct and Other Measures) Bill 2008' (30 January 2009) at 10 para 20, http://www.aph.gov.au/senate/committee/economics_ctte/tpa_cartels_09/submissions/sub10.pdf (accessed December 2010); Beaton-Wells and Fisse, *supra* n. 6, Attachment 1.

[82] A Ashworth, *Principles of Criminal Law* (5th edn, 2006) 40–44.

[83] *Waugh v Kippen* (1986) 160 CLR 156, 165.

[84] TP Act, ss 44ZZRO, 44ZRP.

[85] TP Act, s 76C.

contractual effect. The ACCC argued that this was necessary to prevent firms from escaping liability through the construction of sham joint ventures.[86] However, of equal concern is that it exposes to liability (criminal and civil) firms that make an arrangement or arrive at an understanding that contains a cartel provision or give effect to a cartel provision in the negotiation or implementation of a legitimate joint venture.[87] Limited also to joint venture activity involving production or supply, the exception excludes joint ventures that exclusively involve acquisition, marketing or research and development activity.[88]

The limitations on the joint venture exception have few, if any, justifications on policy or practical grounds. But they are consistent with a tradition of overreach in the Australian formulation of cartel prohibitions. They are also consistent with a prescriptive black-letter law style of statutory drafting that reflects a rule-based rather than a principle-based approach to regulation.[89] This approach in turn reflects shallow faith in the judiciary's capacity to distinguish conduct that the legislature intended to be banned from conduct that is 'innocent' from a competition perspective.

4.2 Legislative Style

The second feature of Australian competition law that is relevant in understanding the debate over the CC & OM Act relates to the style of statutory drafting. Consistent with many other Australian statutes, the TP Act employs a complex, prescriptive, prolix style of drafting. As a result of attempting to define minutely all possibilities and close off any escape routes, most of the provisions are replete with double negatives, proliferating alternatives, multiple cross-references, extensive qualifications and complex statutory interrelationships. The drafting has been criticized

---

[86] ACCC, 'Submission to Senate Standing Committee on Economics on the Trade Practices Amendment (Cartel Conduct and Other Measures) Bill 2008' (12 February 2009) at 5, http://www.aph.gov.au/senate/Committee/economics_ctte/tpa_cartels_09/submissions/sub12.pdf (accessed December 2010).

[87] See B Fisse, 'The Contract Requirement for the Joint Venture Exceptions under Sections 44ZZRO and 44ZZRP of the Cartel Bill' (2009) 17 *Comp & Cons LJ* 22.

[88] See Law Council of Australia, *supra* n. 81, at 7–9. Cf. Supplementary Explanatory Memorandum, 'Trade Practices Amendment (Cartel Conduct and Other Measures) Bill 2008', at paras 1.9–1.11.

[89] J Black, 'Forms and Paradoxes of Principles Based Regulation', LSE Legal Studies Working Paper No. 13/2008, http://papers.ssrn.com/sol3/papers.cfm?abstract_id=1267722 (accessed November 2009).

by both commentators and judges,[90] and provokes comparisons with the brevity that is a hallmark of the prohibitions of the US, the EC and Canada.[91]

The effect of this drafting style is that parties and judges often focus more on semantic parsing and textual analysis than on the fundamental purposes and concepts underlying the legislation.[92] The result is a word-based rather than an outcome-based approach to application of the prohibitions. The reasons for this style of drafting reflect the original concern that judges, unfamiliar with this field of law, would struggle with the economic concepts and theories of antitrust.[93] That fear was borne out in the early years with judges resorting to the dictionary[94] and displaying hostility to the reception of expert evidence from economists.[95] However, that time has passed. There is now a substantial body of jurisprudence in which the basic concepts and purposes of the TP Act have been extrapolated in accordance with mainstream economic theory. There is also now a well-established pool of judges with experience in hearing TP Act cases. To assist, there has been a concerted and sustained effort on the part of the judiciary, together with practitioners and economists, to develop constructive approaches to expert evidence in such cases.[96] In light of this, there is a good case for the view that 'a statute written for interpretation by the judiciary some 30 or 40 years ago might well be quite inappropriate for a statute to be interpreted by our present judiciary'.[97]

That view is not reflected, however, in the provisions of the CC & OM Act. These provisions perpetuate the highly prescriptive and complex

---

[90] See, for example, the comments in *Trade Practices Commission v Tooth & Co Ltd* (1979) 142 CLR 197, 409 (Stephen J); *Visy Paper Pty Ltd v ACCC* (2003) 216 CLR 1; M Brunt, 'Preface' in R Steinwall (ed), *25 Years of Australian Competition Law* (2000) xiii; W Pengilley, 'Thirty Years of the Trade Practices Act: Some Thematic Conclusions' (2004) 12 *Comp & Cons LJ* 1, at 20 et seq.

[91] See, for example, s 45 of the Canadian Competition Act 1985 as amended in 2009, with effect from March 2010.

[92] Pengilley, *supra* n. 90, at 9.

[93] See, for example, M Brunt, 'Lawyers and Competition Policy' in D Hambly and J Goldring (eds), *Australian Lawyers and Social Change* (1976) 266.

[94] See, for example, *Top Performance Motors Pty Ltd v Ira Berk (Qld) Pty Ltd* (1975) 24 FLR 286, 289.

[95] See, for example, *Hecar Investments No. 6 Pty Ltd v Outboard Marine Australia Pty Ltd* (1982) ATPR 40–298, 43,704; *Trade Practices Commission v Australia Meat Holdings Pty Ltd* (1988) ATPR 40–876, 49,479.

[96] For a summary of the development in the approach taken to expert evidence in trade practices cases, see C Beaton-Wells, *Proof of Antitrust Markets* (2003) Ch. 7.

[97] Pengilley, *supra* n. 90, at 9.

drafting style of the existing provisions – the definition of 'cartel provision' runs for 6 pages of dense statutory text including 11 subsections, 36 paragraphs, and 1908 words, suggesting that the legislative drafters are impervious to the criticisms that have been made to date. In the debate over the CC & OM Bill, commentators were critical of the drafting, pointing to the unacceptable level of uncertainty caused for the business people subject to it.[98] The uncertainty will extend also to those charged with applying the law – judges and, in the context of the cartel offences, juries. Evidently, little thought was given by the drafters to the formidable challenge that will arise in preparing comprehensible jury directions. Even if that challenge is met, as one commentator has foreshadowed (tongue in cheek), there is 'a high possibility that . . . the foreman of a jury in a cartel-related criminal trial may well declare a not-guilty verdict with the additional comment to the court that the jury so found because it could not understand the law under which the accused was tried'.[99]

Two further consequences flow from the approach taken to the drafting of these provisions. The first is that overreach is inevitable. By attempting to capture descriptively all of the possible ways in which competitors might engage in a general category of conduct, it is not hard to lose sight of the essence of the conduct motivating prohibition in the first instance.[100] The second consequence of excessively prescriptive drafting is that unexpected errors are made and arbitrary loopholes created. For example, the definition of an output restricting cartel provision under the CC & OM Act covers restrictions in supply, production and capacity, but not in acquisition.[101]

5 ENFORCEMENT BIFURCATION AND EXCESSIVE DISCRETION

The Australian debate over criminalization has been as much concerned with how the new law will be enforced as it has with its scope and

---

[98] See, for example, F Zumbo, 'Submission to Senate Standing Committee on Economics on the Trade Practices Amendment (Cartel Conduct and Other Measures) Bill 2008' (30 January 2009) at 5–7, http://www.aph.gov.au/senate/committee/economics_ctte/tpa_cartels_09/submissions/sub11.pdf (accessed December 2010); Law Council of Australia, *supra* n. 81, at 6 para (e), 7 para (g).

[99] W Pengilley, 'Imperfect Competition' (20 June 2008) *Austr Fin Rev* 9.

[100] See RH Bork, *The Antitrust Paradox: A Policy at War with Itself* (1978) at 26–30, 135–6, Ch. 13.

[101] As pointed out in Beaton-Wells and Fisse, *supra* n. 58, at 179.

drafting. Indeed, the two concerns are inextricably linked. The breadth of the proposed prohibitions as drafted brings to the fore questions about which agencies will decide to prosecute conduct as offences rather than civil contraventions and on what criteria such decisions will be based in practice.

5.1 Enforcement Agency Roles and Relationship

Responsibility for enforcement of Australia's new cartel regime will be divided between two agencies – assigning investigation, instigation of civil proceedings and referral for prosecution to the ACCC, and prosecution, including both the decision to prosecute and the carriage of the prosecution, to the DPP. This is to be compared with an integrated model in which the same agency performs both investigatory and prosecutorial functions and makes all of the relevant decisions pertaining to these functions, best exemplified by the United States' Department of Justice Antitrust Division.

The bifurcated enforcement model reflects the value attributed to independence (including independence from the political process) and consistency in prosecutorial decision-making across the full spectrum of federal criminal offences in Australia, while drawing on the domain-specific expertise and experience of a regulator in investigating potential offences.[102] At the same time there is potential for inefficiency, at best, and conflict generating sub-optimal outcomes, at worst, as a result of having two agencies with traditionally divergent cultures, priorities and perspectives involved in enforcement.[103]

The Canadian experience is proof that a bifurcated system can work. While their roles are clearly distinguished, in practice, staff of the Competition Bureau and the DPP's office in Canada reportedly liaise regularly and cooperate closely on cartel cases, and the system has been said to work smoothly.[104] In particular, it appears that while the DPP retains ultimate independence in decision-making, there is a high degree of consultation with the Bureau throughout the enforcement process, including in the critical areas of leniency policy and sentencing.[105]

---

[102] ALRC, 'Principled Regulation: Federal Civil and Administrative Penalties in Australia', Report No. 95 (March 2003) paras 9.44–9.45.

[103] See id. at paras 9.35–9.40.

[104] See, for example, the account given in P Crampton, 'Canada's New Competition Law Immunity Policy – Warts and All' (2001) 27 *Int'l Tax J* 22.

[105] Canadian Competition Bureau, Leniency Program Bulletin, September 2010.

In the Australian context, there is precedent for cooperation between the ACCC and the DPP in relation to the consumer protection provisions of the TP Act, the breach of some of which carries criminal penalties,[106] as well as in relation to offences associated with obstruction of investigations.[107] However, criminal prosecutions in these areas have been rare and hence it is true to say that, with the introduction of the criminal cartel regime, the ACCC and DPP are entering substantially uncharted territory. Certainly, cartel cases are likely to be more complex and challenging than any others on which the two agencies have worked together previously.

The historically fractured and tense relationship between the Australian corporate regulator, the Australian Securities and Investments Commission (ASIC), and the DPP is evidence of how the separation of roles, absent a positive intra-agency working relationship, can undermine enforcement efforts.[108] For example, it has been reported that ASIC has been frustrated by the number of cases rejected for trial by the DPP.[109] At the same time, ASIC has been criticized for not bringing enough criminal proceedings generally,[110] as well as for failing to refer matters to the DPP for criminal charges in previous high profile cases, the most well known of which is the case involving Australian celebrity figure and businessman Steve Vizard.

In terms of managing the relationship between the ACCC and the DPP, three layers of liaison are contemplated in the ACCC/DPP MOU at the levels of individual cases, regular ongoing review of the organisational relationship in an operational sense and general oversight of the inter-agency relationship.[111] It is debatable, however, whether the MOU is sufficiently detailed or prescriptive in relation to these liaison arrangements and mechanisms for both preventing and resolving disagreements if and when they inevitably arise.[112]

---

106 TP Act, Pt V.

107 TP Act, ss 154R(2), 155(5).

108 See the account given of the ASIC-DPP conflict in P Wood, 'Prosecutorial Predicament' (1 June 2006) *Austr Fin Rev* 62.

109 I McIlwraith, 'Watchdog bares teeth at insurers' (26 February 2001) *The Age* 1.

110 See, for example, V Comino, 'The Enforcement Record of ASIC since the introduction of the civil penalty regime' (2007) 20 *Austr J Corp L* 183; J Overland, 'Two Steps Forward, One Step Back: Assessing Recent Developments in the Fight Against Insider Trading' (2006) 24 *Comp'y & Sec LJ* 207.

111 ACCC/DPP MOU, *supra* n. 26, at para 8.

112 See generally Beaton-Wells and Fisse, *supra* n. 7, at 375.

5.2 Enforcement Decision-making

The scheme of overreaching parallel criminal and civil prohibitions introduced by the CC & OM Act means that significant power is vested in the ACCC and DPP to determine when to pursue a matter as a potential offence and when otherwise to deal with it as a potential civil violation. Guidance on how such determinations will be made in the specific context of cartel conduct has been provided in the ACCC/DPP MOU[113] and in guidelines released by the ACCC in response to the recommendation of the Senate Economics Committee.[114] Reflective of Australian distrust of administrative power generally,[115] both the MOU and the ACCC guidelines have been criticized for failing to provide adequate detail or clarity.[116]

The criteria identified in the ACCC/DPP MOU and ACCC guidelines as relevant to the ACCC's decision to refer a matter for prosecution and the DPP's decision to prosecute (duration and extent of the conduct, effects on the market and the public, and prior similar conduct) are non-exhaustive and are expressed at the highest level of generality. A virtually meaningless threshold of more than AU$1 million value of affected commerce has been set.[117] There are additional criteria contained in other policy documents but it is unclear how the various criteria are intended to interact with each other.[118]

There are also significant gaps in the ACCC/DPP MOU. No reference is made, for example, to when a prosecution should be instituted against an individual, a corporation only, or both; information sharing and the treatment of confidential information as between the ACCC and the DPP and between these agencies and foreign enforcement authorities; or the approach that will be taken to bail.

On a more positive note, a major concern raised early in the debate concerning reconciliation of the DPP's approach to immunity from prosecution with the ACCC's approach has been addressed. Based on the hallmark traits of maximum certainty and minimum discretion, the ACCC

---

113 ACCC/DPP MOU, *supra* n. 26, at para 8.2.

114 ACCC, *supra* n. 30.

115 See, for example, AM Gleeson AC, 'Police Accountability and Oversight: An Overview', http://www.walk.com.au/pedestriancouncil/Page.asp?PageID=339 (accessed December 2010); R Douglas, *Douglas and Jones's Administrative Law* (6th edn, 2009) at 8.

116 M Jacobs and S McKeith, 'Confusion Reigns over Criminal Cartels' (15 July 2009) *Austr Fin Rev* 7. See generally Beaton-Wells and Fisse, *supra* n. 7, at Ch. 9.

117 ACCC/DPP MOU, *supra* n. 26, at para 4.4.

118 Cf. the comment that the ACCC will take a 'holistic' approach: ACCC, *supra* n. 30, at para 17.

Immunity Policy is designed to meet the particular challenges of detecting and proceeding against cartel conduct consistent with the approach taken by antitrust enforcers around the world.[119] By contrast, reflecting maximum discretion and minimum certainty consistent with a traditional prosecutorial approach, the DPP's general policy in determining when to prosecute is to assess whether there is a reasonable prospect of conviction and, if so, whether it is in the overall public interest to prosecute (or not prosecute as the case may be).[120]

Recognizing the difficulties that application of the DPP's policy would pose for immunity in the cartel context in circumstances where the DPP is the final decision-maker on such matters, the ACCC/DPP MOU provides for the ACCC to receive and manage requests for immunity from both criminal and civil proceedings, and make recommendations to the DPP based on the ACCC's assessment as to whether the applicant for immunity meets the criteria set out in the ACCC's Immunity Policy in relation to cartel conduct.[121] The DPP will then make an independent assessment and decide whether to grant immunity from criminal proceedings in accordance with its general policy. Significantly, however, an Annexure has been added to that policy that makes it clear, in making that decision, that the DPP will apply the same conditions as apply under the ACCC Immunity Policy and that the DPP's decision will be communicated to the applicant at the same time as the ACCC's decision on civil immunity.[122] This is the first occasion on which the DPP's Prosecution Policy has been revised in such a substantive way to accommodate 'special' concerns arising in connection with a particular offence.[123]

6 CONCLUSION

As a matter of general policy or principle there appears to be a growing international consensus that cartel conduct warrants criminal sanctions.

---

[119] More than 40 jurisdictions have some type of immunity programme: ICN, Cartel Working Group, Subgroup 1 – General Legal Framework, 'Cartel Settlements', Report to the ICN Annual Conference (April 2008) at 5 et seq. http://www.internationalcompetitionnetwork.org/uploads/library/doc347.pdf (accessed December 2010).

[120] See DPP, *supra* n. 65, at paras 2.7–2.10.

[121] ACCC/DPP MOU, *supra* n. 26, s 7.

[122] See DPP, *supra* n. 65, Annexure B.

[123] For a more detailed account of how the immunity policy operates under the dual criminal/civil regime in Australia, see generally Beaton-Wells and Fisse, *supra* n. 7, Ch. 10.

However, as borne out by the Australian experience, the process by which a country decides to criminalize and the issues that arise in the design of a criminal cartel regime are far less likely to be generalizable or, for that matter, transferable amongst jurisdictions. In short, there are likely to be many different strains of the criminalization contagion.

In Australia the challenges involved in criminalization have been as much political as they have been legal or practical. Under a Conservative government, despite the persuasive efforts of a high profile regulator, political ambivalence towards the notion of treating cartellists as criminal stalled the process of legislative development for over four years, and may have stalled it interminably had it not been for the landmark *Visy* settlement, uncannily timed during a federal election campaign.[124] Under the Labour Government, the process was delayed further, not by lack of political support, but by a commitment by a new Minister to consult and compromise on a range of difficult and technical aspects of the proposed scheme. Over a period of 18 months, two Exposure Drafts of the CC& OM Bill were released, submissions received and published, private consultations conducted and a public parliamentary inquiry held. In this process the majority of commentary was critical and the responses to the criticisms were seen largely as ineffectual.

The criticisms reveal deep-seated divisions amongst stakeholders in Australia as to what conduct should be criminal and how or by which institutions and by what process its criminality should be identified. The debate as to whether dishonesty should be an element of a cartel offence exemplifies this division and perhaps, more profoundly, demonstrates that the case for criminalizing anti-competitive conduct on the grounds of its harmfulness, as distinct from some notion of immorality, has not convinced all in Australia.[125] The debate about whether the characterization of conduct as criminal or civil should be left largely to administrative agencies reinforces the lack of any clear consensus in this country about what

---

[124] See the comments in A Hoel, 'Crime does not pay but hard-core cartel conduct may: Why should it be criminalized?' (2008) 16 *Trade Pract LJ* 102, at 114.

[125] A major survey of the Australian public conducted in 2010 suggests that most Australians respond to cartel conduct and the approach taken to sanctions for such conduct from a moral rather than an economic perspective. See C Beaton-Wells, C Parker, F Haines and C Platania-Phung, *Report on a Survey of the Australian Public Regarding Anti-Cartel Law and Enforcement* (December 2010), http://cartel.law.unimelb.edu.au/go/project-news/project-survey (accessed January 2011). See further C Beaton-Wells and F Haines, 'Making Cartel Conduct Criminal: A Case-Study of Ambiguity in Controlling Business Behaviour' (2004) 42(2) *ANZJIC* 218.

conduct warrants treatment as an offence. Equally, it reflects a degree of trepidation about further empowering the ACCC, seen by some as being too powerful already and as overzealous or dogmatic in the exercise of its power.[126] At the same time, rather than being viewed as a restraining influence, the introduction of the DPP, an agency unknown and inaccessible to most in competition law circles, has only sharpened the nerves.[127]

The criticisms are also in large part a function of long-standing discontent with the approach taken to Australian competition legislation generally. The over-inclusive and simultaneously highly prescriptive and complex formulation of the new prohibitions is symptomatic of the approach taken in relation to many of the prohibitions under the TP Act. In the past the approach has attracted criticism for creating undue uncertainty for business as well as diverting the attention of adjudicators from applying a purposive and principled approach to statutory interpretation. In the present context, not unexpectedly, those concerns have been heightened, given the consequences for individuals prosecuted under the regime, as well as for business and the Australian economy generally. That the new provisions will need to be understood and applied by juries has been an added cause for concern.

There is no doubt that the Australian embrace of criminalization will have flow-on effects for the international movement. Already there are signs of its spread, the New Zealand Government having indicated that it is likely to follow suit.[128] However, once a country embarks on the path of examining closely how to accommodate a criminal cartel regime within its existing legislative framework and enforcement institutions, it should quickly become evident that there is no off-the-shelf model available for adoption.[129] Each

---

126 See the findings reported in C Parker and V Nielsen, 'What do Australian businesses think of the ACCC, and does it really matter?' (2007) 35 *Fed L Rev* 187.

127 Recent controversies surrounding the prosecution of Australian billionaire Richard Pratt for obstruction of the ACCC's investigation into the *Visy/Amcor* cartel (see 'Watchdog receives very painful bite' (28 April 2009) *The Age* 4; 'ACCC pursuit of Pratt raises many questions' (30 April 2009) *Sydney Morning Herald* 5) and bungled charges against terrorism suspects would have done little to calm the nerves; see the report of the inquiry held into the treatment of Dr Mohammed Haneef at http://www.haneefcaseinquiry.gov.au/ (accessed December 2010).

128 See Ministry of Economic Development (NZ), Cartel Criminalisation, Discussion Document (January 2010).

129 Even in the case of New Zealand, despite a longstanding tradition of trans-Tasman harmonization, there are significant differences in both its substance and style of antitrust legislation and the Australian TP Act such that the chances of 'copying' directly from the Australian cartel legislation are minimal. See generally C Beaton-Wells and B Fisse, 'Criminal Cartels: Individual Liability and Sentencing', University of Melbourne Legal Studies Research Paper No. 415 (June

jurisdiction will need to navigate the particular political, social, economic and legal challenges involved in deciding to criminalize and, conceivably to an even greater extent, in designing the law and policy that will implement the decision. In each case, depending on how those challenges are met by political leaders and policy-makers, the outcome is likely to be different.

In Australia's case, despite strong broad-based support for competition policy as well as, it may seem, for the basic idea that cartels should attract criminal sanctions, the process of formulating the new regime has been divisive and the outcome has few public supporters outside of the ACCC. It is difficult to assess what this is likely to mean for the credibility of the criminalization reform going forward. It is conceivable that once the law is enacted, the criticism will dissipate as stakeholders become resigned to dealing with it as best they can. Just as plausibly, the criticism could intensify as the practical reality of the new regime is exposed. One possibility is that the business sector, rather than becoming more compliant, becomes more resistant and actively explores ways in which to avoid the application of the new legislation.[130]

Notwithstanding its distinctiveness, there appear to be two key lessons from Australia's criminalization experience for other countries. The first is that fundamental questions about the design and enforcement of a criminal cartel regime should be considered at the earliest possible stage – if possible, at the same time that the general issue of whether to criminalize is under consideration. This is to be contrasted with a sequential approach in which the general decision whether to criminalize is determined first and if decided in the affirmative, then consideration of questions as to the conduct to be made an offence and the institutional responsibility for, policy and mode of enforcement follow.[131] Depending on the country's particular legal and institutional framework, such questions may include:[132]

2009), http://papers.ssrn.com/sol3/papers.cfm?abstract_id=1433596 (accessed December 2010).

[130] As foreshadowed in B Fisse, 'Avoidance and Denial of Liability for the Cartel Offences: Proactive Lawful Escape Routes Left Open by the Cartel Legislation', Paper presented at the Competition Law Conference, Sydney (May 2009), http://www.brentfisse.com/images/Fisse_Avoidance_&_Denial_of_Liability_for_Cartel_Offences_230509.pdf (accessed December 2010).

[131] The sequential approach was adopted by Australia, and continues to be advocated by the Australian agencies in international fora see ICN, '2008–2009 Member Materials for Conference Call Series', Prepared by Cartel Working Group, Legal Framework Subgroup, Presented at the 8th Annual Conference of the ICN, Zurich, June 2009, at 9–12.

[132] This non-exhaustive list does not include the difficult questions that arise from the interaction between Community and national rules and their enforcement

- what should be the elements of a cartel offence, physical and mental, bearing in mind the objective of criminalizing only 'serious' cartel conduct, as well as the practical constraints of trying such an offence before a jury;
- how would a cartel offence relate to existing civil prohibitions and, in particular, to what extent should it be differentiated on the basis of capturing a narrower and/or different category of conduct;
- what would be appropriate exemptions and defences for a cartel offence and how should these relate to or be differentiated from exemptions and defences for civil prohibitions;
- would liability for a cartel offence attach to corporations and/or individuals and to what extent should liability be fault-based as distinct from vicarious;
- what types of penalty should apply for a cartel offence and what are the appropriate maxima;
- which courts would have jurisdiction, what would be the mode of trial for a cartel offence and to what extent would rules of evidence and procedure, different to those in civil proceedings, apply;
- what protection would be available from double jeopardy if the cartel offence applies to substantially the same conduct as the civil prohibitions;
- which agencies would be involved in enforcement of the cartel offence and, if more than one, what would be the roles and relationship between them;
- what would be the implications for policies that are seen as crucial to anti-cartel law enforcement, such as immunity/leniency policy and settlement policy;
- what would be the appropriate degree of discretion given to enforcement agencies in determining which conduct to prosecute and how should discretion be structured or confined; and
- what approach would be taken to sentencing and are sentencing guidelines likely to be required?

Any decision to criminalize without considering, at least in a general sense, the questions identified non-exhaustively above, inevitably, will be a decision driven primarily by politics (that of the government, as well as

---

in the European Union. See I Simonsson, 'Criminalising Cartels in the EU: Is There a Case for Harmonisation?', in C Beaton-Wells and A Ezrachi (eds), *Criminalising Cartels: Critical Studies of an International Regulatory Movement* (2011), Ch. 9.

the regulator, and conceivably the power struggle between them), rather than by an in-depth and informed assessment of the legal and practical implications of criminalization.

The second lesson is that criminalization requires strong political leadership, together with clear public support from the competition enforcement agency. However, even if these preconditions are met, the challenges in terms of the number, complexity and potentially controversial nature of issues involved are likely to be great. Hence, there are likely to be substantial benefits in referring the matter for examination initially by an independent body that has the expertise and capacity to deal with it thoroughly, openly and sensitively. In Australia, such a body would have been the Australian Law Reform Commission. Instead criminalization was dealt with superficially by the Dawson Committee and then passed back to the government that anointed a cartel-like working party, the procedures and findings of which were marked by secrecy.

The process conducted by such a body should include, at a minimum, the production and release of a discussion paper raising the issues identified above for consideration, the receipt and publication of submissions, followed by the publication of a comprehensive report with recommendations. The government should respond publicly and in detail to the report and its recommendations. Whether further consultation is required at that stage would depend on the response by stakeholders to the process and the extent to which the recommendations and/or the government's response are qualified or ambiguous in any significant respect. There may well be a case for releasing an exposure draft of the legislation to allow for further reflection with the benefit of having the regime in its proposed statutory form.

If these lessons are learnt from the Australian experience, the chances are that the criminalization decision will be more informed, the legislative process smoother, the outcome in terms of the design of the regime more coherent and, ultimately, the prospects of effective enforcement substantially enhanced.

PART 3

Intellectual property and competition law

10. Patent ambush strategies and Article 102 TFEU

Andreas Fuchs

1 INTRODUCTION

In recent years a topic at the interface of antitrust law and IP law has attracted the attention of antitrust authorities on both sides of the Atlantic: the scenario commonly referred to as 'patent ambush'. The strategy underlying this phenomenon, which has become known in connection with the activities of private standard-setting organizations (SSOs), may be characterized by *two steps*. The first is taken during an *ongoing standard-setting procedure* conducted by an SSO or a special committee of it which is about to decide on the possible adoption of a technical or quality standard concerning products or processes in an industry.[1] A firm, usually a member of the relevant SSO, participates in the process of working out the features of the standard, but *does not play* by the rules of the SSO that provide for an *obligation to disclose* any patents or pending patent applications that may be relevant for the potential standard. Rather, it deliberately decides not to disclose its (pending) IP rights in order not to reduce the prospects of its technology becoming part of the standard, and regularly works actively in this direction within the SSO.[2] *Once the standard has been adopted and*

[1] The term 'standard' is used to describe a set of technical specifications that provides or is intended to provide a common design for a product or process. For a more detailed description and definition see, e.g., H Hovenkamp, MD Janis and MA Lemley, *IP and Antitrust* (2001) § 35.1a; Lemley, 'Intellectual Property Rights and Standard-Setting Organizations' (2002) 90 *Cal L Rev* 1889, at 1896.

[2] J Drexl, 'Deceptive Conduct in the Patent World – A Case for US Antitrust and EU Competition Law?', in W Prinz zu Waldeck und Pyrmont, MJ Adelman, R Brauneis, J. Drexl and R Nack (eds), *Patents and Technological Progress in a Globalized World. Liber Amicorum Joseph Straus* (2009) 137; J Farrell, J Hayes, C Shapiro and T Sullivan, 'Standard Setting, Patents, and Hold-Up' (2007) 74 *Antitrust LJ* 603; E Petritsi, 'The Case of Unilateral Patent Ambush under EC Competition Rules' (2005) 28 *World Comp* 25, at 26; T Weck, 'Schutzrechte und Standards aus Sicht des Kartellrechts' (2009) *NJOZ* 1177, at 1186–8.

implemented within the relevant industry, the firm makes use of its exclusive rights as a patent holder and sues anybody using the standard into which its technology is incorporated, unless they are willing to pay *excessively high royalties*. Since the users of the standard have already made considerable investments in adapting their products or services to the proprietary standard and incurred sunk costs, they are caught in a *lock-in effect*.[3] If they had to stop making use of the patented technology implemented in the standard, they would have to write off their previous investments and incur high additional expenses for altering their products and production facilities. In view of the imminent severe losses they probably have no alternative but to pay the excessively high royalties charged by the patent owner. The danger of switching costs becoming prohibitive is extremely high in industries with network effects.[4]

1.1 Competitive Concerns in a Patent Ambush Scenario

One may ask why antitrust lawyers should care about such patent holdup situations. Apart from the fact that some scholars are sceptical about the existence and empirical significance of patent holdup,[5] there are mainly two *competitive concerns* raised by a patent ambush scenario. The first concern relates to the *manipulation of the standard-setting process*. Usually, SSOs attempt to avoid problems resulting from the implementation of patented technologies into a proposed standard. They either exclude such technologies right away or they ask the patent owner for a declaration that it is prepared to grant licences on the patent to every applicant on so-called RAND or FRAND terms, that is, on fair, reasonable and non-discriminatory conditions.[6] By not disclosing those of its intellectual prop-

---

[3] Farrell et al., *supra* n. 2, at 610 et seq.

[4] As to the reasons for such effects see Lemley, *supra* n. 1, at 1899; A Zimmerlich, 'Der Fall Microsoft' (2004) *WRP* 1260, at 1261; J Pohlmeier, *Netzwerkeffekte und Kartellrecht* (2004) 29–31.

[5] JG Sidak, 'Patent Holdup and Oligopsonistic Collusion in Standard-Setting Organizations' (2009) 5 *J Comp L & Econ* 123, at 126; JM Golden, '"Patent Trolls" and Patent Remedies' (2007) 85 *Tex L Rev* 2111; D Gerardin and M Rato, 'Can Standard Setting Lead to Exploitative Abuse? A Dissonant View on Patent Holdup, Royalty Stacking and the Meaning of FRAND' (2007) 3 *Eur Comp J* 101; D Gerardin, 'Pricing Abuses by Essential Patent Holders in a Standard-Setting Context: A View from Europe' (2009) 76 *Antitrust LJ* 329, at 343.

[6] The European Commission stresses the importance of FRAND commitments in its Commission Notice – Guidelines on the applicability of Article 101 of the Treaty on the Functioning of the European Union to horizontal co-operation agreements [2011] OJ C 11/1, paras 280, 283–285, 287 and 291. In addition to

erty rights (IPRs) that are relevant for the proposed standard, the IPR owner increases the chances that its technology will be integrated into the standard, which is of utmost importance for market penetration and commercial success. Thus the competition between different technologies that may be incorporated into the standard is distorted by the non-disclosure, in particular if IP protection already exists for other technologies. In other words, a patent ambush may be viewed as 'a system failure of the standard-setting process'.[7] Furthermore, the deceptive practice may lead to additional barriers to entry for other firms or technologies once the proprietary standard has been adopted. Finally, by using the lock-in effect the patent owner may reach a position that enables it to acquire or maintain monopoly power, which otherwise would not have been the case.

The *second competitive concern* relates directly to the possible *abuse of market power* by charging excessively high royalties once the standard has been successfully implemented. One may ask whether preventing the exploitation of licensees is a true competition concern – in Europe it is, in the United States it is generally not. The controversy whether and, if so, under which circumstances the control of excessively high prices is legitimate and necessary is not to be taken up here and discussed in general terms.[8] The special situation of a patent ambush differs from ordinary abuse cases,[9] and it is rather likely that it does not only inflict harm on

---

securing access to the standard on fair, reasonable and non-discriminatory terms, standardization agreements should, according to the Commission, ensure unrestricted participation in the standard-setting process as well as a transparent procedure for adopting the standard in order to avoid competitive risks under Article 101 TFEU, id. at paras 280–282. Moreover, the rules of the standardization organization should contain a clear IPR policy that requires 'good faith disclosure, by participants, of their IPR that might be essential for the implementation of the standard under development', id. at para 286.

[7] European Commission, 'Antitrust: Commission accepts commitments from Rambus lowering memory chip royalty rates', Press release of 9 December 2009, MEMO/09/544, http://europa.eu/rapid/pressReleasesAction.do?reference=MEMO/09/544 (accessed December 2010).

[8] The issue is usually discussed under the heading 'Antitrust law is designed to protect competition, not competitors' on the one hand, and 'There is no competition without competitors' on the other hand.

[9] A very important point is that entry barriers are extremely high if an industry-wide standard secured by IP rights is firmly established. The underlying rationale of the US Supreme Court that monopoly profits are good and an integral part of the competitive process, because they attract market entry by newcomers which over time will reduce excessive prices, does not work in a patent holdup situation, because there is virtually no chance for an alternative standard to be established in the market by competitors of the patent owner.

individual licensees, but may also, to a certain extent, thwart the benefits of standardization itself, because as a result of the excessively high royalties the product could become more expensive, its acceptance by the consumers reduced and its output restrained. In addition, future standard-setting procedures might be rendered difficult if the participants have to reckon with the possibility that one or more among them will not disclose their IPRs, and, thus, reduce the efforts to implement an industry-wide standard. The prospects of drawing up valuable, efficiency-enhancing standards will be reduced if the threat of patent ambush strategies cannot be eliminated or considerably reduced. Therefore, at least in the context of standard-setting activities, the exploitation of licensees should also be an antitrust concern.

In today's knowledge-based economy featuring a growing importance of IPRs and a considerable expansion of technology licensing markets, patents, their acquisition and enforcement are also used more and more strategically outside a bona fide attempt to protect one's own innovation.[10] In this environment an obvious need exists for an effective protection of competition, in particular against manipulations of standardization procedures. The undistorted establishment of reasonable standards may be very useful, because they facilitate the interoperability and compatibility of different products, increase the market transparency and acceptance of products, make the products more valuable for customers, and stimulate output.[11] On the other hand, an intentional and coordinated private standard defined by a group of cooperating companies or by an acknowledged SSO may entail some competitive risks, with respect to the exchange of sensitive information among competitors, and build barriers to market entry.[12] While such risks of collusion among the members of an SSO, or of a special joint venture of private companies, and the risk of jointly excluding rivals from access to the developed standard are to be judged under the cartel prohibition (Section 1 Sherman Act, Article 101 TFEU), the main issue in cases of *proprietary standards* is the *use of the lock-in effect* to acquire or maintain monopoly power or market dominance. In this regard

---

[10] The strategic use of patents includes, inter alia, 'patent mining' in order to block rivals or extract excessive licence fees, and the acquisition of IPRs by so-called 'patent trolls', cf., inter alia, MA Lemley and C Shapiro, 'Patent Holdup and Royalty Stacking' (2007) 85 *Tex L Rev* 1991 and (2007) 85 *Tex L Rev* 2163 responding to Golden, *supra* n. 5.

[11] For a more detailed survey of the positive and negative effects of standardization see Hovenkamp et al., *supra* n. 1, § 35.2a and 2b.

[12] European Commission, Guidelines on horizontal co-operation agreements, *supra* n. 6, at para 266; A Fuchs in U Immenga and E-J Mestmäcker (eds), *Wettbewerbsrecht, GWB* (4th edn 2007), § 2 GWB para 118.

the competition law tools available in a patent ambush scenario are quite different on both sides of the Atlantic.

1.2 Competition Law Tools for Coping with a Patent Ambush Scenario

In the United States the problem of acquiring monopoly power by deceptive practices may be addressed, at least theoretically, by either Section 2 Sherman Act, which prohibits the wilful acquisition or maintenance of monopoly power as well as attempts to monopolize, or by Section 5 FTC Act, which declares unlawful any unfair methods of competition and unfair or deceptive acts or practices in or affecting commerce.

The legal framework in the European Union is quite different. Article 102 TFEU (ex-Article 82 EC Treaty) covers the abuse of an existing market-dominating position and, therefore, is – at least at first sight – not suitable for directly fighting the manipulation of the standard-setting process as such – at least as long as an IPR owner participating in the standardization process and omitting to disclose its IPRs relevant for the prospective standard does not already hold a market-dominating position. This is usually not the case prior to the adoption and widely dispersed implementation of the standard. Thus, only laws against unfair competition that apply to all firms without regard to their market power might address the deceptive conduct during the standard-setting procedure. So far, however, the provisions of unfair trade laws have obviously not yet been applied to patent ambush scenarios in Europe. Another disadvantage is that the laws applicable in the B2B context may differ considerably from one Member State to the other, since the European efforts to harmonize national unfair trade laws through directives have been restricted to unfair conduct vis-à-vis consumers.

Therefore, at first sight the American antitrust law seems much better prepared to cope with patent ambush strategies. However, a closer look reveals that both approaches have their deficiencies: while Section 2 Sherman Act and Section 5 FTC Act do not require existing market dominance or monopoly power at the time when the exclusionary or deceptive conduct did occur, there is a *causation problem*. The agency, or a private plaintiff, claiming that a firm has engaged in a patent ambush is supposed to demonstrate that the standard would not have been adopted by the SSO 'but for' the deceptive conduct of the patent owner. Proving this is a great problem in practice, as the famous *Rambus* case has shown – a landmark case the FTC unfortunately lost.[13]

---

[13] See *Rambus v FTC*, 522 F.3d 456 (DC Cir. 2008); *cert. denied*, 129 S Ct 1318 (2009).

The situation in Europe is just the other way round: you do *not need a causal link* between dominance and the abusive conduct, but the *market dominance must already have existed at the time of the alleged abuse*. Therefore, Article 102 TFEU is, at the outset, suitable for fighting an abuse of market power by charging excessive royalties. However, price control is in itself always a problem. How do you determine the treshold to price abuses? This is particularly difficult in an IP context because IPRs are intended to allow their holders to exploit their legal monopoly.

The respective legal background in mind, it does not come as a surprise that neither in the United States nor in Europe can the application of competition laws against patent ambush strategies be regarded as a success story yet.

2 RELEVANT PATENT AMBUSH CASES – AN OVERVIEW

2.1 United States

During the last 15 years the antitrust authorities in the United States took up only a few cases involving a patent ambush scenario. After two earlier proceedings under Section 5 FTC Act, against Dell in 1995 involving a deception claim[14] and against Unocal in 2005 with regard to an alleged manipulation of a state rule-making process for low emission standards,[15] the FTC closed the files of the famous *Rambus* case on 14 May 2009 by

---

14 *In the Matter of Dell Computer Corp.*, 121 F.T.C. 616 (20 May 1996); *see* also FTC, 2 November 1995, Docket No. 931-0097, C-3888; press release www.ftc.gov/opa/1995/11/dell.htm (accessed December 2010). In this case Dell's representative in the Video Electronic Standards Association (VESA) was required to sign an *ex ante* statement that the envisaged adoption of the VESA Local (VL) bus standard did not infringe any trademarks, copyrights or patents held by Dell. Later Dell sought to enforce its patents against implementers of this bus standard. The FTC challenged this conduct under Section 5 FTC Act as an unfair method of competition. The proceedings ended with a consent decree.

15 *In the Matter of Union Oil Company of California*, FTC decision of 10 July 2005, Docket No. 9305; see also *In re Union Oil Company of California*, FTC decision of 10 July 2003, Docket No. 9305. In this case Unocal did not disclose that it was adjusting its patent claims and tried to steer the rule-making process towards its own technology. Once the final formula was adopted Unocal started demanding and extracting royalties from other oil companies through successful patent infringement actions. The FTC's claim of violating Section 5 FTC Act finally failed, however, because the conduct occurred during government-sponsored standard-setting proceedings which rendered it immune from antitrust scrutiny

finally dismissing the complaint that was based on integrating a monopolization claim into Section 5 FTC Act.[16] Originally, the FTC had asserted that Rambus had unlawfully monopolized the market for certain computer memory technologies (so-called DRAMS) by deceptive conduct as a member of JEDEC (Joint Electron Device Engineering Council), an industry standard-setting organization. According to the complaint,[17] JEDEC's policy was to avoid the incorporation of patented technologies into its standards, but Rambus participated in the process for over four years without disclosing to the other members of JEDEC that it actually had, or expected to have, patents on technologies under consideration. After its technologies had been incorporated into the standard and the members had made substantial investments to accommodate to it, Rambus demanded very high royalties from them.

The initial decision of an FTC Administrative Law Judge dismissed the agency's complaint, mainly because JEDEC's rules about the disclosure of patents were vague and internally inconsistent.[18] The FTC unanimously reversed the decision and found that Rambus had engaged in a calculated course of conduct that was intended to mislead JEDEC members by fostering the belief that Rambus neither had, nor was seeking, relevant patents that would be enforced against JEDEC-compliant products.[19] The FTC's decision on the appropriate remedy was issued in February 2007.[20]

On appeal by Rambus, the DC Circuit Court of Appeals reversed the decision.[21] The court mainly relied on a single sentence out of the more than 100 pages of the FTC opinion, namely the conclusion that, if Rambus had fully disclosed its IP interests, 'JEDEC *either* would have

---

under the Noerr-Pennington doctrine; for a more detailed overview see Petritsi, *supra* n. 2, at 27 et seq.

16 FTC, Order Returning Matter to Adjudication and Dismissing Complaint, 14 May 2009, available at http://www.ftc.gov/os/adjpro/d9302/090512orderdismisscomplaint.pdf (accessed December 2010). For an earlier discussion of the case see, inter alia, Drexl, *supra* n. 2, at 139–44; ES Mintzer and LM Breed, 'How to Keep the Fox Out of the Henhouse: Monopolization in the Context of Standards-Setting Organizations' (2007) 19(5) *Intell Prop & Tech LJ* 5.

17 Administrative complaint, 18 July 2002, http://www.ftc.gov/os/adjpro/d9302/020618admincmp.pdf (accessed December 2010).

18 Initial decision of the Chief Administrative Law Judge of 24 February 2004, www.ftc.gov/os/adjpro/d9302/040223initialdecision.pdf (accessed December 2010).

19 FTC, 'Liability opinion' of 2 August 2006, www.ftc.gov./os/adjpro/d9302/060802rambusorder.pdf (accessed December 2010).

20 FTC, 'Remedy opinion' and Final Order of 2 February 2007, www.ftc.gov./os/adjpro/d9302/070205opinion.pdf (accessed December 2010).

21 *Rambus v FTC*, *supra* n. 13.

excluded Rambus's patented technologies from the JEDEC standard, or would have demanded an opportunity for ex ante licensing negotiations'.[22] In the Court's view, the first alternative would have supported a monopolization claim, but the second would not. The court reasoned that if Rambus's technology would have been selected as a standard in any event and Rambus's deception affected only the amount of the royalty payments, there was no anticompetitive effect. As long as the FTC could not definitively prove that Rambus's monopoly was actually caused by its deceptive conduct, Rambus ought to be regarded as a lawful monopolist and its use of deception, according to the DC Circuit Court of Appeals, was simply a means of obtaining higher prices. These would normally have no particular tendency to exclude rivals in violation of Section 2 Sherman Act, or Section 5 FTC Act.[23]

The Court's decision has rightly met with a lot of criticism.[24] It appears to be vulnerable on a number of counts, mainly because it fails to recognize that JEDEC's decision to adopt a standard in the first place would inevitably have been affected by considerations of cost. Even though the FTC could not determine whether JEDEC would have rejected Rambus's technology or negotiated lower royalties in the 'but for' world without the deception, there was ample evidence that supported the conclusion that JEDEC would never have adopted patented technology in a standard without any idea of its cost. Moreover, the DC Circuit Court of Appeals did not take into account that its decision is likely to undermine the working of SSOs that are generally assumed to have procompetitive effects. Promoting trust within SSOs by banning deceptive conduct, keeping the volume of royalty rates on a reasonable level and, thus, ensuring access to the technology embedded in the standard would probably be more favourable to innovation and technological progress than the Court's hope of competitors being attracted by monoply royalty rates and trying to replace the current standard.[25] The Supreme Court, however, denied to grant *certiorari*,[26] and the FTC decided to close the case and dismiss the complaint against Rambus.

Thus, the current situation with regard to fighting patent ambush strate-

---

22 *Rambus v FTC*, *supra* n. 13, at 461; see FTC 'Liability opinion', *supra* n. 19.

23 *Supra* n. 13.

24 Cf. Drexl, *supra* n. 2, at 144; A. Chronopoulos, 'Patenting Standards – A Case for US Antitrust Law or a Call for Recognizing Immanent Public Policy Limitations to the Exploitation Rights Conferred by the Patent Act?' (2009) 40 *IIC* 782, at 789.

25 See Drexl, *supra* n. 2, at 154.

26 129 S Ct 1318 (2009).

gies in the United States is rather sobering. While the FTC had assumed that any conduct that undermines the standard-stetting process inevitably harms competition and consumers for the purposes of Section 5 FTC Act as well as Section 2 Sherman Act, the Court of Appeals (DC Circuit) required more explicit proof of causation under the Sherman Act. The consequence is that deceptive conduct in connection with standard-setting is not regarded as prohibited under the Sherman Act if there is no proof that the technology was incorporated into the standard as a result of the deception. As long as the only effect of the patent owner's deception is that it is able to charge higher than RAND licensing fees for its technology, because it would have been incorporated into the standard anyway, even if disclosed during the standard-setting process, the deceptive conduct does not affect, in the eyes of the Court of Appeals, the competitive process or the competitive structure of the market, and thus does not inflict antitrust harm.

2.2 European Union

In an early standard-setting case in 1995 the European Commission demanded changes in the interim IPR policy of the European Telecommunications Standards Institute (ETSI), which required an *ex ante* consent of patent holders to the incorporation of their patents in any subsequent standards. Even though this rule was obviously designed for preventing patent ambush strategies, the Commission took the view that it violated Article 81 EC (now Article 101 TFEU) because it was likely to restrict innovation.[27] ETSI followed the complaint and withdrew the said rule.[28]

It was not till August 2007 that the first actual case involving an alleged patent ambush was initiated by the Commission, which issued a preliminary Statement of Objections to *Rambus* based on the same conduct at issue, but relating to an alleged abuse of Rambus's dominant position by charging excessively high royalties for its patents concerning DRAM chips.[29] The proceedings ended, however, without a formal finding on

[27] European Commission, Case COMP IV/35.006 (1995) – *ETSI interim IPR policy*.

[28] See European Commission, 'Competition: Commission welcomes changes in ETSI IPR rules to prevent "patent ambush"', Press release of 12 December 2005, IP/05/1565, http://europa.eu/rapid/pressReleasesAction.do?reference=IP/05/1565&format=HTML&aged=1&language=EN&guiLanguage=en (accessed December 2010).

[29] Preliminary Statement of Objections of 23 August 2009, see Commission, 'Antitrust: Commission market tests commitments proposed by Rambus concerning memory chips, Press release of 12 June 2009, MEMO/07/330, http://europa.eu/

an infringement of Article 102 TFEU. Rather, the Commission accepted commitments from Rambus lowering its memory chip royalty rates.[30] Thus, Rambus agreed to charge no royalties for the SDR and DDR chip standards that were adopted when it was a JEDEC member; and a maximum rate of 1.5 per cent for the subsequent generations of JEDEC DRAM standards (DDR2 and DDR3) (in comparison to 3.5 per cent for DDR in the existing contracts). After consultation of interested parties on Rambus's commitments,[31] the Commission concluded that the commitments in their final form were adequate to meet the competition concerns expressed in the Statement of Objections and, on 9 December 2009 in a decision pursuant to Article 9 Regulation 1/2003,[32] declared the commitments legally binding on Rambus for a total period of five years.[33] In the meantime, however, a competitor has brought an action for annulment of the decision claiming that the Commission falsely applied Article 9 of Regulation 1/2003.[34]

A similar procedure for an alleged violation of Article 82 EC (now Article 102 TFEU) was initiated against Qualcomm, a company holding IP rights in the CDMA and WCDMA standards for mobile telephones. The WCDMA standard is part of the 3G (third generation) standard for European mobile phone technology (UMTS). The proceedings were initiated following complaints by mobile phone and/or chipset manufacturers alleging that Qualcomm's licensing terms and conditions were neither fair nor reasonable and non-discriminatory and, therefore, violated European

rapid/pressReleasesAction.do?reference=MEMO/09/273&format=HTML&aged=1&language=EN&guiLanguage=en (accessed December 2010).

[30] See Commission, 'Antitrust: Commission accepts commitments by Rambus lowering memory chip royalty rates', Press release of 9 December 2009, IP/09/1897, http://europa.eu/rapid/pressReleasesAction.do?reference=IP/09/1897 (accessed December 2010); see also Commission, 'Antitrust: Commission accepts commitments by Rambus lowering memory chip royalty rates – frequently asked questions', Press release of 9 December 2009, MEMO/09/544, http://europa.eu/rapid/pressReleasesAction.do?reference=MEMO/09/544 (accessed December 2010).

[31] See Press release of 12 June 2009, *supra* n. 29.

[32] Council Regulation (EC) No. 1/2003 of 16 December 2002 on the implementation of the rules on competition laid down in Articles 81 and 82 of the Treaty, [2003] OJ L 1/1.

[33] See Summary of Commission Decision of 9 December 2009, Case COMP/38.636 – *Rambus* [2010] OJ C 30/717; the full (non-confidential) version of the decision is available at http://ec.europa.eu/competition/antitrust/cases/dec_docs/38636/38636_1203_1.pdf (accessed December 2010).

[34] Case T-148/10 *Hynix Semiconductor v Commission* [2010] OJ C 148/41.

competition rules.[35] The Commission investigated whether the royalties charged by Qualcomm were unreasonably high, but closed formal proceedings against Qualcomm without definite result on 24 November 2009 after all complainants had withdrawn or indicated to withdraw their complaints.[36] In view of this and the complexity of the necessary assessments the Commission was not prepared to invest further resources in this case.

This raises the question whether the control of excessive licence fees as an exploitative abuse under Article 102 TFEU can be regarded as a reasonable and feasible approach to prevent patent ambush strategies and diminish incentives to engage in deceptive conduct in connection with standardization procedures, or whether there are any alternative solutions. Is Article 102 TFEU really restricted to assessing anticompetitive conduct after the adoption of the standard and the establishment of market dominance by the patent holder? Or can the use of deceptive practices in the context of standardization procedures be taken into account for assessing patent ambush scenarios under Articles 102 TFEU?

3 THE ASSESSMENT OF PATENT AMBUSH STRATEGIES UNDER ARTICLE 102 TFEU

3.1 Market Dominance

A dominant position is characterized by the European Court of Justice (ECJ) as a position of economic strength that enables a firm to hinder the maintenance of effective competition in the relevant market by allowing it to behave, to an appreciable extent, independently of its competitors and ultimately of consumers.[37] But how to define the relevant market in standardization cases? Is it the market for the (licensing of the) technology

---

35 See Commission, 'Antitrust: Commission initiates formal proceedings against Qualcomm', Press release of 1 October 2007, MEMO/07/389, http://europa.eu/rapid/pressReleasesAction.do?reference=MEMO/07/389&format=HTML&aged=1&language=EN&guiLanguage=en (accessed December 2010).

36 See Commission, 'Antitrust: Commission closes formal proceedings against Qualcomm', Press release of 24 November 2009, MEMO/09/516, http://europa.eu/rapid/pressReleasesAction.do?reference=MEMO/09/516 (accessed December 2010).

37 Case 27/76 *United Brands v Commission* [1978] ECR 207; Case 85/76 *Hoffmann-La Roche v Commission* [1979] ECR 461; Case 322/81 *Michelin v Commission* [1983] ECR 3461, para 30. For a comparison of the differences between dominance under EU Competition Law and monopoly power under US antitrust law see R Bloch, H-G Kamann, J Brown and JP Schmidt, 'A

to be implemented in the standard, the market for the product for which the patented technology is to be used, or is there even a separate market for the (future) standard itself? According to the Commission, one or more of these markets might be affected by standardization agreements. In its new horizontal cooperation guidelines, which contain a redrafted chapter on standardization agreements,[38] the Commission identifies even a fourth possible market (for testing and certification),[39] which, however, is of no relevance in patent ambush cases.

In the process of defining the special features of the future standard it is necessary to take into account all possible alternative technologies that could be used for the product in question and incorporated into the standard. Therefore, in most cases the technologies that are suitable or essential for the envisaged standard seem to be the appropriate frame of reference for the determination of the boundaries of the relevant market. The main competitive concern at this stage refers to the distortion of competition between these technologies with regard to their incorporation into the envisaged standard. Since an SSO always has the option to abstain from developing the intended coordinated private standard at all, or to choose other features to be incorporated, it is hardly conceivable that a patent holder is already in a position of sufficient economic strength during the standard-setting process to exert an undue influence on the SSO's decisions in setting the (features of the) standard. If a member of an SSO conceals an existing patent or patent application for a technology, which is later incorporated into the standard, the member is not dominant at that time, because the mere possibility that the non-disclosure of standard-related patents may lead to market power does not in itself establish a dominant position.[40]

The crucial point in this first stage of a patent ambush scenario is not the market power of the owner of the technology but *deception* about the existence of a patent or patent application with regard to a technology that may be essential for the envisaged standard. This is particularly true in industries where patent thickets of multiple overlapping patent

---

Comparative Analysis of Art. 82 of the EC Treaty and Section 2 of the Sherman Act' (2005) *J Comp L* (*ZWeR*) 325, at 334 et seq., and Petritsi, *supra* n. 2, at 33.

[38] Guidelines on horizontal co-operation agreements, *supra* n. 6, at paras 257–335.

[39] Id. at para 261.

[40] M Hartmann-Rüppel, 'Patentmissbrauch – Neue Entwicklungen an der Schnittstelle von Patent- und Kartellrecht' in B Ahrens, P Behrens, M Kleine and P von Dietze (eds), *Patente, Prognosen, Kooperationen: Aktuelle Entwicklungen der Kartellrechtsanwendung* (2008) 51, at 65.

claims exist and the final product to be sold to the consumer makes use of hundreds or even thousands of IPRs. Moreover, in cases in which the protected technology covers an economic market and enables its owner to dominate the entire industry, it is more likely that a *de facto standard* will be established owing to the overwhelming market success of the product (for example, MS Windows) than a coordinated private standard set by an acknowledged SSO. This is particularly true if the industry involved is in addition characterized by considerable network effects.

Dominance is more likely to be acquired once the standard has been adopted and has become a market success. In this case the IPR owner is able to control – through its exclusive right to the technology incorporated into the standard – the use of the standard for the respective products. There is, however, no guarantee that a standard announced by an SSO will really govern an economic market or a whole industry. It depends on whether alternative technologies and competing standards exist for products that meet the same economic needs and whether one of the differing standards finds considerably more acceptance in the marketplace than others.[41] Moreover, technological changes during the standardization process may lead to transforming markets and prevent the emergence of dominance.

3.2 Abuse of Market Power

As to the determination of abusive behaviour, the general concept under Article 102 TFEU refers to the 'special responsibility' of dominant firms not to allow their conduct to impair undistorted competition.[42] The situation is similar to what an ancient Roman saying described as 'quod licet Iovi non licet bovi'.[43] A certain behaviour in the marketplace that would be perfectly legal if adopted by a firm without significant market power may nevertheless be prohibited – because of its detrimental effects on the remaining but already weakened competition in the market – if it were displayed by the dominant firm. On the other hand, even a dominant company may, of course, aggressively compete on the merits. To draw the line between legitimate competitive acts, the consequence of which may even be to drive other firms out of the market, and the undue impairing of undistorted competition by the dominating firm, is very difficult and

[41] See, e.g., T Loest and M Bartlik, 'Standards und europäisches Wettbewerbsrecht' (2008) *J Comp L* (*ZWeR*) 41, at 50 et seq.

[42] See, inter alia, Case T-65/89 *BPB Industries and British Gypsum v Commission* [1993] ECR II-389; Case 322/81 *Michelin v Commission* [1983] ECR 3461.

[43] 'What Juppiter is permitted to do, an ox is not allowed to do.'

usually depends on the specific circumstances of each case. However, two types of abusive conduct are commonly distinguished: exclusionary and exploitative abuses.

3.2.1 Laying a patent ambush as an exclusionary abuse?

In a patent ambush context one could characterize the deceptive conduct of not disclosing relevant patent rights or applications, as well as the possible breach of other SSO rules (such as the undertaking to grant licences to any applicant on FRAND terms) as a form of exclusionary conduct. The problem, however, is that this conduct usually occurs at a time at which the patent owner (or applicant) does not yet hold a market-dominating position. Even though no causal link between market dominance and abuse is required,[44] this constitutes a major problem for the application of Article 102 TFEU to patent ambush strategies. If there is no way to connect the conduct during the standardization process, i.e. at the time preceding the acquisition of sufficient market power to dominate the market, with the charge of excessive royalties at a later stage after the adoption of the standard, which in itself constitutes an exploitative abuse, then Article 102 TFEU cannot directly address the specific problem of patent ambush scenarios that lies in the deceptive conduct during the standardization procedure.

A conceivable approach could be to draw on cases that involve an *abuse of regulatory procedure*. In *AstraZeneca* the claim was that the pharmaceutical producer fraudulently obtained or got a prolongation of the IPRs concerning its ulcer drug Losec.[45] The anticompetitive effect in such cases is that market entry by competitors with their generic products is blocked or delayed, and the owner of the IPR can enjoy the fruits of its dominant position even longer. In a patent ambush scenario there is a comparable misuse of an ongoing procedure when existing IPRs or pending IPR applications essential for the standard to be developed are not disclosed. And in both cases the firm involved in such deceptive conduct will, as a result of the manipulated procedure, gain an important competitive advantage over outsiders. However, as already mentioned, the dominant position must have existed at the time of the deceptive conduct. This prerequisite was met in the *AstraZeneca* case, but in a patent ambush situation typically no

---

44 Drexl, *supra* n. 2, at 151 et seq. with further references.

45 Commission Decision of 15 June 2005, Case COMP/A.37.507/F3 [2006] OJ L 332/24; confirmed by the General Court in T-321/05 *AstraZeneca v Commission* [2010] ECR II-0000 (not yet officially reported). For a more detailed discussion see also Drexl, supra n. 2, at 147–52; M Negrinotti, 'Abuse of Regulatory Procedures in the Intellectual Property Context: The AstraZeneca Case' (2008) *ECLR* 446.

dominant position exists prior to the adoption of the standard. Therefore, the *AstraZeneca* approach usually cannot be extended to patent ambush cases, even though the forms of abusive behaviour are comparable.

If a dominant firm already controls a market through a proprietary standard, it may try to use its market power to implement a comparable standard in a neighbouring market. It may rely on different means to create *leverage effects* in order to gain control of, or at least a strong position in, the second market and thereby abuse its existing market power. The creation of a patent ambush in the second market, however, does not seem possible in such a situation. In any case, the mere non-disclosure of the existing IPRs (already incorporated into the proprietary standard in the first market) when a comparable standardization procedure is under way in a second market cannot be regarded as a means of transferring market power to this second market.

An interesting alternative suggestion has been made by German authors who argue that the *concept of a 'single and continuous infringement'* should be applied to patent ambush strategies. The concealing of IPRs in a standardization process should be considered as the first step of an integrated abusive behaviour that includes the intended charge of excessive licensing fees after adoption of the standard.[46] The concept of a 'single and continuous infringement' was originally developed by the European Commission in the 1980s to cope with the problem of complex cartels.[47] Under this approach, which was confirmed by the ECJ, diverse acts of different firms are attributed to a 'single and overall agreement' within the reach of Article 101(1) TFEU (ex-Article 81(1) EC). The transfer of this concept to Article 102 TFEU, however, is not possible, because the dominant position must already have existed at the time of the allegedly abusive behaviour. To construe an 'integrated abusive behaviour' would amount to subjecting a firm without market power at the time of the relevant conduct retroactively to the rules that must be obeyed only by dominant enterprises. This is not acceptable. Therefore, it is not possible to infer an infringement of Article 102 TFEU just from the deceptive conduct during

---

46 Loest and Bartlik, *supra* n. 41, at 51 et seq. In the same direction now F Fischmann, 'Die Pflicht zur Lizenzerteilung in Patent-Ambush-Fällen nach deutschem und europäischem Kartellrecht' (2010) *GRUR Int* 185, at 192–4.

47 Commission Decision of 23 April 1986, Case IV/31.149 – *Polypropylene* [1986] OJ L 230/1; Commission Decision of 7 June 2000, Case COMP/36.545/F3 – *Amino Acids* [2001] OJ L 152/24. For an overview see, inter alia, R Wish, *Competition Law* (5th edn 2004) 96; for a detailed analysis see M Dreher, 'Die komplexe und fortdauernde Zuwiderhandlung im europäischen Kartellrecht' (2007) *J Comp L (ZWeR)* 276.

the standardization procedure if, at that time, the patent owner did not hold a market-dominating position yet. However, this does not exclude the consideration of the deceptive conduct applied during the first stage, when it is to be determined whether there is an (exploitative) abuse by charging unusually high royalties in the second stage once the proprietary standard has been implemented.

3.2.2 Control of excessive licensing fees (exploitative abuse)

Any form of price control by competition authorities is a very problematic tool and should be used only as a means of last resort. Since the multifold policy implications cannot be discussed here, I have to constrain myself to some remarks in the special context of patent ambush cases. On the one hand, high prices serve as an incentive for vigorous competition and attract market entry. On the other hand – at least in some circumstances – consumers and other market participants may need protection from being exploited. While US antitrust law follows exclusively the first position, that the charging of monopoly prices is not unlawful in itself, Article 102 lit. a TFEU specifically prohibits the imposition of 'unreasonable' prices.

In its decision in *Trinko*, the US Supreme Court expressed the view that in general the possibility to charge even excessively high prices is 'an important element of the free market system', since the opportunity for monopoly profits '– at least for a short period – is what attracts "business acumen" in the first place; it induces risk taking that produces innovation and economic growth'.[48]

However, the *situation is different if market entry is blocked*, because access to the prevailing or single standard is controlled by a patent. If, in addition, network effects and lock-in effects owing to the implementation of an industry-wide standard reaffirm the dominant position of the incumbent and create a long lasting and firmly entrenched monopoly, then there is good cause for protecting those living at the mercy of the monopolist from being exploited. In such a scenario the *Trinko* rationale does not apply. Therefore, there is good reason for a limited control of excessive prices in exceptional circumstances as a last resort, and that is the situation in Europe, where the Commission is very reluctant in applying Article 102 TFEU to price misuses. Nevertheless, it is the law and one cannot totally do away with the explicit provision of Article 102 lit.

---

48 *Verizon Communications Inc. v Law Offices of Curtis V. Trinko, LLP*, 540 US 398, 405 (2004).

a TFEU.[49] Thus, a legitimate use of this provision, in my view, would be to refer to it as *a means of last resort* in cases of what one may characterize as '*super-dominance*', which goes beyond a mere market-dominating positition but is characterized by *very high and petrified barriers to entry*. Of course, there still is the practical problem of determining which prices or royalties are 'excessive'. Under the general approach taken by the ECJ a price is deemed 'excessive' when 'it has no reasonable relation to the economic value of the product supplied'.[50] In a first step the difference between the costs actually incurred and the price charged is to be determined; if the comparison reveals a very high profit margin, the second step of the analysis encompasses the assessment of whether the price imposed is 'either unfair in itself or when compared to competing products'.[51] The difficulties in ascertaining whether the price charged for a given product is 'unreasonably high' or 'excessive' cannot be discussed here in detail. A generally suitable approach involves a comparison of the price or licensing fee charged, in the case at hand, with that in other regional markets or similar product/technology markets ('yardstick competition'). With regard to identifying exploitation in a patent ambush scenario it is argued that a reasonable royalty would amount to a *fair compensation for the value of the technology* that is transferred, as the European Commission put it in the *Microsoft* case.[52] The *strategic value* stemming from the market power conferred on the patent holder by incorporating its technology into the standard *should be excluded*. Therefore, one ought to differentiate between the value of the invention itself and the demand created by the adoption of the standard, that is, the impact of the lock-in effect.[53] In order to assess which part of the royalty is to be attributed to the incorporation of the

---

[49] See E Paulis, 'Article 82 EC and Exploitative Conduct', in C.-D. Ehlermann and M. Marquis (eds), *European Competition Law Annual 2007: A Reform Approach to Article 82 EC* (2008) 515, at 517; Gerardin, *supra* n. 5, at 345 with further references.

[50] Case 27/76 *United Brands v Commission* [1978] ECR 207, para 250.

[51] Id. at para 252.

[52] Commission Decision of 27 February 2008, Case COMP/C-3/37.792 – *Microsoft*, para 107, http://ec.europa.eu/competition/antitrust/cases/dec_docs/37792/37792_3997_9.pdf (accessed December 2010).

[53] See A Layne-Farrar, AJ Padilla and R Schmalensee, 'Pricing Patents for Licensing in Standard-Setting Organisations: Making Sense of FRAND Commitments' (2007) 74 *Antitrust LJ* 671, at 675; Petritsi, *supra* n. 2, at 38; M.R. Patterson, 'Inventions, Industry Standards, and Intellectual Property' (2002) 17 *Berkeley Tech LJ* 1043, 1056 et seq.; A. Klees, 'Standardsetzung und "patent ambush" im US-amerikanischen und europäischen Wettbewerbsrecht' (2008) *EWS* 449, at 454. For a different view see Gerardin, *supra* n. 5, at 343 et seq.

technology into the standard, one could look, for example, to former but similar technologies or to internal calculations or documents of the patentee prior to the establishment of the standard. An alternative approach refers to a model of an auction-like process for the selection of technologies to be embodied in a given standard.[54] In any case, to determine the value of the technology itself remains a very difficult task.

Normally the burden of proving that the royalties charged by the patent owner are excessive lies with the claimant alleging an exploitative abuse in violation of Article 102 TFEU. However, at least if a clear case of a patent ambush scenario can be established, it seems appropriate to alleviate or shift the burden of proof to the patent holder and require it to show that the royalties claimed are reasonable and not excessive. If the patent holder has not acted bona fide during the standardization procedure by withholding relevant information on its IPRs, in my view a *presumption* is justified that the royalties claimed after the adoption of the standard are indeed excessive, and the patent holder should be required to rebut this presumption. In this way one could provide, at least indirectly, some incentive for a bona fide participation in standard-setting procedures and limit the risk of patent ambush scenarios to a certain extent. However, in order to secure an undistorted procedure of standard-setting, additional measures ought to be taken.

4 ADDITIONAL MEANS TO DISCOURAGE PATENT AMBUSH STRATEGIES

First, it seems necessary to strengthen the enforceability of the IPR policy of SSOs by, for example, providing for mandatory arbitration if a dispute arises as to whether the royalty claimed really is 'fair, reasonable and non-discriminatory'. This is the flaw of any obligation by a patent holder to license its rights on FRAND terms: the concept is so vague that disputes are rather likely on this issue in concrete cases after the adoption of the standard.[55] In any case it remains very difficult to calculate the costs for using the standard in advance. Particularly if a standard contains multi-

[54] D.G. Swanson and W.J. Baumol, 'Reasonable and Nondiscriminatory (RAND) Royalties, Standards Selection, and Control of Market Power' (2005) 73 *Antitrust LJ* 1 (2005). For a critique see Gerardin, *supra* n. 5, at 352–6.

[55] Cf., inter alia, Layne-Farrar et al., *supra* n. 53; D. Geradin, 'Standardisation and Technological Innovation: Some Reflections on Ex-ante Licensing, FRAND, and the Proper Means to Reward Innovators' (2006) 29 *World Comp* 511, at 513; Loest and Bartlik, *supra* n. 41, at 52–4; Patterson, *supra* n. 53, at 1053 and 1054.

ple essential patents, the cumulative royalty rate to be paid by users may quickly become too burdensome. A solution to this problem may be the creation of a patent pool that could issue block licences at a reasonable price level to users, but the design of the pool, the pricing mechanism for licensing and the distribution of the royalties must be undertaken with great care in order to avoid problems under Article 101 TFEU.[56]

Another way to avoid the problem of uncertainty with regard to the cost of implementing a proposed standard would be to provide *ex ante*, prior to the final adoption of the standard, for a *disclosure by the patent owner of the maximum royalty* it would charge *under FRAND terms*. This price information – relating to the cost of the patented input – could then be a permissible topic for potential users of the patent to discuss when deciding whether to select it or to choose an alternative technology to be included into the standard. One could conceive a binding obligation of the patent holder to license its rights on terms already specified in advance, either unilaterally or after a negotiation of licensing terms between the patent holder and the other members of the SSO.

Obviously, in the latter case the question arises whether this would amount to an illegal price-fixing. In connection with standard-setting organizations, in the US, the FTC as well as the Antitrust Division of the Department of Justice and the Antitrust Modernization Commission have proposed to apply a rule-of-reason standard rather than the per se rule against horizontal price-fixing. Others point to the fact that this might conflict with the case-law on anticompetitive information exchanges, and qualify it as an oligopsonistic collusion among competitors concerning the price to be paid for a patented input.[57] In the standardization context, however, the *ex ante exchange of price information* ought to be viewed as an implicit pre-condition of the SSO members' endorsement of that particular technology for adoption in the industry standard. Even if one does not follow the proposition that usually the ancillary restraints doctrine may apply, the danger of a naked price restraint is not very high in connection with standardization procedures. Even if the ex ante licensing amounted to a price restraint, it could probably be justified under the rule of reason, or under Article 101(3) TFEU respectively, as long as it can be demonstrated that the *ex ante* exchange of price information, or

[56] For the evaluation of patent pools under Article 101 TFEU see, inter alia, Commission Notice – Guidelines on the application of Article 81 of the Treaty to technology transfer agreements, [2004] OJ C 101/2, paras 41 and 210 et seq.; H. Ullrich, 'Patent pools – policy and problems', in J. Drexl (ed.), *Research Handbook on Intellectual Property and Competition Law* (2008) 139.

[57] Sidak, *supra* n. 5, at 127–88 with further references.

agreement on royalty rates, is likely to increase efficiency because it makes the adoption of the standard possible, and is likely to benefit consumers as the licensees would be able to pass through royalty reductions in their pricing of the downstream product incorporating the patented technology. The expected social cost of a patent holdup, including the hampering of efficiency-enhancing standardization procedures at large, may well exceed the possible losses owing to an oligopsonistic coordination between the members of the SSO with regard to the royalty rates of specific standard-related IPRs. But, of course, this is a hot topic for further discussion.

Finally, I would like to direct the reader's attention to the possible application of unfair trade laws. To be sure, we have obviously no practical experience yet, neither in Europe nor in the United States, but it could be a promising field for future research and adjudication. In the United States, for example, one might consider a pure Section 5 FTC claim, based solely on the aspect of deception and not recurring simultaneously to an exclusionary practice Section 2 monopolization claim as in *Rambus*; while in the EU Member States the respective unfair trade acts may apply to deceptive acts distorting the standard-setting process and amounting to an unfair obstruction of (potential) competitors (see, for example, Section 4 No. 10 of the German Act against Unfair Competition (UWG), which prohibits unduly hindering competitors in their business activities).

5 SUMMARY AND CONCLUSION

In contrast to Section 2 Sherman Act and Section 5 FTC Act the application of Article 102 TFEU to patent ambush strategies is limited to prevent exploitative price abuses by charging excessive royalties once the standard has been adopted. For at the time of the deceptive conduct (non-disclosure of relevant patents/patent applications during the standard-setting process) the patent holder usually does not yet have a market-dominating position that could be abused. The deceptive conduct itself, therefore, may only be caught by (national) unfair competition rules, as long as market dominance did not exist at the time of the relevant behaviour. On the other hand, also in contrast to US antitrust law, no proof of causation is required under Article 102 TFEU when it is applied to the subsequent price misuse. In this regard it is not necessary to demonstrate that – if the patents or patent applications had been disclosed – the standard would not have been adopted or a different standard would have been implemented. The difficulties in assessing the (amount of) royalty overcharge may be alleviated by shifting the burden of proof to the patent holder trying to enforce its rights in a patent ambush scenario.

Whether the fight against excessive royalties provides sufficient incentives to refrain from engaging in patent ambush strategies in the first place seems doubtful, since the implementation of its own technology in the standard and the prospect of high royalty revenues (even at FRAND terms) remain very attractive to the patent holder. More legal certainty for all participants and maybe an additional incentive to disclose the IPRs could result from *ex ante* negotiations on the licensing terms and their fixing before the standard is finally adopted. Competitive risks of this approach are to be weighed against the advantages of avoiding the difficult task of specifying what 'FRAND' terms actually mean in concrete cases. At least the SSOs should improve the enforceability of the usual obligation to license standard-related IPRs on FRAND terms by providing for a mandatory arbitration clause.

11. Three statutory regimes at impasse: Reverse payments in pay-for-delay settlement agreements between brand-name and generic drug companies

Rudolph J.R. Peritz

Bayer AG recently paid $398 million to generic competitors in exchange for their promise to stay off the market for Ciprofloxacin for the next six years.[1] Cipro, as it is called, is a widely used antibiotic. In these agreements to settle patent infringement cases, Bayer made reverse payments – so called because they were paid *by* the plaintiff patent holder *to* the accused infringers.[2]

There is outrage in the United States over these pay-for-delay agreements. President Obama's proposed budget declares that his 'administration will prevent drug companies from blocking generic drugs from consumers by prohibiting anticompetitive agreements and collusion between brand name and generic drug manufacturers intended to keep generic drugs off the market.'[3] The most recent Bill to prohibit such settlement agreements has recently been sent to the United States Senate from the Judiciary Committee.[4] The public outrage and political responses

---

1 *In re Ciprofloxacin Hydrochloride Antitrust Litigation*, 363 F Supp 2d 514 (EDNY 2005), *aff'd*, 544 F.3d. 1323 (Fed. Cir. 2008).

2 Useful treatments of this subject include CS Hemphill, 'Paying for Delay' (2006) 81 *NYU L Rev* 1553; C Shapiro, 'Antitrust Limits to Patent Settlements' (2003) 34 *Rand J Econ* 31; M O'Rourke and JF Brodley, 'An Incentives Approach to Patent Settlements' (2003) 87 *Minn L Rev* 1767; M Carrier, 'Unsettling Drug Patent Settlements: A Framework for Presumptive Illegality' (2009) 108 *Mich L Rev* 37.

3 http://www.whitehouse.gov/omb/fy2010_key_healthcare/ (accessed November 2009).

4 Reported in 'Senate Judiciary Committee Approves Bill Banning Reverse Payment Agreements' (16 October 2009) *Pat Tradem & Copyr J* BNA Daily Update #198.

are reactions to the spate of federal court opinions approving such payments despite their apparent anticompetitive effects.

I will discuss the legal policies driving these antitrust decisions at the end of this chapter. Antitrust is a late comer to the fierce competition over patented drugs, competition that permeates the approval process in the Food & Drug Administration, the FDA, competition that is restrained by these pay-for-delay settlement agreements. To understand the scenario, we begin with the Patent Act[5] and its relationship with the Food, Drug, and Cosmetic Act[6] – the food and drug act for short – as administered by the FDA. The story of pay-for-delay settlements begins there.

This is a story of three statutory regimes seeking to promote innovation, three clusters of doctrine and policy that have interacted only to reach impasse: the Patent Act, the 1984 amendment to the food and drug act, known as the Hatch-Waxman Act,[7] and finally the Sherman Anti-trust Act.[8]

Let us begin with the patent law, which grants legal monopolies and so is thought to be the antagonist of antitrust law, which promotes competition. But patent law has its own internal competition policy.[9] Most obviously, patent law promotes competition by innovation. One form of this competition is research and development. But there is a fundamental problem, perhaps even a contradiction, in recent judicial expression of patent policy. In 1984, the Federal Circuit Court of Appeals – the special court created by Congress to hear all appeals involving patents – held that unlicensed experimental use of patented inventions is not permitted in commercial settings. In the particular case, the court held that a generic drug producer infringed a pharmaceutical patent when it experimented with one of its active ingredients in preparation for seeking FDA approval.[10]

---

5 35 USC § 1 et seq.

6 21 USC § 301 et seq.

7 Id. at § 355.

8 15 USCA § 1 et seq.

9 See, e.g. RJR Peritz, 'Competition Policy and its Implications for Intellectual Property Rights in the United States' in SD Anderman (ed.), *The Interface Between Intellectual Property Rights and Competition Policy* (2007) (earlier version appearing in *The Intellectual Property/Competition Interface Project*, for the IP Institute of the Republic of Singapore (2003) (consultancy white paper to inform drafting of competition statute for Republic of Singapore). IP policy generally is best understood as clusters of competition policies, beginning with a baseline of free competition. RJR Peritz, 'The Political Economy of Progress: IP Rights and Competition' (work-in-progress).

10 *Roche Products Inc. v Bolar Pharmaceutical Co.*, 733 F.2d 858 (Fed. Cir. 1984).

The decision effectively delayed market entry by generics producers, who compete against brand name manufacturers not only on price but also in litigation to challenge patent validity and scope. Moreover, FDA procedures already required generics producers to go through a lengthy and expensive approval process *de novo* even though their products were chemically identical to brand-name drugs that had already been approved. Combined with the Federal Circuit decision, the requirement of full FDA re-testing effectively delayed competition by generics for years beyond the patent period for brand-name drugs.

At the same time, the lengthy FDA approval process was also affecting the branded companies whose research and development produced the vast majority of new pharmaceuticals. Indeed, the industry claimed an 'innovation crisis' starting in the 1970s, when the number of new pharmaceuticals beginning human testing fell over 80 percent after Congress amended the food and drug act to require the showing that drugs were not only safe but also effective in their intended uses. The declared crisis in pharmaceutical research and development was attributed to the increased time needed for FDA approval and, with it, a steep decline in the patent's effective life to seven years.[11]

Congress amended the food and drug act by passing the Hatch-Waxman Act of 1984, not only to open bottlenecks in the FDA approval process but also to overturn the Federal Circuit decision that prohibited unlicensed experimental use of patented drugs in preparation for seeking FDA approval.

The legislation intended a balancing of policies to promote competition by innovation by brand-name producers and to promote competition on price by generic makers. Experience would show the statute was a flawed attempt to promote both forms of competition in the pharmaceutical industry.

Nonetheless, the effort was well-intended. One the one hand, the 1984 legislation addressed the brand name producers' declared 'innovation crisis' by extending the drug patent term for as much as five years to take into account the lengthy FDA approval process.[12] On average, the period of exclusivity for drugs covered by valid patents would increase from 7 to 12 years.

On the other hand, Congress intended to hasten price competition by generics in three important ways. First, Congress overturned the Federal

---

11 Cf. Carrier, *supra* n. 2.

12 The amendment adds to the patent term half the time taken for clinical trials plus the subsequent waiting period for FDA approval, up to a maximum of 14 additional years.

Circuit decision and opened the door to unlicensed experimental use when it involved drug testing associated with FDA approval. Second, generics producers could now rely largely on branded manufacturers' prior FDA testing. This expedited approval process would permit generic producers to enter the market before patent expiration if the branded manufacturer's patent was either invalid or not infringed by the generic. It should be noted that FDA approval processes as a general matter are confidential. Third, Congress injected an incentive for generic producers to challenge drug patents and seek early entry by granting the first filer a 180-day period of exclusivity in the generics market.[13]

Despite best intentions, the statutory framework quickly began to break down. When the generic producer seeks early entry, the statute requires that notice be given the patent holder, notice spelling out the basis for contending invalidity or non-infringement.[14] If the patent holder sues the first filer for infringement within 45 days of notice, the statute calls for the FDA to halt consideration of the generic's application for 30 months, unless a court earlier finds the patent invalid or not infringed – an unlikely prospect given crowded federal court dockets. Of course such responsive infringement suits have become automatic.

This *automatic* stay is inconsistent as a matter of policy with the recent Supreme Court decision in *eBay* (2006).[15] Interpreting the Patent Act provision concerning the injunction remedy, the Court rejected the Federal Circuit's doctrine that injunctions were granted as a matter of course to protect presumptively valid patents: in the Federal Circuit's view, a property remedy for a property right. But the Supreme Court reminded the Federal Circuit that the Patent Act calls upon judges to issue injunctions only after balancing traditional equitable principles. There is nothing automatic about injunctions in patent cases. Moreover, automatic 30-

---

[13] In 2003, Congress amended the statute by defining a series of events that trigger forfeiture of the exclusivity bonus. 21 USC § 355(j)(5)(D)(i). The 180-day exclusivity bonus provides the first filer with two significant benefits beyond the obvious head start in the generics market. First, market studies have shown that first generics tend to price their products just below the price of brand name drugs. It is the entry of subsequent producers that brings price competition to the market. In consequence, the period of exclusivity delivers six months of high profits to the first filer. Second, firstness promises longevity because pharmacies tend to use only one generics supplier and so there is a formulary inertia that favors the incumbent generic supplier, the first filer, who must typically do no more than meet subsequent suppliers' prices to retain its excusive place on the pharmacy's formulary list.

[14] While notice of the generic's FDA application is public, the substance remains secret.

[15] *eBay Inc. v MercExchange, LLC*, 126 S Ct 1837 (2006).

month stays under the Hatch-Waxman Act make little sense in light of an FTC study showing that pharmaceutical patent holders have lost almost 75 percent of patent infringement cases, despite the strong presumption that requires accused infringers to prove patent invalidity by clear and convincing evidence.[16]

It is not surprising, then, that drug patent holders pay generics – accused infringers – to settle infringement cases that statistics suggest they are likely to lose three times out of four.[17] The Hatch-Waxman Act was passed on the assumption that generics and consumers have a common interest in price competition. But the statute inadvertently changed the game. Now branded and generic producers have the common interest: the pay-for-delay provisions cost the branded companies far less than the profits they would lose from price competition, while generic makers gain far more than they would from competing on the market. In effect, it's the consumer who pays.[18]

In my view, the food and drug act requires further amendment. First, when a case is settled, the first filer's 180-day period of exclusivity should revert to the next generics filer. Restoring this incentive to file would revive the competitive pressure intended by Congress. Second, the automatic 30-month stay should be eliminated; instead, injunctive relief should be available to the drug patent holder only under the same demanding principles applied in other patent cases. Third, the reasons claimed for patent invalidity or non-infringement in a generic filer's FDA confidential application for early market entry should no longer be kept secret. Public disclosure would have two likely benefits. First, free information about a drug patent's infirmities and limitations would improve the conditions for other generics to seek early entry. Second, the size of reverse payments would decrease to the extent branded producers are paying for generics' agreement to maintain secrecy.

16 http://www.ftc.gov/os/2002/07/genericdrugstudy.pdf (accessed November 2009) at p. vi.

17 The settlement has a bonus for the paying patent holder: the patents remain presumptively valid.

18 To make matters even worse, the Hatch-Waxman Act showed an unintended loophole that permitted the first filing generic to keep the 180-day period of exclusivity even after settlement. As a result, all other generics were blocked from entering the market until 180 days after the first filer's delayed entry – years later, if at all. And so the brand name drug-maker had another valuable reason to settle. Congress did pass an amendment in 2003 that narrowed the loop hole prospectively. The first filer would now forfeit the exclusivity bonus if it failed to market its generic drug within 75 days of FDA approval or of an appellate court determination that the patent is invalid or not infringed.

It is in this context that federal courts have heard antitrust challenges to the reverse payments in agreements settling patent infringement cases. Both the Federal Trade Commission and private plaintiffs have filed numerous lawsuits claiming that settlements with pay-for-delay provisions violate the antitrust laws as agreements in restraint of trade or conspiracies to monopolize.

The first appellate decision, handed down in 2003, concluded that the agreement was 'a classic example of a per se illegal restraint of trade.'[19] The FTC has taken the more moderate position that these agreements are presumptively illegal.[20]

But all federal appeals courts since 2003 have rejected the views that such agreements are per se or presumptively illegal under Sherman Act § 1 and its FTC § 5 equivalent. For example, the Eleventh Circuit in reversing the FTC applied a truncated rule of reason to conclude that the pay-for-delay agreement was reasonable and thus legal. The primary rationale given was that when the agreement stays within the scope of the patent, the patent holder is merely exercising its statutory right to exclude others from making, using, or selling the patented invention. Exercising patent rights cannot be a violation of the antitrust laws. The court also relied on policies in favor of settling lawsuits.[21]

In the past few years, these two rationales – patents as exclusionary rights and settlements as deserving deference – have been taken up by the 2nd Circuit in New York and the powerful Federal Circuit in Washington to conclude that such agreements are per se *legal* unless the patent is a sham or the infringement case is entirely baseless. This standard has a profound impact that goes beyond the antitrust injury to consumers, the higher prices for pharmaceuticals.[22] It spills over into patent policy. The courts, in refusing to consider the reasonableness of the agreement, have also put aside the question of patent viability. The 2nd Circuit stated explicitly that its policy of favoring settlement is so strong that it extends to 'fatally weak' patents, 'even though such settlements will inevitably protect patent monopolies that are, perhaps, undeserved.' This overwhelming judicial deference to case settlements, which are, after all, just private contracts, creates the perverse incentive to litigate and settle rather than innovate and compete.[23]

There are two recent class action suits brought by purchasers of

---

19 *In re Cardizem*, 332 F.3d 896 (6th Cir. 2003).

20 See *supra* n. 15.

21 *Schering-Plough Corp. v FTC*, 402 F.3d 1056 (11th Cir. 2006).

22 *In re Ciprofloxacin Hydrochloride Antitrust Litig.*, 544 F.3d 1323 (Fed. Cir. 2008); *In re Tamoxifen Citrate Antitrust Litig.*, 466 F.3d 187 (2d Cir. 2006).

23 *In re Tamoxifen litigation*, 466 F.3d at 211.

Cipro, the subject matter of Bayer's $398 million reverse payment that I mentioned to open the chapter. In one, the Supreme Court refused to review the Federal Circuit's determination of per se legality[24] even though 54 law, economics, and business scholars filed an *amicus* brief urging the Court to overturn the decision. In the other Cipro class action, the 2nd Circuit affirmed the lower court's decision approving the settlement agreement. Many thought the Court would take a more skeptical attitude toward the agreement and depart from precedent because the Court prior to oral argument addressed an extraordinary letter to the Solicitor General of the United States inviting 'the Executive Branch to address the question.'[25] The invitation is highly unusual if not unprecedented in its acknowledgement of criticism – here by the Solicitor General that the 2nd Circuit's influential opinion in its prior reverse payments case was 'incorrect.' An open letter from ten large consumer rights organizations urges the government to accept the invitation and confute the view that these settlement agreements are legal under the antitrust laws.[26]

The 54 scholars' *amicus* brief urged the United States Supreme Court to reject the view of per se legality, arguing that the public policy in favor of settlement does not merit such weight. In light of the 73 percent failure rate of pharmaceutical patents in cases actually litigated, there is a more powerful public interest in invalidating weak patents, stopping unearned monopoly profits, and bringing to a halt the perverse incentives produced by these reverse payments.

Indeed, it was five years ago that the Supreme Court affirmed the doctrine that patents do not grant antitrust immunity.[27] Moreover, there is longstanding Supreme Court precedent that IP licensing cannot provide a pretext for agreements in restraint of trade.[28] The Second and Federal

---

24 *Arkansas Carpenters Health and Welfare Fund v Bayer AG*, 129 S Ct 2828 (2009).

25 *Arkansas Carpenters Health and Welfare Fund v Bayer AG*, 2d Cir., No. 05-2851-cv(L), reported in (BNA 1 September 2010) 80 *Patent, Tradem & Copyr J* 636. Letter re: In re Ciprofloxacin Hydrochloride Antitrust Litigation to the Office of the Solicitor General of the United States from Clerk of the Court, on behalf of a three-judge panel for the United States Court of Appeals for the Second Circuit, dated 6 April 2009.

26 Letter re: Need for the Administration's Views in Pharmaceutical 'Exclusion Payments' cases written on Behalf of [10 named consumer rights organizations] to United States Attorney General Eric H Holder, Jr, US Department of Justice, dated 17 April 2009, on file with the author.

27 *Illinois Tool Works Inc. v Independent Ink, Inc.*, 547 US 28 (2006).

28 *Palmer v BRG of Ga., Inc.*, 498 US 46 (1990) (finding per se illegal copyright licensing agreement as pretext for territorial market allocation).

Circuits thus seem to have got it wrong in declaring that every patent holder has an absolute right to prevent competition within the 'exclusionary zone' of all patents, including the many that are weak. This approach takes the rebuttable status of patent validity and treats it as irrebuttable, even though the Supreme Court has long characterized a patent as something closer to a probable property right.[29] Moreover, it seems pretty clear that the generics' promises to delay entry are in consideration for the large reverse payments, not in concern for the restraining effects attributable to weak patents.

So, what is the prognosis? If the Supreme Court had granted the petition in the Federal Circuit's *Cipro* case to resolve the conflict in the circuit courts, the outcome would have been in deep doubt, in my view. Why? Because there are two powerful policies that collide, two policies each of which the Court has supported independently. For one, there is the strong support for property rights, especially intellectual property rights. And so the Court is inclined to find as reasonable an agreement whose restraints fall within the so-called 'exclusionary zone' of the patent. The second policy is procedural rather than substantive. In recent years, the Supreme Court has moved away from clear rules and toward balancing tests in both antitrust and patent cases. Per se rules have given way to more fact-intensive inquiries. In patent cases, for example, the Supreme Court has rejected bright line rules fashioned by the Federal Circuit for injunctions, prosecution history estoppel, and prior art reference materials to determine non-obviousness.[30] In antitrust, the Court's rejection of the century-old doctrine that resale price maintenance is per se illegal is only the most recent example of a shift toward the rule of reason.[31]

Does this shift make sense? In theory, a rule of reason calls for a flexible approach intended to take into account the particular commercial circumstances. And that's good. But, in practical terms, a rule of reason analysis

---

[29] A patent represents a 'legal conclusion by the Patent Office, . . . often ex parte, . . . on factors as to which reasonable men can differ widely. Consequently, it does not seem to us to be unfair to require a patentee to defend the Patent Office's judgment . . .' *Lear, Inc. v Adkins*, 395 US 653, 670 (1969).

[30] See, e.g. *eBay* (more flexible approach to injunctive remedy), *supra* note. 15; *KSR Int'l. Co. v Teleflex Inc.*, 127 S Ct 1727, 1742 (2007) (less rigid approach to determining prior art for nonobviousness inquiry; *Festo Corp. v Shoketsu Kogyo Kabushiki Co., Inc.*, 535 US 722 (2002) (more open approach to determining extent of prosecution history estoppel).

[31] See, e.g. *Leegin Creative Leather Products, Inc. v PSKS, Inc.*, 551 US 877 (2007) (applying rule of reason to minimum resale price maintenance); *State Oil Co. v Khan*, 522 US 3 (1997) (applying rule of reason to maximum resale price maintenance).

in antitrust amounts to de facto legality because it produces high cost and high risk cases, which deters litigation. This closing of the court house door in my view is inconsistent with the longstanding US policy favoring and, indeed, depending on private plaintiffs, often small firms and consumers unable to afford the expensive litigation of rule of reason cases; moreover, the standards for class action suits have become exceedingly difficult to attain. And so I am disinclined from a full-blown rule of reason.

The best solution in the antitrust cases, in my view, would be adoption of the FTC's approach of presumptive illegality, which would shift some cost and risk to the brand-name manufacturer and, as a result, improve conditions for generics to challenge weak patents and compete on price. Moreover, the approach would mitigate the perverse incentives that result from shielding weak patents from scrutiny. Indeed, a *strong* presumption of illegality would reflect judicial experience, in particular the 73 percent failure rate in cases litigated to date. Finally, the FTC would become an even more forceful arbiter of these settlement agreements.

Together with amendments to fix the food and drug act, what would be the result of an antitrust analysis that begins with a strong presumption that reverse payments in pay-for-delay settlements are illegal? The market for pharmaceuticals would sooner become price competitive, weak drug patents would be more open to challenge, and as a result consumers would save billions of dollars annually without taking from branded drug companies legitimately earned incentives to engage in research and development.

12. Patent ambush and reverse payments: Comments

Gustavo Ghidini

My comments are very short and address both topics jointly. I believe that, in the case of both reverse payment and patent ambush, antitrust enforcement should not take into consideration, as arguments for defence, the questions of validity and/or scope of the patent concerned, or the degree of market power it may embody or has come to embody.

In either case, indeed, on the one hand, the competitor's behaviour is not based, in a proper sense, on the exercise of her/his statutory patent rights (see below). On the other hand, symmetrically, the rationale of antitrust enforcement rests on *different and independent* legal grounds, not essentially influenced by 'strictly IP' questions. Of course, patents come into play, but in relation to the *factual*, rather than the *legal*, framework.

Take, for example, the issue of reverse payments: what has this practice to do, in a proper sense, with the exploitation of patent rights? Patent rights allow the exclusion of free riders, and not of lawful entries. In other words, contractual exclusion is not a legal exercise of patent rights. Therefore, a pay-for-delay settlement is just *a straightforward horizontal agreement* in restraint of competition, which would be equally illicit – this is a counterproof of my assumption – even if no patent existed. Wouldn't pay-for-delay settlements violate antitrust rules even if they took place between two producers of generics? As Abbott and Michel of the FTC have convincingly argued in 2006,[1] 'the payment and not the patent provides exclusion resulting from the agreement'.

Analogously in patent ambush cases: here, thanks to his fraudulent

[1] AF Abbot and ST Michel, 'The right balance of competition policy and intellectual property law: a perspective on settlement of pharmaceutical patent litigation' (2005) 46 *IDEA* 1, also available at: http://nessiteras.piercelaw.edu/assets/pdf/idea-vol46-no1-abbott-michel.pdf (accessed December 2010). Mr Abbott was Associate Director, and Ms Michel Chief Counsel at the Federal Trade Commission. See also *In re Cardizem CD Antitrust Litigation*, 332 F.3d 896 (6th Cir. 2003), *cert. denied*, 543 US 939 (2004).

behaviour, the patent holder more easily achieves the adoption of his technology as the standard ('as all non-IPR holders would prefer an IPR-free standard'[2]) and then, after that standard has been adopted and diffused, forces competitors to pay 'unreasonable' royalties[3] 'after they have incurred the sunk costs they would have to write off if they refused the licensing offer'.[4]

Again, in order to qualify this practice as a type of anti-competitive abuse (as the FTC did in the *Rambus* case[5]), one does not need to get involved in any properly patent-related questions, in particular, whether or not the patent has given rise to specific market power in consequence of the adoption of the standard.[6] And again – even apart from contractual, pre-contractual and unfair competition remedies (the last autonomously emerging in case the patentee does not hold market power in the antitrust sense) – the real McCoy of the antitrust violation lies in the deception that 'harmed competition by distorting a standard-setting process designed to serve consumers welfare through *ex ante* competition among rival technologies',[7] rather than in an undue exercise of patent rights.

Under EU law, one might directly apply Article 102 TFEU, since the imposition of the higher licence fees constitutes, as indicated above, an abusive pricing practice where the price is 'unfair' because it is the outcome of the deception. As one can see, the ultimate rationale is basi-

---

[2] D Guellec and B van Pottelsberghe de la Potterie, *The economics of the European patent system: IP policy for innovation and competition* (2007) at 106.

[3] See the European Commission's 'Statement of Objections' issued against Rambus in 2007. 'Antitrust: Commission confirms sending a Statement of Objections to Rambus', Press release MEMO/07/330 of 28 August 2007.

[4] Guellec and de la Potterie, *supra* n. 2.

[5] See http://www.ftc.gov/os/adjpro/d9302/index.shtm. Eventually, in May 2007, as is well known, the FTC dropped the case after the Supreme Court refused to reverse the April 2009 decision of the District of Columbia Circuit of Appeals dismissing the charge. The pendulum, though, has swung in the other direction in Europe. See Commission Decision of 9 December 2009, Case COMP/38.636 – *Rambus*, http://ec.europa.eu/competition/antitrust/cases/dec_docs/38636/38636_1203_1.pdf; see also Summary Decision, OJ C 30/17. For an early discussion of the patent ambush as a competitive tort in the US and EU framework see E Petritsi, 'The Case of Unilateral Patent Ambush Under EC Competition Rules' (2005) 28 *World Comp* 25.

[6] Andreas Fuchs rightly speaks of a 'possible acquisition' of such power. See also *Broadcom Corp. v Quallcom, Inc.*, 501 F.3d 297 (3d Cir. 2007), which refers to 'the likelihood' that the inclusion in the standard will confer monopoly power upon the patent holder.

[7] Reply Brief for the Petitioner in *FTC v Rambus*, at 8 http://www.ftc.gov/os/caselist/0110017/0902rambusreplybrief.pdf (accessed December 2010).

cally the same under both regimes – even under US law the practice ultimately consists of a 'deception over price'.[8] And, again, we are facing a fraudulent conduct that would lead to the very same conclusion had it been referred to any other factual circumstance whose distortion was relevant for determining or manipulating the consent of the contracting party or competitor, as well as that of the standard-setting organisation, to the detriment of the consumers.[9]

In conclusion, it is the fraudulent manipulation that leads to the distortion of competition: inter alia, 'suppression of information about competition can be as anticompetitive as direct suppression of competition itself'.[10]

The foregoing remarks might also encourage a stricter than usual definition of the IP/competition law intersection, characterised by the joint occurrence of two conditions, namely (1) a restriction of competition that is or may be caused, albeit exceptionally, by the exercise – be it contractual or unilateral – of IPRs' inherent exclusionary faculties and (2) the possibility to remove such restriction through the imposition of a duty to exercise the patent rights in a non-exclusionary manner, that is, by granting FRAND licences.

---

8 Brief for Twenty Scholars as Amici Curiae in Support of Petitioner, *FTC v Rambus*, at 7.

9 See the *Unocal* case, where the FTC charged the Union Oil Company, California, of having manipulated the standard-setting process by providing misleading data relating to emission research that eventually led to the adoption of Unocal's technology as the standard for low emission gasoline. FTC docket No. 9305, 4 March 2003.

10 Amici Scholars Brief, *supra* n. 8, at 11.

13. Intellectual property in competition: How to promote dynamic competition as a goal

Josef Drexl

1 INTRODUCTION: THE 'IDEAL WORLD' OF SCHUMPETEREAN COMPETITION

Ever since Joseph Schumpeter published his theory of 'creative destruction',[1] it should have been clear that the protection of innovation by intellectual property rights (IPRs) does not as such contradict the competition principle. Schumpeter rejected the focus of traditional competition policy on price competition and highlighted the role of dynamic competition for better products as the driving force of economic growth. According to his ideas, even if superior technology leads to market dominance, continuous pressure by other innovators, who may 'destroy' the existing market position of the incumbent at any time, will keep the market competitive.

In the Schumpeterean worldview, patents – as IP rights that are expected to create incentives for innovation – are hence pro-competitive. Indeed, they exclude only a specific form of competition, namely competition by imitation based on price as the parameter of competition. Simultaneously, by pushing competitors to bring products to the market that are technologically superior and serve consumer interests better than the pre-existing ones, patents ideally promote competition by substitution. Hence, Schumpeterian 'dynamic' competition is based on a trade-off. Patents have the potential of restricting price competition and thereby enhance competition based on innovation. In line with these theories, modern competition policy accepts a theory of 'complementarity', according to which intellectual property and competition serve the same objectives, or as phrased in the EU Technology Transfer Guidelines:

[1] See J Schumpeter, *Capitalism, Socialism, and Democracy* (1942, new edn 1976) at 81–6.

> The fact that intellectual property laws grant exclusive rights of exploitation does not imply that intellectual property rights are immune from competition law intervention. . . . Nor does it imply that there is an inherent conflict between intellectual property rights and the Community competition rules. Indeed, both bodies of law share the same basic objective of promoting consumer welfare and an efficient allocation of resources. Innovation constitutes an essential and dynamic component of an open and competitive market economy. Intellectual property rights promote dynamic competition by encouraging undertakings to invest in developing new or improved products and processes. So does competition by putting pressure on undertakings to innovate. Therefore, both intellectual property rights and competition are necessary to promote innovation and ensure a competitive exploitation thereof.[2]

However, the functioning of Schumpeterean competition relies on particular assumptions that correspond to the economic assumptions of traditional patent law. In particular, it is assumed that each product competing in a relevant market is protected by a single, discrete patent. In this 'ideal world of Schumpeterean competition', patent-holding manufacturers only compete in product markets and use their patents as instruments for protecting investment in better products against imitation for free. This form of dynamic competition is depicted by Figure 13.1, below.

In real life, however, there are many markets for which this 'one patent = one product' assumption will not hold true. For instance, in the 'brave new world' of standardized technology all manufacturers who compete in a given product market have to rely on access to the standardized technology for being able to even enter the market. This technology will regularly be patent-protected. The patent holder, as the holder of an

---

[2] Commission Notice – Guidelines on the application of Article 81 of the EC Treaty to transfer of technology agreements, [2004] OJ C 101/1, para 7. The same principles are expressed in the US IP Licensing Guidelines:

> The intellectual property laws and the antitrust laws share the common purpose of promoting innovation and enhancing consumer welfare. The intellectual property laws provide incentives for innovation and its dissemination and commercialization by establishing enforceable property rights for the creators of new and useful products, more efficient processes, and original works of expression. In the absence of intellectual property rights, imitators could more rapidly exploit the efforts of innovators and investors without compensation. Rapid imitation would reduce the commercial value of innovation and erode incentives to invest, ultimately to the detriment of consumers. The antitrust laws promote innovation and consumer welfare by prohibiting certain actions that may harm competition with respect to either existing or new ways of serving consumers.

See US Department of Justice and US Federal Trade Commission, 'Antitrust Guidelines on the Licensing of Intellectual Property (6 April 1995) at Ch 1.0.

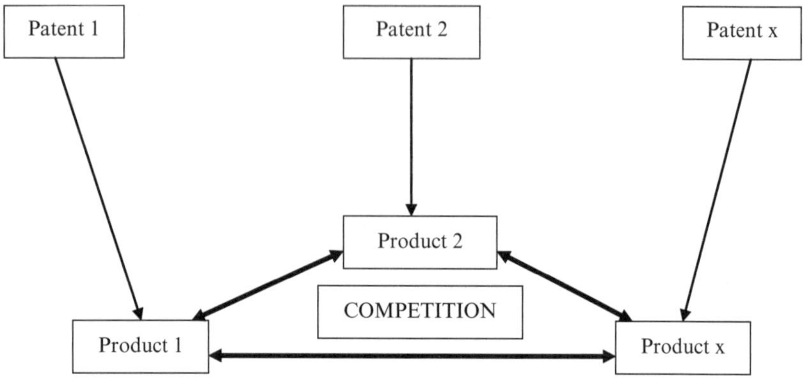

Figure 13.1 Competition in the 'one patent = one product' world

indispensable input for manufacturing standard-compatible products, has power to decide on who will be allowed to enter the market, whether it will retain ('monopolize') the secondary product market for itself and, finally, which prices will be charged for the use of the patented technology without feeling the pressure from competition. Even worse: in the information technology sector in particular, a technological standard may be controlled by several complementary patents that are held by different patentees. Accordingly, and as depicted by Figure 13.2, manufacturers may still compete in a product market characterized by technological standards, but competition in this market may easily be distorted by the

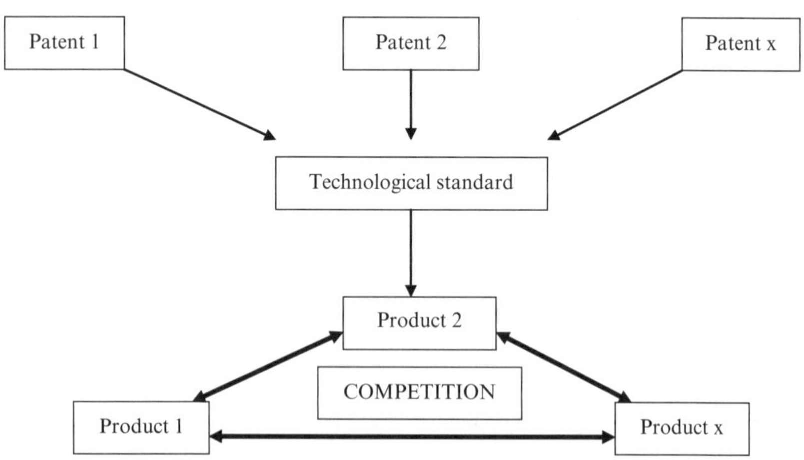

Figure 13.2 The brave new world of technological standards

use of the patent(s) controlling the standard. In such a situation, the patented technology itself becomes a commodity that has to be licensed in a technology market dominated by each holder of a complementary patent that is indispensable for entering the product market. This raises the competition law issue of how to deal with possible abuses of this market dominance.

If, as just described, complementary patents control a technological standard and if these patents are held by different persons, each patent holder can try to charge the monopoly price as the royalty fee for using the whole technology. Hence, in such a situation, patent protection leads to suboptimal use of the technology. This problem is characterized in economics as a 'tragedy of the anti-commons'.[3] The accumulation of too many rights in the hand of several owners may lead to inefficiency.

A market solution for this problem would be the creation of a technology pool. Competition law has to guarantee that such pools, in principle, contain only complementary patents and do not restrain competition by taking in patents that are technological substitutes.[4] Pooling is facilitated if the patent owners have already participated in selecting the patent in the framework of a standard-setting organization (SSO).[5]

Hence, standard-setting may be part of a solution to the competition problems related to technological standards. However, standard-setting by SSOs creates new competition problems, in particular the one of 'patent ambush'.[6] In the following analysis I will consider whether and how the pro-competitive rationale of patents, as described above by reference to Schumpeterean competition and the theory of complementarity, can be translated for a market characterized by network effects and standardization (at 2, below).

---

[3] See MA Heller, 'The Tragedy of the Anticommons: Property in the Transition of Marx to Markets' (1998) 111 *Harv L Rev* 621; MA Heller, *The Gridlock Economy: How Too Much Ownership Wrecks Markets, Stops Innovation and Costs Life* (2008); MA Heller and R Eisenberg, 'Can Patents Deter Innovation? The Anticommons in Biomedical Research' (2008) 280 *Science* 5364.

[4] On this difficult role of competition law see H Ullrich, 'Patent pools – Policy and problems', in J Drexl (ed.), *Research Handbook on Intellectual Property and Competition Law* (2008) 139. See also S Anderman, 'Industrial standards and technology pools: A regulatory challenge for EU competition law', in this volume, Ch. 14, below.

[5] This does not exclude that there are outsiders who hold complementary patents.

[6] See A Fuchs, 'Patent ambush strategies and Article 102 TFEU', in this volume, Ch. 10, above.

The other issue to be discussed (at 3, below) is a less obvious candidate for deepening the understanding of dynamic competition. When agencies, mostly in the US and the EU, nowadays identify pay-for-delay settlements between originator companies and generics producers in the pharmaceutical industry as a problem for competition law, they do not worry about Schumpeterian dynamic competition but price competition.[7] The argument goes that price competition is delayed by a settlement agreement that pays off the generics company for withdrawing the invalidity claim against the patent.[8] However, the analysis below will demonstrate that such settlements may also have a harmful effect on dynamic competition among originator companies.

2 PATENT AMBUSH

2.1 Why Standard-setting through SSOs Should Be Preferred to De Facto Standards

As indicated above, patent ambush occurs within standard-setting organizations (SSOs).[9] Technological standards appear in markets that are characterized by network effects, most typically experienced in markets of the information technology (IT) industry. In such markets efficiency is enhanced if all consumers are able to communicate with each other, transfer

---

7 See RJR Peritz, 'Three statutory regimes at impasse: "Reverse payments" in "pay-for-delay" settlement agreements between brand-name and generic drug companies', in this volume, Ch. 11, above.

8 The probably most convincing argument against the conformity of such settlements with competition law is that patent infringement cases are settled in a situation of uncertainty. The argument therefore goes that if the parties settled the case without a reverse payment to the generics company, in assessing the likelihood of losing or winning the case, they would allow the generics company to enter the market earlier. Hence, competition law does not prevent the parties from entering into a settlement as such. The parties are prevented from combining such settlement only with a reverse payment that would delay the market entry of the generics. Such settlement, therefore, has the same effect as a price cartel since it excludes price competition for said period. Also in favour of a competition law violation: J Drexl, '"Pay-for-Delay" and Blocking Patents – Targeting Pharmaceutical Companies Under European Competition Law', in: (2009) 40 *IIC* 75; J Drexl, '"Pay for Delay" – Zur kartellrechtlichen Beurteilung streitbeilegender Vereinbarungen bei Pharma-Patenten', in D Stauder, S Abel and T Friede (eds), *Sektorenuntersuchung Pharma der Europäischen Kommission – Kartellrechtliche Disziplinierung des Patentsystems?* (2010) 13.

9 Cf. the detailed description of this conduct by Fuchs, *supra* n. 6, at Part 1.

and consume information by using interoperable devices. Interoperability requires implementation of the same technological standard.[10]

In such instances, where network effects are present, the brave new world of standardization is economically superior to the ideal world of Schumpeterean competition. Given the efficiency gains emerging from the use of technological standards, competition law should not try to prevent standardization. Markets characterized by network effects will unavoidably migrate towards technological standards. The market position gained by the person controlling the standard based on IPRs is therefore to be considered a natural monopoly, which is economically superior to forced competition.

Yet competition law enforcers should be interested in the way in which technological standards emerge. Apart from legally defined standards, there are two forms by which markets can produce standards. Standardization through an SSO, which is run by the undertakings active in the relevant market, is only one form. The other option consists in de facto standardization. In the framework of the latter, each firm *competes for the standard* and, thereby, *for the market* by trying to convince all market participants to adopt the particular technology. Once a specific technology has attracted a critical number of customers, the benefits accruing from the high number of persons already using this technology will be the decisive competition parameter for convincing all other customers to accept this technology. Once the market is 'tipped' in this sense, the holder of the standardized technology will control the market. Even technologically superior products will then have problems being accepted by the industry. Such a market entry barrier will be even higher if the implementation of the standard involves high investment by the industry. In such situation there is an additional 'lock-in effect' since all the investment – as 'sunk costs' – would get lost, if the industry later migrated to another standard.[11]

De facto standardization avoids the problem of patent ambush. But this is not an argument for preferring de facto standardization to standard-setting through SSOs. Although it may seem that standard-setting through SSOs restricts consumer choice,[12] such standard-setting

---

[10] This is not the place for elaborating in more detail the economics of network effects. See, e.g., M-O Mackenrodt, 'Assessing the effects of intellectual property rights in network standards', in J Drexl (ed.), *Research Handbook on Intellectual Property and Competition Law* (2008) 80.

[11] See Fuchs, *supra* n. 6.

[12] On the criterion of 'consumer choice' in competition policy see RH Lande, 'Consumer choice as the best way to recenter the mission of competition law', in

is potentially more efficient than de facto standardization. In competition policy, we should prefer the procedure that is better suited to identifying superior technology – of course, by also taking account of the costs of the implementation of said technology in marketable products. Intuitively, one might think that markets and, hence, de facto standardization offers the better approach. However, the process of competition *for the market* is highly susceptible to market failures. Technological superiority is only one parameter that will influence the choice of consumers in the race for the market. In general, the market will be captured by the competitor who develops the best business strategy to 'tip' the market. For instance, in markets that have to rely on complementary products, such as the markets for video and DVD products, it is crucial for consumers that they have access to a large variety of compatible products. Hence, when Sony and JVC competed for the video market, these two technology holders faced the challenge of convincing as many video producers as possible to implement the respective technology. In such situation, ease and price of access to the technology may turn out to be the decisive factor. Thus, a technologically inferior technology can conquer the whole market if the technology is licensed for free to the manufacturers of complementary products while the holder of the technologically superior technology would charge a significant price for the licence. The 'Betamax/VHS war' was finally won by JVC and its VHS format, although it did not necessarily offer the superior technology.[13]

In contrast, standard-setting through SSOs has particular virtues: it may not only be helpful for better addressing the problem of a tragedy of the anti-commons, as explained above.[14] It also offers a collective process for innovation, in which all markets participants can participate. SSOs usually begin to work a considerable time before potential technology has attained a degree of maturity that would allow for its implementation in tradable products. SSOs often take several years to discuss the pros and cons of technological options before they fix the standard. Although individual SSO members may continue to work on different technological formats, they meet within the SSO and discuss the technological problems to be solved and the pros and cons of different technology for solving these problems. Such discussions produce innovation gains that cannot

this volume, Ch. 2; NW Averitt, 'Protecting consumer choice: Competition and consumer protection law together', in this volume, Ch. 3.

[13] On reasons that can explain why the market finally preferred the VHS technology see D Owen, 'The Betamax vs. VHS format war' (2008), http://www.mediacollege.com/video/format/compare/betamax-vhs.html (accessed December 2010).

[14] At 1, above.

be achieved if firms develop their technology in isolation. Similar to other forms of collective arrangements for innovation such as R&D agreements in particular, standardization through SSOs should, in principle, be considered pro-competitive.[15]

2.2 Why Does Patent Ambush Occur?

Yet the interests of the individual members of an SSO are not necessarily the same. In general, three different groups of members can be distinguished: (i) vertically integrated firms that engage both in R&D for the development of standardized technology and the implementation of the said technology in tradable products; (ii) firms that engage only in manufacturing and selling in the downstream product market and are therefore only purchasers of technology; and (iii) firms that engage exclusively in the development of technology and then sell that technology to manufacturers by licensing their patents.

For guaranteeing that the SSO will identify the best technology, it is crucial that firms of the second group (pure manufacturers) are also allowed to become SSO members. They are most likely to push the standard towards the technology that is most preferred by consumers and to prevent the R&D developers from anti-competitively excluding superior technology from being adopted as the standard. Participation of firms of the third group (pure technology developers) is also crucial. However, these firms are characterized by a very specific incentive structure that may lead to a patent ambush. On the one hand, these firms share the common interest of all members in identifying a new standard. In particular, for their own strategic planning, they have to know in which direction the standard will develop. This information is available to them only if they become members of the SSO. However, and in contrast to the other two groups of firms, they are not interested in keeping the prices for the licences low. While the SSO will try to impose on individual members a duty to inform on patents and patent applications as well as a duty to license the patents on FRAND terms, that is, at 'fair, reasonable and non-discriminatory' terms, in order also to solve the problem of monopoly pricing, purely R&D firms have incentives to cheat by acquiring patents on the standardized technology without informing the other SSO members

[15] Cf., in particular the most recent Commission Regulation No. 1217/2010 of 14 December 2010 on the application of Article 101(3) of the Treaty on the functioning of the European Union to categories of research and development agreements, [2010] OJ L 335/36.

and by later charging excessive royalty fees for the use of the patents (so-called patent ambush).[16]

2.3 Assessing the *Rambus* Case under US and EU Law

In the *Rambus* case, the US-based technology firm was accused of having engaged in such patent ambush by both the US Federal Trade Commission and the European Commission. Whereas the US courts rejected the antitrust claim of the FTC,[17] the European Commission managed to convince Rambus to make considerable concessions regarding the royalty fees in the framework of a so-called commitments decision.[18]

In the field of unilateral conduct, it is usually no surprise that US courts argue against a violation of Section 2 of the Sherman Act, whilst European institutions – in *Rambus* even in the same case – confirm a violation of Article 102 TFEU. *Rambus*, in particular, highlights both the specific competition problems of patent ambush and the fundamental differences between US and European law on unilateral conduct in general. The specific issue of patent ambush is one of price control.[19] In *Rambus*, the members of the SSO (JEDEC), which had been established for identifying better technology for coordinating the speed of data processing and data storing in the micro-chip industry, made a conscious and informed decision on the technology to be implemented in the future. However, what they did not know was that Rambus, a technology firm that had been a member for some time, but had left the SSO later and still tried to receive information on the discussions in the SSO, held patents controlling the standard and later charged excessive royalty fees vis-à-vis the

---

[16] Accordingly, two stages of conduct need to be distinguished. See Fuchs, *supra* n. 6, at Part 1.

[17] *Rambus v FTC*, 522 F.3d 456 (DC Cir. 2008); *cert. denied.* See also A Chronopoulos, 'Patenting Standards – A Case for US Antitrust Law or a Call for Recognizing Public Policy Limitations to the Exploitation Rights Conferred by the Patent Act?' (2009) 40 *IIC* 782; J Drexl, 'Deception in the Patent World – A Case for US Antitrust and EU Competition Law?' in W Prinz zu Waldeck und Pyrmont, MJ Adelman, R Brauneis, R Drexl and R Nack (eds), *Patents and Technological Progress in a Globalized World. Liber Amicorum Joseph Straus* (2009) 137; Fuchs, *supra* n. 6, at Part 2.1 (see also on the facts of the case).

[18] Commission Decision of 9 December 2009, Case COMP/38.636 – *Rambus*, http://ec.europa.eu/competition/antitrust/cases/dec_docs/38636/38636_1203_1.pdf (accessed December 2010) (subsequent citations follow this full version); see also Summary Decision, [2010] OJ C 30/17.

[19] Correctly seen by Fuchs, *supra* n. 6, at Part 3.2.2 (characterizing patent ambush as a case of excessive pricing).

chip manufacturers. Of course, the FTC should also have been aware that Section 2 Sherman Act on monopolization does not allow banning monopoly pricing as such. Yet the FTC was seemingly of the opinion that anti-competitive conduct in the form of exclusion could also be proven by the fact that JEDEC might have chosen another technology as the standard if its members had known that Rambus had applied for patents.[20] The Court of Appeals for the District of Columbia (DC Circuit) rejected the FTC decision by holding that the FTC had not demonstrated that both 'but for' hypotheticals in the FTC decision constitute an antitrust violation. Indeed, the FTC had argued that, if the JEDEC members had been informed about Rambus' patents, JEDEC would either have chosen another technology as the standard or imposed FRAND obligations upon Rambus. The Court concentrated on the second hypothetical and argued that Rambus would not violate the antitrust laws by simply charging supra-competitive prices. According to the Court, for an antitrust violation the plaintiff has to show that the conduct causes harm to competition. However, charging supra-competitive prices as such has the potential of attracting competition rather than harming competition by excluding competitors. The Court stated: 'Indeed, had JEDEC limited Rambus to reasonable royalties and required it to provide licenses on a non-discriminatory basis, we would expect *less* competition from alternative technologies, not more; high prices and constrained output tend to attract competitors, not to repel them.'[21] In contrast, excessive pricing is banned as a competition law violation in EU under Article 102(a) TFEU. However, also in Europe, agencies and courts are hesitant to intervene in the pricing mechanism of markets given the difficulties of identifying the 'as if' competitive price. This may explain why the Commission in its *Rambus* decision did not exclusively rely on the excessive pricing allegation, but obviously justified its intervention also by Rambus's previous deceptive conduct:

> The Commission took the view that Rambus may have been abusing its dominant position by claiming royalties for the use of its patents from JEDEC-compliant DRAM manufacturers at a level which, *absent its allegedly intentional deceptive conduct*, it would not have been able to charge. In the preliminary assessment, the Commission provisionally concluded that claiming such royalties was incompatible with Article 102 TFEU, in light of the specific circumstances of this case, including Rambus' intentional breach of JEDEC policy and the underlying duty of good faith in the context of standard-setting,

---

[20] The FTC was actually able to demonstrate that alternative technology existed.

[21] *Rambus v FTC*, *supra* n. 17, at 466.

> which resulted in a deliberate frustration of the legitimate expectations of the other participants in the standard-setting process.[22]

Indeed, generally accusing patent holders of charging over-competitive prices would amount to a problematic competition law concept. Rather, in a system of competition for substitution, supra-competitive pricing is very much part of the pro-competitive patent system. After all, it is the ability to charge such prices that triggers investment in new products as part of dynamic competition in the first place.[23] The Commission seems to be aware of this problem by justifying invervention in Rambus's allegedly excessive pricing strategy by the firm's previous deceptive conduct in the framework of the standard-setting process. The Commission explains this in more detail:

> Furthermore, the Commission considered that such alleged behaviour by Rambus undermined the confidence in the standard-setting process, given that an effective standard-setting process is, in the sector relevant to the present case, a precondition to technical development and the development of the market in general to the benefit of consumers.[24]

The Commission then goes on to explain the pro-competitive effects of standard-setting in the framework of an SSO.[25] Hence, the theory of harm developed by the Commission is not based on the pricing strategy and exploitation alone. Rather, Rambus was accused of having distorted the decision-making procedure within JEDEC. In this context, the price remedy appears as a sanction to force firms like Rambus not to engage in deceptive conduct in SSOs. Without such sanctions, pure technology firms could live out their incentives to cheat, trust within SSOs would be undermined, and, finally, industries would have to prefer de facto stand-

---

22 Case COMP/38.636 – *Rambus*, *supra* n. 17, at para 28 (emphasis added).

23 This idea was most clearly expressed by Justice Scalia in *Verizon Communications Inc. v Law Offices of Curtis V. Trinko, LLP*, 540 US 398, at 407 (2004):

> The mere possession of monopoly power, and the concomitant charging of monopoly prices, is not only not unlawful; it is an important element of the free-market system. The opportunity to charge monopoly prices – at least for a short period – is what attracts "business acumen" in the first place; it induces risk taking that produces innovation and economic growth. To safeguard the incentive to innovate, the possession of monopoly power will not be found unlawful unless it is accompanied by an element of anticompetitive *conduct*.

24 Case COMP/38.636 – *Rambus*, *supra* n. 17, at para 29.

25 *Id.* at paras 30–34.

ardization to organized standard-setting. There is also an increasing need for such sanctions, given that the number of non-vertically integrated technology firms is increasing. Maintaining pressure on them to make sure that they do not destroy trust within SSOs is therefore crucial.

Hence, in contrast to the DC Circuit, the Commission takes full account of the innovation dimension of the case. In addition, the counter-argument of the DC Circuit, according to which high prices would attract competitors rather than harming competition, misses the point. In a patent ambush case, high entry barriers based on the network effects and the sunk costs incurred by the whole industry after the implementation of the standard make it practically impossible that a competitor of Rambus might show up with better or cheaper technology and would convince the chip industry to switch to a new standard. Controlling prices is therefore well justified in the particular case.[26]

2.4 In Favour of an 'Incentives-balancing' Approach

However, the Commission's decision in Rambus also has a problematic side, which is clearly identified by Andreas Fuchs in his contribution.[27] Article 102 TFEU requires market dominance at the time of the abusive conduct. Rambus had no market dominance at the time when it engaged in its deceptive conduct. Market dominance was present only after the standard was identified and when Rambus started to charge excessive royalty fees.[28] This is why the Commission seems to rely on the whole strategy, including the deceptive conduct plus the charging of royalty fees. Yet the Commission remains surprisingly silent on whether mere temporary overlap of an abusive strategy with the existence of market dominance is sufficient for applying Article 102 TFEU. At least in this regard, US antitrust law would offer obvious advantages by also banning anti-competitive acquisition of monopoly power under Section 2 Sherman Act.

Although Andreas Fuchs, in his contribution to this book, opposes the view that already the deceptive conduct of Rambus prior to the acquisition of its market dominance can be relied upon as a basis for an abuse, he is still in support of a violation. He argues in the sense of a violation of the excessive pricing prohibition contained in Article 102(a) TFEU. The real challenge he has to live up to is to draw the line between cases where the

---

26 See also Fuchs, *supra* n. 6, at n. 9. Note that the opinion expressed in this chapter nonetheless differs from the one by Fuchs as to the role deceptive conduct plays in applying Article 102(a) TFEU. See at 2.4, right below.

27 Fuchs, *supra* n. 6, at Part 3.2.1.

28 As confirmed by the Commission, *supra* n. 17, at para 26.

patent holder is allowed to charge any price and where competition law enforcers are allowed to intervene. His argument in favour of intervention is the existence of the standard as such. He argues:

> However, the *situation is different if market entry is blocked* because access to the prevailing or single standard is controlled by a patent. If, in addition, network effects and lock-in effects due to the implementation of an industry-wide standard reaffirm the dominant position of the incumbent and create a long lasting and firmly entrenched monopoly, then there is good cause for protecting those living at the mercy of the monopolist from being exploited.[29]

These arguments seem to be in line with the concept of dynamic competition. Fuchs seems to argue that control of the pricing policy of the patent owner is justified where, owing to the specific market conditions, dynamic competition by substitution does not work. However, there remains a serious problem. According to Andreas Fuchs price control would be justified in all cases in which patents control the use of an industry-wide standard, including de facto standards and standards controlled by patent pools. In contrast, I would clearly distinguish between these last cases and patent ambush cases. While Andreas Fuchs relies on the deceptive conduct of the later patent holder only as a presumption for excessive pricing,[30] I think that deceptive conduct prior to the acquisition of market dominance is relevant for the abuse and can be taken into account for the test to be applied in the framework of Article 102(a) TFEU. In principle, I agree that patent ambush cases should be dealt with as exploitative abuse under Article 102(a) TFEU. However, in contrast to Andreas Fuchs, I would not argue in the sense of a per se violation of Article 102(a) TFEU in case of an industry-wide standard that is caused by network effects and sunk costs. Rather, I would advocate an application of an *incentives-balance approach*, according to which the pro-innovation incentives of patent protection, which generally involve the ability to charge supra-competitive prices, need to be balanced with the anti-innovation incentives that would emerge if patent ambush was allowed. This incentives balance approach can be seen as an adaptation of the approach taken by the Commission and the former Court of First Instance (now General Court) in the *Microsoft* case,[31] where the effects on the incentives for follow-on innovation within

---

29 Fuchs, *supra* n. 6, at Part 3.2.2.

30 Id.

31 Commission Decision of 21 April 2004, Case COMP/C-3/37.792 – *Microsoft*, http://ec.europa.eu/competition/antitrust/cases/dec_docs/37792/37792_4177_1.pdf (accessed December 2010); Case T-201/04 R *Microsoft v Commission* [2007] ECR II-3601.

the standard were weighed with potential negative incentives for Microsoft to invest in innovation if it had to share the interoperability information with competitors.[32]

It has to be noted that the lack of market dominance at the time of deceptive conduct does not argue against this approach. Both kinds of incentives produce an *ex ante* effect on technology providers before they acquire market dominance. After all, it is the prospect of being able to charge supra-competitive prices that made Rambus both invest in the technology and acquire patents, and engage in deceptive conduct for controlling the standard.[33] For applying Article 102 TFEU it suffices that the charging of supra-competitive prices would take place after acquisition of market dominance. This argumentation corresponds with the Commission's reasoning in its commitments decision in *Rambus*, where it justified the intervention into Rambus's pricing policy by the distortion of the standard-setting process as a pro-competitive, innovation-enhancing mechanism.

2.5 Looking beyond Competition Law

It is true that patent ambush could also be addressed by other legal remedies. These remedies include contract fraud,[34] unfair competition laws or the exceptional denial of injunctive relief.[35] From a European perspective, such remedies are clearly insufficient, since these alternative remedies, given the lack of harmonization within the EU, would have to be applied according to the legal principles of the EU Member States despite the European and even global scope of patent ambush cases. Hence, for the time being, Article 102 TFEU is the only legal basis that allows for EU-wide protection of dynamic competition in a standard-setting context.

---

[32] In favour of such an 'incentives balance in' in particular see F Levêque, 'Innovation, Leveraging and Essential Facilities: Interoperability Licensing in the EU Microsoft Case' (2005) 28 *World Comp* 71.

[33] Similar to the arguments made here, in *Microsoft*, the CFI accepted that Microsoft may, in principle, rely on potential negative effects on its own incentives to innovate in the framework of an objective justification. See Case T-201/04 R, *supra* n. 31, at para 696. See also the Commission Decision, *supra* n. 31, at paras 709–12.

[34] In the US *Rambus* case, such remedy was denied in *Rambus, Inc. v Infineon Techs. AG*, 164 F. Supp. 2d 743, 767 (ED Va. 2001) (holding that JEDEC's rules on a duty to inform were too vague to justify a case of contract fraud).

[35] On the latter see *eBay Inc. v MerckExchange, LL.C.*, 547 US 388 (2006) (defining a four-factor test under which courts are authorized to deny an injunction as equitable relief in patent infringement proceedings).

In the long run, additional instruments could be considered for better guaranteeing dynamic competition where technological standards play a role. There are basically two further reaching legislative options. First, the legislature could *amend patent law* by cutting back the exclusivity of the patent and introducing a statutory licence scheme (also 'liability rule') where patents control industry-wide standards. The second option would consist in a regulatory approach. From an economic standpoint, markets characterized by network effects do not differ from industries based on physical networks. The latter are the classical field of regulation, which typically includes access and price regulation. The only argument against extending regulatory approaches to markets characterized by technological standards in the IT sector in particular is that the incumbents in the traditional network industries gained dominance as state-protected monopolies, whilst the owners of patents that control industry-wide standards gained market dominance in a competitive environment. Nevertheless, both approaches would be in line with the pre-cited ideas of Andreas Fuchs, who seems to advocate price control in all these instances.

3 REVERSE PAYMENTS FOR SETTLING PATENT INFRINGEMENT CASES

The discussion on pay-for-delay settlements, especially in the United States, has so far concentrated on scenarios involving patent infringement proceedings between originator pharmaceutical companies and generics producers.[36] In addition, the anti-competitive effect of such agreements is usually assessed in the light of the effects such settlements have on price competition by delaying the market entry of generics. The following analysis will demonstrate that effects on dynamic competition should also be considered. In this regard, it is appropriate to distinguish between the two cases of competition between originator and generics companies on the one hand and among originator companies on the other hand.

3.1 Settlements between Originator Companies and Generics Producers

The argument that, in the framework of assessing pay-for-delay settlements between orginator companies and generics producers, the dynamic aspects

---

[36] Cf. Peritz, *supra* n. 7.

of patent law also need to be taken into account may come as a surprise. These aspects have neither attained any attention in the US nor in the EU. In the US, courts have largely concentrated on the pro-competitive nature of court settlements as such,[37] and, in addition, have avoided any deeper analysis of the dynamic aspects by maintaining an assumption of patent validity. In the light of the latter argument, any market entry of generics before the expiry of the patent term has to appear as a particular concession of the patent holder.[38] In the EU, the Commission made pay-for-delay settlements a major target of its criticism expressed in the Pharma Sector Inquiry Report. However, the Commission refrained from any legal assessment and only argued that such settlements potentially violate EU competition law.[39]

Dynamic aspects may be relevant in particular under EU law. From a purely normative perspective, EU competition law does not recognize any per se illegality of restrictive agreements. According to Article 101(3) TFEU, at least in principle, there is not any type of agreement for which the application of this specific European efficiency defence could be excluded as such. Under the four cumulative requirements of Article 101(3) TFEU, a restrictive agreement can be justified if it 'contributes to the production or distribution of goods or to *promoting technical or economic progress*'. This formula was recently applied by the ECJ to pharmaceutical companies in the *GlaxoSmithKline* case.[40] There, the Court held that the Commission, in assessing whether an agreement between an originator company and drug wholesalers that restricts the abilities of the latter to export drugs to other Member States, has to take into account the probability that the agreement would encourage innovation on the part of the pharmaceutical company.[41]

---

[37] *See Schering-Plough Corp. v FTC*, 402 F.3d 1056 (11 Cir. 2006).

[38] *See In re Ciprofloxacin Hydrochloride Antitrust Litigation*, 544 F.3d 1323 (confirming that the settlement does not violate the antitrust laws as long as it remains within the 'exclusionary zone' of the patent).

[39] See European Commission, 'Pharmaceutical Sector Inquiry Final Report' (8 July 2009) at para 1573, http://ec.europa.eu/competition/sectors/pharmaceuticals/inquiry/staff_working_paper_part1.pdf (accessed December 2010).

Agreements that are designed to keep competitors out of the market *may* also run afoul of EU competition law. Settlement agreements that limit generic entry and include a value transfer from an orginator company to one or more generic companies are an example of such *potentially anticompetitive agreements*, in particular where the motive of the agreement is the sharing of profits via payments from originator to generic companies to the detriment of patients and public health budgets. (Emphasis added.)

[40] Joined Cases C-501/06 P, C-513/06 P, C-515/06 P and C-519/06 P *GlaxoSmithKline v Commission* [2009] ECR I-9291.

[41] Id. at para 95.

Already some years earlier, in the *Syfait* case,[42] Advocate General Jacobs had argued in favour of allowing restraints on parallel trade for pharmaceuticals by highlighting the role of innovation as the most important parameter of competition in the pharmaceutical industry.[43]

This recent development demonstrates that the ECJ is willing to apply Article 101(3) TFEU in favour of pharmaceutical companies in defence of an agreement that contains a hard-core restraint. The argument is very straightforward. Originator pharmaceutical companies compete, above all, by investing in innovation. Conduct that leads to higher profit margins can therefore be considered pro-competitive, since competition will push such firms to reinvest their return in innovation.

Indeed, the case of parallel trade is similar to the one of pay-for-delay settlements. In both cases, originator companies face price competition – in one case by generics, in the other case by parallel imports of original drugs. But is this sufficient reason for accepting the efficiency defence also in pay-for-delay cases?

The answer is no. Justifying the possibility of an originator company to save high income from potentially invalid patents, with the argument that this company has to compete with other originator companies and can only do so if it is able to invest as much as possible in R&D, would completely overlook that pay-for-delay settlements have the potential of distorting dynamic competition among originator companies. According to the logic of the opinion of Advocate General Jacobs, originator companies should be allowed to generate income only in the framework of patent law. Patent law therefore plays a crucial role in establishing a level playing field for dynamic competition among originator companies. This requires that single undertakings can invest only what they can generate from justified patents and do not generate additional and unjustified income by artificially delaying price competition with generics. Hence, dynamic competition among R&D-intensive originator companies should be regarded an argument in favour of acting against pay-for-delay settlements rather than against such intervention.

---

42 Case C-53/03 *Syfait and others* [2005] ECR I-4609.

43 AG Jacobs, Case C-53/03 *Syfait and others* [2005] ECR I-4609, para 89. It is not the place here to discuss the assessment of restraints of parallel trade in pharmaceutical products between EU Member States. See, however, the critical view expressed in J Drexl, 'Healing with bananas – How should Community competition law deal with restraints on parallel trade in pharmaceuticals?' in J Drexl, RM Hilty, L Boy, C Godt and B Remiche (eds), *Technology and Competition – Contributions in Honour of Hanns Ullrich* (2009) 571.

3.2 Settlements among Originator Companies

Of course, patent infringement disputes do also accur among originator companies; and sometimes such disputes are settled. There is nothing wrong about such settlements, especially if the settlement results in a cross-licensing arrangement that is designed to overcome a blocking situation. However, patent infringement claims against other originator companies may also harm dynamic competition in case of a vexatious infringement claim that has the sole purpose of deterring the research activities of the competitors.

In its Sector Inquiry Report, the European Commission also looked into settlements between originator companies. In this regard the inquiry produced an enormous variety of different kinds of settlements.[44] Despite the data the Commission was able to gather, it refrained from commenting on the illegality of any kind of these settlements. This, however, does not mean that such settlements never have any anti-competitive effect. Where licensing agreements are involved, the law on technology transfer agreements may be applied for assessing the case.[45] In contrast to settlements between originator companies and generics companies, the existence of a value transfer is no sign of a restrictive agreement, given the complexity of the competitive relationship of originator companies. According to the Technology Transfer Guidelines, a settlement agreement that contains a non-challenge clause is even generally considered to fall outside Article 101(1) TFEU.[46] In contrast, in the *AstraZeneca* case, the Commission reported that AstraZeneca consequently prosecuted competitors that were most likely to come up with as efficient drugs for patent infringement and entered into a series of settlements.[47] The Commission seems to report these facts in the context of its market analysis and the assessment of AstraZeneca's market dominance, without arguing that any of these litigations was vexatious and potentially abusive.

In sum, it may be concluded that it will be much more difficult to assess the potentially anti-competitive effect of dispute settlements among

---

44 Commission, *supra* n. 39, at paras 1216–88.

45 Commission Regulation (EC) No 772/2004 of 27 April 2004 on the application of Article 81(3) of the Treaty to categories of technology transfer agreements, [2004] OJ L 123/11; Commission Notice – Guidelines on the application of Article 81 of the EC Treaty to technology transfer agreements, [2004] OJ C 101/2.

46 Guidelines on technology transfer agreements, *supra* n. 45, at para 209.

47 Commission Decision of 29 July 2006, Case COMP/A.37.507/F3 – *AstraZeneca*, paras 87–96, http://ec.europa.eu/competition/antitrust/cases/dec_docs/37507/37507_193_6.pdf (accessed December 2010).

originator companies, which is essentially owing to the general difficulties of assessing the effects of specific behaviour on future incentives to innovate.

4 CONCLUSION

The analysis of the two cases of patent ambush and patent infringement settlements has turned the attention to the challenges of assessing the effects of specific behaviour on the dynamic aspects of competition. It is to be concluded that, where patent law and competition law intersect, competition agencies should strive to develop tests that focus on the incentives to innovate rather than on pure price analysis.

Both cases present good examples for this need. Although patent ambush has to be assessed as a unilateral price restraint, the mere fact of supra-competitive pricing cannot explain the need for intervention. In the framework of an incentives-balance test, the anti-competitive effect of excessive pricing is rather explained by the impact it produces on the incentives to distort the pro-competitive and innovation-enhancing character of the standard-setting process. By excluding liability for exploitative abuses under Section 2 Sherman Act, US law does not provide any antitrust remedy against patent ambush and thereby fails to enhance trust among the members of SSOs. It still needs to be seen whether US law will be able to provide other legal remedies to combat patent ambush. One option would be to deny injunctive relief to patent holders under the rules of equity as developed by the US Supreme Court in the *eBay* case.[48]

In the debate on pay-for-delay settlements between originator pharmaceutical companies and generics companies the dynamic aspects of competition have so far been largely ignored. These aspects argue in favour of banning such settlements. This should not be a surprise if we take the idea according to which patent law and competition law pursue complementary goals seriously. Patent law is meant to establish a level playing field for dynamic competition between originator companies. Competition for better drugs would be distorted if the law allowed originator companies to restrain price competition with generic companies based on potentially invalid patents and, therefore, to gain unjustified competitive advantages in dynamic competition with other originator companies.

Dispute settlement agreements among originator companies would be a most obvious candidate for applying competition law with the objective

48 *Supra* n. 34.

of promoting dynamic competition. However, given the difficulties of predicting the effects of a great diversity of agreements on the incentives for innovation, it is understandable that enforcers have so far refrained from intervening and rather accept a generous approach to settling patent dispute cases. At least, the law on transfer technology agreements provides some guidance on how to assess settlements that include a licensing arrangement.

14. Industrial standards and technology pools: A regulatory challenge for EU competition law

Steven Anderman

1 INTRODUCTION

Producing industrial standard products through patent and technology pools has on occasion dramatically awakened competition concerns on both sides of the Atlantic in recent years. The most obvious examples in the EU are the recent but now closed cases of *Rambus*[1] and *Qualcomm*[2] and the interchange between the European Commission and ETSI in relation to IPCom's role in the UMTS pool after it accepted Bosch's commitment to a FRAND license of essential patents.[3] These cases all raised specific questions about the role of obligations within patent or technology pools. However, away from the more dramatic incidents that have occasioned investigations by the Commission, the development of technology pools as an autonomous process of collaboration amongst competitors producing considerable innovative benefit with occasional risks of anticompetitive harm raises demanding questions concerning how the innovative and therefore procompetitive benefits of such collaborations should be

[1] The Commission adopted a 'commitments' decision in respect of *Rambus Inc.* which, inter alia, put a cap on royalties it could charge the JEDEC SSO for certain patents for 'Dynamic Random Access Memory Chips' (DRAMS). See 'Antitrust: Commission accepts commitments from Rambus lowering memory chip royalty rates', Press Release IP/09/1987, 9 December 2009), http://europa.eu/rapid/pressReleasesAction.do?reference=IP/09/1897 (accessed December 2010).

[2] Commission, 'Antitrust: Commission closes formal proceedings against Qualcomm', Press Release MEMO/09/516, 24 November 2009, http://europa.eu/rapid/pressReleasesAction.do?reference=MEMO/09/516 (accessed December 2010).

[3] See Commission, 'Antitrust: Commission welcomes IPCom's public FRAND declaration', Press Release MEMO/09/549, 10 December 2009, http://europa.eu/rapid/pressReleasesAction.do?reference=MEMO/09/549&format=HTML&aged=1&language=EN&guiLanguage=en (accessed December 2010).

assessed in relation to their anticompetitive risks. There is evidence of two distinct schools relating to the role of competition law: a relatively non-interventionist approach[4] and a relatively interventionist approach.[5]

There are undoubted competition concerns raised by the prospect of competitors cooperating to producing industrial standards. Some of these concerns have been reflected in the R&D Joint Venture Block Exemption,[6] the Horizontal Guidelines and the Technology Transfer Block Exemption and Guidelines. However, in a situation where a particular industry has created a process by which thousands of patents are relevant and potentially essential to a new technology, it may be procompetitive for competitors to cooperate in R&D after a preliminary planning stage, and in a technology pool with a standard-setting organisation (SSO) after the various contributory technologies have been identified as relevant to choosing a new technology. It has been estimated that 2G mobile telephony involved cooperation between almost 5000 patent holders and 3G involved cooperation between more than 9000 patent holders. In those and even smaller groups there are overlapping patents and a plethora of micro patents that will impede the achievement of a technical innovation unless some kind of novel form of cooperation can be instituted. The procompetitive benefits of a technology pool are that a new product can be created that might not otherwise be realised. It constitutes a defeat for the 'tragedy of the anti-commons' in certain sectors. A technology pool offers the benefit of attaining and improving product interoperability since many pools are aimed specifically at created interoperable standards. An economist would argue that this process also lowers transaction costs and thereby contributes to consumer welfare. The EU regulators have recognised these contributions in a series of 'safe harbours' in the three regulations mentioned above while at the same time stipulating guidelines as to what types of collaborative activity are potentially anticompetitive.[7]

---

[4] See, e.g. SD Anderman and J Kallaugher, *Technology Transfer and the New EU Competition Rules* (2006) Ch. 9; D Teece and E Sherry, 'Standard Setting and Antitrust' (2003) 87 *Minn L Rev* 1911; See too M Carrier, 'Why Antitrust Should Defer to the Intellectual Property Rules of Standard Setting Organisations: A Commentary on Teece and Sherry' (2005) 89 *Minn L Rev* 2017.

[5] See P Chappatte, 'FRAND Commitments – The Case for Antitrust Intervention' (2009) 5 *Eur Comp J* 319.

[6] See now the new R&D Block Exemption Regulation of 14 December 2010 on the application of Article 101(3) of the Treaty on the functioning of the European Union to categories of research and development agreements (not yet published in the OJ on 1 January 2011).

[7] These safe harbours and guidelines have been analysed in detail in Anderman and Kallaugher, *supra* n. 4, Ch. 9.

However, the purpose of my remarks here is not to analyse the framework created by the competition law instruments but rather to try to sketch out a picture of how collaboration in standard-setting and technology pools occurs over several separate but interrelated stages since this has been infrequently done. For the purposes of this brief sketch of the stages in the technology pool process, I am taking a composite of a number of different patent pools in recent years.

2 STAGE ONE: THE PRELIMINARY MEETING

The first stage of a patent or technology pool is often a form of preliminary meeting in which actual or potential competitors meet to identify what type of product is being aimed at and what types of research activity may be necessary to produce the technology to create the product. The organisations that engage in research at this stage are often drawn from three disparate groups: university scientists engaged in contracted out research; the research departments of manufacturing firms planning to manufacture a new product using the results of the pooled technology, two examples of which are Nokia and Sony Ericsson; and 'research led' firms, that is, firms that concentrate essentially on research and often do not plan to manufacture a new product based upon the technology resulting from the pool. Two examples of this last category are Qualcomm and increasingly Phillips. As a result of the preliminary stage, we have a potential type of R&D agreement and the decision to engage in collaborative research or contract out research or even engage in independent research based on a pre-established set of parameters is regulated if at all for competition purposes by the R&D Block Exemption Regulation (R&D BER) and Horizontal Guidelines.

This research stage often results in a series of patents covering the technologies discovered in the research. Other patent holders, not originally in the pool, may be enticed to enter either as research-led-patentees or as manufacturer-patentees. Yet other patentees may gamble that it is in their interests to remain outside the pool and reap the benefits of higher royalties if their patents should prove essential to the selected technology. These decisions are made once the project moves to the standard-setting stage and the members of the technology pool have accepted an obligation to disclose their ownership of all patents relevant to the proposed technology, to license at a FRAND rate any patents chosen for the standard and in some cases to search for relevant patents.

3 STAGE TWO: THE CREATION OF THE STANDARD AND THE SELECTION OF ESSENTIAL PATENTS

The next stage consists of the creation of the standard by an SSO based on the evaluation of the results of the research and the selection of the essential patents in the pool. The SSO will sometimes consist of an entity based on an association of patentees within the pool. Increasingly, specialist organisations such as MPEGLA, are contracted specifically for the purpose of forming and running an SSO. In either form the SSO will normally concentrate on identifying an optimal technological solution to create the product and the patents that are 'essential' to the creation of a new product because there is no known substitute. At this stage, the SSO will also identify those patents that are needed to license the technology but that are non-essential because of the existence of substitutes.

Before the selection of essential patents, the SSO will have secured an obligation from all those participating in the pool that they will license their patents chosen as essential to the pool on FRAND terms or will disclose at an early stage that certain of their patents are unavailable on FRAND terms so as to allow the SSO and contributors to the technology pool to invent around the unavailable patent. In some cases, the patentees may have to undertake an obligation to search for relevant patents but this obligation is increasingly being assigned to the SSO. What is palpably unacceptable conduct, either as a matter of contract or under an Article 102 TFEU analysis, is to give the appearance of being a member of the pool and then once the SSO selects the chosen technology to 'ambush' the other pool members by proclaiming that the patents essential held were never disclosed to the pool and were therefore never subject to a FRAND obligation. Of course, it is incumbent on the SSO to obtain a contractual obligation to disclose all relevant patents – not only those held but also those applied for during the selection process. In addition, there needs to be convincing evidence that those commitments were undertaken by the patentee. In the US *Rambus* case, Court of Appeals for the DC Circuit annulled the FTC's ruling that *Rambus* had deceived the JEDEC SSO and breached Section 2 Sherman Act by failing to disclose its ownership of essential patents because the extent of the patent disclosure rules of the JEDEC SSO were not sufficiently established by the evidence.[8] The CCA did not rule out a claim under Section 5 of the Fair Trade Act.

---

[8] *Rambus v FTC*, 522 F.3d 456 (DC Cir. 2008).

After *Rambus* ETSI made it a point to recommend to technology pool coordinators to tighten their rules of disclosure and to bind contributing patent holders more closely to contractual commitments to license their patented technology to the pool on FRAND terms.

4 STAGE THREE: LICENSING OUT

Once the technology has been chosen and the essential and relevant patents selected, the next stage is for the SSO or other entity to license out the pooled technology to manufacturers to produce and distribute a product based on the technology. These licenses will be subject to payment of a royalty to the SSO based on a commercial rate and influenced by the demands of the patentees for their royalties. This royalty will tend to be offered to non-member manufacturers on the same terms as pool member manufacturers. The latter may be single firms with two hats but are treated as operating separately for the purposes of the technology pool licensing process. It is not clear whether this parity of treatment of non-members by the SSO is a matter of commercial practice but clearly once the licensed product of the SSO achieves dominant market power in a market, then a failure to offer access on non-discriminatory terms would be an infringement of Article 102 TFEU.

They will receive royalties for their individual patent that they contribute to the pool on the basis of their FRAND commitments. They will pay royalties for licensing the pooled technology as a manufacturer. Finally, the SSO normally will place the manufacturer/licensees under an obligation to grant back a license of their improvements in the form of a non-exclusive license and that can be secured contractually on FRAND terms. All members of the pool will receive a cross license of the technology for research purposes from the SSO. Moreover, all members of the pool with essential or relevant licenses will receive a grant back in the form of a non-exclusive license of the improvements discovered by the manufacturer licensees.

The competition issues here depend upon the degree of market power of the standard. Some standards are private and compete against other private standards. Some standards are quasi public and some standards achieve the status of industrial standard. The greater the market power of the standard, the greater the 'special responsibilities' of the SSO or licensing entity to offer access to non-member manufacturers and on terms that are non-discriminatory and 'fair' within the Delphic meaning of Article 102(a) TFEU. If the new standard is one of a number of competing standards, its obligation to grant access will be decreased and it is not altogether certain that it will have a legal obligation to grant a license to non-member manufacturers on non-discriminatory terms. It may, however, have a commercial incentive.

5 THE FRAND COMMITMENTS

One relatively novel element in these relationships within the process of standardisation technology pools is the measurement of the various FRAND commitments. The patent holders joining a patent pool do so normally on the basis of an agreement to license essential patents on FRAND terms to the SSO. This is a recommended course of action by ETSI and a desired one by the Commission in the TT Guidelines. The FRAND obligation normally extends to the return commitment of the SSO/licensor to license back to individual patent holders. If the SSO becomes a true industrial standard it will have FRAND obligations to manufacturers, particularly if some of the essential patent holders have begun to manufacture, Finally, the FRAND obligation will extend to the manufacturer/licensees to grant back licences for their improvements and to the SSO or licensing entity to grant back improvements to the patent holders who have contributed essential patents to the pool.

In all cases the FRAND commitment is contractual, which allows for the commitment to vary with the nature of the contractual arrangement. Even assuming that all essential patents chosen from contributors in a technology pool are bound by FRAND commitments, the nature of what is reasonable can vary with the nature of the parties. For example, a research-led company with no stake in the technology as a manufacturer may argue that it is reasonable to have a higher royalty than a firm that participates both as a contributor of essential patents and as a manufacturer. Alternatively, a firm that has contributed a greater number of patents to the technology pool may argue that size or quantity matters. Another patentee contributing to the pool may argue that it is reasonable for the qualitatively most important contribution to receive a bigger share. All three arguments may be made within the framework of a FRAND commitment and each SSO must work out a dispute settling mechanism as part of its contractual arrangements.

Consequently, participation in technology pools by inventing firms is often based on uncertainty about the actual share of the royalties received and distributed by the SSO or licensing entity as well as uncertainty about the period of time that will elapse before the royalties will be paid out.

Finally, the role of lawyers in the process is variable. The process thus far seems to be driven by the technologists who are instrumental in choosing the technologies to be researched, the optimal product from a technological perspective and the selection of the 'essential' patented technologies. Lawyers thus far seem to be more active at the stage when things go wrong. It is possible that some lawyers are becoming more successful in being heard in the earlier planning stages of the process.

There are undoubtedly competition issues concerning the role of the essential patent holder as a potential abuser of a dominant position as well as collaborators adding non-essential patents to the essential patents to create a potentially unlawful bundled product. Also, there are exclusionary and exploitive risks when cooperation at the research and SSO stage spills over into the production and marketing stages. Finally, there is an exclusionary risk if the licensed technology is dominant in the product or technology market and the standard-setting organisation licenses out to manufacturers who compete with the patentee/manufacturers within the pool. The task for the regulatory framework is to protect against those risks using methods that do not place the autonomous process of patent and technology pools into a regulatory straitjacket.

PART 4

Promoting competition policy nationally and across borders

15. International antitrust solutions: Discrete steps or causally linked?

Michal S. Gal*

1 INTRODUCTION

In the past two decades a growing number of jurisdictions explored and experimented with solutions to competition problems created by the internationalization of trade. The level of cooperation among jurisdictions has arisen in parallel with the realization that unilateral enforcement provides a limited solution to competition law challenges with an extra-territorial dimension. Indeed, increasing levels, or 'steps', of international antitrust cooperation have been taken or have been suggested, ranging from unilateral extra-territorial enforcement of domestic laws to the yet theoretical possibility of a supra-national competition authority. The step analogy suggests that lower steps lead to higher ones. This chapter explores to what extent this is true: whether international competition law solutions based on lower levels of cooperation provide a catalyst and sometimes even a basis for higher ones, or whether cooperation levels are not causally linked to each other. It does so, inter alia, by focusing on one specific cooperative competition law solution: regional competition law agreements and exploring their effects on higher cooperative steps.

Accordingly, the first part of the chapter identifies five different levels of international antitrust cooperation. The second part focuses on a specific example of such cooperation: regional competition law agreements. The proliferation of such agreements in recent years is so profound that it can be termed 'the new wave of regionalism'.[1] The third part ties the two previous ones together by exploring whether and to what extent regional

* The author would like to thank Doron Rentsler for excellent research assistance. This research was partly supported by the Israeli Science Foundation.

[1] On regional competition law agreements see, e.g. MS Gal, 'Regional Competition Law Agreements: An Important Step in International Antitrust' (2010) 60 *U Toronto LJ* 239.

competition law agreements might serve as a catalyst for higher levels of international cooperation on competition law.

2 LEVELS OF ANTITRUST COOPERATION

2.1 Setting the Stage: International Antitrust Challenges

Several high-profile antitrust cases, such as the vitamins cartel[2] and the *Microsoft* decisions[3] serve as striking examples of the complex and significant effects on one's jurisdiction that result from conduct that takes place elsewhere. These cases also exemplify the externalities imposed by the regulatory acts of one jurisdiction on another. As elaborated elsewhere, foreign regulation determines the ability of one's firms to enter or expand in foreign markets ('the access effect'). It can also affect the conduct of international firms in other markets in which they trade ('the conduct effect').[4] Indeed, the vitamins case exemplifies the conduct effect: prosecution of the vitamins cartel by several jurisdictions, which led to the cessation of its operations, created positive externalities on all the countries in which the cartel operated. The purpose of this section is to identify, using a very broad brush, the different competition law problems created by internationalization of trade. Such identification will serve as a basis for understanding and analysing the effectiveness of the different regulatory tools developed to tackle such issues.

Seven main antitrust problems created by the internationalization of trade that exist in a system based on unilateral enforcement can be identified.[5] Let us first assume that all countries have non-clashing regulatory incentives. Several regulatory challenges can still be identified. The first

---

[2] See, e.g. JM Connor, *Global Price Fixing: Our Customers are the Enemy* (2nd edn, 2007).

[3] *US v Microsoft Corporation*, 84 F Supp 2d 9 (DDC 1999) (findings of fact); 87 F Supp 2d 30 (DDC 2000) (conclusions of law); 97 F Supp 2d 59 (DDC 2000) (final judgment); on appeal (DC Cir. 2001); Case T-201/04 *Microsoft v Commission* [2007] ECR II-3601.

[4] For a broader exposition of such externalities see MS Gal and AJ Padilla, 'The Follower Phenomenon: Implications for the Design of Monopolization Rules in a Global Economy' (2010) 76 *Antitrust LJ* 899.

[5] For exposition of some of these problems see generally Int'l Competition Policy Advisory Comm. (ICPAC), US Department of Justice, 'Final Report to the Attorney General and Assistant Attorney General for Antitrust' (2000), http://www.justice.gov/atr/icpac/finalreport.htm (accessed December 2010). See also EM Fox, 'Linked-In: Antitrust and the Virtues of a Virtual Network' (2009) 43 *Int'l L* 151.

and most basic one involves a lack of a legal basis to reach conduct that takes place elsewhere. Many jurisdictions have overcome this problem by adopting the effects doctrine or a variation thereof.[6] But, even if this problem is overcome, others abound. The second is the duplication of enforcement resources. Under a unilateral enforcement system all jurisdictions affected by an anti-competitive conduct might need to invest parallel regulatory resources in order to prevent its continuation or to create deterrence of similar acts in the future. This can be exemplified by the costs of proving the existence of an international cartel which must be borne by all countries prohibiting the cartel.[7] The third, related problem involves burdensome regulatory costs borne by the regulated firms. This is especially problematic in the merger area, since international mergers might need to be approved in multiple jurisdictions. The regulatory costs involved might even result in the abandonment of pro-competitive transactions.[8] Information gathering is also problematic when the anti-competitive conduct takes place elsewhere. If information cannot be reached, it might not be possible to prosecute the firm for its anti-competitive conduct.

The fifth problem involves under-deterrence of international anti-competitive conduct. Studies clearly indicate that only a handful of jurisdictions actually apply their competition laws to prohibit anti-competitive conduct of international firms.[9] Limited enforcement provides firms with incentives to engage in global anti-competitive conduct. This is because the sanctions imposed by a handful of jurisdictions on cartel members are significantly disproportional to the profits to be gained. As the OECD

---

[6] A Guzman (ed.), *Competition, Comity and Cooperation* (2010).

[7] For a suggested solution to this problem see, e.g. MS Gal, 'Free Movement of Judgments: Increasing Deterrence of International Cartels Through Jurisdictional Reliance' (2010) 51 *Va J Int l L* 57.

[8] For analysis of the regulatory costs involved in approving international mergers see, e.g. ICN, Notification and Procedures Subgroup, Report on the Costs and Burdens of Multijurisdictional Merger Review (2004) at 4–9, http://www.internationalcompetitionnetwork.org/uploads/library/doc332.pdf (accessed December 2010); WJ Rowley and AN Campbell, 'A Comment on the Estimated Costs of Multi-Jurisdictional Merger Reviews' (September 2003) *Antitrust Source*, http://www.abanet.org/antitrust/at-source/03/09/comment.pdf (accessed December 2010).

[9] Such arguments were recognized by the US Supreme Court in 1978. See *Pfizer v India*, 434 US 308, 315 (1978). See also OECD, Hard Core Cartels – Recent Progress and Challenges Ahead (2000) at 38; they were also raised in the *Empagran* case. See Brief of Amici Curiae Economists JE Stiglitz and PR Orszag in Support of Respondents, *F Hoffmann-La Roche Ltd v Empagran S.A.*, 542 US 155 (2004) (No. 03–724); Brief for Certain Professors of Economics as Amici Curiae in Support of Respondents, *Empagran*, 542 US 155 (No. 03-724).

observed with regard to international cartels, 'unless a multinational cartel participant is prosecuted and fined in most or all of the countries in which the cartel had effects, the cartel still might have been profitable after paying fines in only some of the countries affected'.[10] Indeed, since the decision to join a cartel is primarily a financial one, if anti-cartel enforcement leaves significant profits in the hands of the cartelists, they have strong incentives to engage in such conduct.[11]

Let us now relax the assumption of non-clashing regulatory incentives of the different jurisdictions that are affected by the anti-competitive conduct. This raises an additional set of issues, the first of which arises from the veto power held by a handful of jurisdictions, which allows them to determine the outcome in many cases. If, for example, a merger is prohibited by a large jurisdiction, it would usually not take place, despite its potential pro-competitive effects elsewhere, and vice versa.

Finally, unilateral enforcement might lead to clashing remedies that might affect consumers and firms in all jurisdictions involved. The *Microsoft* case provides a good example, where the EU and the US authorities analysed some aspects of Microsoft's conduct differently. The European decision, which prohibited Microsoft from tying together the media player into its operating system, had a conduct effect: it prevented the tie in all other markets in which Microsoft sold similar products.[12] Such an effect might occur when two conditions are met:[13] (1) the international firm sells the same product in several markets. This may be the case, for example, if it is too costly to design and market differentiated products in different jurisdictions; (2) the jurisdiction prohibiting the conduct is sufficiently large that it would not be profitable for the firm to simply exit it and only sell its products elsewhere. It is noteworthy that the clashing remedies problem also captures situations in which the clash of interests arises from the non-enforcement of competition law. For example, if a jurisdiction does not prohibit the abuse of dominance by its firms that prevents the access of foreign competitors into its markets, then a negative

---

[10] OECD, Report on the Nature and Impact of Hard Core Cartels and Sanctions Against Cartels under National Competition Laws (2002) at 14.

[11] Other factors might also affect the motivation of cartelists to enter into anti-competitive agreements, such as the criminal sanctions imposed on individuals and the morality perceptions of such conduct. See, e.g. ME Stucke, 'Morality and Antitrust' (2006) *Col Bus L Rev* 443.

[12] *Microsoft* decision, *supra* n. 3; see, e.g. D Spluber, 'Competition Policy and the Incentive to Innovate: The Dynamic Effects of Microsoft v. Commission' (2008) 25 *Yale J Reg* 247, at 275.

[13] See Gal and Padilla, *supra* n. 4.

access effect is created on the foreign jurisdictions in which the foreign competitors domicile.

2.2 International Antitrust Solutions

The responses to the challenges of international competition law explored above have not been immediate. Rather, they developed in stages in parallel with the growth of international competition law challenges and the realization that traditional unilateral enforcement of competition law provides a meagre solution to the challenges posed. Accordingly, this section introduces five discrete partial solutions taken or to be taken in international competition law.

Notably, not all jurisdictions have adopted all the new regulatory tools. Moreover, the order of their adoption has sometimes varied. Still, they exemplify a growing level of cooperation on international antitrust issues (and thus will be referred to as steps). Accordingly, their analysis enables us to put international antitrust developments in perspective.

Interestingly, the US and the EU have been the first to adopt most of the new regulatory tools to deal with such challenges. This is not surprising: both jurisdictions have a strong interest in remedying international antitrust issues given the size of their markets and their levels of trade with other jurisdictions as well as their power to enforce the newly created regulatory tools. Many other jurisdictions followed suit, at least with regard to some of the regulatory tools adopted.

2.2.1 The five international antitrust regulatory tools

The development of international competition law can be illustrated graphically in accordance with the regulatory tools adopted or that might be adopted in the future, which are ordered in accordance with the level of cooperation needed in order to implement them. The relative size of the steps is discussed below.

The starting point (not exhibited in the figure) is unilateral application of domestic competition law to firms operating within domestic borders. Despite the fact that countries have always traded with each other and that international cartels are not a new phenomenon, international antitrust tools are relatively recent. In the mid-20th century courts still rejected the extra-territorial application of competition law. This is illustrated in the famous US case of American Banana,[14] in which the court,

---

[14] *American Banana Co. v United Fruit Co.*, 213 US 347, 53 L. Ed. 826, 29 S Ct 511 (1909).

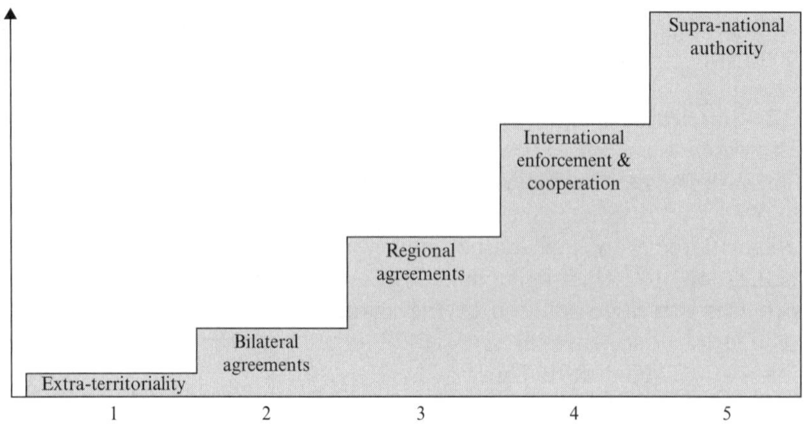

Figure 15.1 International competition law regulatory tools in order of level of cooperation

rejecting an application of US antitrust law to a cartel that was created outside US borders but affected US markets, stated that: '[t]he general and almost universal rule [is] that the character of an act as lawful or unlawful must be determined wholly by the law of the country where the act is done'. This ruling comported with then-established doctrines of public international law under which objective territoriality was the main basis for the application of domestic law. The limited ability to deal effectively with competition law issues with an international aspect, as well as the increase in international trade levels, have served as important catalysts in the development of the regulatory tools of international competition law elaborated below.

The first step taken was unilateral enforcement coupled with extra-territoriality. Each jurisdiction still applies its competition laws by itself, but now the scope of cases that come under its jurisdiction is extended. Doctrines of extra-territoriality differ somewhat from one another, but their core is the extension of jurisdiction to capture conduct that affects one's jurisdiction or is implemented in it, even if the parties to the anti-competitive conduct are located elsewhere or the conduct was agreed upon outside one's borders.[15] This subjective territoriality basis for international competition law can be exemplified by the first case in which it was adopted, the US case of ALCOA.[16] ALCOA involved agreements

[15] Guzman, *supra* n. 6.
[16] *United States v Aluminum Co. of America,* 148 F.2d 416 (CA2 1945).

among the Canadian subsidiary of a US firm and several European firms to limit production of aluminum ingot in the US. No US-domiciled company was found to have participated in the agreement. The court found that the agreements nonetheless violated US competition law despite the fact that there was no basis for application under the objective territoriality principle. The ruling extended the application of US law to conduct that affects domestic commerce so long as the conduct was meant to produce and did in fact produce direct, substantial and reasonably foreseeable effect on US commerce. This test, which has come to be known as the 'effects doctrine', was later applied in many other cases both in the US and elsewhere.[17]

Extra-territorial application of one's laws is, however, fraught with problems. Small and developing jurisdictions can rarely apply their laws to prohibit the conduct of large, international firms that takes place outside their borders owing to their limited ability to create a credible threat of enforcement and their limited enforcement resources.[18] Even large, established jurisdictions face significant obstacles to extra-territorial application of their laws. For example, they may face obstacles to obtaining information and enforcing remedies to firms located elsewhere.[19] In addition, firms trading within their markets might face clashing remedies that create negative externalities on their markets. This has been the main catalyst for the adoption of more cooperative regulatory tools.

The second step is bilateral or multilateral agreements. Indeed, many jurisdictions are currently party to such agreements, which include some antitrust-related provisions.[20] Such agreements are, however, often quite limited in the extent of cooperation they create. Most include provisions for notification and exchange of information and some include traditional or positive comity. Positive comity provisions require jurisdictions in essence to apply their laws in a non-discriminatory fashion. Accordingly,

---

[17] *Continental Ore Co. v Union Carbide & Carbon Corp.*, 370 US 690, 704 (1962); Foreign Trade Antitrust Improvements Act 1982. The effects doctrine has been tempered by a jurisdictional rule of reason, which takes into account some comity considerations. See, e.g. *Timberlane Lumber Co. v Bank of America*, 549 F.2d 597, 611–12 (9th Cir. 1976). For the EU test see, e.g. Case C-89/85 *A Ahlström Osakeyhtiö and others v Commission*, 1988 ECR 5193; Case T-102/96 *Gencor v Commission* [1997] ECR II-879. For its application in other jurisdictions see Guzman, *supra* n. 6.

[18] See MS Gal, 'Antitrust in a Globalized Economy: The Unique Challenges of Small and of Developed Economies' (2010) 33 *Fordham Int'l LJ 1*.

[19] ICPAC, *supra* n. 5.

[20] Guzman, *supra* n. 6.

they do not change the substance of foreign laws, although they might sometimes change enforcement priorities.[21]

Interestingly, some bilateral agreements affected the existence and content of competition laws in other jurisdictions. Agreements that require all parties to adopt and apply some form of a competition law often act as a catalyst for jurisdictions that have not adopted or applied such a law to do so. Such requirements are most commonplace in trade agreements between a large, developed jurisdiction such as the EU and the US and small or developing jurisdictions. Singapore, for example, adopted a competition law as a result of trade pressures from the US. Malaysia experienced similar requirements.

Yet such agreements generally provide poor tools for solving most international competition law challenges. While they reduce information-gathering problems, most other problems of international antitrust identified above abound. This results, to a large extent, from the fact that the model on which such agreements are based is unilateral enforcement: each jurisdiction continues to apply its own laws, in its own territory. Accordingly, the problem of clashing remedies is not solved but might even be aggravated if more jurisdictions are required to apply their laws. For the same reason the duplication of resources, both of the competition authorities and of private parties subject to regulation, is generally aggravated, although positive comity can sometimes reduce such duplication. While gathering information might be made easier owing to cooperation and coordination between jurisdictions, bilateral agreements generally also prove a poor solution to the issue of under-deterrence that result from limited resources or a limited ability to create a credible threat of enforcement.

The third step, which exhibits a higher level of cooperation, involves regional agreements. Regional agreements differ from bilateral agreements explored above in two related aspects. First, they are, as their name indicates, regional in scope. This fact implies that parties will often have a larger cadre of cases with cross-border effects, given that business does not follow national borders but rather demand patters and trade barriers. Indeed, geographic proximity often strengthens the benefits to be had from joint enforcement and competition advocacy. This leads to their second characteristic, which is that they often exhibit a higher level of cooperation on antitrust enforcement. Indeed, this article uses this

---

[21] On positive comity see, e.g. OECD, Committee on Competition Law & Policy, Report: Making International Markets More Efficient Through 'Positive Comity' in Competition Law Enforcement, DAFFE/CLP(99)19 (1999) at 2, http://www.oecd.org/dataoecd/40/3/2752161.pdf (accessed December 2010); ICPAC, *supra* n. 5, at 235.

characteristic as their defining feature in order to differentiate them from bilateral agreements among neighbouring states. While in many regional agreements the parties retain the discretion and ability to apply their laws unilaterally, a growing number of regional agreements involve some form of joint enforcement as well (such agreements will be termed Regional Competition Law Agreements (RCAs)). Such regional agreements are, in essence, a microcosm of a supra-national authority. Their ability to provide a viable solution to international antitrust problems faced by their members will be elaborated in the second part of this chapter.

The fourth step involves international cooperation and harmonization efforts. It includes both current efforts, most notably through the International Competition Network (ICN) and the Organisation for Economic Co-operation and Development (OECD) and past efforts, most notably through the World Trade Organization (WTO). It comes after RCAs because of its global scope of cooperation and the potential it has for reducing international antitrust problems.

So far, however, such international efforts have not succeeded in significantly solving the problems of international antitrust. This is because, once again, current solutions are based on unilateral enforcement. Nonetheless, they reduce, to some extent, clashing remedies and reduce the problem of under-deterrence as they serve, to a large degree, as international institutions for technical assistance and harmonization, which often strengthen and streamline unilateral enforcement by their members. The OECD, for example, has been one of the first to create proposals for harmonized antitrust rules and has long pointed out some of the obstacles to efficient deterrence of international cartels in an effort to increase overall deterrence.[22] The OECD, however, is quite limited in its membership and has not applied any mandatory antitrust rules upon its members. The ICN is an important platform, especially for competition law harmonization, yet it is a mechanism for soft convergence with no enforcement powers.[23]

The most interesting suggestion that came close to being adopted involves the inclusion of a mandatory requirement to prohibit hard-core cartels in the WTO agreement.[24] This would have enabled jurisdictions to apply trade sanctions through the WTO mechanism to other jurisdictions that did not prevent the existence of cartels in their jurisdiction. The possibility that some form of competition law requirements would be included

---

[22] See www.oecd.org.

[23] See, e.g. Fox, *supra* n. 5.

[24] See, e.g. SJ Evenett, MC Levenstein and VY Suslow, 'International Cartel Enforcement: Lessons from the 1990s' (2001) 24 *World Economy* 1221, at 1243.

in the WTO was seriously discussed, but was taken off the table several years later owing, inter alia, to the opposition of developing countries that were concerned they would be sanctioned through the suggested WTO mechanism for their low levels of unilateral enforcement.[25]

The final step is, as of yet, a virtual one. It involves the establishment of a supra-national antitrust authority: a global enforcement authority that will have powers to collect evidence, conduct interviews, and then compute the global gains from cartelization and levy the appropriate fines.[26] This idea, which has been raised by many scholars,[27] involves a great leap from all other steps, since it would require all jurisdictions to give up some of their sovereignty to deal unilaterally with their competition law problems and transfer some of the regulatory powers to an international body. This option holds promise to solve many of the problems of international antitrust, at least on a global-welfare basis. However, it is fraught with problems that have so far prevented its adoption. Most importantly, jurisdictions do not easily concede their decision-making power to an international body and give up sovereignty.[28] It also limits the veto power that some jurisdictions currently have.

The five steps described above may represent an increase in several different values (on the vertical axis in Figure 15.1). One option, suggested above, is the level of cooperation among jurisdictions: the higher the step, the stronger the cooperation. Cooperation might be measured by the number of jurisdictions that cooperate or the strength of the cooperation among them – the steps can apply to both.

Alternatively, they may represent potential increases in global welfare – the higher the step, generally the higher the positive impact on global welfare. To illustrate, unilateral enforcement creates under-deterrence of

---

[25] The issue was placed on the agenda in 2001: WTO, Ministerial Declaration, WT/MIN(01)/DEC/1 Doha (2001), paras 1, 3, 23–5. It was taken off the agenda in 2004: Doha Work Program – Decision Adopted by the General Council, 1 August 2004, WT/L/579, para 1(g). For analysis on why WTO negotiations have failed see e.g. A Bradford, 'International Antitrust Negotiations and the False Hope of the WTO' (2007) 48 *Harvard J Int'l L* 383.

[26] Evenett et al. *supra* n. 24, at 1241.

[27] For a discussion of such proposals see, e.g. Evenett et al. *supra* n. 24; A Bhattacharjea, 'The Case for a Multilateral Agreement on Competition Policy: A Developing Country Perspective' (2006) 9 *J Int'l Econ L* 293; R Anderson and F Jenny, 'Competition Policy, Economic Development and the Possible Role of a Multilateral Framework on Competition Policy: Insights from the WTO Working Group on Trade and Competition Policy' in EM Medalla (ed.), *Competition Policy in East Asia* (2008) 61.

[28] Evenett et al. *supra* n. 24.

international cartels. Empirical studies indicate that most jurisdictions do not bring cases against such cartels but rather rely on the enforcement activities of a small number of large, developed jurisdictions to stop their operation.[29] While such enforcement decisions are generally rational on the part of each jurisdiction, they create negative spillover effects on other jurisdictions, since the fines imposed on such cartels are extremely low relative to their profits. Bilateral agreements on information sharing can increase the number of jurisdictions that bring such cartels to trial, although marginally. RCAs have a stronger potential to increase the practical ability of jurisdictions to adopt regulatory measures, given that they join forces in enforcement. Finally, if such cartels were prosecuted by a supra-national antitrust authority, they would have been fined based on the overall damage that they created worldwide and deterrence would have been much closer to the optimum. Likewise, if mergers were decided by a supra-national authority, the decision would have maximized total global welfare, since it would have balanced the harm to some jurisdictions with the benefits to others, thus solving the veto problem created by merger decisions of large jurisdictions. It would also have solved the problem of duplication of resources and of burdensome parallel notifications currently faced by merging parties, thereby further increasing total welfare.

An interesting question is whether the regulatory tools explored also represent increases in domestic welfare. The short answer is no, although it might differ among jurisdictions and much depends on the rules that will emerge at each stage. Increased cooperation and coordination of enforcement is likely to increase the domestic welfare of small and developing jurisdictions, since it would overcome their enforcement problems and would take into account their interests in cases in which they were unlikely to enforce their laws unilaterally.[30] For large jurisdictions with a strong veto power and enforcement resources, domestic welfare will not always be increased by higher levels of cooperation. The last step in particular, the creation of a supra-national competition authority, might not increase their domestic welfare. This is because their interests would then be balanced against those of small and developing jurisdictions, which generally do not apply their laws to prohibit international conduct that affects their jurisdictions. This effect might be especially problematic in merger cases. In contrast, a joint enforcement against international cartels would generally increase both global and national welfare, since it would significantly amplify the deterrence of such cartels. One conclusion that emerges from

---

29 Gal, *supra* n. 18, 15–26.
30 Id.

the above is that the creation of a supra-national authority to prohibit international cartels has the strongest potential given that it has the potential to increase the domestic welfare of all jurisdictions.

The values we choose the figure to represent also affect the relative size of each step. For example, extra-territorial application of competition laws can significantly increase the domestic welfare of those jurisdictions that apply it in practice. Its effects on global welfare are, however, often minimal, with the exception of cases in which the incentives of all jurisdictions are aligned, such as those involving international cartels or mergers of firms that operate in international markets that increase market power without offsetting efficiency benefits. The effects of the existing bilateral and multilateral agreements on domestic and global welfare are generally considered to be quite minimal.[31] The effects of the current international cooperation on domestic and global welfare are also relatively small. In contrast, the potential effects of regional agreements and of a supra-national antitrust authority on global welfare are quite significant.

2.2.2 Interrelation between the regulatory tools

When climbing stairs, one must generally step on a lower step in order to reach a higher one. As elaborated above, this analogy fits well when each step represents a potential growth in the level of international cooperation relative to a previous one. Yet it does not apply with regard to the international antitrust steps adopted by specific jurisdictions. While some jurisdictions have experienced a gradualization in competition law tools that paralleled the level of international cooperation, most jurisdictions have not adopted the full menu of regulatory tools currently available. Furthermore, some jurisdictions have adopted regulatory tools that require a higher degree of cooperation before lower ones. This can be illustrated by the EU Member States, which entered into a regional agreement for competition law enforcement well before adopting other tools, such as extra-territoriality and bilateral agreements. Likewise, many west African countries have recently entered into a regional agreement for joint enforcement even before most had a competition law regime. These facts illustrate the flexibility of international competition law responses given that the diverse characteristics of different jurisdictions might require them to take different routes to solve their international antitrust problems. Furthermore, they illustrate the possibility that jurisdictions can avoid the adoption of some regulatory tools if they observe their limits as experienced by other jurisdictions.

---

[31] See, e.g. Guzman, *supra* n. 6; ICPAC, *supra* n. 5.

An interesting question is whether one step leads to another – that is, whether a lower step can (rather than must) serve as a catalyst for a higher one. The answer is a qualified yes. Both the success and the limitations of a lower step may lead to the adoption of a higher one. Let us explore both possibilities. A successful relationship based on a bilateral or multilateral agreement, for example, can lead jurisdictions to seek a deeper level of cooperation and thus take a higher step. Likewise, a successful regional agreement, such as the EU, might increase incentives for international cooperation based on an expanded model of regional cooperation.

Yet, in most cases, it is the experienced or perceived limitations of previous steps that served as a catalyst to the adoption of more cooperative ones. The limited promise that extra-territorial application brought to the US has, indeed, led to the creation of the ICN and to the strengthening of bilateral agreements for sharing of information.[32] Likewise, the limited ability of small and developing jurisdictions to use in practice extra-territoriality to tackle international competition law problems they face and the limited refuge provided by bilateral agreements has led to the growing phenomenon of regional competition law agreements.

These causal connections are explored in more detail in the next chapters, which focus on regional agreements and their ability to serve as catalysts for higher levels of international cooperation.

3 REGIONAL ANTITRUST AGREEMENTS

Regional competition law agreements hold an important key for solving some of the most significant problems of competition law enforcement for their parties. Indeed, the past two decades have witnessed the proliferation of RCAs. Examples include COMESA (Common Market for Eastern and Southern Africa), WAEMU (West Africa Economic and Monetary Union) and the CARICOM (the Caribbean Community). This trend is so significant that it can be termed the 'new wave of regionalism'. This new wave is not only characterized by an increased dynamism but also by more ambitious and deeper levels of integration, taking steps that go beyond tariffs or non-tariff border measures.

This new wave of competition law regionalism raises the question of the motivations for their creation. Nonetheless, to meet their promise, RCAs

[32] ICPAC, *supra* n. 5.

need to be structured efficiently. This part explores the potential held by such agreements, as well as their possible limitations.[33]

3.1 Types of Regional Competition Law Agreement

There are many types of RCAs. Such agreements differ along important dimensions, including the breadth of their membership; the institutional arrangements they create (supra-national institutions, joint committees, etc.); trade-related objectives (elimination of tariffs on goods, liberalization of trade in services, or even creation of a customs union and a joint market); and the types of competition provision they include (notification, formal cooperation, comity, establishment of supranational competition rules, harmonization, dispute settlement, etc.).

The figure below focuses on the last dimension and illustrates some possible types of cooperation on competition issues that might be included in a regional agreement, which are arranged in accordance with the level of cooperation involved. Agreements may include some or (almost) all of these mechanisms.

The first two – notification and information sharing – are low-level forms of cooperation, since they do not require the notifying jurisdiction to change its decisions. Nonetheless, information sharing might carry an important potential for increased enforcement in the requesting jurisdiction, if it provides access to information that is necessary in order to prove anti-competitive conduct. Information sharing is often, however, plagued with practical and legal issues, especially if it enables a foreign jurisdiction to take one's domestic firms to court. The third type of cooperation, comity, also does not require significant changes in one's conduct, although positive comity may require a change in enforcement priorities and might serve to overcome discrimination against one's firms. The next two represent joint efforts. Cooperation in enforcement allows

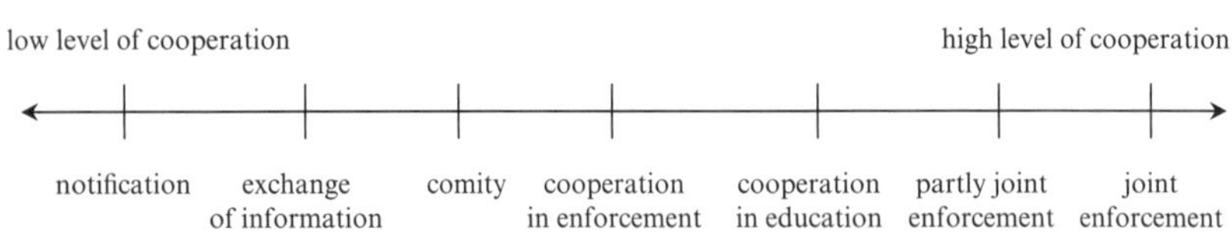

Figure 15.2 Types of cooperation in regional agreements

[33] On regional competition law agreements see, e.g. Gal, *supra* n. 1; P Brusick et al. (eds), *Competition Provisions in Regional Trade Agreements: How to Assure Development Gains* (2005).

jurisdictions, for example, to coordinate dawn raids and investigations. Cooperation in educatory measures allows jurisdictions to pool together their resources in order to create a competition culture, which is an essential element for a successful competition law.[34] Other elements, such as technical assistance, might also be included in the agreement.

The most interesting forms of cooperation are the last two: partly joint enforcement and complete joint enforcement, which create a much deeper level of integration. The first one pertains to a situation where a joint enforcement agency is created but member states can also apply their competition laws where no joint action is taken. This is the model adopted, for example, in the EU and in the CARICOM. Complete joint enforcement is much less common and applies where a joint enforcement authority is formed and member states do not have or might even be prohibited from having their individual competition laws. The Organization of Eastern Caribbean States' proposed agreement exemplifies voluntary forbearance, while the WAEMU regional agreement exemplifies mandatory forbearance. We shall focus on these two forms of agreements, which differentiate regional from bilateral or multilateral agreements and which generally include all or almost all other less cooperative types of agreements.

3.2 Potential Benefits of Joint Enforcement Agreements

RCAs for joint enforcement can potentially create strong benefits to their members. There are several different reasons for this effect. The most important one involves scale economies in enforcement, which allow its members to significantly reduce their enforcement costs by pooling their enforcement budgets on issues of mutual interest. This is especially important for small and developing economies that usually have limited budgets to monitor and limit anti-competitive conduct.[35] Such scale economy effects can be broken down into several sub-categories: the six Es.

Expertise: Competition law enforcement is not easy. Rather, since it combines law and economics, its efficient enforcement requires expertise.

---

[34] See, e.g. MS Gal, 'The Ecology of Antitrust: Preconditions for Antitrust Enforcement in Developing Countries' in P Brunsick et al. (eds), *Competition, Competitiveness and Development: Lessons from Developing Countries* (2004) 22.

[35] See, e.g. MS Gal, 'When the Going Gets Tight: Institutional Solutions When Antitrust Enforcement Resources Are Scarce' (2010) 41 *Loy U Chicago LJ* 417; WE Kovacic and D Eversley, 'An Assessment of Institutional Machinery: Methods Used in Competition Agencies and What Worked for Them' (2007), http://www.internationalcompetitionnetwork.org/uploads/library/doc368.pdf (accessed December 2010).

RCAs might overcome this problem, as they enable countries to pool their limited expert human resources.[36]

Evidence: Oftentimes evidence of anti-competitive conduct might be spread in different jurisdictions. For example, foreign firms might divide the regional markets among them. If they do so, joint efforts to seek evidence might strengthen the case for anti-competitive conduct or enable it to be proven. Also, evidence necessary in order to prove anti-competitive conduct might be found in a country other than the one in which the anti-competitive conduct occurred. This may happen, for example, when the parties meet outside the jurisdiction in order to avoid getting caught. Information-sharing agreements can overcome this obstacle to enforcement. The agreement will increase the chances that the investigation will be successfully concluded and that the costs for the parties and for the competition authorities in the countries involved are reduced.

Enforcement: If the anti-competitive conduct takes place in several jurisdictions, fines imposed in one jurisdiction might not be a sufficient deterrent for such conduct. Joining forces, and thereby multiplying the penalties for anti-competitive conduct, create a much more forceful deterrent. Take, for example, the vitamins cartel, which was found to affect all countries worldwide. The cartel imposed billions of dollars in damages. However, only six jurisdictions brought it to trial and imposed fines that were based on the damages incurred to their own citizens. All other countries chose not to bring suit, given that the cartelistic agreement was brought to an end and that prosecuting the cartel would have entailed high enforcement costs. However, this meant that most of the profits of the cartel were never confiscated, and thus there still exist strong motivations for future cartelists.[37] The same is true for abuse of a dominant position that takes place in several jurisdictions. Joint enforcement can help increase enforcement, thereby increasing domestic as well as global welfare.

Empowerment: A joint competition authority is better suited to deal with large multinational companies. Where a domestic competition authority could not easily take on such cases, this task could more easily be tackled by a joint authority, as its members can create a joint credible threat to the foreign company. This is especially important for small or

---

[36] Id.

[37] See, e.g. JM Connor and CG Helmers, 'Statistics on Modern Private International Cartels' (2007), http://papers.ssrn.com/sol3/papers.cfm?abstract_id=944039 (accessed December 2010).

developing jurisdiction, given their limited ability to create a credible threat of enforcement.[38]

Externalities: If regulators ignore impacts beyond their own jurisdictions, the standards they set will be systematically suboptimal on a regional basis. This implies that each jurisdiction might suffer from the decision of its neighbouring jurisdictions. This may create a snowball effect whereas jurisdictions attempt to 'punish' their neighbours by imposing negative externalities upon them. Such externalities might be overcome by joint competition law enforcement.

Educational efforts: Necessary to create a competition culture, such as workshops, press releases, seminars – might all benefit from the pooling of scarce resources.

In addition, to these benefits from scale economies, RCAs create additional benefits: the four Cs.

Common market: A joint competition agency has the potential to further the goal of creation of a common, single market, as in the case of the EU market.

Certainty and compatibility: Decentralized implementation increases the risks of inconsistent application of competition rules. Without cooperation, each jurisdiction might apply its own rules and outcomes might differ owing, for example, to differences in technical standards. This creates, of course, incompatibility of outcomes, which may impose high costs on firms operating in the market and even prevent them from engaging in welfare-enhancing projects. Again, a joint competition law can overcome such problems.

Costs are reduced: Joint enforcement avoids duplication of efforts, while increasing enforcement chances. Additionally, companies operating within a region that applies joint enforcement may enjoy lower costs of compliance. For instance, joint mergers and acquisition procedures might significantly reduce costs and time required for an approval of a merger. Such reduced costs may encourage mergers and acquisitions that improve efficiencies, better allocate resources and reduce consumer prices.

Credible commitments: One of the main obstacles to incentives to invest and compete in developing jurisdictions involves their inability to create credible commitment to support such investments in the long run. Changes in commitments may take many forms such as changes in the regulatory framework that alter the business assumptions on which investors based their predictions or the erection of artificial barriers in

---

38 MS Gal, *Competition Policy in Small Market Economies* (2003) at Ch. 6.

the market based on protectionism or favoritism. This creates a strong risk for potential investors that might significantly reduce their incentives to invest in such jurisdictions, despite their economic potential. An RCA might create a stronger commitment that will increase incentives to invest. Once again the reason is the aggregation of different incentives, which reduces the ability of a domestic group to exert pressures on the regulator. Of course, overcoming commitment problems requires that the joint authority has powers of enforcement to override local decisions.

Given all these benefits, joint enforcement through regional competition law agreements is becoming increasingly popular.

3.3 Costs and Limitations

Are the benefits of such regional agreements costless? Of course not. Creating a joint authority involves the direct costs of building a new institution and funding its operation. Moreover, it requires allocating appropriate staff. This is possibly the highest cost for developing countries, as human and financial resources are normally scarce therein.

The indirect cost involves some harm to the sovereignty of the parties to the regional agreement. Indeed, once enforcement is implemented by a joint authority, generally the parties will not be able to apply their own laws to the same conduct. But harm to sovereignty may extend further, given the possible conflicting interests joint enforcement might create. Assume, for example, that a merger benefits consumers in some member states, since their markets are less concentrated, and harms consumers in others. Any standard set for review of such a merger will harm some members and benefit others. Setting a joint standard for review in such cases is highly problematic. There are several ways to overcome such problems. One solution is to jointly enforce only those cases that further the interests of all countries involved, and leave others outside the scope of the agreement. However, this solution reduces the benefits from the agreement. A more effective, although not simple, way of tackling such issues is by ensuring that an overall balance of social welfare exists. While, for example, a merger might not be blocked if it benefits most jurisdictions, those jurisdictions that are harmed might be otherwise compensated, whether by transfer payments or by other enforcement decisions in which their interests are given priority.[39]

Accordingly, the costs of entering into regional agreements are undeni-

---

[39] Guzman, *supra* n. 6.

ably high. Yet, such costs might be justified if they enable more efficient implementation and enforcement of competition laws.

4 REGIONAL COMPETITION LAW AGREEMENTS: CATALYSTS FOR A SUPRA-NATIONAL AUTHORITY?[40]

This part ties the two previous ones together and focuses on whether RCAs carry the potential to move international competition law beyond the level it currently reaches, that is, towards the creation of some sort of supra-national competition authority. As elaborated below, the answer is a cautious yes.

RCAs allow jurisdictions to escape the dilemma of choosing between extreme decentralism (unilateral enforcement) and extreme centralism (global enforcement): they allow jurisdictions to explore an intermediate solution to the many competition law problems created by the internationalization of trade by creating a form of participatory and cooperative governance on competition issues. Accordingly, they enable countries to experience and refine different joint endeavors for solving competition issues that extend beyond their borders. Furthermore, regional agreements are based on different degrees of coherence and diversity. Most agreements attempt to provide joint solutions for internationalized markets without eroding the diversity of players, institutions and responsibilities. The experience gained in RCAs might thus serve as an important building block for developing a more centralized solution to joint competition problems. Indeed, it may come as no surprise that the EU was the main torch-bearer for the inclusion of some competition law provisions in the WTO.[41]

A necessary condition for the strengthening of motivations for the creation of an international authority that result from an RCA is a positive experience in a regional agreement or, at least, an observation that a successful joint authority may increase the welfare of its parties. This is a necessary but not a sufficient condition.

An additional condition requires that the experience in the agreement can be carried over to a larger scale of cooperation. This condition is much less trivial than the previous one. For one, the RCA must not be too successful in solving all or almost all the problems of its members, as

40 This section builds upon Gal, *supra* n. 1.

41 See, e.g. Fox, *supra* n. 5.

otherwise they will have limited incentives to take another step, especially if it involves placing additional limits on one's sovereignty.

Furthermore, geographic proximity might play an important role in the success of a regional agreement, for several reasons. First, the socio-economic culture is often relatively similar. While geographic proximity does not ensure socio-economic similarity, ideological patterns often follow geographical locations. Second, and more importantly, neighboring jurisdictions oftentimes deal with relatively similar market players. Business does not comply with national borders but rather with demand patterns and entry barriers. Accordingly, when trade barriers are not prohibitively high, firms often trade in regions that allow them to take advantage of scale and scope economies in marketing, transport, technical service, etc. Accordingly, similar conduct may take place in several neighboring countries and similar solutions may be effective. The higher the similarity of trade patterns between different jurisdictions, the higher the incentives to give up some degree of sovereignty in order to reach joint solutions, and vice versa.

These observations strengthen our above conclusion that an international anti-cartel authority is the most likely type of international authority to emerge, if at all. This observation comports with the conditions elaborated above. First, anti-cartel prohibitions worldwide are based on relatively similar socio-economic ideologies. While there is some confusion with regard to the definition of abuse of dominance, and merger review often poses issues of clashing interests, there is a consensus that international cartels generally harm all countries involved. If an agreement can be reached with regard to export cartels, then a good case for international cooperation can be made. Second, in such cases geographic proximity is not a necessary condition for economic incentives to be intertwined. Rather, global cartels might harm jurisdictions that are far apart. Furthermore, the enforcement actions of one jurisdiction in which the cartel operates affect others. This is because the aggregation of under-enforcement at the domestic level has global implications. Accordingly, the motivation to cooperate in prosecuting international cartels extends beyond one's region.

RCAs might provide a further catalyst for stronger cooperation on international competition law issues, resulting from the aggregate bargaining power they provide their members in the inter-governmental arena. The same forces that enable members to create a stronger opposition to anti-competitive conduct relative to each member's unilateral enforcement also allow them to present a stronger and more credible joint position in international negotiations. This, in turn, might increase their willingness to take the more cooperative steps in international competition law since their position will be given more weight. It might also strengthen the motivation of other jurisdictions to enter into global enforcement agreements, given that the agreement might provide a higher degree of information sharing and of credible enforcement, which might be necessary for global enforcement.

Indeed, RCAs might overcome the main obstacle to the inclusion of competition law provisions in the WTO. Attempts to use the WTO as a vehicle for increasing anti-cartel enforcement have so far failed owing, in part, to the concern of developing jurisdictions that their special concerns will not be addressed.[42] In particular, two issues arose. First, developing countries were concerned that a WTO rule that would mandate them to apply their competition laws to prohibit cartels might aggravate their problems, given that their limited resources might not enable them to prohibit all cartels that affect other jurisdictions as well, and they might then be subject to international sanctions for their limited enforcement. A successful regional agreement can reduce such concerns, as it can increase enforcement against cartels and thus reduce the concern for sanctions. Second, developing countries were concerned that a global anti-cartel policy would interfere with their industrial policy and would not enable domestic firms to grow to efficient sizes. RCAs can weaken this concern by enabling their members to come to the international negotiation table with a stronger, unified position that would enable them to strike a better balance between competing considerations.

5 CONCLUSION

The internationalization of trade has created a cadre of new competition law issues with an international dimension. To deal with these issues, jurisdictions have developed and adopted a set of new regulatory tools that go beyond the traditional model of unilateral enforcement of competition laws to conduct that takes place within one's borders. The level of cooperation between jurisdictions is growing in parallel with the growth in international trade levels and the realization that traditional regulatory tools are sometimes ineffective in dealing with such issues.

This chapter explored the main challenges to competition law created by the internationalization of trade. It then examined five different solutions adopted or suggested as partial solutions to such challenges, with rising

---

42 See, e.g. E Elhauge and D Geradin, *Global Competition Law and Economics* (2007) at 1108.

levels of cooperation. The question was then posed whether regulatory tools characterized by a lower degree of cooperation led to higher ones. In particular, the potential of RCAs to increase international cooperation was analysed. This example is timely, given that in the past few years a new wave of RCAs has taken place. As elaborated, RCAs have much to offer. They allow for a better utilization of meager resources in the quest for effective and efficient enforcement of competition law. Interestingly, they might also create a stronger motivation for increasing the level of cooperation in international competition law – the creation of a supra-national competition agency.

16. Penumbras of European Union competition law: External governance, extraterritoriality, and the shifting borderlands of the internal market

Clifford A. Jones

1 INTRODUCTION: THE ROLE OF COMPETITION POLICY IN THE EU

Competition policy in the European Union finds its origins in the fundamental purposes of the original EEC Treaty to integrate the separate national markets of its Member States into a single or 'common market'. Prior to the seminal ECSC Treaty in 1952, cartels in Europe were favourably regarded as engines of industrial development driving the economic growth of Europe, especially in Germany.[1] Indeed, cartels were respected economic institutions, and economy by cartel was the rule in Europe prior to 1945.[2] Harding and Joshua's literature review on the behaviour of cartels in Europe portrays cartel history from private systems of transnational trade regulation to government-encouraged market stabilization to the compulsory cartelization in Nazi Germany.[3]

When the 'Schuman Plan' for the creation of the European Coal and Steel Community (1952–2002), precursor to the former European Community and present European Union, was presented to US Secretary

---

1 See, generally, C Trebilcock, *The Industrialization of the Continental Powers 1780–1914* (1981).

2 HG Schröter (1996), 'Cartelization and decartelization in Europe, 1870–1995: Rise and decline of an economic institution' (1996) 25(1) *J Eur Econ Hist* 129, at 137. See, also, CA Jones, Clifford, *Private Enforcement of Antitrust Law in the EU, UK, and USA* (1999) at 23–8.

3 C Harding and J Joshua, *Regulating Cartels in Europe: A Study of Legal Control of Corporate Delinquency* (2003) at 63–82.

of State Dean Acheson on 7 May 1950, Acheson's first reaction was the fear that the plan was a clever cover for a 'gigantic European cartel'.[4] Although Acheson's concerns were satisfied, and the plan went forward, the history of cartels in Europe to that point would have supported Acheson's initial reluctance.[5]

Acheson's concerns were assuaged by the introduction of competition rules modelled on the Sherman Act. These rules were predominantly aimed not at securing competition for its own sake, but to secure economic integration:

> A genuine single market cannot be brought about except through free competition. If the market were to remain subject to the arbitrary decisions of the cartels, or to the restrictive practices of monopolies, then the benefits of the single market would soon be offset by the effects of price-fixing and production quotas. This of course was understood by the framers of the Treaty, who provided in Articles 65 and 66 a set of standards and guiding procedural principles which together constitute the first effective anti-trust law in Europe. (There is a resemblance to American models here. Article 65, which relates to combinations in restraint of trade, and Article 66, which relates to illegal concentrations of economic power, respectively correspond somewhat to Articles 1 and 2 of the Sherman Anti-Trust Act.)[6]

In the EU, the 'first principle' of competition law is single market integration and the elimination of private practices that interfere with integration.[7] As Deringer has commented, 'the basic sin in Europe is not

---

[4] D Acheson, *Present at the Creation: My Years in the State Department* (1969) at 383; D Dinan, *Ever Closer Union? An Introduction to the European Community* (1994) at 23. Acheson feared objections by the Antitrust Division, which took a dim view of cartels controlling essential war material in light of then recent experience with the powerful cartelized German economy.

[5] Acheson's reaction to the Schuman Plan for the ECSC was not without basis: '. . . [T]he ECSC then substituted a supranational system of extensive public management. Part of the latter entailed the ability of the new supranational body, the High Authority [later the Commission], to require conformity with arrangements reminiscent of a conventional business cartel. Article 58 of the ECSC Treaty enabled the High Authority to impose production quotas in response to crisis conditions or decline in demand. Article 61 allowed the High Authority to fix maximum and minimum prices. Article 63 enabled the High Authority to specify conditions of sale. To that extent the ECSC organized coal and steel producers into a kind of public cartel.' Harding and Joshua, *supra* n. 3, at 94. Competition rules were added to the ECSC Treaty.

[6] High Authority, European Coal and Steel Community, *Memorandum on the Anti-Trust Policy of the High Authority* (1954), at 1 (Translation by the High Authority).

[7] B Hawk, *United States, Common Market and International Antitrust*, vol. II (2nd edn, 1990) 6.

so much restricting competition but creating an obstacle to integration'.[8] Competition law serves the purpose of integration by preventing private concerns from erecting or maintaining private barriers to free trade after or as governmental barriers are dismantled under the Treaty of Rome.[9] The Court of Justice has said:

> An agreement . . . which might tend to restore the national divisions in trade between Member States might be such as to frustrate the most fundamental object of the Community. The Treaty, whose preamble and content aim at abolishing the barriers between States . . . could not allow undertakings to reconstruct such barriers. Article 85(1) [EEC, now Article 101(1) TFEU] is designed to pursue this aim . . . .[10]

The importance of antitrust policy to the EU and other less economically integrated global (WTO) or regional trade arrangements is similar – private practices that have the effect of blocking or restricting access to markets by foreign traders may either substitute private trade barriers for governmental ones or prevent the elimination of governmental barriers from having the desired effect.[11] Hence, when the EU reaches less ambitious (less than full membership) trading arrangements such as free trade area agreements with neighbouring countries, there remains the market integration or 'level playing field' goal for competition rules.

The second major objective of EU competition law is the promotion of effective competition in the Union,[12] and more recently the Commission has brought a 'more economic' approach to competition analysis reflecting to a certain extent the emphasis on economic analysis found in modern US antitrust law.[13] While some may feel that the economic goals of efficiency have displaced the market integration goals of EU competition

---

[8] A Deringer, in conference discussions in F Rowe, F Jacobs and M Joelson (eds), *Enterprise Law of the 80s: European and American Perspectives on Competition and Industrial Organization* (1980) at 65.

[9] N Green, T Hartley and J Usher, *The Legal Foundations of the Single European Market* (1991) at 201; V Korah, *EC Competition Law and Practice* (5th edn, 1995) at 1.

[10] Joined Cases C-56 and C-58/64 *Consten and Grundig v Commission* [1966] ECR 299, 340.

[11] CA Jones and M Matsushita (2002), 'Preface', in CA Jones and M Matsushita (eds), *Competition Policy in the Global Trading System* (2002) v, at v–vi.

[12] Hawk, *supra* n. 8, at 5.

[13] See CA Jones, 'Foundations of Competition Policy in the EU and USA: Conflict, Convergence, and Beyond', in H Ullrich (ed.), *The Evolution of European Competition Law – Whose Regulation, Which Competition?* (2006) 17; CA Jones, 'The Second Devolution of European Competition Law: The Political Economy of Antitrust Enforcement Under a "More Economic Approach"', in D Schmidtchen,

policy, the enlargements of 2004 (the 'big bang' of ten new Member States at once) and two more in 2007 suggest that this is not necessarily the case. The market integration goal remains important in EU competition policy as enlargements expand the borderlands of the internal market.

Over time, the EU has extended its competition policy outside the confines of its geographic borders, casting its shadows first through the adoption of extraterritoriality rules[14] not dissimilar to the notorious 'effects' doctrine at one time practised only by the United States. A second type of shadow was cast by the enlargement processes, as new Member States were required to adopt the *acquis communautaire* of European law in its entirety, including competition rules. A related type of shadow was the European Economic Area Agreement, in which certain EFTA Member States adopted Single Market rules of the EU, including the competition rules. All former EFTA and EEA states except Iceland, Switzerland, Liechtenstein and Norway have become full EU Member States, and Iceland appears poised to join the EU.

The farthest reaching penumbra of EU competition law is found in the so-called European Neighbourhood Policy (ENP), a multi-faceted approach to foreign policy and trade relations between the EU and 16 of its neighbours[15] to the south (Mediterranean countries) and to the east (eastern European countries). It does not include Russia, candidate countries (Croatia, Turkey, former Yugoslavian Republic of Macedonia), or the western Balkan countries viewed as probable candidate countries for full membership (Albania, Bosnia and Herzegovina, Montenegro and Serbia including Kosovo).

Within the general confines of the ENP are subsets (and supersets) of countries, some of which predate the ENP as such. The ENP per se is a bilateral process, but it is accompanied by multilateral agreements that seek to enhance ENP objectives. For example, the 'Union for the Mediterranean' declared in 2008 is a re-launch and 'upgrade' to the so-called Barcelona Process (dating from 1995) with the goal of setting up

---

M Albert and S Voigt (eds), *The More Economic Approach to European Competition Law* (2007) 65.

[14] See Case 48/69 *ICI v Commission* ('*Dyestuffs*') [1972] ECR 619 (economic entity doctrine); Joined Cases 104/85, 114/85, C-116/85, C-117/85 and C-125/85 to C-129/85 *A Ahlström Oy et al. v Commission* ('*Woodpulp*') [1988] ECR 5193 (Community implementation doctrine); Case T-102/96 *Gencor v Commission* [1999] ECR II-753 (merger jurisdiction).

[15] The 16 'neighbours' in the ENP are Algeria, Armenia, Azerbaijan, Belarus, Egypt, Georgia, Israel, Jordan, Lebanon, Libya, Moldova, Morocco, the Occupied Palestinian Territory, Syria, Tunisia and Ukraine.

a free trade area with its Mediterranean neighbours by 2010 and other specific tangible projects, including a Euro-Mediterranean University in Slovenia. These countries include the Arab countries around the southern and eastern Mediterranean plus Israel and the Occupied Palestinian Territories. The original 12 members were Morocco, Algeria, Tunisia, Egypt, Israel, Jordan, the Palestinian Authority, Lebanon, Syria, Turkey, Cyprus and Malta. Since then, Cyprus and Malta have become full EU members, while Turkey is an EU candidate country. The countries involved in the Union for the Mediterranean include Albania, Algeria, Bosnia and Herzegovina, Croatia, Egypt, Israel, Jordan, Lebanon, Libya, Mauritania, Monaco, Montenegro, Morocco, the Occupied Palestinian Territories, Syria, Tunisia and Turkey. There is a 'co-presidency' with one EU-member president and one from the non EU participants.

In addition, the 'Eastern Partnership', encompassing eastern Europe and the southern Caucasus, holds out the prospect of free-trade pacts, financial aid, help with energy security and visa-free travel to the EU for Armenia, Azerbaijan, Belarus, Georgia, Moldova and Ukraine.

2 OVERVIEW OF COMPETITION POLICY IN THE ENP: SHIFTING BORDERLANDS OF THE INTERNAL MARKET

The ENP as such dates from near the completion of the 2004 enlargement which added ten Member States to the EU, and reflects the recognition that the 2004 and 2007 enlargements create new borders and thus new borderlands to the Internal Market. The ENP has been referred to as the 'shadow of enlargement'.[16] In anticipation of these successful enlargements, then-President of the Commission Roman Prodi famously spoke of a 'wider Europe – A Proximity Policy' as a key to international security and 'lasting and sustainable stability in the European region' as the 'crowning achievement of the European Union'.[17] Prodi's vision was that the 'proximity policy' would surround the EU with a 'ring of friends' to

---

[16] A Magen, 'The Shadow of Enlargement: Can the European Neighborhood Policy Achieve Compliance?' (2006) 12 *Col J Eur L* 384.

[17] R Prodi, 'A Wider Europe – A Proximity Policy as the Key to Stability', Speech to the 6th European Community Studies Association World Conference, Brussels (6 December 2002), *http://europa.eu/rapid/pressReleasesAction.do?reference=SPEECH/02/619&format=HTML&aged=0&language=EN&guiLanguage=en* (accessed December 2010).

whom would be offered 'more than partnership and less than membership, without precluding the latter', and its centrepiece would be a '*common market* embracing the EU and its partners; it would offer a single market, free trade, open investment regime, approximation of legislation, interconnection of networks and the use of the euro as a reserve and reference currency in our bilateral transactions'.[18]

The coming into force of the Lisbon Treaty in December 2009 marks the raising of the profile of the ENP in several ways. New Article 8 of the TEU as amended at Lisbon explicitly empowers the EU to enter into specific agreements with the aim of 'development of a special relationship with neighbouring countries aiming to establish an area of prosperity and good neighbourliness, founded on the values of the Union and characterised by close and peaceful relations based on cooperation'. The EU's new External Action Service essentially creates a diplomatic corps and in conjunction with the appointment of a High Representative of the Union for Foreign Policy and Security Policy and the naming of a Commissioner for Enlargement and European Neighbourhood Policy, there is expected to be a new coherence to the ENP.

The 'approximation'[19] of legislation sought by the ENP process was meant to include competition rules among many others, and competition rules have been included in free trade area (FTA) agreements, partnership and cooperation agreements (PCA) and association agreements (AA) preceding the ENP as well as in the 'Action Plans' that are specific to the ENP.[20] The level of penetration in the competition field is shown by the fact that despite the diversity in conditions obtaining in the 16 ENP States,[21] 12 of them, or 75 per cent have agreed on Action Plans that include 'commitments to implement or support reform measures in many areas directly relevant to economic integration', including 'competition policy and state aid'.[22] The Commission views 'deeper economic integration with our ENP partners' as 'central to the success and credibility of the [ENP] policy', considering that a 'key premise of the ENP was that

18 Id. (emphases in original).

19 'Approximation' is 'Euro-speak' for uniformity or harmonization of laws.

20 In general, the Eastern European neighbours sign PCAs and the southern (Euro-Med) neighbours sign AAs. Action Plans are political documents, not intended to be legally binding, but are negotiated bilaterally between the EU and each ENP partner country. Magen, *supra* n. 16, at 395.

21 See *supra* n. 15.

22 Commission, 'Non-Paper Expanding on the Proposals Contained in the Communication to the European Parliament and the Council on Strengthening the ENP, COM(2006)726 final of 4 December 2006, p. 5 and n. 5.

economic integration should go beyond free trade in goods and services to also include "behind the border" issues: addressing non-tariff barriers and progressively achieving comprehensive convergence in trade and regulatory areas (such as . . . *competition policy* . . .)'.[23]

Even with respect to those four ENP States that have not yet agreed on Action Plans (Algeria, Belarus, Libya and Syria), Algeria has an Association Agreement from the Euro-Med programme, and has adopted competition rules mirroring the EC Treaty rules (see part 3, below). With regard to Libya, the Commission has now proposed negotiations on an Action Plan and suggests that progress can be made in Syria on the basis on an existing draft Association Agreement. The internal situation in Belarus does not yet appear to permit any progress at ministerial level.[24]

On a formal level at least, the ENP and its related policies have produced a very substantial if incomplete adoption of TFEU competition rules. Table 1 summarizing the adoption by ENP States of EU competition rules appears in part 3, below. While formal identity of rules does not always result in consistent interpretation and application in practice, the rules are quite new in most ENP States and there is not yet a sufficient body of judicial or administrative rulings in most of the ENP countries to form a judgment about whether formal adoption results in a truly level playing field outside the shifting borderlands of the internal market. This may also be true regarding some of the newer Member States as well.

However, many of the ENP States still have much to do before it can be said that they really have a functioning market economy, and much more frequent application of the competition rules will be needed to determine if they are applied consistently with the *acquis communautaire* in the competition field. With regard to both the formerly communist eastern neighbours and the southern neighbours, the most probable competition problems initially are likely to concern former state-owned enterprises who abuse their dominant positions. This seems to be the experience in the former communist countries that are now full EU Member States, and economic reform in the Neighbourhood is even less advanced than in those new Member States.

---

23 See *supra* n. 22, p. 5 (emphasis supplied).

24 Commission, 'Communication from the Commission to the Parliament and the Council on Implementation of the European Neighbourhood Policy in 2007', COM(2008) 164 of 3 April 2008, p. 9.

3 COMPETITION RULES OF THE ENP PARTICIPANT STATES

3.1 Algeria

Algeria's first national competition provisions date from 1989, when it adopted the *Act on Prices*[25] as a legislative framework for liberalizing its economy; although not a competition law as such, the legislation contained provisions concerning cartels and dominant positions.[26] In the following 1995 Competition Decree,[27] a competition authority (the Competition Council) was created and received the authority to make decisions and impose sanctions in competition matters. However, the 1995 Competition Decree was greatly criticized, which led to further reforms designed in particular to bring the Algerian legislation closer to the rules in the EU. Competition Ordinance 2003[28] followed the signing of the 'Euro-Med' Association Agreement with the EC[29] in April 2002, and the December 2002 issuance of a 'Declaration on Co-operation between Algeria and the EFTA States', the purpose of which is to lead to a free trade area between Algeria and the EFTA States.[30] The text of the 'Euro-Med' Agreement specifically defines the competition rules in language drawn from Articles 101 and 102 TFEU (ex-Articles 81 and 2 EC)[31] and Annex 5, Chapter I, the 'implementing rules' for Art. 41 of the Agreement make specific reference to ex-Articles 81 and 82 EC (now

---

25 Law No. 89–12 of 5 July 1989.

26 R Qalyoubi *Competition Law in the Arab Countries – Jordan As a Case Study* (2008) at 514.

27 Competition Decree No. 95–06 of 23 Sha'ban 1415 corresponding to 25 January 1995.

28 Ordinance No. 03–03 of 19 July 2003. See MM Dabbah, *Competition Law and Policy in the Middle East* (2007), at 126.

29 Euro-Mediterranean Agreement establishing an Association between the European Community and its Member States, of the one part, and the People's Democratic Republic of Algeria, of the other part, [2005] OJ L 265.

30 Dabbah, *supra* n. 28, at 127.

31 Art. 41 of the EC-Algeria 'Euro-Med' Agreement provides in part that:

> 1. The following are incompatible with the proper functioning of the Agreement, insofar as they may affect trade between the Community and Algeria:
>
> (a) all agreements between undertakings, decisions by associations of undertakings and concerted practices between undertakings which have as their object or effect the prevention, restriction or distortion of competition;
>
> (b) abuse by one or more undertakings of a dominant position in:

Articles 101 and 102 TFEU) and the Merger Regulation then in effect. The language of Article 41 of the Euro-Med agreement with Algeria is essentially identical to Article 18 of the EFTA Convention and represents a subset of Articles 101 and 102 TFEU (ex-Articles 81 and 82 EC).[32]

The history of the Algerian competition rules makes it clear that, at least in their current form, they owe their content to the TFEU (ex EC Treaty) competition rules. Their adoption predates the formal commencement of the ENP, but is clearly a product of the Barcelona Process, which is now related to the ENP and reformed into the Union for the Mediterranean. The Commission considers that the difficulties encountered by Algeria in ratifying the Euro-Med Association Agreement make it premature to adopt a specific Action Plan under the ENP at this stage.[33] For purposes of this chapter, Algeria will be treated as having adopted its competition rules pursuant to the ENP.

3.2 Armenia

Armenia became independent from the Soviet Union following its 1991 collapse, although it remains a member of the Confederation of Independent States. Armenia entered into a PCA with the EU in 1996,[34] and Title V, Article 43 of the PCA obligated Armenia to converge with EU competition rules. Armenia adopted its 'Law on Protection of Economic Competition' in 2000 as partial implementation of that obligation.[35] The

---

- the whole of the territory of the Community or in a substantial part thereof;
- the whole of the territory of Algeria or in a substantial part thereof.

[32] Article 18 EFTA Convention, http://www.efta.int/legal-texts/efta-convention.aspx (accessed December 2010). The EFTA States are Norway, Iceland, Switzerland and Liechtenstein. All but Switzerland are also Members of the EEA. Iceland's government has announced its intent to join the EU as a Member State, subject to a national referendum.

[33] Commission, 'European Neighbourhood and Partnership Instrument Algeria Strategy Paper 2007 – 2013 & National Indicative Programme 2007–2010', http://ec.europa.eu/world/enp/pdf/country/enpi_csp_nip_algeria_en.pdf (accessed December 2010).

[34] Commission, 'European Neighbourhood and Partnership Instrument Armenia Country Strategy Paper 2007–2013', http://ec.europa.eu/world/enp/pdf/country/enpi_csp_armenia_en.pdf (accessed December 2010).

[35] Articles 5 and 6 of the Law of the Republic of Armenia on Protection of Economic Competition correspond to Articles 101 and 102 TFEU respectively. See unofficial translation at http://www.competition.am/uploads/resources/Law_of_SCPEC_new_engl.pdf (accessed December 2010).

ENP Action Plan for Armenia[36] called upon Armenia to strengthen its state aid transparency provisions and increase the independence, legal capacity and legal powers of the State Commission on the Protection of Economic Competition. Armenia amended its law in 2007. To date, it is not clear that there is any significant enforcement or application of the Armenian competition law,[37] but it clearly was adopted and strengthened pursuant to the PCA/ENP process. An Association Agreement is being negotiated with Armenia since July 2010, and negotiations on a DCFTA are expected to begin as soon as possible.

3.3 Azerbaijan

Azerbaijan also dates its independence from the 1991 collapse of the Soviet Union. Azerbaijan entered into a PCA[38] with the EU which came into force 1 July 1999[39] and in Article 43 obligated Azerbaijan to converge its competition rules with the EC Treaty, now TFEU. The EU-Azerbaijan ENP AP was agreed on 14 November 2006. Azerbaijan has not adopted a competition law that approximates the TFEU provisions. It currently has a competition law that seems more aimed at state-owned monopolies.[40] It has drafted a new EU-compatible competition code and submitted it to Parliament.[41] The EU-Azerbaijan Action Plan calls for Azerbaijan to adopt the draft Code and align its antitrust legislation to modern EU standards, as well as increase the transparency of its state aids and enhance the administrative capacities, independence and legal powers of

[36] EU/Armenia Action Plan, Ch. 4.4.5, p. 23 (2006), http://ec.europa.eu/world/enp/pdf/action_plans/armenia_enp_ap_final_en.pdf (accessed December 2010).

[37] The total number of administrative actions involving anticompetitive agreements (1) and abuse of dominant position (4) is 5, according to the website of the Armenian State Commission for the Protection of Economic Competition, found at http://www.competition.am/index.php?menu=156&lng=2 (accessed 10 June 2009).

[38] [1999] OJ L 246/3.

[39] Commission, 'European Neighbourhood and Partnership Instrument Azerbaijan Country Strategy Paper 2007–2013', http://ec.europa.eu/world/enp/pdf/country/enpi_csp_azerbaijan_en.pdf (accessed December 2010).

[40] The text of the Azerbaijan law in English may be found at http://siteresources.worldbank.org/INTCOMPLEGALDB/Resources/competitionlaw.pdf (accessed December 2010).

[41] Commission, 'Commission Staff Working Document Accompanying the Communication from the Commission to the Council and the European Parliament "Implementation of the European Neighbourhood Policy in 2007" – Progress Report Azerbaijan', SEC(2008)391 of 3 April 2008, http://ec.europa.eu/world/enp/pdf/progress2008/sec08_391_en.pdf (accessed December 2010).

its competition agency.[42] An Association Agreement is being negotiated with Azerbaijan since July 2010.

3.4 Belarus

Belarus has been offered participation in the ENP, conditioned on restoration of a democratic government, but has not accepted an AP. A Draft PCA was completed in 1996, but following the 1996 Presidential elections, Belarus appears to have ceased functioning as a democracy, and ratification of the agreement has been suspended.[43] Limited EU assistance, primarily humanitarian assistance to cope with the aftermath of the 1986 Chernobyl disaster is provided, but no current prospect for participation by Belarus in the ENP exists. Belarus has a competition law, but it cannot be regarded as modelled after or convergent with the TFEU.[44]

3.5 Egypt

Egypt's first cooperation agreement (1977) predated even the Barcelona Process, and it subsequently signed an Association Agreement in 2004. Egypt's first competition law was enacted in 2005, and is broadly capable of being interpreted consistently with TFEU rules. Although the text is somewhat different, the EU model is discernible.[45] The EU/Egypt ENP Action Plan (2007) calls for Egypt to adopt implementing rules on competition as required by Article 34.2 of the Euro-Med AA, to enforce the law in line with that of the EU, to establish an independent adequately-funded competition authority, and to adopt state aid definitions and an information collection mechanism.[46] Enforcement of the law has barely begun; in

---

42 EU/Azerbaijan Action Plan (2006), Ch. 4.4.5, p. 26 et seq. http://ec.europa.eu/world/enp/pdf/action_plans/azerbaijan_enp_ap_final_en.pdf (accessed December 2010).

43 See 'What the EU Could Bring to Belarus', http://ec.europa.eu/delegations/belarus/documents/eu_belarus/non_paper_1106.pdf (accessed December 2010).

44 The English text may be found at http://web.worldbank.org/WBSITE/EXTERNAL/TOPICS/EXTLAWJUSTICE/EXTCOMPLEGALDB/0,,contentMDK:21266760~pagePK:2137398~piPK:64581526~theSitePK:2137348,00.html (accessed December 2010).

45 See Articles 1, 6–8 of the Law No. 3–2005, Law on Protection of Competition and Prohibition of Monopolistic Practices, Egypt OJ 6(Bis) of 15 February 2005, found at http://www.eca.org.eg/ECA/StaticContent/View.aspx?ID=5 (accessed December 2010).

46 EU/Egypt Action Plan, (March 2007), ¶ 2.2.4b, p. 19, found at http://

2007 only one decision, the first Egyptian anti-cartel decision involving a cement cartel was issued.[47]

3.6 Georgia

Georgia signed a PCA in 1996, and it came into force in 1999. Articles 43 and 44 of the PCA require convergence with EU competition rules. Georgia adopted its Law on Monopolistic Activity and Competition in 1996, and it prohibits agreements or decisions that restrict competition and the abuse of a monopolistic position, to a limited extent in accordance with EU competition law. However, the law is limited in scope and does not regulate restrictive agreements, concerted practices, the abuse of a dominant position, or mergers. There is no comparable state aid surveillance or control regime comparable to that of the EU. The institutional arrangements for enforcing the competition policy are weak and insufficient, with no legal mechanisms to enforce decisions. An EU-Georgia AP was agreed under the ENP, but no significant progress has been reported.[48]

3.7 Israel

Israel's first cooperation agreement dates from 1975, although it later signed a Euro-Med AA in line with the Barcelona Process. Israel's competition law, the Restrictive Trade Practices Law,[49] began life in 1959 as a transplant of the UK's competition laws of the period. Israel revised its laws in 1988, although the UK did not change its own domestic law until 1998. While some[50] consider the 1988 Israeli law analogous to the

---

ec.europa.eu/world/enp/pdf/action_plans/egypt_enp_ap_final_en.pdf (accessed December 2010).

[47] Commission, 'Commission Staff Working Document Accompanying the Communication from the Commission to the Council and the European Parliament "Implementation of the European Neighbourhood Policy in 2007" – Progress Report Egypt', SEC(2008)395 of 3 April 2008, p. 10, http://ec.europa.eu/world/enp/pdf/progress2008/sec08_395_en.pdf (accessed December 2010).

[48] Commission, 'Commission Staff Working Document Accompanying the Communication from the Commission to the Council and the European Parliament "Implementation of the European Neighbourhood Policy in 2007" – Progress Report Georgia' SEC(2008)393 of 3 April 2008, p. 14, http://ec.europa.eu/world/enp/pdf/progress2008/sec08_393_en.pdf (accessed December 2010).

[49] The text of the law is found at http://www.antitrust.gov.il/Files/HPLinks/RTP%20Law.pdf (accessed December 2010).

[50] D Geradin and N Petit, 'Competition Policy in the Southern Mediterranean Countries' (2004) 3(1) *Rev Network Econ* 65, at 76.

EU competition rules, this is true only in part; it might more accurately be described as descended from the UK, US and EU law, sharing traits with each. However, substantively it permits regulation of restrictive agreements and abuse of dominance to at least the same degree as EU competition law, even if the text diverges. An EU-Israel AP[51] was adopted in April 2005 under the ENP. The AP addresses only the need to develop state aid surveillance and control mechanisms, thus the Commission appears to consider the competition law is otherwise convergent with the TFEU.

3.8 Jordan

The Jordan Competition Law[52] began with the Barcelona Process, with the EU-Jordan Euro-Med AA signed in 1995 and coming into force in May 2002.[53] Ex-Articles 81 and 82 of the EC (now Articles 101 and 102 TFEU) were its primary model, although it also drew from the Common Arab Rules on Competition.[54] The EU-Jordan AP calls on Jordan to adopt implementing rules on competition, develop a state aid monitoring and control system, strengthen the institutional antitrust enforcement regime, assess the effectiveness of current legislation and its implementation, and ensure the right to appeal decisions to an independent court.[55] Amendments to the legislation are in process. Enforcement is not particularly active.[56]

3.9 Lebanon

Lebanon entered into an Association Agreement with the EU in 2002, and it came into force in 2006. Its Competition Act, still in draft form, was

---

[51] EU-Israel Action Plan (2005), p. 13, http://ec.europa.eu/world/enp/pdf/action_plans/israel_enp_ap_final_en.pdf (accessed December 2010).

[52] The Competition Law of the Year 2004, Law No. 33 of the Year 2004, http://web.worldbank.org/WBSITE/EXTERNAL/TOPICS/EXTLAWJUSTICE/EXTCOMPLEGALDB/0,,contentMDK:21039964~pagePK:2137398~piPK:64581526~theSitePK:2137348,00.html (accessed December 2010).

[53] OJ [2002] L 129/3. See Articles 53 and 54.

[54] Qalyoubi, *supra* n. 26, at 34–7.

[55] EU-Jordan Action Plan (2005), p. 13, found at http://ec.europa.eu/world/enp/pdf/action_plans/jordan_enp_ap_final_en.pdf (accessed December 2010).

[56] Commission, 'Commission Staff Working Document Accompanying the Communication from the Commission to the Council and the European Parliament "Implementation of the European Neighbourhood Policy in 2007" – Progress Report Jordan', SEC(2008)396 of 3 April 2008, p. 9, http://ec.europa.eu/world/enp/pdf/progress2008/sec08_396_en.pdf (accessed December 2010).

prepared to meet the terms of the AA and is modelled on the Articles 101 and 102 TFEU.[57]

3.10 Libya

Libya has no AA with the EU, as it was under UN sanctions when the Barcelona Process commenced. Although Libya is now eligible, there have not been any negotiations to join the BP, the Union for the Mediterranean, or the ENP. Libya has no ENP Action Plan, and no competition law, although one was being drafted for possible future adoption.[58]

3.11 Moldova

Moldova is a former republic of the USSR and remains a member of the Confederation of Independent States (CIS). Moldova first entered into a PCA in 1994, which came into force in 1998. It adopted an Action Plan under the ENP in 2005, which called for implementation of the commitment to conform its domestic competition laws to the requirements of the EU, including requirements concerning state aids and politically independent enforcement. The Moldovan competition authority, the National Agency for the Protection of Competition (NAPC), was finally established as an independent body only in February 2007, despite having been formally created in 2000. The NAPC drafted a competition law to upgrade the 2000 Law on Competition in order to comply with EU law, but the law was not approved after revision and has been returned to Parliament by the President's office.[59] Parliament supposedly is reviewing Presidential comments with an eye toward further revision. The Draft Law is considered by Moldova to be fully compliant with the EU *acquis communitaire*, including Council Regulation (EC) No. 1/2003 of 16 December 2002,[60] although it has not yet been finally adopted. It is expected to be finalized in 2011.[61]

---

57 Dabbah, *supra* n. 28, at 261–3.

58 Dabbah, *supra* n. 28, at 166–7.

59 Commission, 'Commission Staff Working Document – Progress Report Republic of Moldova', SEC(2009) 514/2 of 23 April 2009, p. 13, http://ec.europa.eu/world/enp/pdf/progress2009/sec09_514_en.pdf (accessed December 2010).

60 National Commission on European Integration [Moldova], 'Report on Progress in the Implementation of the EU-Moldova Action Plan 2008' (January 2009), p. 42, http://integrare.gov.md/file/final_report_150108.pdf (accessed 10 June 2009).

61 Commission, 'Commission Staff Working Document – Progress Report

3.12 Morocco

Morocco's first cooperation agreement predated even the Barcelona Process, and it signed a new Euro-Med Association Agreement[62] in 1996 that came into force in 2000 and required the adoption of EU-convergent competition rules. Its competition law, the Law on Freedom of Prices and Competition, is modelled on the TFEU (ex EC Treaty) provisions and was adopted in 2000.[63]

3.13 Occupied Palestinian Territory

Although an Action Plan under the ENP exists with the Palestinian Authority, it is largely theoretical, and there is no reported progress in the area of competition policy.[64] This is unsurprising given the fact that there is no Palestinian State as of yet, the Palestinian Authority does not exercise many governmental prerogatives – owing to Israeli occupation and two competing governments – in Ramallah and in Gaza – and progress in most areas must await a resolution of the Israeli-Palestinian peace process, which assuredly means a very long wait indeed.

3.14 Syria

Syria initially signed a cooperation agreement with the EC in 1977. Syria later negotiated an AA with the EU in 2004, but the agreement has not been ratified. Syria nonetheless drafted a Law on Competition and Prevention of Monopolistic Practices and submitted it to Parliament in 2005. The

---

Republic of Moldova', SEC(2010) 523 12 May 2010, p. 12, http://ec.europa.eu/world/enp/pdf/progress2010/sec10_523_en.pdf (accessed December 2010).

[62] Article 36 Euro-Mediterranean Agreement establishing an association between the European Communities and their Member States, of the one part, and the Kingdom of Morocco, of the other part [2000] OJ L 70/2.

[63] Law No. 06–99 of 6 July 2000. The text may be found at http://web.worldbank.org/WBSITE/EXTERNAL/TOPICS/EXTLAWJUSTICE/EXTCOMPLEGALDB/0,,contentMDK:20973121~pagePK:2137398~piPK:64581526~theSitePK:2137348,00.html (accessed December 2010).

[64] See Commission, 'Commission Staff Working Document – Progress Report on the Occupied Palestinian Territory', SEC(2009) 519/2 of 23 April 2009, pp. 1–3, http://ec.europa.eu/world/enp/pdf/progress2009/sec09_519_en.pdf (accessed December 2010); Commission, 'Commission Staff Working Document – Progress Report on the Occupied Palestinian Territory', SEC(2010) 515 of 12 May 2010, http://ec.europa.eu/world/enp/pdf/progress2010/sec10_515_en.pdf (accessed December 2010).

preamble of the draft competition law recites that it is required to meet the conditions of the proposed EU-Syria AA.[65] In April 2008, Syria adopted the Competition and Anti-Trust Law (Law 7/2008).[66] Syria has no AP under the ENP and no ENP Progress Reports have been prepared.

3.15 Tunisia

Tunisia was the first country to sign a Euro-Med AA in July 1995 under the then-Barcelona Process, and it entered into force in 1998. Tunisia first had a competition law in 1991, making it one of the most experienced Arab countries with regard to competition law.[67] Tunisia has six times amended its Competition and Prices Act, most recently in 2005, and it now more closely mirrors Articles 101 and 102 TFEU, in compliance with Articles 36–38 of the Euro-Med AA. The Tunisian law goes somewhat beyond the TFEU provisions and also borrows from the French Competition Ordinance of 1986.[68]

3.16 Ukraine

Ukraine, another former USSR republic, adopted its first competition law shortly after its 1991 separation from the USSR. Ukraine's current Competition Law was adopted in 2002 and is generally modelled after the TFEU with some provisions taking after the German national law.[69] Ukraine has not eliminated individual exemptions or abolished its notification system as of yet to track the adoption of EC Reg. 1/2003.

Ukraine initially entered into a PCA with the EC in 1994, and it became effective in 1998. After the Orange Revolution, Ukraine intensified its efforts aimed toward EU integration, and adopted an ENP Action Plan in 2005. Negotiations on a more comprehensive Association Agreement began in 2007, and negotiations for a Deep and Comprehensive Free

---

65 Dabbah, *supra* n. 28, at 279.

66 The complete text in Arabic may be found at http://www.syria-report.com/doc/Competition_and_Anti-Trust_Law.pdf (accessed December 2010). The law apparently came into force on 11 November 2008.

67 Qalyoubi, *supra* n. 26, at 502–14.

68 Dabbah, *supra* n. 28, at 150–55.

69 OECD, *Ukraine – Peer Review of Competition Law and Policy* (2008), p. 42, http://www.oecd.org/dataoecd/44/26/41165857.pdf (accessed December 2010).

Table 16.1 Summary of competition rules in the ENP States

ENP Members N=16	Comp Law	EU Model	Source	Agreement
Algeria	Y	Y	ENP/BP	Euro-Med AA
Armenia	Y	Y	ENP/PCA	ENP-AP/PCA
Azerbaijan	Y/Draft	N/Y	ENP/PCA	ENP-AP/PCA
Belarus	Y	N	N/A	PCA Draft
Egypt	Y	Y	AA/ENP	AA/AP
Georgia	Y	Y	PCA/ENP	PCA/AP
Israel	Y	N	AA/ENP	AP
Jordan	Y	Y	BP/ENP	Euro-MedAA/AP
Lebanon	Draft	Y	AA/ENP	AA/AP
Libya	N	N/A	N/A	N/A
Moldova	Y/Draft	Y	ENP	ENP/AP
Morocco	Y	Y	ENP/BP	Euro-Med AA
Occupied Palestinian Territory	N/A	N/A	N/A	ENP-AP
Syria	Y	Y	Proposed AA	Proposed AA
Tunisia	Y	Y	BP/ENP	Euro-Med AA
Ukraine	Y	Y	ENP-AP	PCA/ENP-AP

Trade Area (DCTA) agreement began in February 2008.[70] Ukraine's objective is ultimately to become an EU Member State.

4 CONCLUSION

The long-range goal of the ENP is a very ambitious 'Neighbourhood Economic Community', which will be achieved through 'deeper economic integration' produced by implementation of APs and Deep and Comprehensive Free Trade Agreements (DCFTAs), which will 'liberalise substantially all trade and codify regulatory alignment through binding commitments and a dispute settlement mechanism'.[71] Given that the

[70] Commission, 'Commission Staff Document – Progress Report Ukraine', SEC(2009) 515/2 of 23 April 2009, p. 8, http://ec.europa.eu/world/enp/pdf/progress2009/sec09_515_en.pdf (accessed December 2010).

[71] Commission, 'Non-Paper Expanding on the Proposals Contained in the Communication to the European Parliament and the Council on "Strengthening the ENP"', COM(2006)726 final of 4 December 2006, p. 1.

regulatory alignment will be progressive at diverse rates to be determined by the ability and willingness of each ENP State individually, the time frame of the Neighbourhood Economic Coummunity (NEC) process is indeterminate. The first DCFTA is presently under negotiation with Ukraine.

At least for a period of time, military disputes between Russia and Georgia over breakaway provinces cast a cloud over the entire process, especially since some ENP States, including especially Ukraine and the western Balkans, have hopes for a membership perspective. While Russian muscle-flexing could prevent or slow the progress of some of the eastern ENP States in the ENP and/or NEC process, it appears that tensions have eased since the 2008 clash in south Ossetia. Russia itself is outside the ENP process, but these events highlight more than ever the importance of the ENP in promoting stabilization in the Neighbourhood.

From a competition policy perspective, the ENP and its progress to date is a forceful reminder that the underlying purposes of competition laws in the EU and in the Neighbourhood remain focused on European integration as well as economic efficiency in the Chicago or post-Chicago sense. Actual enforcement on the ground of EU-inspired competition rules in the 16 ENP states is limited or non-existent but at least there is a beginning. No approximation of the neighborhood to EU competition policy can occur until the basic competition rules are in place. It is also well for competition law aficionados to recall that the ENP states are not adopting competition rules for their own sake or out of devotion to arcane economic theory, but in order to reap the benefits of economic integration and international peace and stability. This is not so different in some ways from the motivation for the original 6 to enter into the ECSC and EEC some 60 years ago.

17. The role of non-governmental organizations in the development of competition law

Albert A. Foer

1 BACKGROUND

An earlier version of this chapter was originally published as an American Antitrust Institute (AAI) working paper,[1] elaborating on the desirability of creating an international network of competition advocacy non-governmental organizations (NGOs) and explicating the model of the AAI as one type of independent, non-profit competition advocacy organization, offering suggestions to others yet to be formed, and recognizing that what works in the United States will not necessarily be appropriate in other nations. The first part describes the AAI model. The second discusses the need for competition advocacy NGOs worldwide. A third section poses foreseeable questions and offers some responses. And the final section describes the AAI's efforts to reach out to NGOs in other nations to foster their growth. An edited version of this was published in the *Boletín Latinoamericano de Competencia*.[2] Modifications were made for presentation to ASCOLA's fourth conference held at George Washington University Law School, June 16 and 17, 2009.

The above brief history of the chapter provides in itself an example of how a competition advocacy NGO, in this case the AAI, can participate in the development of competition law and policy through the

[1] AA Foer, 'AAI Working Paper No. 08-04, International Consumer Advocacy for Competition Policy: Learning from the AAI Model', AAI Working Paper No 08-04 (2008), retrievable at: http://www.antitrustinstitute.org/search/node/Working%20Paper%2008-04 (accessed January 2011).

[2] Albert A Foer, 'International Consumer Advocacy for Competition Policy: Learning from the AAI Model' (February 2009) 25 *Boletín Latinoamericano de Competencia* 62. Also see Albert Foer, 'Toward Independent Competition Advocacy in the Mediterranean World: Learning from the AAI Model' (November 2010) 2 *Mediterranean Competition Bulletin* 117.

origination of an idea (the need for competition advocacy NGOs), the fleshing out of the idea (through a working paper published on the NGO's own website) and further distribution to a wider audience (through the Latin American Competition Bulletin), the recycling of the work (through a paper presented to a different antitrust audience) and the further distribution (through publication of this revision and a further revision in the Mediterranean Competition Bulletin). Indeed, the initial working chapter was prepared with the primary intention of delivering it to advocacy NGOs and potential advocacy NGOs whenever and wherever possible. A secondary intention was to explain to those who are interested in public interest advocacy what the AAI is and how its model works, in conjunction with our tenth anniversary.

In June 2008, the AAI celebrated its tenth anniversary as a not-for-profit independent education, research and advocacy organization. The booklet created for this anniversary event summarizes its first decade of experience as a leading advocate of post-Chicago, activist antitrust policy.[3] For those who might be contemplating the creation of a pro-consumer NGO in the rapidly developing field of competition policy, please review this booklet on the AAI website.[4]

I do not claim that the AAI model is appropriate in all circumstances, but something similar to AAI, customized to local needs, would seem beneficial in every nation that has adopted a competition policy. In this chapter, I will describe the salient features of AAI, suggest why similar organizations are needed and comment on some lessons learned that might be useful to competition NGOs.

2 ABOUT THE AAI

The AAI was founded in 1998 in Washington DC.[5] At the time, antitrust in the USA seemed to be recovering from its capture by what is generally

---

3 Recognizing that the rest of the world often tends to speak of 'competition policy' rather than 'antitrust', I will nevertheless use the American term frequently in this chapter. References to 'Chicago' or 'the Chicago School' pertain to the school of thought popularized by such conservative, neoclassical economists and law professors as George Stigler, Robert Bork and Richard Posner, who have been closely associated with the University of Chicago.

4 At http://www.antitrustinstitute.org/content/10th-anniversary-booklet (accessed January 2011).

5 For a detailed history of our first five years, see AA Foer, 'The American Antitrust Institute: The First Five Years of a Virtual Public Interest Network', http://www.antitrustinstitute.org/node/10233 (accessed January 2011).

referred to as 'the Chicago School', whose dominance was enthroned by the administration of President Ronald Reagan and continued in slightly milder form during the administration of the first George Bush. By 1998, the Clinton administration was providing a somewhat more progressive variety of antitrust enforcement, as exemplified by the Government's monopolization suit against Microsoft. In other words, the AAI was born at a time of hope that antitrust policy could be reshaped and reinvigorated to become a more important part of US economic policy, of particular advantage to consumers and independent businesses that would benefit from an open competitive system.

Clearly, the opponents of vigorous antitrust within the USA were then (and are now) strong politically, economically and legally, in the sense that their views dominated large parts of the government, the courts and even academia. Moreover, a significant percentage of lawyers and economists with expertise on matters of competition policy have always worked in the private practice of law or economic consulting associated primarily with the defense side of litigation and counseling; while many of these individuals are public-regarding, official institutions (such as the American Bar Association's Section on Antitrust Law) tend to imbibe and reflect the minimalist antitrust sympathies of large clients. The founders of the AAI responded to the perceived need for a rallying point for those who believe in a more activist role for antitrust in order to sustain the movement that was reflected by the Microsoft litigation.

The second Bush administration proved a disappointment from the perspective of the AAI, with the Government's acceptance of a weak remedy in the *Microsoft* case becoming the iconic moment.[6] Although there were bright spots in the administration that the AAI was pleased to support, including the continued battle against cartels and several important cases brought by the Federal Trade Commission, by and large the Chicago School's cramped vision of antitrust policy prevailed – and still prevailed in 2008. At this writing, the Obama administration seems to be moving in what the AAI would consider a more positive direction.

A statutory study commission, the Antitrust Modernization Commission (AMC), reviewed the state of US antitrust and concluded, in April 2007, that as long as the conservative line is followed all is essentially well with

6 The *Microsoft* case was successfully prosecuted by the US Government, which proved illegal monopolization by Microsoft when it used improper methods to promote its own browser at the expense of its Netscape rival. However, the remedy phase was handled by a different administration and many people believe the remedy actually arrived at in a settlement was ineffective.

US antitrust.[7] The AAI monitored and attempted to influence the work of the AMC by establishing a dozen working groups, which filed public comments with respect to each topic the AMC addressed. The AAI's own answer to the Bush administration and to the AMC has recently been published as 'The Next Antitrust Agenda: The American Antitrust Institute's Transition Report on Competition Policy to the 44th President'.[8]

What else does the AAI do besides monitoring study commissions and publishing books on antitrust policy? A lot! The AAI website contains its entire work product in its archives section, as well as full background on who is involved and how it is organized.[9] A research section provides links to a wealth of information about antitrust. In a nutshell, the AAI:

- testifies before Congress and other legislative bodies;
- prepares white papers on matters under investigation or policy consideration;
- writes and otherwise generates articles, commentaries and editorials;
- responds to questions from the media;
- conducts seminars, symposia, and major conferences;
- develops educational materials;[10]
- submits friend-of-the-court briefs to appellate courts;
- moderates an email listserv for its network of advisors; and
- provides speakers for public forums.

Its efforts serve not only to provide the public with an enforcement-oriented view of competition issues, but also to provide a useful check on the overwhelming pro-business advocacy that legislators, administrative policy-makers, and law enforcers persistently receive from major corporations and their advocates.

The AAI does this with a very low overhead, operating as *a virtual network of experts*. The office, such as it is, is located in the home of the president. Other paid employees (the vice president, the director of legal

---

[7] Antitrust Modernization Commission, Report and Recommendations (2007).

[8] This 415-page book can be viewed at www.antitrustinstitute.org and is also available for purchase on www.Amazon.com and elsewhere.

[9] In order to receive periodic email updates on AAI activities, visit the website and click on the button at the top of the homepage for 'e-Bulletin'.

[10] See the AAI's secondary website, www.fairfightfilm.org, which provides enrichment material for the award-winning movie we produced about antitrust. This material is available for use by competition NGOs and others. It includes translations of the transcript of the film into many languages.

advocacy, and the director of communications) operate from their own homes and offices, each in a different city. There is a five-person board of directors and an active advisory board of more than 100 professors of law, economics, and business, as well as practicing lawyers and economists. We communicate almost exclusively via email. There is no strict ideological test to become an advisory board member or a loosely-connected supporter of the AAI (that is, a person who chooses to be on our listserv), although its positions on issues tend to draw people who are sympathetic to a centrist but activist orientation. Formally, it does not have members.

The question always arises: how does the AAI obtain its funding? First of all, none comes from a federal agency that it may wish to criticize or influence. It has benefitted from grants from courts under the doctrine of cy pres[11] and it raises funds through the sponsorship (primarily by law firms and economics consulting firms) of some of its conferences. It receives donations to its general treasury from corporations, trade associations, law firms (both plaintiff and defense-oriented[12]), individuals, and individually-directed foundations. So far, it has not received grants from public foundations. The AAI makes available on request a list of all contributors of $1,000 or more, cumulatively from the beginning. The list now contains more than 150 entities. In 2010, the AAI's expenses were approximately $800,000.

In the next section, I summarize some of the conditions that contribute to the design of the AAI model, but which may not necessarily be present in other countries. Each country, I stress, must design its own model.

3 THE NEED FOR SIMILAR NGOs WORLDWIDE

The AAI model has proven itself for over a decade in the US context. A virtual network does not require a large paid staff or expensive facilities, so operating costs can be kept low. This is likely to be true in most other countries as well. Funding is available in the USA; however, through a

11 See AA Foer, 'Enhancing Competition through the Cy Pres Remedy: Suggested Best Practices' (2010) 24(1) *Antitrust* 88, retrievable at http://www.antitrustinstitute.org/content/enhancing-competition-through-cy-pres-remedy-suggested-best-practices-albert-foer-published- (accessed December 2010).

12 In the US, certain lawyers specialize in representing businesses and consumers who allege they have been injured by antitrust violations. Others (a much larger number) tend to specialize in representing businesses that are defending themselves against governmental investigations or private lawsuits. Some law firms and individual lawyers represent both plaintiffs and defendants.

variety of sources, without the need to rely on the government, whose financial contributions might reduce the independence of the NGO. With a mature antitrust system in place in the USA, a large and diverse base of experts is available because – with private enforcement accounting for 90 percent or more of cases – so many people earn a living in the antitrust industry and so many have a viewpoint that is to a large degree shared. The role of independent think tanks (such as the AAI) is well-established in the USA and even generally appreciated as a significant part of democratic governance. I am quite aware that these conditions would not apply in all or even most of the other antitrust jurisdictions. It may take many years for comparable conditions to evolve, if ever, in countries with new competition regimes.[13] This does not in the least diminish the need for public interest NGOs focused on competition policy; it simply suggests that each one will have to be designed to reflect the local context and constraints.

At first the AAI's focus was strictly domestic. It did not take long, however, to realize that the antitrust field was so tied to globalization that the AAI had to become knowledgeable about how other jurisdictions were enforcing (or not enforcing) competition policies. It began to recruit international experts to its advisory board and to reach out to an increasingly international network, including having foreign experts participate in its programs. The AAI's president travels abroad to speak face-to-face with competition officials and experts and frequently meets with foreign visitors to Washington. As a result of all of this, I have become convinced that something like the AAI model would be beneficial in every nation that has adopted antitrust laws. Why?

As nations create market institutions, they typically and now almost universally recognize that the government must set some rules for how competition should operate within a free market and must have the ability to intervene from time to time to assure that markets are operating as intended. Cartels occur everywhere where they can be formed and maintained without effective government opposition and they inevitably

[13] There is a chicken-and-egg problem here. Having a mature antitrust regime may be a condition precedent for developing a sturdy antitrust NGO. But a sturdy antitrust NGO may be necessary to facilitate development of a sturdy antitrust regime. Both need to be brought into being conjunctively and they can be expected to grow and evolve conjunctively. Without effective enforcement of competition laws that are on the books, it is likely to be especially difficult to motivate people to participate in or fund a competition NGO. It may take the active participation of a strong current or former enforcement official to jump-start a nation's first competition NGO.

have the effect of taking money from the consumer's pocket and transferring it to companies that are acting anticompetitively. Private monopoly is common in nations around the world. Sometimes monopoly is the necessary structure in a small economy or the result of uncommonly large economies of scale. Sometimes monopoly is the creation of privatization that transfers public monopoly power to private hands, which is not likely to improve economic performance because monopoly usually leads to higher prices and less innovation than would be found in a more competitive structure. Not only in privatization but in many day-to-day regulatory activities, governments themselves often create anticompetitive situations that end up harming both small and medium-sized businesses and consumers. Often, it is the poorest and least powerful members of a community who are most disadvantaged by anticompetitive activity. The alternative is a well-run antitrust regime, which should bring four values to any market-oriented economy: lower prices, better service, more choice, and innovation leading to growth in the economy.[14]

In most of the hundred or more competition policy jurisdictions, antitrust is still a fairly new idea. The basic institutions are in the process of being molded. The number of experts is limited. Enforcement efforts may be feeble, garnering little attention or support from the public. Enforcement, in any event, is still largely the monopoly of government, with little opportunity for persons injured by anticompetitive activities to obtain private remedies.[15] The public at large has minimal understanding of and perhaps little natural sympathy for the somewhat arcane concept of competition policy. Even in mature market economies, institutions continue to evolve.[16] Those who support antitrust will need to work together to educate the public at large and to increase the sophistication of the emerging antitrust community. I suggest three interrelated tasks that should be undertaken by a new competition NGO.

The initial mission of a competition NGO should be to identify and bring together a self-identifying antitrust community that can provide part of the

---

[14] For further discussion on the value of competition and antitrust see the introductory chapter of the the AAI's report: 'The Next Antitrust Agenda: The American Antitrust Institute's Transition Report on Competition Policy to the 44th President of the United States', http://www.antitrustinstitute.org/node/11001 (accessed December 2010).

[15] The AAI has recently produced a book intended to promote the development of private remedies. See AA Foer and JW Cuneo (eds), *The International Handbook of Private Enforcement of Competition Law* (2010).

[16] In the US, with all of its educational advantages, relatively few members of the public have a sophisticated understanding of basic economics, much less antitrust.

infrastructure for making antitrust succeed. Where does one start? The central characters in the antitrust community will likely include the following: high enforcement officials and staffers at the national competition authority and any subsidiary authorities; lawyers and economists who practice in the field; professors of law, economics, or public affairs who teach competition policy; journalists who cover business and legal developments; consumer and public interest advocacy organizations (the existing NGOs I am most directly addressing); legislators and their staffs who have oversight responsibility or general interest in competition policy; and businesses and trade associations that can benefit from enforcement or recognize the strategic benefit to themselves of high-quality professional enforcement.

A second mission is strengthening the local antitrust enterprise. In particular, private enforcement of competition law is at best severely limited in most countries outside of the US and (to a lesser extent) a few other common law nations. The lack of treble damages removes a strong incentive for gifted trial advocates to develop a specialization in competition law, and the English Rule requiring losing plaintiffs to pay attorneys' fees provides a strong deterrent to action. The absence of laws supporting class actions, contingent fees, and discovery processes – which are often dismissed as American inventions amounting to a 'toxic cocktail' – all help account for the non-existence of a plaintiffs' antitrust bar. Thus, the pro-corporate bias of the private bar is likely to be even more pronounced outside of the US. Developing a workable private enforcement component would seem to be a high priority if a system of antitrust is to find a reliable political base.

One domestic role a competition NGO can play is to help overcome regulatory capture, a problem that might be even more important in developing countries. By providing a voice for consumers – a task that normally would be that of the antitrust authority, but that benefits from external support – the NGO can help curb anticompetitive political influences, both directly and indirectly (for example, by educating a large consumer body who are also voters).[17]

If the first mission of self-identification and the second mission of enhancing the domestic antitrust effort are local in nature, *the third mission is international.* International developments will be moving during the next period of time toward consensus on best practices and eventually toward new institutions for harmonizing the different national approaches to both

---

[17] It might be useful if the NGO were granted official standing in regulatory bodies. In Israel, for example, the consumer association has such standing in antitrust matters.

substantive and procedural law. NGOs can learn from each other and can work together both to improve their national systems and to influence the consensus that will drive international developments. Right now at the International Competition Network (ICN), where much of the informal harmonization work is proceeding, the players are the national competition authorities and a group of non-governmental advisors (NGAs) that are mostly defense-oriented lawyers and a few public interest spokespersons, including the AAI's president. The national competition authorities must hear from consumer and public interest advocates as well, or the consensus that emerges will be driven by the well-funded defense lawyers and their large multinational clients, without a significant counterweight of consumer concerns.[18] The third mission, therefore, should be to assure that, both in domestic and international policy making, the voice of proponents of vigorous antitrust policies is heard.

I am not aware of many NGOs similar to the AAI. The leading example may be the Consumer Unity and Trust Society (CUTS) in India, a consumer advocacy organization that pays much attention to antitrust issues, not limited to India.[19] IBRAC is an independent NGO in Brazil that does not deal with current cases, but has a journal, and conducts workshops and an annual international event.[20] The Consumers' Association, UK, which trades as *Which?* (the name of the consumer magazine it publishes that helps subsidize consumer protection activities), has frequently intervened in European antitrust matters,[21] just as several consumer organizations in the US have advocated their own antitrust positions in US courts and agencies.[22] A recent entry on the scene is StopCartel, a Greek NGO.[23] Various universities have created centers that focus on

---

18 Donors both multilateral and bilateral have funded ICN participation of officials (including NGOs) from developing countries but the point remains that such funding has been sporadic and not sufficient.

19 See http://www.cuts-ccier.org (accessed December 2010).

20 See http://www.ibrac.org.br (accessed December 2010).

21 See http://en.wikipedia.org/wiki/Consumers%27_Association (accessed November 2009).

22 The author is informed that the Dutch, Danish, French, Polish, Slovene and Italian consumer protection organizations (among others) have all had domestic influence in competition discussions. BEUC, the European Consumers' Organisation, http://www.beuc.org, has sporadically intervened in European competition cases. Thus a European model may be said to exist, in which established consumers organizations to a greater or lesser degree become involved in competition policy issues as an extension of their consumer protection focus. Often the activities of these organizations are funded by governments.

23 See http://www.stopcartel.net (accessed December 2010).

antitrust but are academic rather than advocacy organizations (notably, Loyola University Chicago Institute for Consumer Antitrust Studies; the Competition Policy Center at the University of California, Berkeley;[24] George Washington University's new Competition Law Center; the Centre for Competition Policy at East Anglia University; and the British Institute for International Comparative Law's Competition Law Forum; ASCOLA represents an international version of these other centers). Another model that is developing is that of the FIPRA Group, an international but Brussels-based independent for-profit network of senior public policy and regulatory affairs advisors specializing in strategic government relations.[25] FIPRA employs several well-known consumer advocates and increasingly represents corporate interests within the European Union that coincide with consumer interests. The American Bar Association's Antitrust Section is yet another model, and a highly successful one at that.[26] In many nations, the first step toward developing an antitrust community would be to organize a section within the bar whose sole focus is competition policy.

The AAI model is distinct from these other models in that it is not-for-profit and focuses solely on antitrust and competition policy issues, always from a consumer-driven perspective. Competition regimes will vary by objectives, maturity, budget, staffing, cultural attitudes toward markets and government, and in many other ways. I do not suggest that the AAI model is superior to or should be adopted ahead of alternative models, especially where competition policy is relatively new and it is deemed more important to develop an initial sense of community among its supporters than to espouse a particular perspective on how policy should be directed.

My purpose, rather, is to encourage the development of NGOs in each nation with an antitrust regime, as an initial step. Secondarily, I urge the linkage of such NGOs in some fashion so that they will communicate with each other and eventually work cooperatively in support of common goals. A start has been made by the International Network of Civil Society Organisations on Competition (INCSOC),[27] whose driving force has been Pradeep Mehta of CUTS International and Alan Asher of EnergyWatch, UK. Although INCSOC has individual members in a number of countries who have met several times in Geneva and elsewhere, the organization has

---

24 See http://iber.berkeley.edu/cpc (accessed December 2010).

25 See http://www.fipra.com (accessed December 2010).

26 See http://www.abanet.org/antitrust (accessed December 2010).

27 See http://www.cuts-international.org/incsoc.htm (accessed December 2010).

been hampered by difficulty in finding funds and seems to be languishing at the moment.[28]

4 SOME FORESEEABLE QUESTIONS AND RESPONSES

4.1 How Large an Office and Staff Are Needed?

Given the availability of the Internet, it should not be necessary to invest very much in overhead. A physical office outside of the home of the organization's coordinator may not be necessary. Staffing can begin with one person on a part-time basis, although full-time is better. Additional staff can be added as funding increases. A written publication such as a mailed newsletter is probably not needed; reliance on the Internet and email, together with a telephone, should provide the necessary communications infrastructure.

4.2 What Qualifications Are Needed for Staffing?

The AAI emphasizes quality of antitrust experience, relying on a balanced mixture of legal and economic experts, with a variety of experiences within the antitrust community. If the staff is to be limited to a single individual, it should probably be an attorney or industrial organization economist, preferably with some experience in a competition policy agency.

It is important that the head of the competition NGO and the board of directors be largely impartial. Otherwise, the NGO might be viewed as yet another body representing a special interest and not the general public.

4.3 How Can Experts Be Enticed To Participate?

Personal contacts are extremely important and one leads to another. The AAI tries to make participation in the organization a social experience as well as a satisfying professional experience that adds to one's knowledge of antitrust on a continuing basis. This is accomplished in a variety of ways, including having a listserv for its advisory board, on which people are encouraged to present information and discuss current events, out

---

28 The author takes some responsibility for this as co-chair of INCSOC's capacity building committee, which has thus far failed in its efforts to raise funds for additional international meetings.

of which the AAI often determines its public positions. It also provides an annual luncheon at the time of the spring antitrust meeting of the American Bar Association in Washington and a barbecue at the time of its annual conference, also in Washington. It has never attempted to have a meeting of all advisors but it waives registration fees for them to attend its conferences.

The AAI has intentionally kept its board of directors small and nimble – able to make decisions quickly. The directors make decisions but rely on the advisory board, which has grown to over 100 members. Others might fashion a much tighter leadership group, or, indeed, a more widespread membership organization.

The AAI has designated certain of its advisors as Senior Fellows, based on their commitment of time and energy. Another title it bestows is Research Fellow for various lesser or briefer commitments of pro bono effort.

4.4 How Much Advocacy Should the Organization Undertake?

A first question is whether the organization should engage in advocacy with respect to (a) policy matters, or (b) policy matters and specific cases and investigations, or (c) whether it should merely be a clearinghouse for the exchange of information, that is, research and education without advocacy. The AAI has found that the advocacy function helps differentiate it and responds to the media's desire for opinionated exposition and commentary. It has also found that it learns more about current enforcement thinking and current issues of policy and analysis by directing a portion of its activity to cases and investigations that are ongoing. Its role is that of an independent commentator rather than a litigant, consultant, or representative of a party. Finally, it is important to its funding that it takes positions, in that corporations and associations that agree with our positions will sometimes make contributions.

Nevertheless, taking positions in ongoing investigations and cases has its negatives. First, it creates enemies, as well as friends. Second, it can keep certain members of the antitrust community from participating because of actual conflicts of interest or the perception that their clients will feel threatened by such an affiliation.[29] Third, the taking of positions requires the development of an organizational ideology, and this is likely to repel some potential supporters. And fourth, because the AAI accepts

29 Even our law professors often have clients, either on their own or as 'of counsel' members of law firms.

contributions from corporations and others with a direct financial or perhaps ideological interest in matters at hand, there is a risk that its role will be perceived as less than independent. It is very sensitive to this possibility and has taken steps in its internal governance to minimize this risk.

A decision on the role of advocacy needs to be developed at the outset, as its communication to potential supporters will help determine whether and how they will participate. It may also affect funding possibilities.

A related concern is whether to include enforcement officials within the membership. Having them as members adds to the prestige and to the knowledge base, but makes it very difficult to take positions with respect to governmental policies and decisions. The AAI excludes federal officials, but includes several state officials, in that it rarely if ever take positions before state agencies. If enforcement officials are excluded, the NGO should nonetheless be diligent about maintaining cordial and, to the extent possible, supportive relationships with them.

4.5 Should There Be an Ideological Test for Members/Supporters?

Presumably, all members and supporters will agree that antitrust is an important part of the national economic structure, which itself may be considered an ideological test. There would be no point, for example, in trying to attract people who oppose in principle either markets or government intervention via antitrust.

Beyond this, the question is how narrow or broad an ideological test is appropriate? The AAI welcomes onto its advisory board a wide range of perspectives, although all are of a self-identified 'post Chicago' sensibility. A broad umbrella provides the selection metaphor for an organization that will not function as an advocate. Advocacy requires a narrower mission statement, in order to give predictability to policy positions being advocated.

If possible, a competition NGO should function on a non-partisan basis, neither the cheerleader for the party in power nor for an opposition. It should focus on competition policy in an objective manner.

4.6 The AAI Raised Several Millions of Dollars over a ten-year Period. But How Can a New Foreign NGO Raise Money?

This is not going to be easy. Once one has identified an antitrust community, he or she will have identified most of those with a self-recognized stake in making antitrust succeed. Some will likely be willing and able to make annual financial contributions. Others will have client interests they will need to protect, but they may be willing to buy a table[30] at an essentially academic event, even if unable to be a sponsor of the organization itself.

A starting place could be the Internet. Every advocacy group needs a website to provide a focal point for activities, an archive of the group's work products, and an attraction to supporters. Once an audience is attracted, it may be possible to sell ads on the website, as a funding source. The AAI has not attempted this, but the various law firms and others who stand to benefit if there is an active antitrust practice might pay to be listed. The downside is that this might cause the NGO to be viewed as biased.

If there is a private right of recovery of damages in a jurisdiction, there may be a specialized private bar that has a financial interest in being supportive. In those few jurisdictions where consumer class actions are permitted, it may be possible to create a cy pres tradition, such that an antitrust NGO can seek this source of funding. In a number of countries, provisions exist or may be created for recognized consumer associations to represent their members in private remedy actions. At the moment, this has not proven to be especially useful, because the representative actions are on an opt-in basis that makes it difficult to recruit claimants. One can imagine legal and procedural reforms that would turn consumer associations into powerful advocates of consumer interests in competition cases. Accomplishing the necessary reforms and building the skills and reputation for bringing monetary compensation to injured consumers should be a high priority for consumer associations now existing or new ones created with this purpose in mind.

An organization can charge a fee for symposia and conferences, but these also have expenses, and making a net profit on events can be difficult. The AAI has found it useful to charge more for private lawyers and others who can afford it; less for government officials and academics; and to offer scholarships as necessary.

While the AAI has avoided seeking government funding (which may not be available anyway), other jurisdictions may have different traditions, in which such funding is expected and not considered undesirable. In additional to national governments (for example, US AID, the EU, the UK, Japan), there are intergovernmental groups (for example, The World Bank, OECD, UNCTAD, the Asian Development Bank, the Inter

[30] The AAI 'sells' tables as well as individual tickets to its annual conference. A table sponsor, most often a law firm, receives ten seats for the full conference, including a gala luncheon, coffee and snacks, invitations to an informal barbecue, and bound papers and materials associated with Continuing Legal Education credits.

American Bank) that are, at least in theory, potential donors to well-conceived projects. In Europe, it is not uncommon for consumers' organizations to be government-funded. In developing countries, funding often tends to be donor/project specific.

Foundations that are interested in economic liberalization could be another possible resource.[31] Universities offering courses in competition policy may be approachable to create centers for competition policy that could perform at least some of the functions served by the AAI. It would be possible to conduct antitrust courses on a clinical basis, with law students participating in actual advocacy projects (for example, preparation of a letter to a government agency commenting on the likely effects of a proposed regulation). The principal difficulties with this are (a) timing of assignments to relate the intervention need to the availability of the students and (b) possible concerns of the university that certain interventions might be controversial or created problems with donors or government. An example of a successful clinical program that focuses on regulatory intervention at the state level is the Center for Public Interest Law at the University of San Diego Law School.[32]

It is possible to self-organize as a membership organization, charging an annual membership fee. This has some drawbacks. First, the transaction costs can be high, especially if the annual fee is low. Second, a membership organization generally must provide voting rights, which can put the continuing leadership, management, and policy standards into question. The AAI avoided being a membership organization for these reasons. It does, however, consider its mailing list to be a compilation of friends of the AAI and it solicits these friends (albeit with very limited success) for voluntary contributions.

5 THE AAI AND INTERNATIONAL COMPETITION NGOs

The AAI has created an international outreach committee for the purpose of working with international competition NGOs that seek its assistance.[33] At this point in time, such assistance is limited to information and

---

[31] Our experience in the US was that foundations were unlikely to donate capital funds or start up operating funds, but were more willing to consider funding specific projects in specific industrial sectors, depending of course on the programmatic interests of the foundation.

[32] http://www.cpil.org (accessed December 2010).

[33] Communications may be directed to aai@antitrustinstitute.org.

advice via its website and email. Alas, the AAI has no funding to offer. It would be pleased to provide links from its website to others' sites and it is prepared to participate in the future to help coordinate linkages between international competition NGOs. Individual committee members may be identified who will be able to be responsive to a particular NGO.

The AAI looks forward to the day when there is at least one competition NGO in each nation and to when they will all come together in a loose confederation tied through the Internet and even occasional global conventions. Is this too much of a dream?

6 CONCLUSION

In this chapter, I have focused almost exclusively on what I call competition advocacy NGOs without giving due regard to other types of NGOs that might influence competition policy in the interests of those who wish to restrain governmental enforcement of competition policy laws or who might actively oppose adequate budgets for enforcement, improvement of the laws, or the expansion of antitrust to private remedies. They, too, will play a role in the development of competition law.

There is a huge need for civil society to support the antitrust enterprise if it is to succeed over the long term. By its very nature, the antitrust enterprise will bring into existence powerful opponents – those large and powerful or perhaps small and protection-seeking businesses that want to avoid fair competition, on the one hand, and government interference with their freedom, on the other. That side of the table we can take for granted will be crowded. Countervailing influence by competition advocacy NGOs, bringing to bear the tools of education, research, and a variety of advocacy techniques, is essential to provide public enforcers the space in which they can exercise their informed, independent professional judgment.

Index